ILLUSTRATED VENTURA 3.0 (Windows Edition)

George Sheldon

Wordware Publishing, Inc.

Library of Congress Cataloging-in-Publication Data

Sheldon, George
Illustrated Ventura 3.0 / George Sheldon.
p. cm.
"Windows edition."
Includes index.
ISBN 1-55622-212-2
1. Desktop publishing--Computer programs. 2. Ventura publisher (Computer program). I. Title.
Z286.D47S576 1991
686.2'2544536--dc20 90-23959
CIP

1506 Capital Avenue
Plano, Texas 75074

Printed in the United States of America

ISBN 1-55622-212-2

10 9 8 7 6 5 4 3 2 1
9103

All inquiries for volume purchases of this book should be addressed to Wordware Publishing, Inc., at the above address. Telephone inquiries may be made by calling:

(214) 423-0090

Contents

Contents (Cont.)

Contents (Cont.)

Recommended Learning Sequence

Recommended Learning Sequence (Cont.)

Recommended Learning Sequence (Cont.)

Module 1
ABOUT THIS BOOK

INTRODUCTION

Illustrated Ventura 3.0 Windows Edition is a reference and self-instruction book for Xerox Ventura Publisher 3.0, an electronic page composition program for PC-DOS-, MS-DOS-, and OS/2-compatible computers. This book is designed for a wide range of Ventura Publisher users—first time users who want to learn Ventura Publisher from the very beginning, experienced users who need an easy-to-use reference containing examples of every Ventura Publisher command, and classroom instructors who want an instructionally designed text for Ventura Publisher.

ORGANIZATION OF MODULES

Illustrated Ventura Publisher 3.0 Windows Edition is divided into 88 modules. The first three modules contain a general introduction to Ventura Publisher 3.0.

Module 1 describes how to use this book as a reference manual or a self-instructing educational handbook. *Illustrated Ventura 3.0* can also be used as a textbook in a classroom environment.

Module 2 contains an overview of Ventura Publisher. With text, pictures, and illustrations, this module describes the features of Ventura Publisher. This module also demonstrates how all the pieces of a Ventura Publisher document fit together. The description places emphasis on the use of Ventura Publisher's frames and style sheets, as these two features control the power and usefulness of the program. To master these two main concepts is to master Ventura Publisher. Although there are many other things to learn about using the program, once you master the principle of using Ventura Publisher's frames and style sheets, you will find your work with the program to be much smoother and faster. Module 2 also discusses the user interface with the program, which is how you communicate and control Ventura's various commands. You will learn about using the mouse, pull-down menus, dialog boxes, and control keys. Although this may seem elementary, it is important to master this information if you are ever to become proficient at using Ventura Publisher.

Module 3 presents a sample session with Ventura Publisher. Easy-to-follow step-by-step instructions take you on a tour through Ventura Publisher. This module leads you through the creation, saving, editing, and printing of an entire document.

Modules 4 through 88 are self-contained descriptions of each Ventura Publisher command and feature. The modules are in alphabetical sequence for easy reference. You can follow the Recommended Learning Sequence for a step-by-step learning guide through the program. After completing the Recommended Learning Sequence, this book can then be used as a reference guide.

Appendix A contains a glossary of terms and definitions for quick reference. Most of the terms listed in the glossary are not covered by their own module within this book.

Appendixes B, C, D, E, and F provide additional information and reference resources for you when using Ventura Publisher.

Appendix G is provided for both classroom and self-teaching exercises. It presents questions about each module, which, if correctly answered, indicate you are ready to move on to the next module. Classroom instructors may want to include these as part of assignments. If you are studying alone, these questions will help you realize if you have clearly grasped the important concepts of each module.

CONTENT OF MODULES

Beginning with Module 4, each module follows a consistent format to make this book easy to use. The parts of each module are:

Description
Applications
Typical Operation

The Description section of each module contains general information about a command. The Applications section describes the different ways to use a command. The Typical Operation section contains an example related to the module topic and the learning sequence of this book. Most of the examples provided in the Typical Operations are simple and easy-to-follow, to minimize the amount of time it takes for you to master the program.

Each module provides insight into Ventura Publisher's use in solving practical, everyday publishing problems or needs. Hundreds of useful examples and illustrations are presented within the Description, Applications, and Typical Operation sections of the modules. These examples help you master Ventura Publisher quickly.

By first following these examples, you will be able to design, create, and publish your own documents to meet your own needs. The examples permit you to experiment with the special features of Ventura Publisher and remove the mystery from what may at first look like difficult, confusing, or impossible operations. As you conduct and learn from the actual hands-on experiments, do not be surprised if you are suddenly having fun with the program. Not only is Ventura Publisher a powerful page composition program, it is also fun to use, once you master it.

WHAT YOU NEED

To use this book to its greatest potential, you will need:

- A PC-DOS-, MS-DOS-, or OS/2-compatible computer with at least 2 megabytes of RAM (memory). This RAM must be configured as extended memory.
- A fixed or hard disk with at least 1.6 megabytes of storage capacity available to hold the Ventura Publisher Program. You should also have 5 megabytes of storage available after installation, as this space is needed to hold the document files you create.
- A high-resolution monitor
- A graphics board in your computer, so you can see graphics and not just text on your computer screen
- A mouse
- A current copy of Ventura Publisher 3.0 Windows Edition
- Microsoft Windows Version 3.0. Windows must be installed prior to the installation of Ventura Publisher.

NOTE

An earlier version of Microsoft Windows (such as version 2.0 or Runtime versions) will not work. The display, printer, and fonts available in Ventura Publisher depend entirely on the capabilities you have installed for Microsoft Windows.

In addition to this minimum hardware configuration, you also need a full-featured word processor.

NOTE

Although Ventura can be used without a mouse, it is not recommended. Trying to do so greatly decreases your productivity. This book assumes you will be using a mouse, and if you choose not to use a mouse with your computer, you should reconsider that decision.

WHAT YOU SHOULD KNOW

The descriptions and examples in this book assume you know how to use your PC-DOS-, MS-DOS-, or OS/2-compatible computer. You should be familiar with your computer's operating system, the keyboard, and the mouse. You should know simple DOS commands, such as DIR, COPY, REN, and CD\. You should have a good working knowledge of creating, using, removing, and making directories. Further, you should have developed some expertise with at least one powerful word processor, such as WordPerfect, Microsoft Word, WordStar, XyWrite, or DisplayWrite 4. If you know all of these things, you are ready to proceed with Ventura Publisher. If not, you should read the appropriate user manuals, or refer to the related book in the Illustrated series from Wordware Publishing, Inc. before attempting to move on to Ventura Publisher.

PROPER INSTALLATION

In Module 2, information is provided about how to install Ventura Publisher. To use this book, you must have first properly installed the program. In addition, it is assumed that you have installed and still have on your hard disk the sample documents and chapters that are included with your copy of Ventura Publisher 3.0. These documents should be located in the TYPESET directory. These samples are the files and documents that are used in the Typical Operation sections of the modules.

> **NOTE**
>
> If you have altered, changed, or deleted these original samples supplied with your copy of Ventura Publisher, you should copy them from the examples diskette into the TYPESET directory. To do so, insert the examples diskette in the A: drive, and at any DOS prompt, type: COPY A:\EXAMPLES*.* C:\TYPESET.

THE FIVE VENTURA PUBLISHER PRODUCTS

With the release of Ventura Publisher 3.0, there are now five versions of the product available. They are Ventura Publisher 3.0 Gold Series DOS/GEM Edition, Ventura Publisher 3.0 Gold Series Windows Edition, Ventura Publisher 3.0: Network Server, Ventura Publisher Gold Series OS/2 Edition, and Ventura Publisher Macintosh Edition. No matter which version of Ventura Publisher 3.0 you might be using, this book will get you started.

Should you be using a release of Ventura Publisher earlier than 3.0, you may still find this book helpful, particularly in the beginning modules. Many of the basic features and modes are the same from the earlier to later releases. Some of the more advanced features, however, are not available on earlier releases of Ventura Publisher. Also, before release 3.0, Ventura Publisher worked under the GEM operating environment. With the release of version 3.0, Ventura Publisher now works under the Windows graphics environment.

Module 2
VENTURA PUBLISHER OVERVIEW

VENTURA PUBLISHER AND DESKTOP PUBLISHING

Xerox Ventura Publisher is a high-end desktop publishing computer program. Today, the term "desktop publishing" is a muddied, confused phrase, and means many different things to many different people. Some high-end word processors are now self-proclaimed desktop publishing packages.

This book was prepared with the approach that desktop publishing refers to the use of a personal computer to create near-typeset-quality documents that are "camera-ready." In other words, the documents you create with Ventura are of such high quality that they will look much like they were created with a commercial typesetter and are ready to be turned over to a printer, so they can be mass reproduced. Sometimes, the mass reproduction is done with a printing press, and other times, the reproduction may be done with a standard photocopying machine.

Desktop publishing is also called *electronic page composition.* Ventura was designed to be the electronic equivalent of the layout table used by a graphic artist. Ventura contains many different types of tools that allow you to perform the electronic composition of your documents. Some of these tools are equivalent to the tools used by graphic design layout artists and designers, as well as typographers. And, in some special instances, these electronic tools permit you to create documents that will have a better appearance than if they were produced by traditional methods. If you are currently using a typewriter or a computer and dot matrix or letter quality printer, you will be amazed and more than satisfied with the new, quality appearance of your documents.

By using Ventura to produce these materials, you save time (by eliminating the waiting period when you send your job to a typesetter for completion) and you cut costs (by eliminating the expense of commercial typesetting). You can produce a wide array of documents—everything from raffle tickets to books, from business reports to luxurious sales brochures. You will soon be able to produce just about any type of document you may want or need—the only thing that limits you when using Ventura is your imagination.

One of the very best things about Ventura is the simple fact that it is available to everyone. You need not be a graphic designer or a commercial typesetter to create decent, graphically correct documents. Even though you may not have "gifted talents" or the natural ability to design outstanding documents, almost everyone can master the design, layout, and production of basic, high-quality, camera-ready pages.

LEARNING VENTURA PUBLISHER

Learning Ventura takes time, patience, and a willingness to experiment. The program is not intuitive, but if you follow the learning sequence of this book, you will be able to produce documents in a short time. But the author cannot emphasize enough that it does take a significant amount of time to master Ventura. Do not be surprised if it takes longer to learn to use and to be able to produce documents with Ventura than it took you to learn any other computer program.

Ventura is not the sort of program in which you can learn only a "few pieces" and then try to pick up the rest later or as you work in a document. You will probably be disappointed with your results if you do not learn most of the features of the program before attempting to produce your own documents. Unlike a word processing program, where you can learn the basics, such as cursor movements, spell checking, printing, and block movements, to effectively use Ventura you must learn most of the features of the program first.

If you take the time to learn Ventura Publisher, it will have taken a lot of effort, but the results you achieve with your final documents will prove it was worth the undertaking.

As mentioned in Module 1, to use Ventura effectively, you should be comfortable and experienced with MS-DOS or PC-DOS, as well as with a powerful word processor, such as WordPerfect, Microsoft Word, WordStar, XyWrite, or Multimate. Unless you know DOS and a word processor very well, you are limiting your use of Ventura.

"WYSIWYG"

Ventura offers what is called WYSIWYG (pronounced wizz-ee-wig). The term WYSIWYG is an acronym which stands for "What You See Is What You Get." It means that what you see on your screen is what you get when you print your document. Although this is the principal of how Ventura works, there is no such thing as true WYSIWYG. Since the method of displaying graphics and text on your screen is different from the technique used to print them, and because of the differences between your screen and printer resolution (the number of dots per inch is different on each), there is no true WYSIWYG.

So what you see on your screen is not what you will really get, but it will be fairly close. Do not be surprised if you find some differences between what you create on your screen and what you receive from your printer. But in most cases, it will approach WYSIWYG.

Ventura Windows Edition requires that you have installed Microsoft's Windows 3.0. The way you have installed and set Windows will determine what printer is available and what colors you will see on your Ventura screen. Windows 3.0 drives and supports color displays if your computer equipment includes a color monitor and a VGA, EGA, or DEB graphics adapter.

Of course, even if you are using a monochrome monitor with Ventura Publisher, the text prints in the chosen color if a color printer is used. The user interface, which means the menus, windows, rulers, and dialog boxes, displays in monochrome even on a color monitor. Text, graphics, and other page elements appear in the color assigned to each.

PRINTER LIMITATIONS

Many laser printers are not capable of printing to the edge of the standard size paper. Accordingly, if you place text, pictures, or graphics near the edge of the page, they may not print properly, even though they show correctly on the screen. In the next module, you will be instructed to print a file called CAPABILI.CHP so you can see exactly what your printer can and cannot do.

You must know the limitations of your laser printer to work effectively with Ventura. For example, you may not be able to produce documents 12x18 on one single sheet of paper. This is because your laser printer probably cannot print on a piece of paper that large. If your laser printer only prints in black toner, you cannot print in red from the laser printer. Rather the printer's ink will place red on your finished document.

INSTALLING VENTURA

Before you can begin the sample session or the learning sequence presented in this book, you must make certain that Ventura has been properly installed on your computer.

Before installing Ventura Publisher, make sure that you have properly installed Microsoft Windows 3.0 on your computer. Windows must be installed for your individual system, including the type of monitor, graphics adapter board, mouse, and printer you have.

If you have not yet installed Ventura Publisher, you should do so now. Before starting the installation, you should:

- Make backup copies of your master disks received in the Ventura package. Read the Software License and Warranty Agreement included within your copy of Ventura to understand the legal restrictions governing copying and installing Ventura.
- Make sure you have between 4 and 5 megabytes of space on your computer's hard disk to hold all the printer fonts, screen fonts, program software, and examples provided with Ventura. You will use another 1 to 3 megabytes for the program (depending on the type and number of printers installed). You should have another 2 or 3 megabytes available to hold document files and any additional fonts you might add later.
- Make sure MS-DOS or PC-DOS version 3.1 or higher has been installed on your computer.

You can proceed with the installation by inserting the Ventura Disk #1 into the A drive. Close the drive door.

Start Microsoft Windows 3.0.

NOTE

Make sure you are running Windows in the protected mode. Do not run windows by typing WIN/R.

Once Windows is running, select the Windows Program Manager. From the Program Managers's File menu, select the Run Option. On the Run option's Command line, type **A:\SETUP** and press **Enter**. If you must use the B drive because of incompatible disk size on your A drive, type B:\SETUP and you can install Ventura from the B drive.

You are then presented with three options:

Store Preference In:
Destination Drive Letter:
Examples

Unless you are installing Ventura on a network operation, do not make any changes in the Store Preferences In option.

If you want to install Ventura on a drive other than C:, specify the desired drive in the Destination Drive Letter: option.

If you do not want to install the Example files (they are required for the Typical Operations sections of this book), remove the x from the Examples box.

Within 10 to 15 minutes, the Ventura installation will be complete.

CHECKING YOUR INSTALLATION

The instructions in this book assume you are using a standard Ventura installation, which includes two standard Ventura directories, VENTURA and TYPESET. Ventura places the programs and associated files in the VENTURA directory and places the style sheets and sample text and graphic files in the TYPESET directory. You can check whether these directories are on your hard disk by typing DIR at the DOS command line.

Also, make sure you have a copy of the original default style sheet called DEFAULT.STY installed in the TYPESET directory. If you have altered or changed this style sheet, then recopy it from the working copy master diskette into the TYPESET directory.

STARTING VENTURA

Before starting Ventura Publisher, make sure you are logged on to your computer's hard drive (usually C) and you have changed to the root directory. To do this:

1. Type **C:** and press **Enter**.
2. Type **CD** and press **Enter**. (Make sure you typed \ and not /.)

To begin running Ventura Publisher, you must first start Windows. To start Windows,

1. Type **WIN**.
2. Press **Enter**.

NOTE

Make sure you run Windows in protected mode by typing WIN.
Do not type WIN/R to start Windows.

Select the Windows Applications icon from the File Manager menu. Within the Windows Application program manager window, select the Ventura Publisher icon and then select Run from the File Manager File menu. Type **C:\VENTURA\VPWIN.EXE** and click **OK**. Or you can simply point and double-click your mouse on the Ventura icon located with the Windows Application program manager window.

Depending on your computer, Ventura takes anywhere from 10 to 60 seconds to load.

VENTURA MAIN SCREEN

After starting Ventura Publisher, the first thing you see is the main screen:

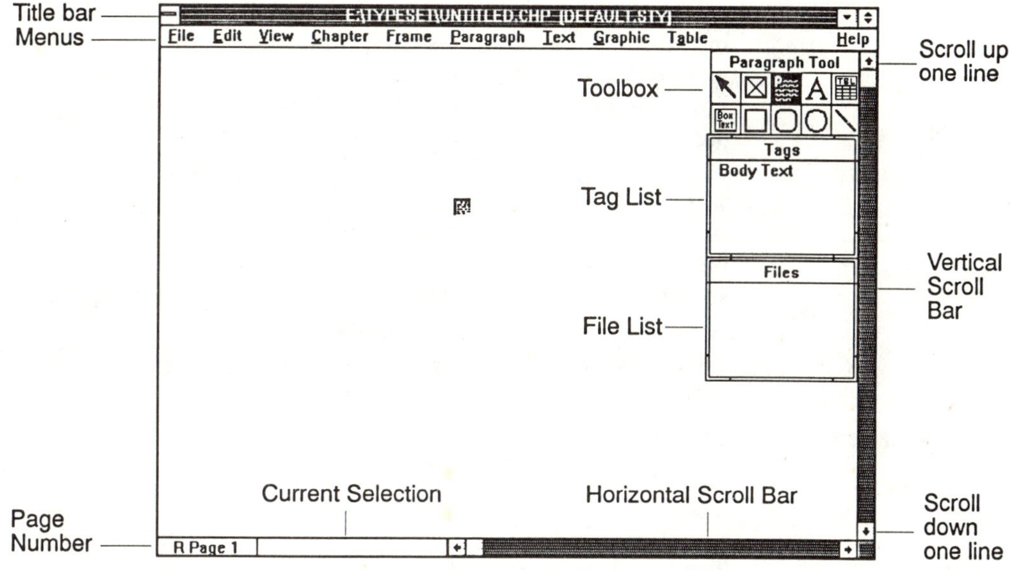

NOTE

The screens displayed in this book were captured using E: as the default directory.

This screen provides the user interface (how you work with, command, and control Ventura Publisher).

The parts of the screen are:

Title Bar	Located just above the menu names, the Title Bar displays the name of the current Ventura document and the name of the current style sheet.
Menus	At the top of your computer screen, the various menu names are displayed. When you point the mouse cursor at one of the menu names and press the left mouse button, the menu drops down. As you move the mouse cursor down through the menu, the available menu options change appearance from black on

white to white on black. This reverse highlighting indicates that the item is available for selection.

Scroll Up One Line	Located just above the Help menu, this feature moves the screen up over the page in increments of approximately one line at a time. Point the mouse cursor to this feature and click once to move the screen one line. To continue scrolling, press and hold the mouse button until the display is where you want it, then let go. For large screen movements, use the Vertical Scroll Bar.
Vertical Scroll Bar	Located on the right side of the screen, the Vertical Scroll Bar moves the screen up or down over the page. The grayish area in the scroll bar indicates the portion of the page that is not visible. Move the mouse cursor to the scroll bar and press and hold the mouse button to drag the scroll bar up or down, depending on which direction you want the screen to move over the page. When you see the area of the page that you want, release the mouse button. You can also reposition the page by moving the mouse cursor to the grey area in the scroll bar and clicking once. The page will move approximately one screen length. (This operation is quite similar to using PgDn in most word processing programs.)
Scroll Down One Line	This works like Scroll Up One Line, described before, except that the screen moves down.
Horizontal Scroll Bar	This works like the Vertical Scroll Bar, except it moves the screen horizontally.
Toolbox	The Toolbox consists of ten icons (pictures), each representing a tool you can use to create or modify your documents. The Toolbox can be moved to any convenient location on your screen. To move it, point to the word Toolbox, and click and hold your mouse. Then drag the Toolbox to the desired location, and finally let go of the mouse button. The icons represent the five major operating modes and indicate which is currently enabled and ready for use. You can also change modes by clicking on the icons. The modes are Frame Setting, Paragraph Tagging, Text Editing, Graphic Drawing, and Tables. The operation of each of these major modes is described in detail in later modules.
File List	The File List shows, in alphabetical order, the names of all files currently available and ready to be placed within your chapter. The File List can be moved to any location on your computer screen by pointing to the word Files at the top of the File List box, then press and hold the mouse button, dragging the File

	List box to its new location, and finally releasing the mouse button.
	The File list box can be enlarged or reduced by pointing to any edge of the box until the mouse changes to a two-directional arrow, and then pressing and holding the mouse button, dragging the edge of the File List box to its new size and finally releasing the mouse button.
Tag List	The Tag List shows, in alphabetical order, the names of all paragraph tags available to be assigned to each paragraph within your chapter. Tags can be added or removed from the Tag List box by using menu options available in the Paragraph menu.
	The Tag List can be moved, enlarged, or reduced in the same manner as the File List.
Current Selection	Located on the bottom left side of your computer screen, the Current Selection indicator displays which item is currently assigned to a specific frame, paragraph, text, or graphic that you have selected.
Page Number	Located at the left bottom of the computer screen, this shows the page number of the currently displayed page and if the page is a left or right page.

KEYBOARD COMMANDS AND KEYS

You can use various commands available from the different keyboard keys to perform special functions. They are:

Key	*Function*
Cursor keys	Control the movement of the text cursor.
Home	Go to the first page of the document.
End	Go to the last page of the document.
PgUp	Go to the previous page.
PgDn	Go to the next page.
Del	Delete the character to the right of the text cursor when using the Text tool.
	Similar to selecting Cut in the Edit menu when a block of text, frame, or graphic is selected.
	Similar to selecting Copy in the Edit menu when Shift is pressed simultaneously with Del.
Ins	Similar to selecting the Paste option in the Edit menu.
Backspace	Deletes the character to the left of the text cursor.

Key	*Function*
Esc	Stops the printing operation for the current chapter. Halts a "go to page" operation. Within a dialog box, Esc is equivalent to Cancel. **NOTE** Esc reformats the current page at all other times.
Shift	When used with the mouse, press Shift to select multiple paragraphs, frames, or graphics. Press and hold down either Shift key while selecting to choose several items. When using the Text tool, Shift is used to extend or decrease the range of text selected. Press and hold down either Shift key and then press the mouse button. The text selected extends to the current text cursor location. Press Shift when adding frames or graphics to keep the Add New Frame or graphic tool enabled. Press Shift plus any keyboard arrow key to change the spacing between letters or to change the font size of selected text.
Tab	Inserts horizontal tab characters. Within a dialog box, Tab moves the text cursor forward to the next line or, if Shift is pressed simultaneously, back to the previous line.
Function keys	Used to tag paragraphs if the style sheet has assigned tags to these keys. **NOTE** F1 calls the Help index.
Ctrl	Use with Enter to insert a line break. Use with the Hyphen key to insert a discretionary hyphen. Press and hold Ctrl while selecting graphics or frames with the mouse to select graphics which are "hidden" beneath other graphics. Press and hold Ctrl and then press X to perform the last menu action, including recalling the last dialog box.
Alt	Use with the mouse to move cropped pictures within frames. Press and hold Alt, move the mouse cursor to the center of the image to be moved, press and hold the mouse button, and then move the image. Release both Alt and the mouse button when finished.

Key	*Function*
Alt	Constrain graphics. Press and hold Alt while drawing graphics using any of the Graphic tools. The graphic is constrained to absolute proportions (for example, a box becomes a perfect square). Add characters that are not on the keyboard. Press and hold Alt, and type the numeric equivalent on the keypad for the character you wish to enter, and then release Alt.

Special Characters

Ventura provides the keyboard shortcuts shown below for commonly used typographic characters.

NOTE

These shortcuts can be used instead of typing a number with Alt pressed.

To use these commands, press and hold Ctrl, then press the second key.

Shortcut Command	*Typographic Character*
Ctrl-Shift-2	Trademark
Ctrl-Shift-C	Copyright mark
Ctrl-Shift-F	Figure space
Ctrl-Shift-M	Em space
Ctrl-Shift-N	En space
Ctrl-Shift-R	Registered trademark
Ctrl-Shift-T	Thin Space
Ctrl-Shift-[	Quote, open
Ctrl-Shift-]	Quote, closed
Ctrl-Spacebar	Non-breaking space
Ctrl-[	En dash
Ctrl-]	Em dash
Ctrl- -	Discretionary hyphen

Keyboard Shortcuts

Many of Ventura Publisher's functions can be controlled directly from the keyboard. Those commands are:

Command	*Function*	*Command*	*Function*
Ctrl-2	Addition button	Ctrl-A	Bring to Front
Ctrl-B	Renumber Chapter	Ctrl-C	Insert Special Item
Ctrl-D	Edit Special Item	Ctrl-E	Enlarged View
Ctrl-F	Fill Attributes	Ctrl-G	Go to Page

Command	*Function*	*Command*	*Function*
Ctrl-K	Update Tag List	Ctrl-L	Line Attributes
Ctrl-N	Normal View	Ctrl-O	Text Tool
Ctrl-Q	Select All (graphics)	Ctrl-R	Reduced View
Ctrl-S	Save	Ctrl-T	Show/Hide Tabs & Returns
Ctrl-V	Show/Hide Tags List	Ctrl-W	Show/Hide Side-Bar
Ctrl-X	Recall Last Dialog	Ctrl-Y	Show/Hide Files List
	Box	Ctrl-Z	Send to Back
Del	Cut	End	Go to Last Page
Esc	Redraw Screen	Home	Go to First Page
Ins	Paste	PgDn	Go to Next Page
PgUp	Go to Previous Page	Shift-Del	Copy

Cursor Keys

When using the Text Tool, move the text cursor to another location on the screen by moving the mouse cursor to the desired new position and clicking the mouse button once. When the text cursor is positioned, use the keyboard cursor keys to move the cursor back and forth one character at a time and up and down one line at a time.

USING THE MOUSE

A mouse is a computer peripheral that connects to your computer. It is called a mouse because it has a long thin wire that looks like a mouse tail which attaches to your computer. A mouse is small and fits within your hand. It is electronically attached to a pointer on the computer screen. The shape of the pointer or cursor on the screen is determined by which Ventura function you are currently using. There are currently 13 different shapes for the mouse cursor. They are:

Frame Tool		Text Tool	
Add Frame Tool	 Fr	Selection Tool	
Re-size Frame		Box Text Tool	 Te
Pan Image		Line Tool	
Move Frame		Circle Tool	
Paragraph Tool		Rectangle Tool	
		Rounded Rectangle Tool	

To operate a mouse, you move it around on a flat surface near your computer. Either a ball attached to tiny sensors or a light emitting diode within the mouse tells the computer which way the mouse is moving. Each time you move the mouse, the pointer or mouse cursor on the screen moves in the same direction.

The mouse has two separate functions within Ventura Publisher. They are:

- Move the mouse cursor to items on the screen that you want to select and use.
- Draw frames and graphics.

To select items with the mouse, simply move the mouse cursor to anywhere within the item and click the left mouse button once. Exact or precise placement of the mouse cursor is not critical as long as the cursor lies within the item you have selected. Pressing the mouse button twice in a row, very quickly, is equivalent to selecting the item and then selecting OK. This is also called a *double click.*

There are five basic operations you do to make the mouse work. They are:

Point	Move the mouse until the pointer rests on an item you want to select or choose.
Click	Press and release the left mouse button.

NOTE

If your mouse has multiple buttons, only the left button works with Ventura.

Click and Hold	Press and hold the left mouse button.
Drag	Move the mouse while holding the left mouse button.
Double Click	Click the left mouse button twice in a row (quickly).

The mouse, with these operations, is used to select commands, work with text, tag paragraphs, size, resize, and move graphics and frames.

Selecting Commands

Commands are picked in the pull-down menus. They provide access to most of the functions available within Ventura. To select commands with a mouse, follow these steps:

1. Point to the desired menu name in the Menu Bar, and click and hold the left mouse button once. Ventura then automatically displays the associated pull-down menu.
2. Continue to hold the left mouse button and move the mouse cursor down through the various options on the menu until you are pointing at the command you want to execute.
3. Release the left mouse button to finish the selection process.

The following illustration depicts selecting an item within a pull-down menu:

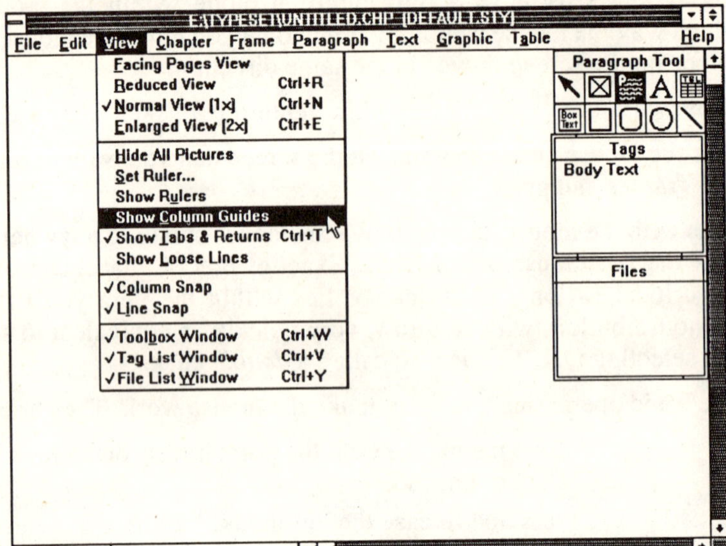

Working with the Toolbox

Although the Toolbox is described in detail in Module 81, the following chart depicts each tool available:

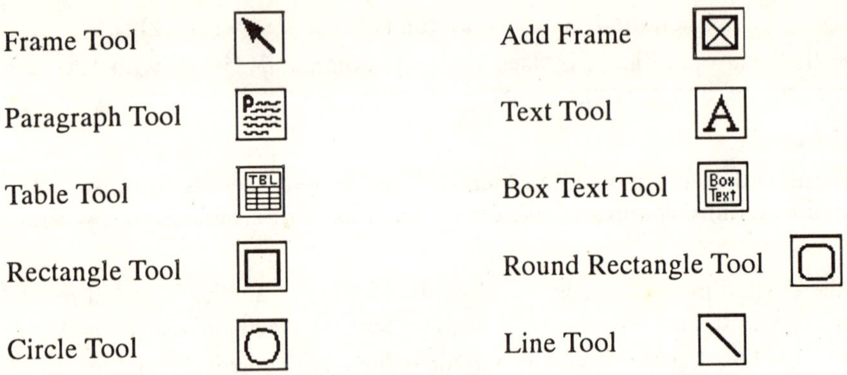

Drawing, Resizing, and Moving Frames

Frames hold either text or graphics. In most cases, the text has been imported from a file previously created in a word processor, but text can also be typed directly into a frame within Ventura. However, graphics placed within a frame must always be imported into Ventura from a graphics file. Frames are easily drawn, resized, and moved. To work with frames, first choose the Frame Tool. The mouse cursor changes to its Frame selection shape.

To draw a frame:

1. Click on the Add Frame Tool in the Toolbox.
2. Point to the position where you want the upper left corner of the frame.
3. Click and hold the mouse button.
4. Drag the mouse cursor to the position where you want the lower right corner of the frame.
5. Release the mouse button.

Your screen will resemble this illustration:

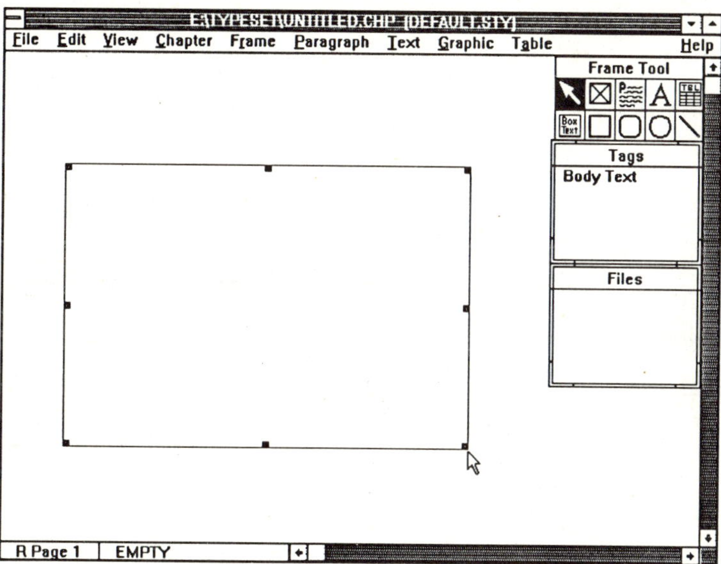

To resize a frame:

1. Position the mouse cursor within the frame you want to resize.
2. Click the left mouse button once. Eight dark boxes appear around the edge of the frame. The corner boxes permit you to resize the height and width of the frame at the same time, while the edge boxes allow you to push or pull one edge of the frame to resize it. If the frame is extremely small, you may only see the corner boxes.
3. Point to one of the boxes around the edge of the frame.
4. Click and hold the left mouse button.

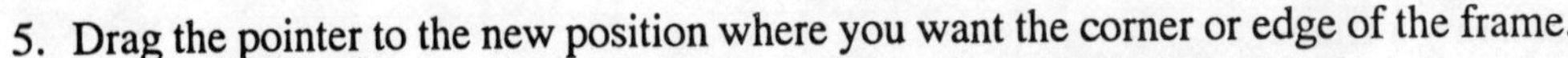

5. Drag the pointer to the new position where you want the corner or edge of the frame.

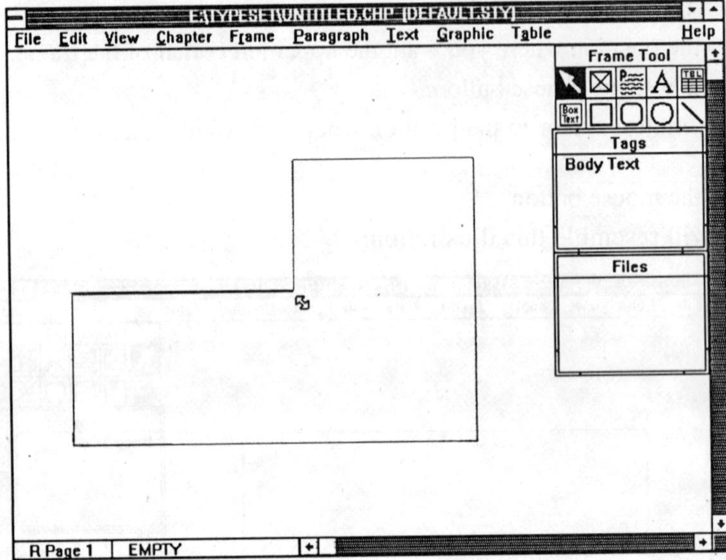

6. Release the left mouse button.

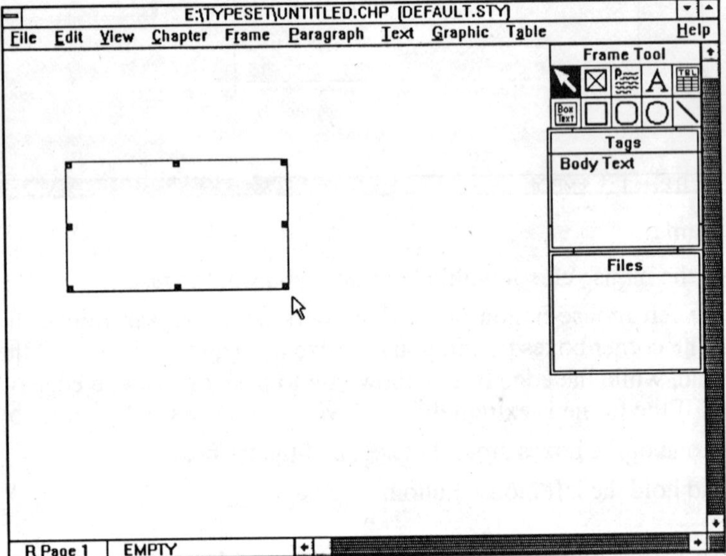

To move a frame:

1. Position the mouse cursor within the frame you want to move.
2. Click and hold the left mouse button. The mouse cursor will change shape to the Move Frame cursor.
3. Drag the frame to the new position.
4. Release the mouse button.

Working With Paragraph Tags

Paragraph tags are used to define the appearance of any paragraph. In Ventura Publisher, a paragraph is any text that ends with a *required carriage return* (which is entered whenever you press Enter). To tag a paragraph, first choose the Paragraph Tool in the Toolbox. The mouse will change to its paragraph tagging shape. Then move the mouse to any point within the paragraph and click the left mouse button once. The entire paragraph is displayed in reverse or highlighted background and the current tag name is identified in the Current Selection within the Tags window.

You can select additional paragraphs for the same tag by pressing and holding Shift, then pointing to the next paragraph to be tagged and clicking the left mouse button. This procedure can be continued until you have selected all the paragraphs you need to change. The word Multiple appears in the Current Selection beside the bottom scroll bar. You can then work with all the selected paragraphs at one time, rather than selecting each individually.

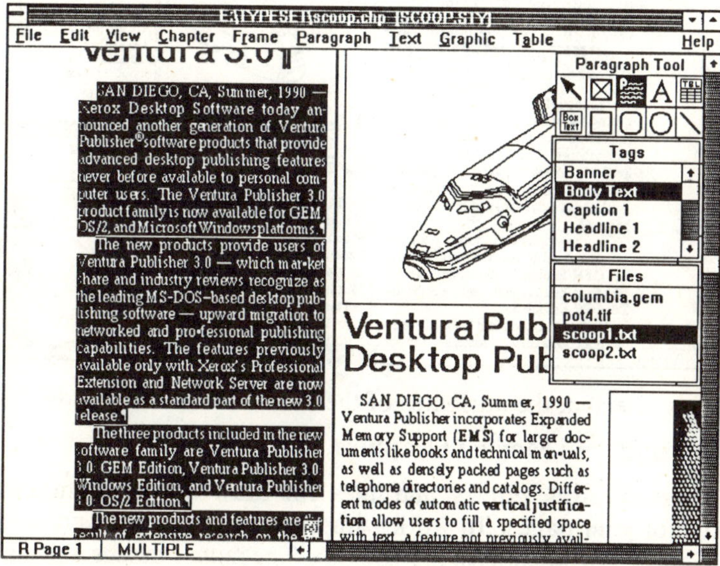

Working with Text

Ventura provides basic text editing functions including adding text, adding bold or italic styles, copying, cutting, and pasting text. When working with your text, first choose the Text Tool in the Toolbox (the uppercase "A"). The mouse cursor will change to its text selection shape. To select an entry point for typing or pasting text, simply point to the beginning place in the text and click. To select a block of text for assigning attributes, copying, or cutting, follow these steps:

1. Point to the beginning position in the text.
2. Click and hold the left mouse button.
3. Drag the mouse point to the ending position within the text. As you drag the pointer, Ventura shows the selected text by displaying it on a highlighted background. You can only select text that is displayed on the screen. You cannot select text that is not on the screen, as Ventura does not automatically scroll forward or backward.
4. Release the left mouse button.

When text has been selected, your screen will look like this:

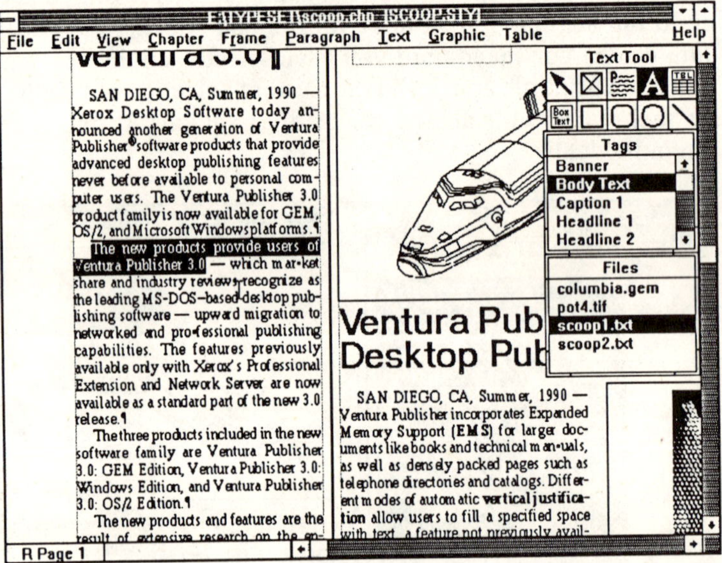

Once the text is selected, the attributes of the text can be changed, deleted, or pasted.

Drawing, Resizing, and Moving Graphics

Graphics consist of boxes, circles, and lines you draw within Ventura to enhance the graphic design of your pages. To work with Ventura Publisher's graphics, first select one of the graphic drawing tools in the Toolbox. The mouse cursor will change to match the tool selected.

To draw a box, circle, or line:

1. Select the Round Rectangle Tool.
2. Point to the position where you want the upper left corner of the graphic.
3. Click and hold the left mouse button.
4. Drag the mouse cursor to the position where you want the lower right corner of the graphic.
5. Release the left mouse button.

After drawing a box, your screen looks like this:

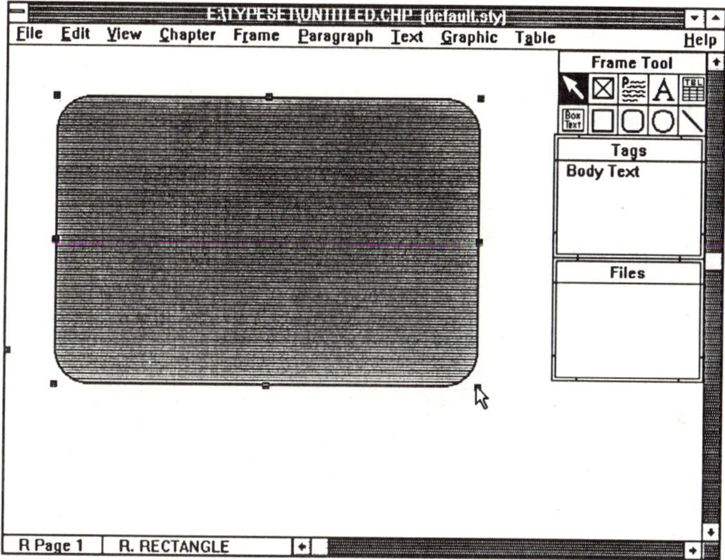

When drawing a line, your screen looks like this:

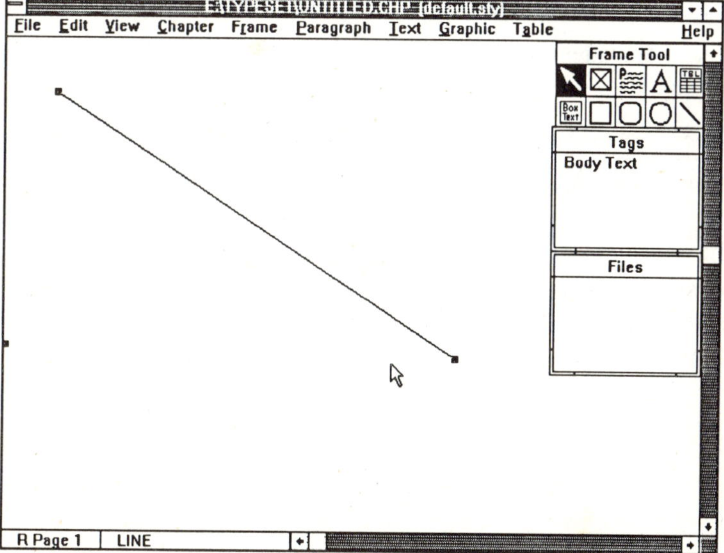

To resize a box, circle, or line:

1. Point to the object you want to resize.
2. Click the left mouse button. Eight dark boxes appear around the edge of the object. The corner boxes permit you to resize the height and width of the box or circle at the same time, while the edge boxes allow you to push or pull the edge of the box or circle to resize it. If the box, circle, or line is extremely small, you may only see the corner boxes.
3. Point to one of the boxes around the edge of the object.
4. Click and hold the left mouse button.
5. Drag the pointer to the new position where you want the corner or edge of the box, circle, or frame.

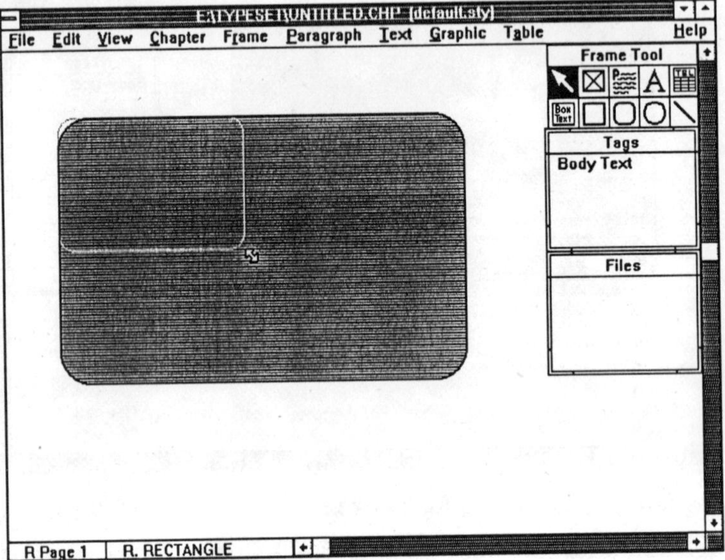

6. Release the left mouse button.

To move a graphic:

1. Point the mouse cursor to the object you want to move.
2. Click and hold the left mouse button. The mouse cursor changes shape to the Re-size Frame cursor.
3. Drag the object to the new position.
4. Release the mouse button.

USING THE PULL-DOWN MENUS

Ventura Publisher's pull-down menus are the primary means of selecting commands. The following menu names are listed at the top of your computer screen:

File
Edit
View
Chapter
Frame
Paragraph
Text
Graphic
Table

When you point and click the mouse cursor at a menu name, Ventura displays the entire pull-down menu. Some items in the menu are solid black, while others are gray. The items displayed in solid black are available as commands. The items displayed in gray are not available in the current mode, but are available when Ventura is operating under a different mode. In the following illustration, only Cut Text, Copy Text, Update Counter, Re-Anchor Frames, and Set Preferences are available:

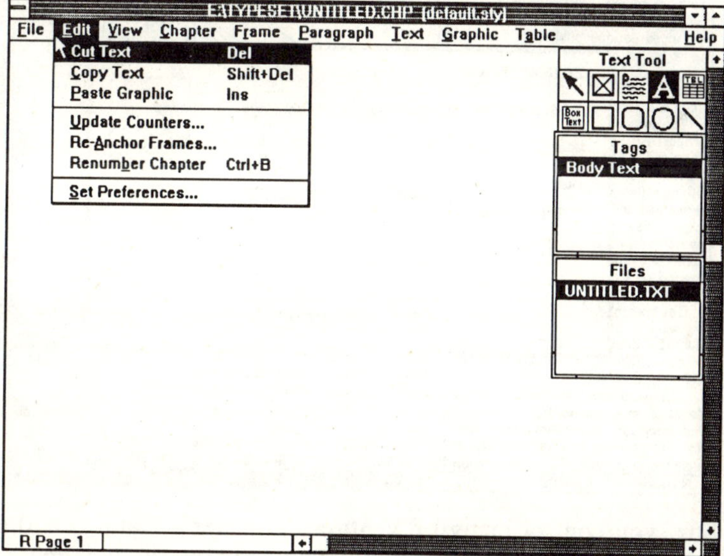

Some of the items on some menus also have keyboard equivalents. Some commands can be executed by pressing Ctrl in combination with other keys. For example, Ctrl-S executes the Save command without using the mouse to make the selection in the File menu.

For a complete list of the various keyboard shortcuts available within Ventura Publisher, see Appendix D.

SCROLLING AROUND THE PAGE

Ventura lets you view the screen in three different sizes: reduced, normal, and enlarged. In the normal and enlarged views, Ventura shows only part of the page. To see the other parts of the page, it is necessary to use the scroll bars. To scroll up or down, click on the scroll bar or scroll arrows on the right edge of your computer screen. To scroll to the left or right, click on the scroll bar or scroll arrows on the bottom edge of the screen. You can also click in the gray area of the scroll bar to move the screen a fixed amount with each click. You can click and hold in the solid area of the scroll bar and then drag the mouse to move the screen the amount you want to move it. You can also scroll up one line or down one line by clicking on the Scroll Up or Scroll Down One Line Arrows at the ends of the Vertical Scroll Bar.

USING VENTURA'S DIALOG BOXES Although some of the menu options within Ventura function as simple commands which are executed as soon as you select them, many menu options contain features that require you to specify additional information. To allow you to do so, Ventura displays a dialog box.

The following illustration depicts a typical Ventura dialog box:

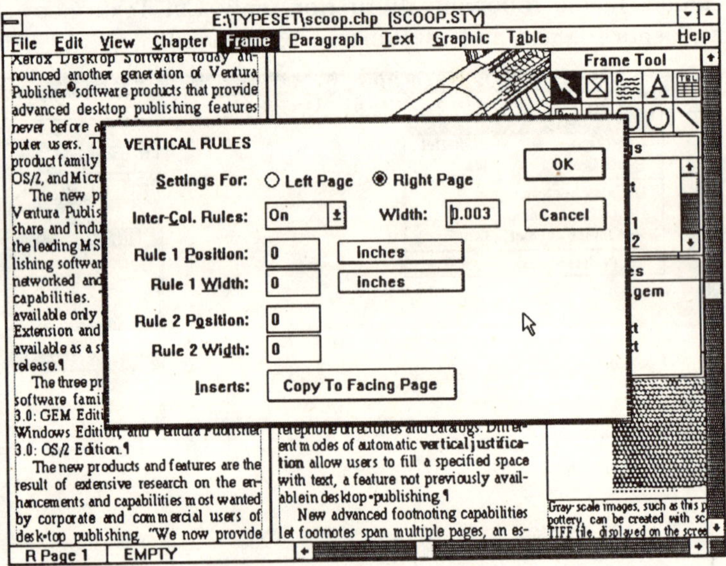

In a dialog box, you control many of Ventura Publisher's features and options. The dialog boxes follow standard Microsoft Window conventions. For more information about working in the Windows dialog boxes, see Module 4.

Using Help

Help menus and associated help screens provide on-line assistance concerning the functions and operations of each feature within Ventura. Help is accessed by pressing F1 anytime while working in Ventura. The following illustration depicts a Ventura Help screen:

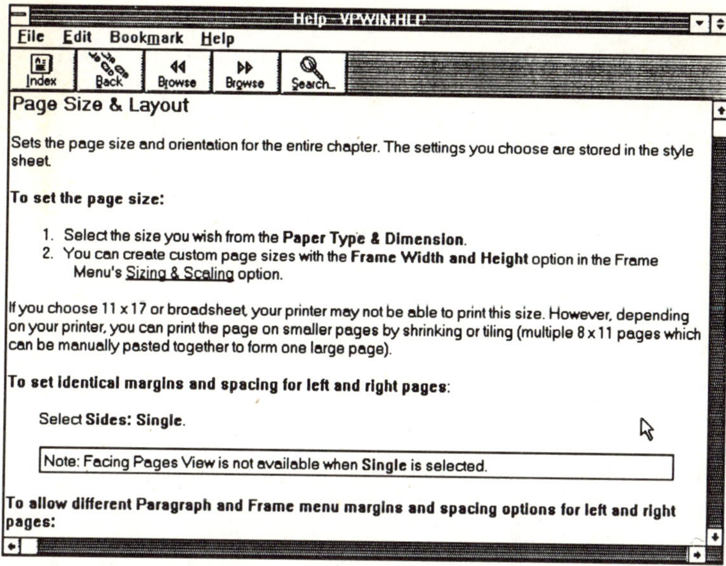

PRINTING MEASUREMENTS

In printing, *points* and *picas* are the standard. For those not familiar with points and picas, there are 12 points to a pica, and there are 6 picas to an inch. Accordingly, there are 72 points to an inch. So 6 picas and 72 points each equal one inch.

When setting measurements in picas in Ventura, the numbers to the left of the comma are picas and to the right of the comma are points. Thus to set 5 picas and 3 points, type 5,03.

If you were to type 2,12, Ventura would change your setting to 3,00, since 2 picas and 12 points actually equals 3 picas.

Sometimes, you may see a tilde character (~) appear in a measurement setting within a dialog box. The reason for this is that the setting is too large to be displayed in the chosen measurement unit. For example, if you set the top margin to 3.00 inches and then change your measurement units to fractional points, you will see only ~~.~~ because three inches is larger than 99.99 points, the largest setting possible with the fractional points measurement unit. When these characters are displayed (~~.~~) the settings are not lost or discarded by Ventura. To see them, change the measurement unit to another setting.

STYLE SHEETS

Ventura uses *style sheets* to control the appearance of your documents. By mastering the use of Ventura's style sheets, you will be able to easily control the appearance of your documents, especially when similar documents need to be produced. For example, if you were to use Ventura to produce a magazine, each issue of the magazine would look similar to the others because the same style sheet would be used, the headlines, body text, bylines, justification, line spacing, and so on to always be the same.

You will learn more about Ventura Publisher's style sheets in later modules, but remember now that by using them, your documents will develop a consistent appearance.

This diagram depicts how a style sheet fits into the Ventura document.

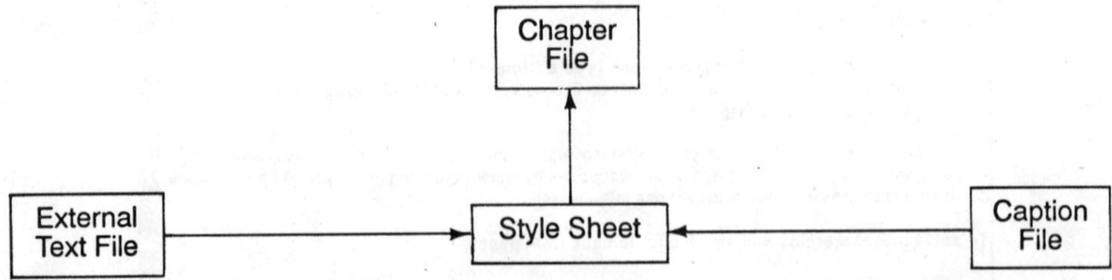

VENTURA MODES OF OPERATION

One of the sometimes confusing concepts of Ventura is the program's use of modes of operation. There are five modes of operation: Frame Setting, Paragraph Tagging, Text Editing, Graphic Drawing, and Tables mode.

These modes of operation determine which mouse cursor will be available and which commands can be executed. For example, when in the Text Editing mode, you cannot move or resize a frame. Rather, you would need to leave the Text Editing mode by selecting the Frame mode. Then you could move or resize the frame, as well as complete any other command dealing with frames.

FITTING IT ALL TOGETHER

Each Ventura document is comprised of several files. The complete document is called a *chapter*.

Since many different files can make up a Ventura chapter, the file that directs, or controls the final output of the document to the printer is the *chapter file*. Ventura creates this file, and it is always assigned the extension .CHP. Each chapter file contains a link, or directions, to Ventura Publisher, telling the program where to look for the various files that make up the chapter.

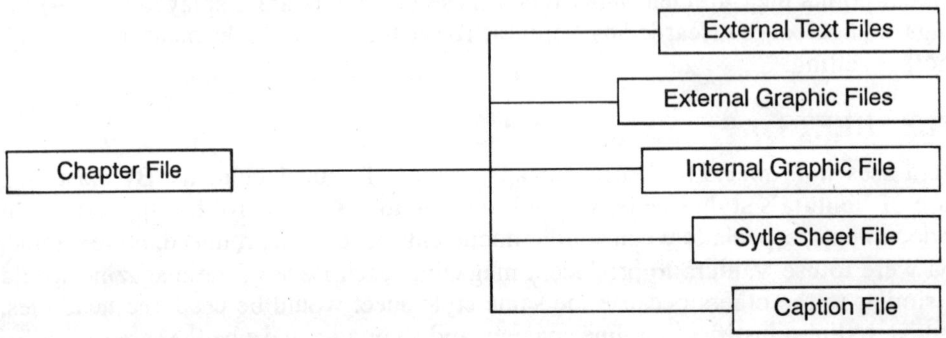

As you can see from reviewing this illustration, many different files are connected or linked to the chapter file. External text and graphic files (those created outside of Ventura and imported into the program) are used, as well as files created within Ventura. The style sheet file, caption file, and internal graphics file are created within Ventura. The style sheet file contains the paragraph tag information. The caption file contains the frame information, including the frame text. The internal graphics file contains the graphics created within the Ventura Graphic Drawing mode.

Since the chapter file acts as a director of the various files used to make the final Ventura document, all the various files need not be located in any single directory or subdirectory. The chapter file will direct Ventura to go to different directories or drives to get the documents required to create the final document. In addition, you can continue to edit or modify the files used within the final document after they have been merged into Ventura. For example, no matter how much a graphic has been scaled, resized, or distorted, the original graphic file remains unchanged by Ventura.

Module 3
SAMPLE SESSION

INTRODUCTION

Using Ventura becomes easy, once you have mastered the concepts of using a computer to do page composition. You will also have to learn how to use Ventura's various modes, how to enter commands, and how to work with Ventura's style sheets. This module is intended to provide a tour through Ventura 3.0 Windows Edition and to let you practice using the mouse and entering commands.

CREATE A TEXT FILE WITH YOUR WORD PROCESSOR

Ventura has a text editing function, but its word processing capabilities are very limited. Using Ventura as a word processor is not recommended. In fact, if you do, you may be disappointed with the results and the limited power of Ventura's text editing function. The program was never intended to be a word processor, rather, it was designed to be used as a page composition program. Accordingly, you should prepare your text with a word processor and import it into Ventura.

Review this list:

MicroSoft Word	.DOC
Multimate	.DOC
WordPerfect (4.2, 5.0 & 5.1)	.WP
WordStar	.WS
WordStar UK	.TXT
Xerox Writer	.XWP
Xywrite	.TXT

If the word processor you will be using is on the list, you can save your text document in the standard file format of the word processor. Ventura can work with the file created by the word processor. If your word processor is not on the list, then you will need to save your text file in either ASCII (.TXT extension) or DCA (.RFT extension).

Type the following text pressing Enter only where <Enter> appears:

Here Comes Desktop Publishing!<Enter>

Page Composition by Personal Computer<Enter>

by George Sheldon<Enter>

Just as Morse changed the world of communications with the invention he called the telegraph, desktop publishing is changing the way we communicate today.<Enter>

Being able to use a personal computer linked to a laser printer to produce near-typeset-quality documents is what desktop publishing promises...and delivers!<Enter>

Name the file DTP and add the proper extension for your word processor format. For example, if you are using WordPerfect as your word processor, name the file DTP.WP. Place the text file, with the proper filename extension, within the TYPESET directory.

REMOVE THE VPWIN.INF FILE

Ventura creates a file called VPWIN.INF to hold the default information you were using during your last session in the program. To make this sample session easier for you to use and to learn, you should start Ventura without a VPWIN.INF file in the \VENTURA directory. By deleting VPWIN.INF, you will cause Ventura to start with the DEFAULT.STY style sheet and with all the paths, filenames, and file types set with the installation defaults. To remove the VPWIN.INF file:

1. At the DOS command prompt type **Del C:\VENTURA\VPWIN.INF** and press **Enter**.
2. Ventura will automatically recreate this file for you each time you use the program.

Before you can start Ventura, you must first start Microsoft Windows.

START WINDOWS

To start Microsoft Windows 3.0 begin at the DOS command prompt:

1. Type **WIN** and press **Enter**.

START VENTURA

To start Ventura within Windows:

1. Select the Windows Applications icon from the Program Manager.
2. Select the Ventura icon from within the Windows Publication window.

3. Select **Open** from the Program Manager **File** menu.

TIP:

Any of the Microsoft Windows shortcuts can also be used to start Ventura. For example, you can double click on the Ventura icon to start the program.

Depending on your computer configuration, it could take up to 60 seconds to see the main screen.

Ventura's main screen looks like this illustration:

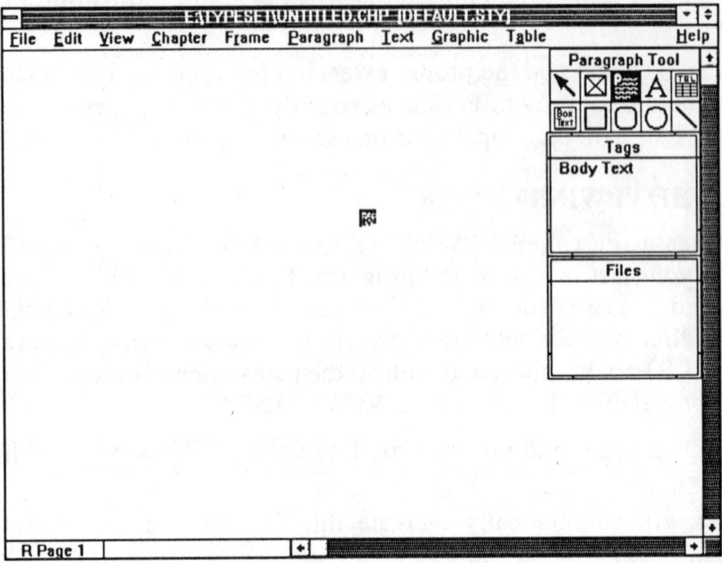

Look at the Title Bar. It shows that you are working with a Ventura file called C:\TYPESET\UNTITLED.CHP and that you are using DEFAULT.STY as your style sheet. (For a detailed description of the parts of this opening screen, see Module 2.)

LOAD THE TEXT FILE

To load the text file that you created with your word processor:

1. Click on the **Frame** Tool in the Toolbox. Your screen should look like this:

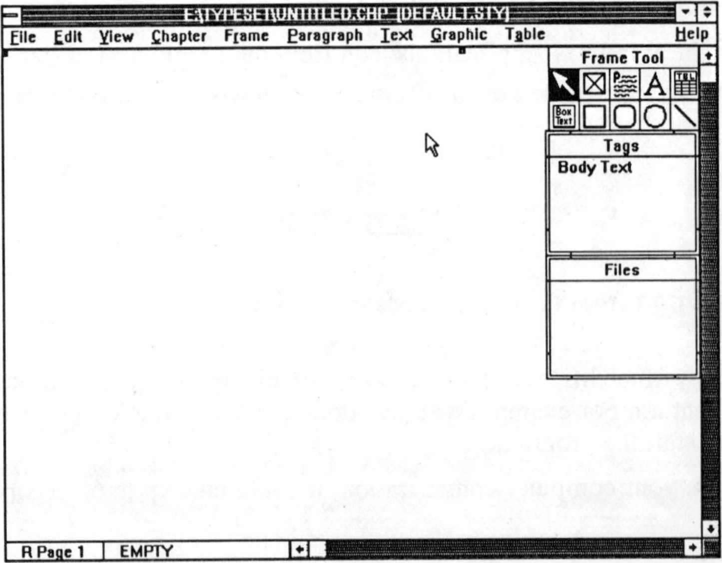

2. Click on the **File** menu and select **Load Text/Picture**. The Load/Text Picture dialog box is displayed.

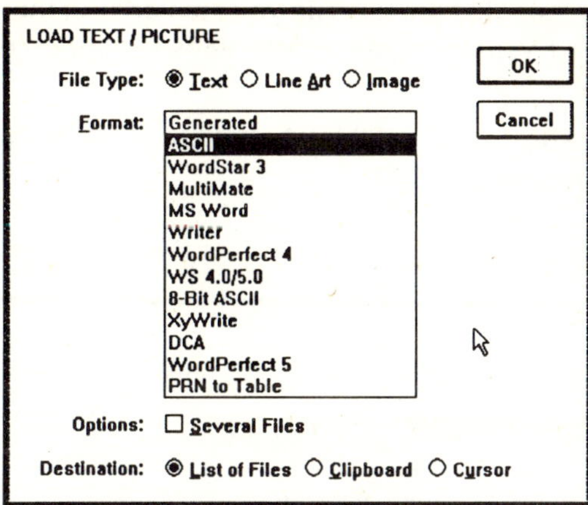

3. Click on **Text** for File Type, **WordPerfect** (or the word processor you used) for Format, and **List of Files** for Destination.
4. Click **OK** to display the Open File dialog box.

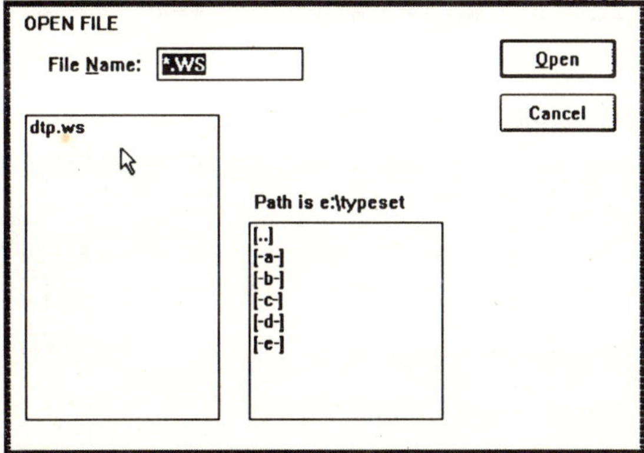

Notice that the Path entry within the Open File dialog box contains the TYPESET path name. The File Name entry contains the asterisk (*) wild card filename and the extension associated with the selected word processor file format. The window below File Name displays the list of files with extensions matching the one associated with the word processor file format that was selected.

NOTE

If the path name is not TYPESET, exit from Ventura by selecting Quit from the File menu. Delete VP.INF from the VENTURA directory. Be sure that the text file you created is in the TYPESET directory. Start Ventura again, repeat steps 1-4 under load the text file.

5. Click on the text file called DTP.XXX (where XXX is the extension for your particular word processor).
6. Click on **OPEN**.

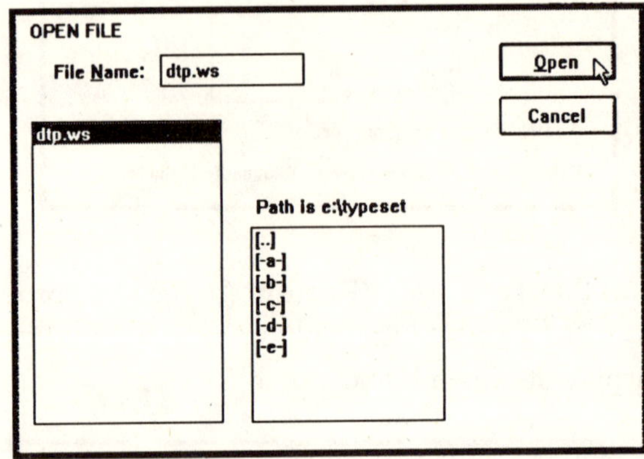

Within a moment, the text appears on your screen:

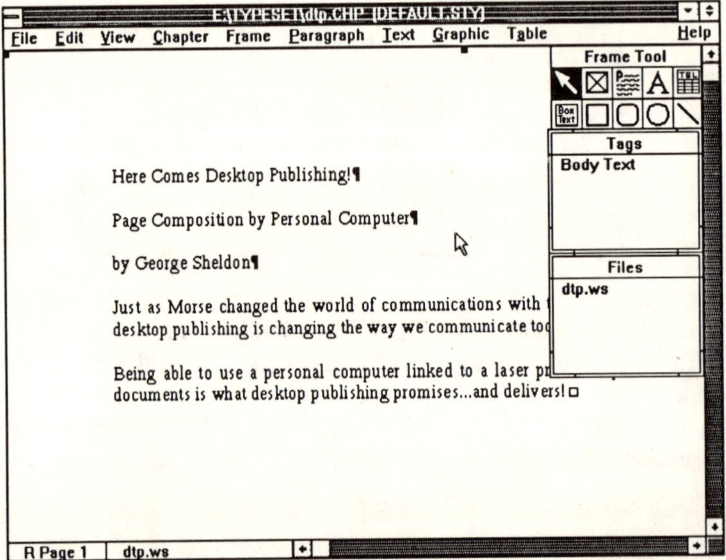

Notice that space appears between the paragraphs, even though there were no blank lines inserted within the text. This space has been created by the paragraph tag for Body Text. Also note that the name of your text file DTP.XXX now appears in the Files Window.

NOTE

> If the text does not appear on your screen, press Ctrl-U to select the Frame Setting mode. Then click on the middle of the working part of the screen, and click on the name of your text file within the Files Window. The text should then appear on your computer screen.

SELECT TEXT ATTRIBUTES

To change the attributes of the selected text:

1. Click on the **Text** Tool from the Toolbox (or press Ctrl-O).
2. Select the words **Page Composition by Personal Computer**. To do so, click and hold at the front of the word "Page" and drag to the end of "Computer" and release the mouse button.

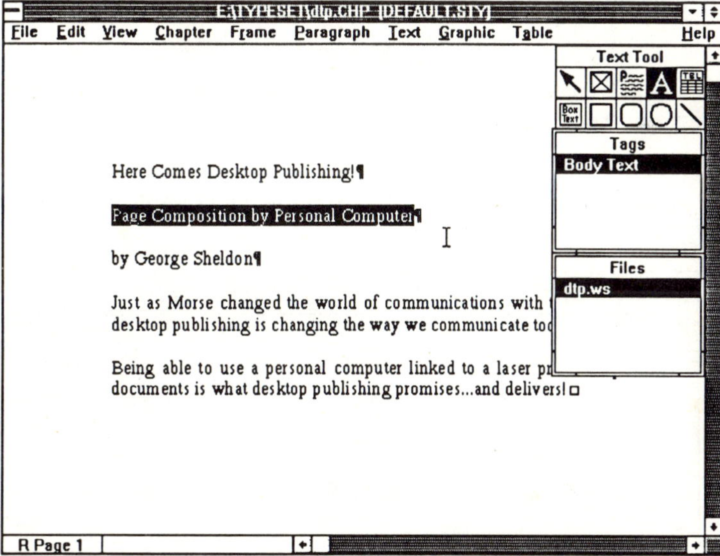

3. Click on the **Text** menu and click on **Italic**.

Notice that the text has now changed from normal to italic.

ALTER THE STYLE SHEET

To alter the style sheet:

1. Click on the **Paragraph** Tool in the Toolbox (or press Ctrl-I).

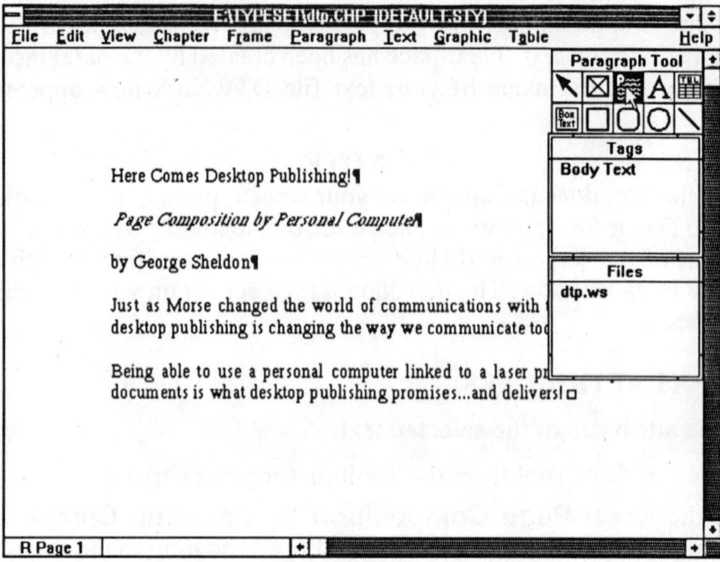

2. Click on the **File** menu and click on **Save Style As**. Ventura displays the Save File As dialog box.

NOTE

To keep DEFAULT.STY from being altered, it is necessary to create a new style sheet.

3. Type **textdoc1.sty** in the File Name area and press **Enter** or click **Save** to save the new style sheet. Notice that the new style sheet name is now displayed in the Title Bar on the computer screen.

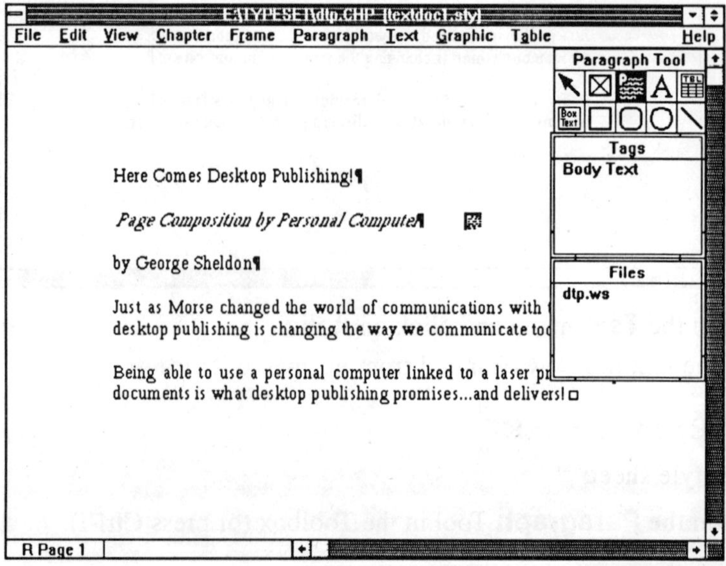

4. Click anywhere on the words **Here Comes Desktop Publishing!** to highlight the paragraph.

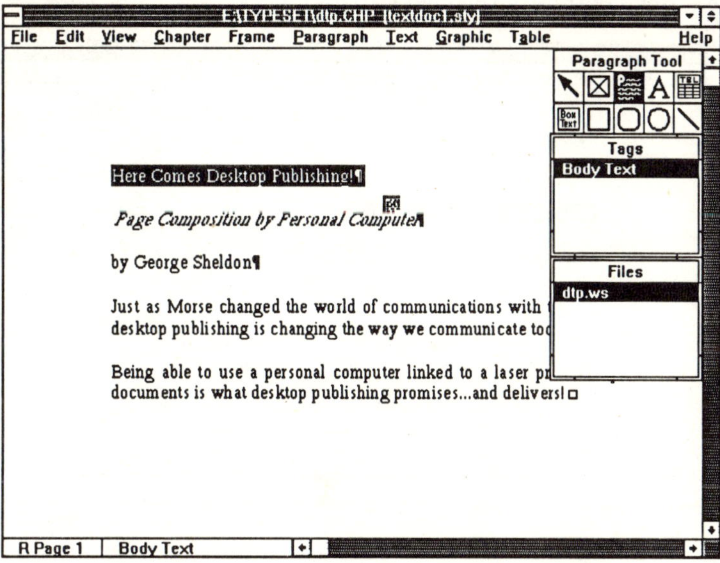

5. Click on the **Paragraph** menu and select **Add New Tag**.

TIP:
You can also press Ctrl-2 to display the Add New Tag dialog box.

ADD NEW TAG
Copy From: Body Text
Name to Add:
OK
Cancel

6. Type **Headline** in the Name to Add section of the Add New Tag dialog box.

ADD NEW TAG
Copy From: Body Text
Name to Add: Headline
OK
Cancel

7. Click **OK** or press **Enter**. Notice that Headline now appears in the Tags Window. Headline is also displayed in the Current Selection Indicator to show that it is assigned to the currently selected paragraph.

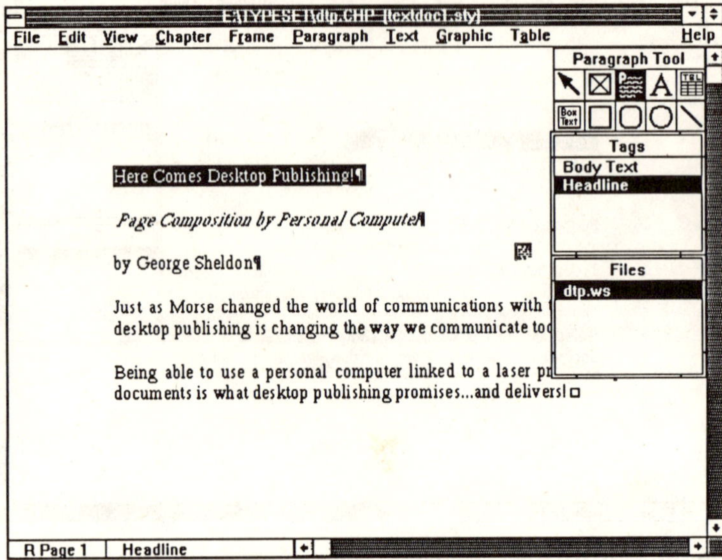

8. Select the **Paragraph** menu and click on **Font** to display the Font dialog box.

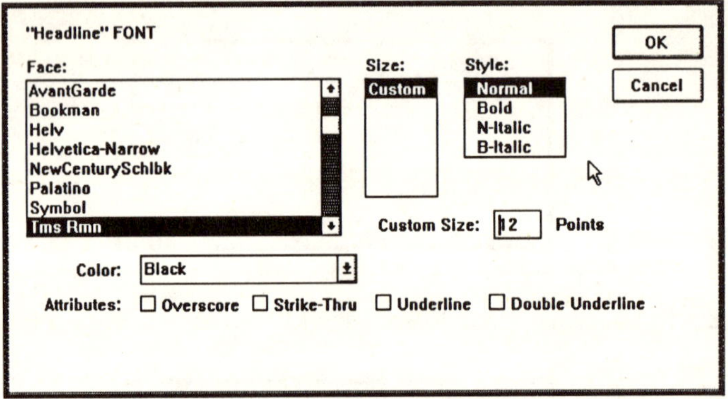

NOTE

The next step assumes that you have installed Ventura on a PostScript Printer. If you have not, click on other values for Face, Size, and Style.

9. Click on **Tms Rmn** for Face, **Normal** for Style, and type **24** for Custom Size. Click **OK** or press **Enter**.

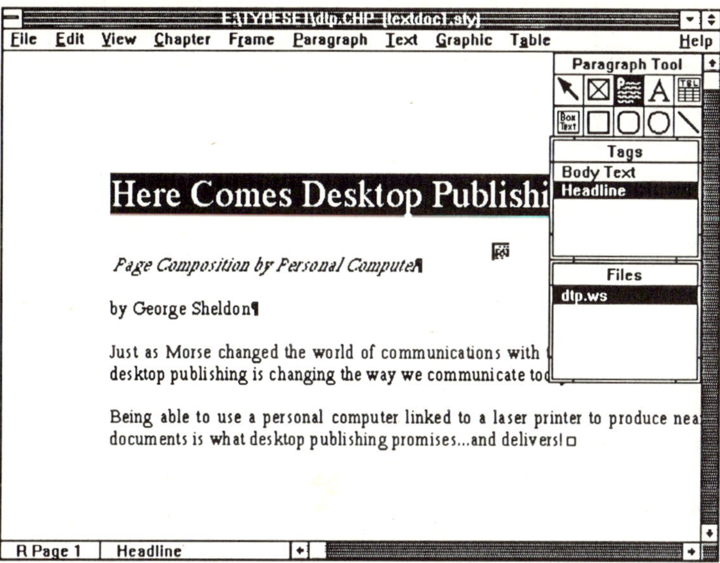

Notice the new appearance of the selected paragraph.

10. Save the changes to the style sheet by selecting the **File** menu and clicking **Save**.
11. Click anywhere on the words **by George Sheldon** to highlight them.
12. Press **Ctrl-2** to display the Add New Tag dialog box.
13. Type **Byline** in the Tag Name to Add area and click on **OK**. Notice that Byline is now included within the Tags Window. Byline is also displayed in the Current Selection Indicator to show that it is assigned to the highlighted paragraph.
14. Select the **Paragraph** menu and click on **Font** to display the Font dialog box.

NOTE

The next step assumes that you have installed Ventura on a PostScript Printer. If you have not, click on other values for Face, Size, and Style.

15. Click on **Tms Rmn** for Face, **Bold** for Style, and type **10** for Custom Size. Click **OK**.
16. Select the **Paragraph** menu and click on **Alignment** to display the Alignment dialog box.

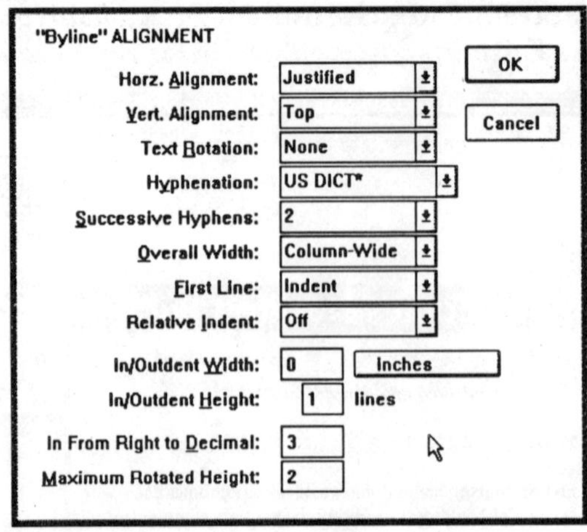

17. Click and hold on the arrow beside **Justified** and drag the pointer down to **Center** in the pop-up menu for Horizontal Alignment. Do the same to select **Off** for Hyphenation. Click **OK**.
18. Click anywhere on the first paragraph which begins "Just as Morse changed the world of communications..." to highlight and select the paragraph.
19. Click on **Paragraph** menu and select **Add New Tag**.
20. Type **First Para** in the Tag Name to Add area and click on **OK**. Notice that First Para is now included within the Tag Window. First Para is also displayed in the Current Selection Indicator to show that it is assigned to the highlighted paragraph.
21. Click on the **Paragraph** menu and click on **Special Effects** to display the First Para Special Effects dialog box.

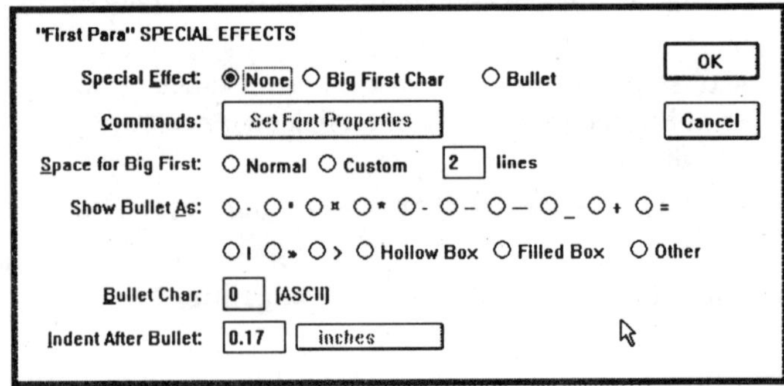

22. Click on **Big First Char** for Special Effect and **Set Font Properties** for Commands. Ventura displays the Font Setting for Big First Character dialog box.

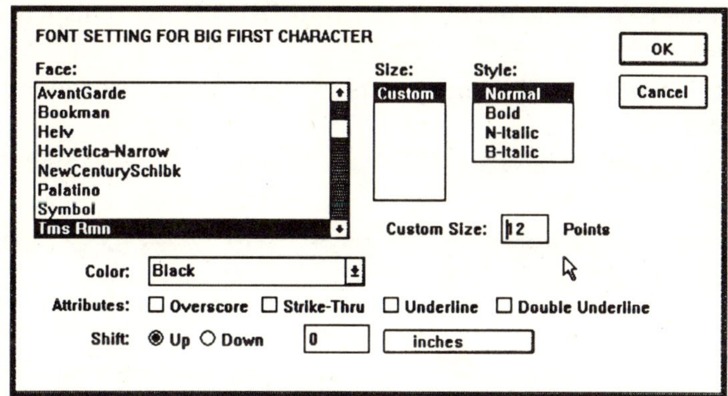

NOTE

The next step assumes that you have installed Ventura on a PostScript Printer. If you have not, click on other values for Face, Size, and Style.

23. Click on **Tms Rmn** for Face, type **18** for Custom Size, and **Bold** for Style. Click **OK** to redisplay the First Para Special Effects dialog box.
24. Click on **Custom** for Space for Big First, **1** for lines, and click **OK**.
25. Click once anywhere in the margin to remove the highlight from the selected paragraph. Your screen should now resemble this illustration:

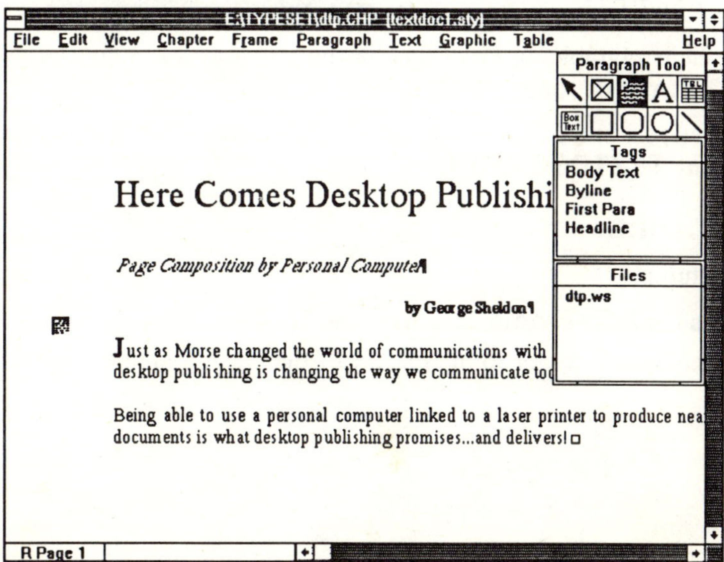

USE ANOTHER STYLE SHEET

To use a different style sheet:

1. Click on the **File** menu and click on **Load Diff. Style** to display the Open File dialog box.
2. Click **Save** when the VP Alert appears asking to Save or Abandon changes to this style sheet.
3. Double click on **&NEWS-P2.STY**. Notice the changes made to the entire document.

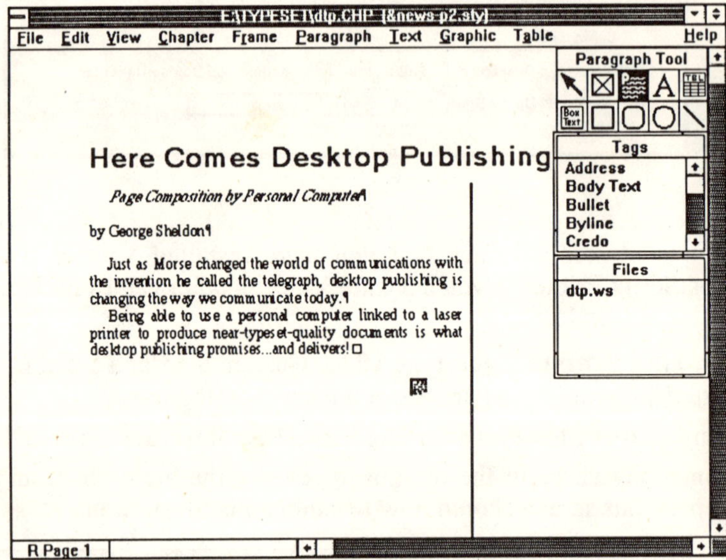

Notice that the paragraph tag First Para has no effect as it has not been defined in the &NEWS-P2.STY style sheet.

4. Repeat steps 1 and 3 for several other style sheets. When done, repeat steps 1 and 3, loading **TEXTDOC1.STY**.

LOAD A PICTURE

To load a picture:

1. Click on the **Add Frame** Tool from the Toolbox.
2. Move the mouse cursor to the middle of the page, and click and hold the mouse button.

3. Drag the mouse button down and to the right to draw a new frame.

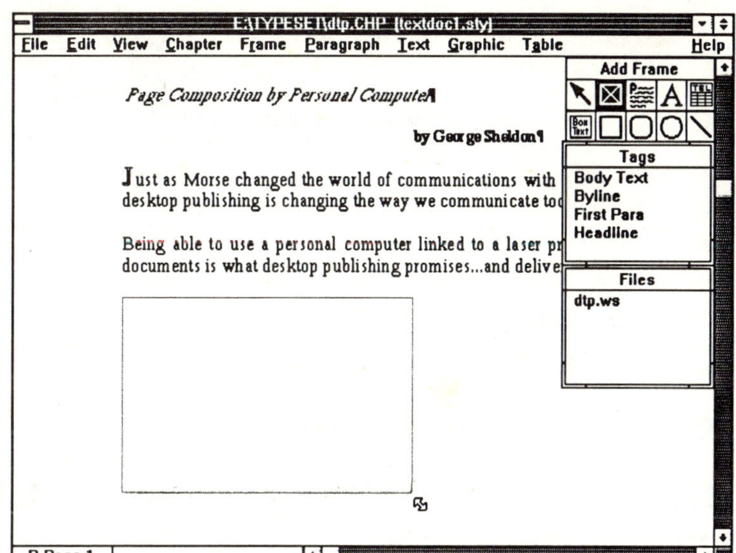

4. Release the mouse button.
5. Select the **File** menu and click on **Load Text/Picture** to display the Load Text/Picture dialog box.
6. Select **Line-Art** for Type of File, and **GEM** from Line-Art format. Click **OK**. The Item Selector is displayed.
7. Double click on **NOZZLE.GEM**. The picture of the nozzle will appear in the frame drawn in steps 2 and 3.

NOTE

If the nozzle picture does not appear in the frame, point to the middle of the frame and click the mouse once. Then point to the Files Window and click on NOZZLE.GEM. The nozzle picture should then appear in the frame.

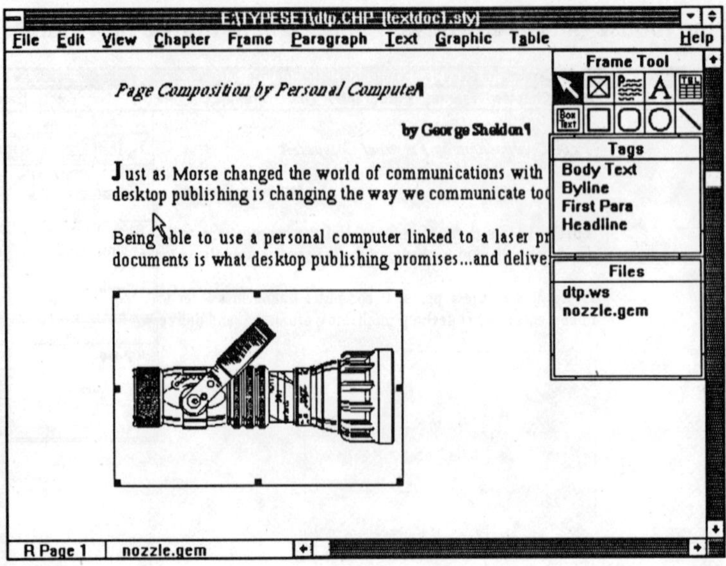

SIZE A FRAME

To change the size of a frame:

1. Click in the middle of the frame. Eight boxes appear along the edge of the frame.
2. Click and hold on the box located in the bottom right corner. Drag the mouse down and to the right to make the frame larger.

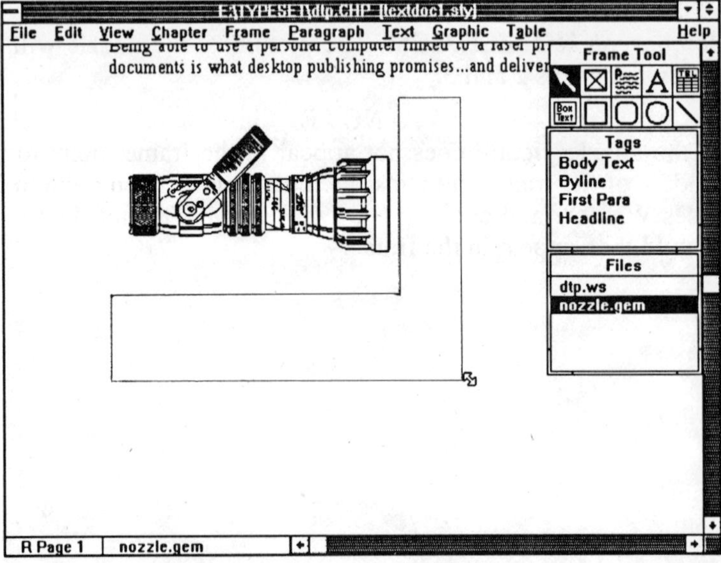

3. Repeat step 1. Click and hold on the box located in the bottom right corner. Drag the mouse to make the frame smaller.

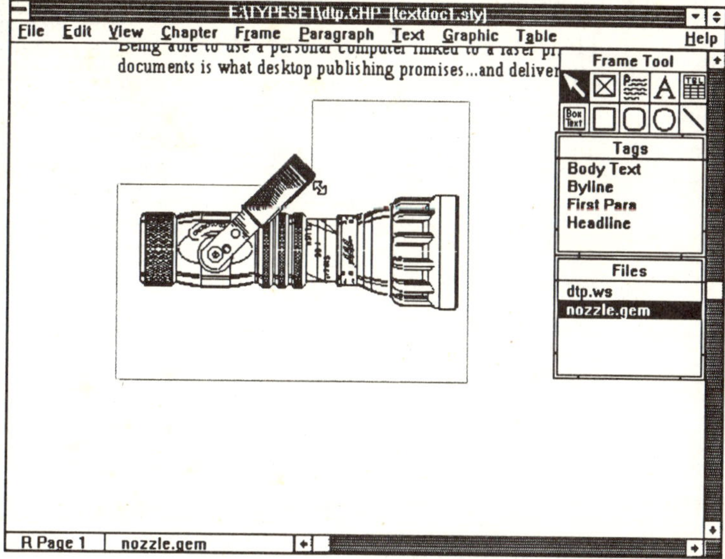

4. Repeat step 1, and click and hold one of the other boxes to practice sizing the frame. Continue practicing sizing the frame until you feel comfortable with the procedure.

CHANGE VIEWS

To change the view of a Ventura document:

1. Click on the **View** menu and click on **Reduced View.**

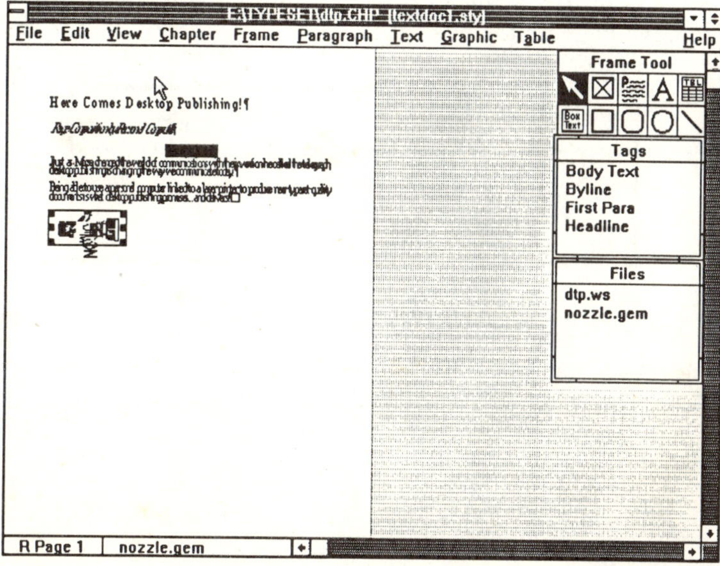

2. Click on the **View** menu and click on **Normal View**.

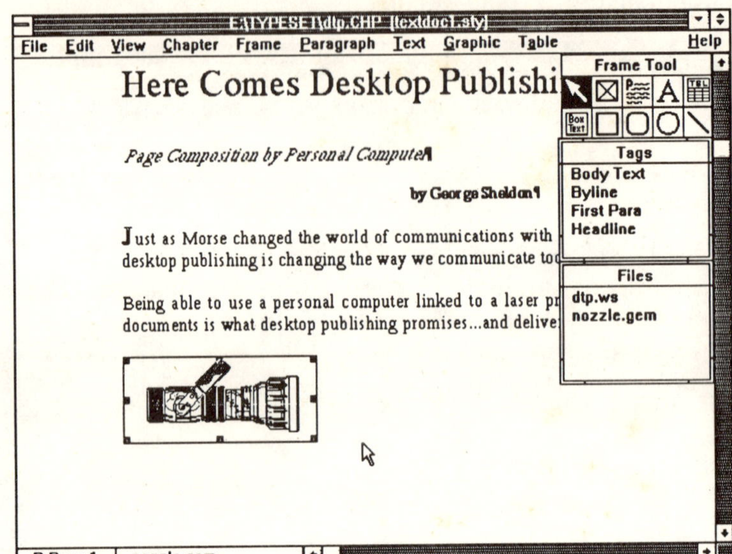

3. Press **Ctrl-R** to select Reduced View.
4. Press **Ctrl-N** to select Normal View.
5. Press **Ctrl-E** to select Enlarged View.
6. Press **Ctrl-N** to return to Normal View.

INSERT A PAGE

To insert a new page:

1. Click on the **Chapter** menu and click on **Insert/Remove Page** to display the Insert/Remove Page dialog box.

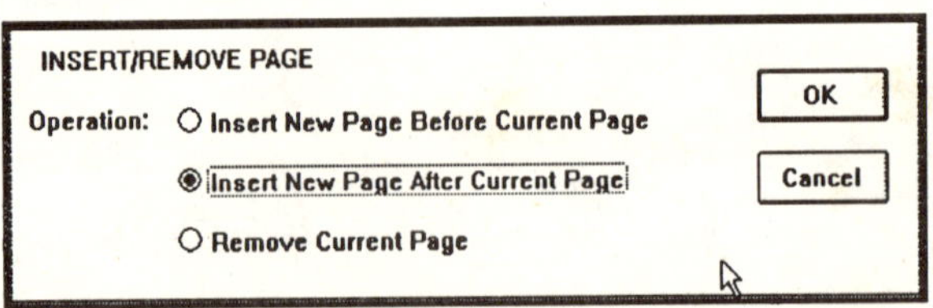

2. Click on **Insert New Page After Current Page** and then click **OK**.

Notice that a new page has been inserted and Ventura is now on page 2.

CREATE A GRAPHIC

To create a graphic within Ventura:

1. Click on the **Add Frame** Tool from the **Toolbox**.
2. Move the mouse cursor to the middle of the page and click and hold the mouse button.
3. Drag the mouse button down and to the right to draw a new frame, and release the mouse button.
4. Click on the **Rectangle** drawing tool within thc Toolbox.
5. Move the mouse to the middle of the frame and click and drag the mouse. A box appears as you drag.

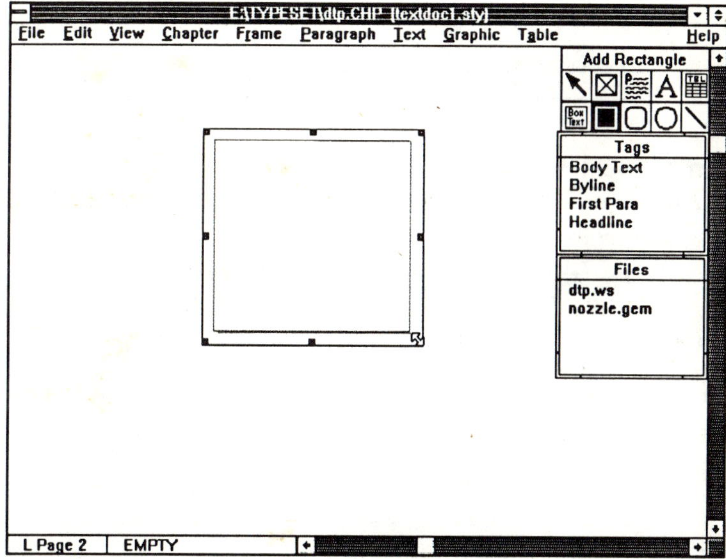

6. Release the mouse button.

SAVE THE DOCUMENT

To save the Ventura document with a new name:

1. Point to the **File** menu and click on **Save As**. Ventura displays the Save File As dialog box.

The dialog box should display the various chapters located with the TYPESET directory.

2. Type **firstdoc.chp** as the name of the document you are now saving in the File Name area.

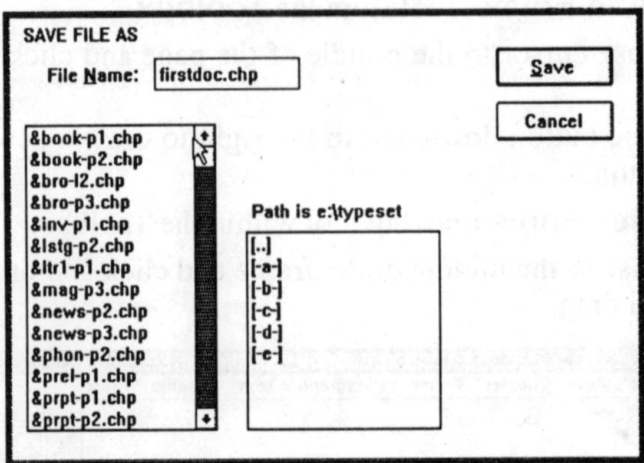

3. Press **Enter**. Ventura displays messages telling you what documents it is now saving. After the files have been saved, the main screen shows the document name and style sheet name in the Title Bar.

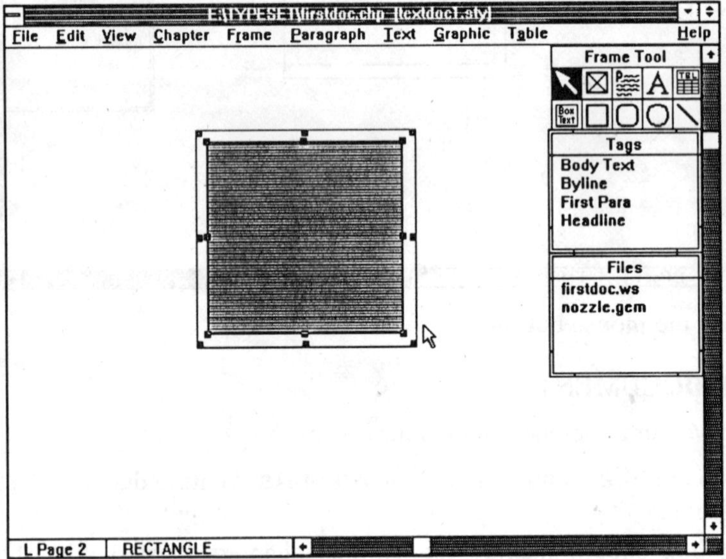

PRINT A DOCUMENT

To print a Ventura document:

1. Select the **File** menu and click on **Print**. Ventura displays the Print dialog box.

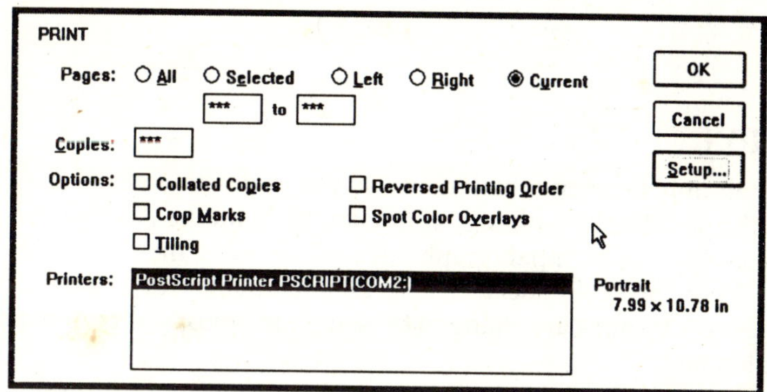

2. Click on **All** for Pages. Click **OK** to start printing. Ventura displays different messages to tell you what it is doing.

EXIT VENTURA

To exit Ventura:

1. Select the **File** menu and click on **Exit**. Ventura returns you to the Windows Applications.
2. Press **Alt-F4** to exit Windows. Select **OK** to return to the DOS prompt.
3. Turn to Module 88 to continue the learning sequence.

Module 4
ADD NEW TAG

DESCRIPTION

Ventura's Paragraph Tagging function allows you to design, create, change, and assign attributes to the paragraphs within your document. With the Add New Tag option, you can add and create your own paragraph tags. When using the Paragraph Tool, you can assign a tag from the style sheet. Those tags available are selected from the Tags Window. The tag attributes are changed by using the options or commands available in the Paragraph menu.

Ventura contains two types of tags. They are user-defined tags, which you create, and Ventura-generated tags, which are automatically created when you use certain commands, such as Headers & Footers or Auto-Numbering.

User-defined tags can be added anytime to a style sheet. To add a new tag:

- Select the Paragraph Tool.
- Select the Add New Tag option in the Paragraph menu. The Add New Tag dialog box appears:

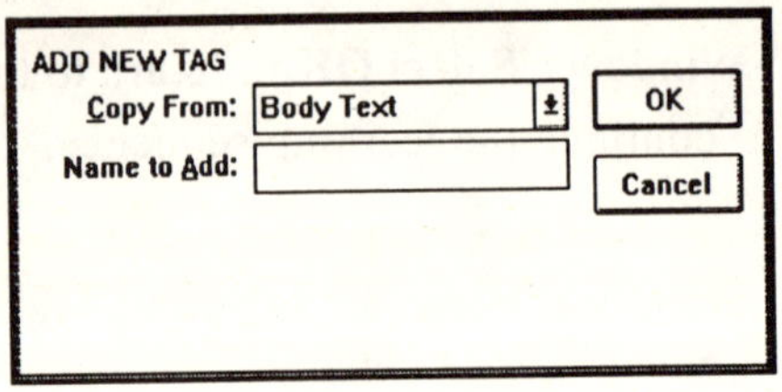

ADD NEW TAG
Copy From: Body Text
Name to Add:
OK
Cancel

TIP:

You can also press Ctrl-2 to make the Add New Tag dialog box appear.

- Type the name of the new tag you want to add. You can also copy the settings from a tag by typing the name of that tag on the Copy From line.
- Select OK when finished. The new tag name automatically appears in the Tag list within the Tag Window.

For more information about paragraph tags, see Module 55.

APPLICATIONS

Ventura makes formatting text easier by using paragraph tags. Because each tag can be set to assign a different style to a paragraph, you are able to take advantage of design freedom. And since more than one paragraph can be assigned with the same tag, you assure a uniform appearance throughout the current document, as well as any other document using the same style sheet.

Obviously, you are going to want to create and use your own paragraph tags. The Add New Tag command allows you to add tags to your style sheets.

TYPICAL OPERATION

In this example, you use the Paragraph mode and select a paragraph. Then, you assign a new paragraph tag to the style sheet. The Ventura sample chapter &NEWS-P2.CHP is used. The example begins with &NEWS-P2.CHP already open and in use. Use the command Open Chapter in the File menu to retrieve and open &NEWS-P2.CHP. You may need to adjust your screen using the scroll bars to make your computer look like the illustrations.

1. Press **Ctrl-I** to select Paragraph mode.
2. Point to the **Paragraph** menu and click on **Add New Tag**.
3. Type **Sm Body Text** in the Name to Add. Your screen should resemble this illustration:

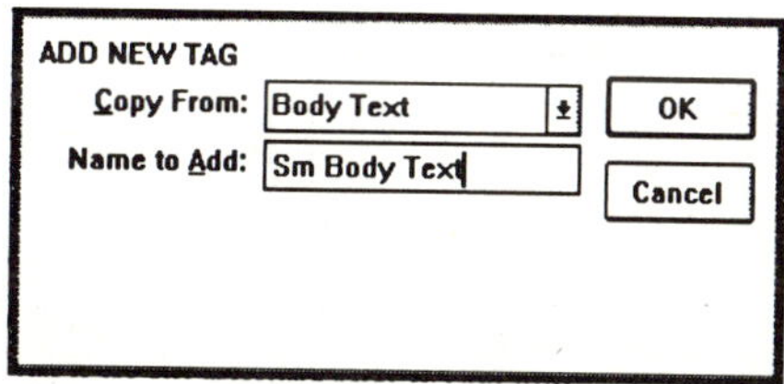

4. Point and click on **OK** in the Add New Tag dialog box. The words Sm Body Text now appear in the Tag Window.
5. Turn to Module 74 to continue the learning sequence.

Module 5
ALIGNMENT

DESCRIPTION

The Alignment command controls the positioning of text within a column or frame. This command also turns on and off hyphenation, sets the language rules to use for hyphenation, and determines the number of successive lines that can be hyphenated.

The Alignment command in Ventura is accessed by tagging a paragraph and then selecting the Alignment command. The changes made with this command affect the paragraph tag associated with the selected text. When a paragraph tag is changed, it affects all text marked with that paragraph tag in your Ventura document, as well as in other Ventura documents that use the same style sheet.

"Subhead" ALIGNMENT

OK

Cancel

Horz. Alignment:	Left
Vert. Alignment:	Top
Text Rotation:	None
Hyphenation:	Off
Successive Hyphens:	Unlimited
Overall Width:	Column-Wide
First Line:	Indent
Relative Indent:	Off
In/Outdent Width:	0 Inches
In/Outdent Height:	1 lines
In From Right to Decimal:	0
Maximum Rotated Height:	0

The Alignment dialog box contains these options:

Horz. Alignment — Select how the text lines up horizontally in the column or frame: Left, Center, Right, Justified, or Decimal. The following describes the five types of alignments available in Ventura:

Left aligns all the text along the left margin and keeps the right margin ragged.

Centered aligns all the text in the middle of the left and right margins and keeps both margins ragged.

Right aligns all the text along the right margin and keeps the left margin ragged.

Justified aligns all the text along the left and right margins. Justified text has no ragged edges. Justified adds spaces between words and letters as needed to align the left and right margins.

You can also select *Decimal*. This option within the pop-up menu positions the first decimal point in a line at a distance from the right margin specified by In From Right To Decimal (also located within the Alignment dialog box). This setting allows easy alignment on the decimal point.

Vert. Alignment — Text is aligned vertically within a page or frame. This command allows you to position vertical text anywhere on the page or frame. (For some printers, this command does not work). Use Vertical Alignment in conjunction with the Horz. Alignment command to position your vertical text.

Text Rotation — Choose the degree of text rotation desired.

Hyphenation — Choose between the hyphenation rules for US English or another language. Select Off to disable the automatic text hyphenation available in Ventura.

Successive Hyphens — Select the number of successive lines that end with hyphens. For example, if you select 3, Ventura never hyphenates the last word in more than three text lines in a row.

Overall Width — Select whether the text should be aligned within the column or within the frame. By selecting Frame-wide as the Overall Width, column settings are ignored and the paragraph is printed across the entire frame or page.

NOTE

Text continues to flow after the frame-wide paragraph. For that reason, frame-wide paragraphs in other columns will print over the paragraphs in the left column. Column Balance should always be turned on whenever frame-wide tags are applied to paragraphs which are not at the top of a frame.

First Line — Select Indent or Outdent if either the first line of the paragraph should be offset to the right (Indent) or to the left (Outdent). An outdent is sometimes called a hanging indent. The following text illustrates the indent and outdent:

This paragraph is indented text where the first line of the paragraph is offset to the right.

This paragraph is outdented text where the first line of the the paragraph is offset to the left.

Relative Indent	Select On if you want the indent of the paragraph to be exactly the length of the last line in the previous paragraph. If there is an amount specified in the Indent Width, that amount of space is added in addition to the length of the previous line. Select Off for the last line in the previous paragraph to have no effect.
In/Outdent Width	Select the amount of space desired for the indent or the outdent.
In/Outdent Height	Enter the total number of lines to indent or outdent. In most cases, the typical number of lines is one.
In From Right to Decimal	Enter the amount of distance from the right margin to align the decimal within the text.
Maximum Rotated Height	Enter the maximum height desired for the text that is rotated.

The Alignment command is located in the Paragraph menu.

APPLICATIONS

The text Alignment command affects the final appearance of the text. Justified text generally looks neater in appearance and certainly looks typeset.

Center-aligned text is useful for headlines in most publications. Right-aligned text is often used in advertisements and picture captions on the left side of the picture. Left-aligned text is still used in many applications, for both style and for ease of reading. Decimal alignment is used to create easy-to-read tables containing numbers.

This command is also used to create both indented and outdented paragraphs. Such paragraphs are often used to enhance the design of a publication. Outdents are also used in combination with bullets to make items on a list easy to read.

The Alignment command also sets the hyphenation of text within the Ventura document. Depending on the width of your columns, you may need more hyphenation to eliminate white "rivers of space" within your text. Also, you should turn the hyphenation off for most headlines.

TYPICAL OPERATION

In this example, you change the alignment of text. The example begins with &LSTG-P2.CHP already open and in use. Use the Open Chapter command in the File menu to retrieve and open &LSTG-P2.CHP. So your view matches the screen depicted in this book, press Ctrl-N. Adjust the scroll bars to make your computer screen look like the illustration.

1. Press **Ctrl-I** to select the Paragraph Tool.
2. Click on the text "PC-Eye" in the left column.
3. Click on the **Paragraph** menu and select **Alignment**.

4. Click and hold on **Horz. Alignment** and select **Right**. Press **Enter**. Your screen should resemble this illustration:

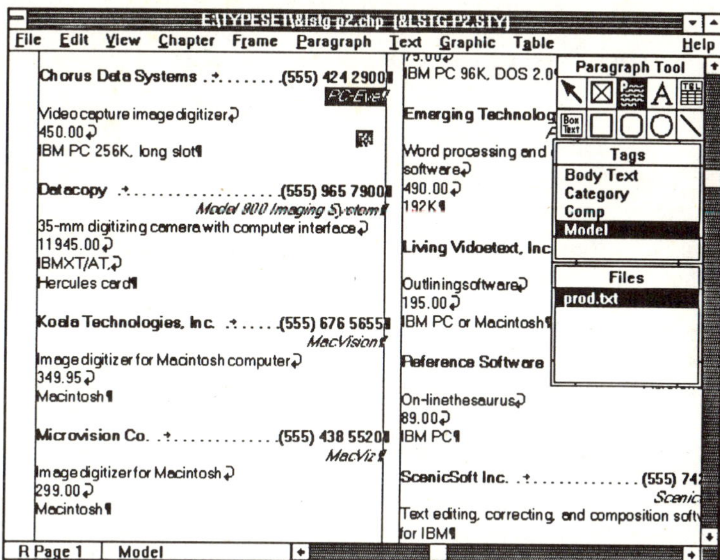

5. Click on the **Paragraph** menu and select **Alignment**.
6. Click and hold on **Horz. Alignment** and select **Left**. Press **Enter**.
7. Turn to Module 4 to continue the learning sequence.

Module 6
ANCHORS & CAPTIONS

DESCRIPTION

The Anchors & Captions command assigns an anchor name and creates a caption for any frame. The anchor name is used to associate a frame with a specific point in the text on the underlying page.

If the location of the text changes within the Ventura document, the associated frame can be moved by using the Re-Anchor Frames command (see Module 58 for more information). With the captions option located within the Anchors & Captions command, a caption can be attached to any side of the frame. The captions are included in a frame Ventura produces adjacent to the anchored frame. The caption frame moves with the main frame, even if the frame is cut and pasted.

Each caption frame consists of two basic parts: one with Ventura automatically generated information (such as table or figure numbers), and the other part with the text typed into the caption frame. Many captions in a document consist of both the automatically generated and manually typed text. The manually typed text can be as long as you want it to be.

NOTE

> Anchor names and captions cannot be assigned to the underlying page.

All captions for a chapter are stored in a separate caption file. This file can be edited and even spell checked later in a word processor.

There are two different caption counters used in this command. The Table Counter and the Figure Counter can be used to automatically number frame captions. These counters are automatically updated as captions are deleted or added. See Module 83 for more information about the Update Counter command.

The Anchors & Captions command is accessed from the Frame menu. To access the command, Ventura must first be in Frame mode, and a frame must be selected. When the Anchors & Captions command is selected, the Anchors & Captions dialog box appears:

ANCHORS & CAPTIONS

Anchor: [ ] OK

Caption: Off Cancel

Label: [ ]

Inserts: ○ Table # ○ Figure # ○ Chapter # ○ Text Attr.

The options in the Anchors & Captions dialog box include:

Anchor — Type the name of the anchor to be assigned to the selected frame. This name must exactly match the anchor name that was inserted in the text with the Insert/Edit Anchor command. (See Module 37 for more information about Insert/Edit Anchor.)

Caption — Select the location where the caption is to appear in relation to the frame. The choices are: Above, Below, Left, and Right.

Label — Type the information Ventura is to enter automatically into the frame caption. The information can include the inserts described below.

TIP:

If you are creating a series of figures or tables, enter this generated information in the same format for all figures and tables to create a uniform appearance.

Inserts — Select the type of information Ventura is to enter automatically into the caption. Also, the appearance of the caption can be defined. The information Ventura inserts into the Label area each time an item is clicked in the dialog box is:

Item	*Inserted Characters*
Table #	[T#]
Figure #	[F#]
Chapter #	[C#]
Text Attr.	<D>

For [T#], Ventura substitutes the current table number.

For [F#], Ventura substitutes the current figure number.

For [C#], Ventura substitutes the current chapter number.

For <D>, you must substitute for "D" the characters associated with the various text attributes Ventura supports. The letters and attributes are described in Appendix B.

NOTE

If no text appears in the caption frame, select the Frame mode and then select the caption frame. Then lengthen or widen the caption frame as necessary until the caption text can be seen.

Two paragraph tags are automatically generated by Ventura when a caption is added to a frame. The tag names are Z_LABEL FIG and Z_CAPTION. The basic attributes for these two tags are copied from the Body Text, but the attributes can be changed if desired.

APPLICATIONS

The Anchors and Caption command provides several useful tools when working with frames. The first is that it assigns an anchor entered into the text to a frame. By doing so, this completes the process and allows a frame to be anchored to specific text within the Ventura document. Then, as the text moves through editing, formatting, or realignment, the frame moves with the text.

The Anchors and Captions command also provides a way to add captions to the frames created within the document. Captions make illustrations, tables, and charts easier to understand for the reader of documents. Ventura can automatically number the captions, such as Figure 1-1, Figure 1-2, etc.

This command also allows you to decide where the captions should appear on your document. A caption can be on either side of a frame, or the top, or bottom.

TYPICAL OPERATION

In this example, you change a caption and insert an anchor. The Ventura sample chapter &BOOK-P1.CHP is used. The example begins with &BOOK-P1.CHP already open and in use. Use the Open Chapter command in the File menu to retrieve and open &BOOK-P1.CHP. You may need to adjust your screen using the scroll bars to make your computer look like the illustration.

1. Click on the **Frame** Tool.
2. Click in the middle of the frame containing the nozzle to select it.
3. Click on the **Frame** menu and select **Anchors & Captions** to display the Anchors & Captions dialog box.
4. Press **Del** three times to erase Map and type **Nozzle** in the Anchor section.
5. Press **Tab** twice to move to Label. Press **Del** to erase the text in the Label section.
6. Click on **Figure #**, press **Spacebar** once, and type **An Example of a Graphic**. Press **Enter**. Your screen should resemble this illustration:

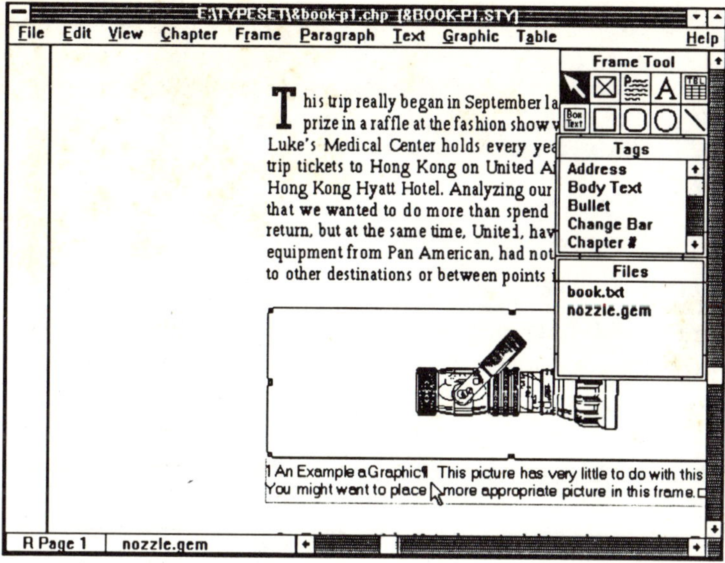

7. Click on the **File** menu and click on **Save**.
8. Turn to Module 37 to continue the learning sequence.

Module 7
ATTRIBUTE OVERRIDES

DESCRIPTION

The Attribute Overrides command allows you to modify your text by changing the overscore, strikethrough, underline, small text, superscript and subscript text attributes.

To select the Attribute Overrides command, first select the Ventura Paragraph Tool and then select a paragraph. The Attribute Overrides command can then be selected from the Paragraph menu. When selected, the Attribute Overrides dialog box appears:

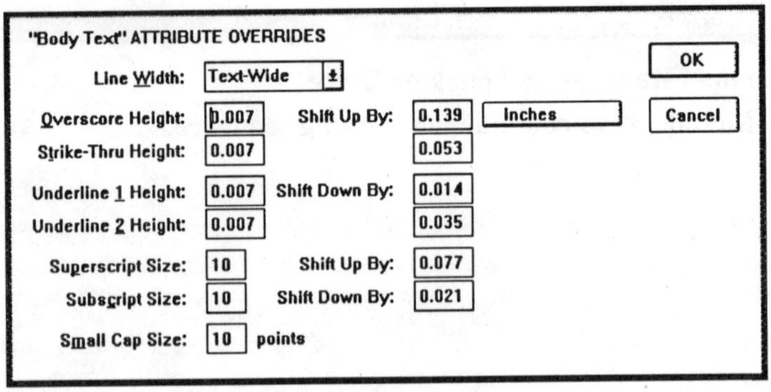

"Body Text" ATTRIBUTE OVERRIDES

Line Width: Text-Wide ±
Overscore Height: 0.007 Shift Up By: 0.139 Inches
Strike-Thru Height: 0.007 0.053
Underline 1 Height: 0.007 Shift Down By: 0.014
Underline 2 Height: 0.007 0.035
Superscript Size: 10 Shift Up By: 0.077
Subscript Size: 10 Shift Down By: 0.021
Small Cap Size: 10 points

OK
Cancel

The following options are available within the Attribute Overrides dialog box:

Line Width — Select Text-Wide to set the length of lines to the width of text. Select Margin-Wide if the line is to extend from the left margin to the right margin.

Overscore Height — Type in the height or thickness of the overscore height and the amount of distance the overscore is to shift from the text baseline.

Strike-Thru Height — Type in the height or thickness of the Strike-Thru Height and the amount of distance the Strike-Thru Height is to shift from the text baseline.

Underline 1 Height — Type in the height or thickness of the Underline 1 height and the amount of distance the underline is to shift from the text baseline.

Underline 2 Height	Type in the height or thickness of the Underline 2 height and the amount of distance the underline is to shift from the text baseline.
Superscript Size	Type in the font size of the superscript and the amount of distance the superscript is to shift from the text baseline.
Subscript Size	Type in the font size of the subscript and the amount of distance the subscript is to shift from the text baseline.
Small Cap Size	Type in the font size to be assigned to the Small Cap setting.

APPLICATIONS

The Attribute Overrides command provides several different ways to fine-tune the typography of your Ventura document. For example, you can precisely adjust the super and subscript characters of your document to prevent them from touching the adjacent lines of type.

The Attribute Overrides command allows you to determine how thick or thin an underline should be and how far under the word it should be placed. This precise control is available to you with this command.

TYPICAL OPERATION

In this example, you change the attributes of selected text within the Ventura sample chapter <R1-P1.CHP. The example begins with <R1-P1.CHP already open.

1. Press **Ctrl-O** to select the Text Tool.
2. Highlight the street address paragraph within the letterhead.
3. Click on the **Text** menu and select **Underline**.
4. Press **Ctrl-I** to select the Paragraph Tool.
5. Select the street address paragraph within the letterhead.
6. Click on the **Paragraph** menu and select **Attribute Overrides** to display the Attribute Overrides dialog box.
7. Type **0.1** for the **Underline 1 Height**. Click **OK**. Notice that the underline thickness has increased.
8. Click on the **File** menu and click on **Revert to Saved**. Click on **OK** when prompted to revert back to the last saved version.
9. Turn to Module 20 to continue the learning sequence.

Module 8
AUTO-NUMBERING

DESCRIPTION

The Auto-Numbering command defines the automatic numbering of tagged paragraphs in the underlying page. With automatic numbering, you create numbered headlines and paragraphs, such as those used in technical manuals, scholarly outlines, and business documents.

Auto-Numbering automatically inserts the section numbers for you. These section numbers can contain combinations of numbering styles, as well as punctuation.

NOTE

> Only text in the underlying pages can be auto-numbered. Text in frames and box text cannot be auto-numbered. This command never affects the text in regular frames.

A computer training manual might have these headlines:

1.0 Personal Computers
    1.1 Major Components
        1.1.2 C.P.U.
        1.1.3 Input Devices
        1.1.4 Output Devices
    1.2 How They Work
2.0 Mainframe Computers

As a scholarly outline, these topics might use this numbering scheme:

A. Personal Computers
    1. Major Components
        a. C.P.U.
        b. Input Devices
        c. Output Devices
    2. How They Work
B. Mainframe Computers

The numbers or letters can be any variety of styles such as legal (1.0, 1.1., 1.2, 1.2., and so on), Harvard (I., II., III., and so on), or numeric (1, 2, 3, and so on).

Your numbering scheme is associated with a particular paragraph tag (see Module 55 for a description about paragraph tags). When the paragraph tag is assigned to a paragraph, Ventura precedes the paragraph with the numbering scheme. Ventura automatically increases the number or letter by one each time it encounters a paragraph marked with the paragraph tag. For example, if the first paragraph is numbered with I, the second paragraph is automatically numbered with II.

The numbering scheme is created by typing information in the Auto-Numbering dialog box.

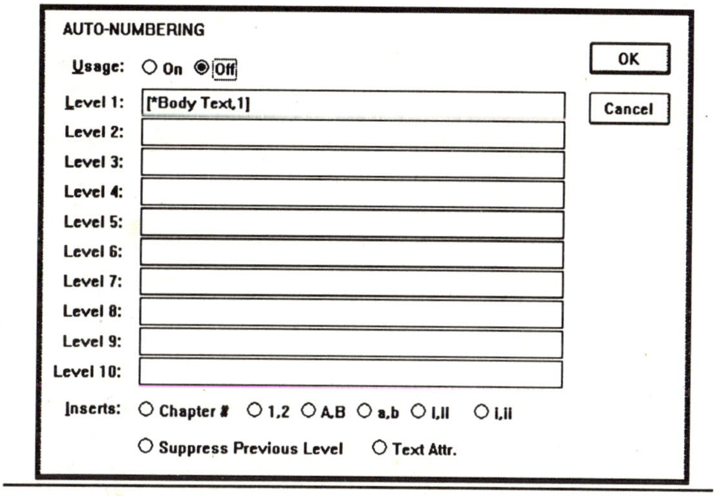

AUTO-NUMBERING

Usage: ○ On ◉ Off — OK — Cancel

Level 1: [*Body Text,1]
Level 2:
Level 3:
Level 4:
Level 5:
Level 6:
Level 7:
Level 8:
Level 9:
Level 10:

Inserts: ○ Chapter # ○ 1,2 ○ A,B ○ a,b ○ I,II ○ i,ii

○ Suppress Previous Level ○ Text Attr.

The Auto-Numbering dialog box contains these options:

Usage	Select On or Off. To use the auto numbering, Usage must be On.
Level 1 through 10	The multiple levels establish different numbering definitions for different paragraph tags. You can create a maximum of 10 levels of section numbering by typing a different tag name on each level line. The tag names entered must match paragraph tags associated with the current style sheet.
Inserts	Select the type of numbering scheme to place into the auto-number definitions. Also, define the appearance of the numbers. The information Ventura inserts into the auto-numbering definition each time you click on the item on the dialog box is:

Item	*Inserted Characters*
Chapter #	[C#]
1,2	[*tag name,1]
A,B	[*tag name,A]
a,b	[*tag name,a]
I,II	[*tag name,I]
i,ii	[*tag name,i]
Suppress Previous Level	[-]
Text Attr.	<D>

For [C#], Ventura substitutes the current chapter number.

For any definitions containing [*tag name,x], replace "tag name" with the name of the paragraph tag you are associating with the numbering scheme. For example, if you want to define a numbering scheme for the paragraph tag named Headline, replace [*tag name,x] with [*Headline,x]. The x in[*tag name,x] is the type of numbering scheme to use.

The following table shows the different types of numbering schemes available:

What You Enter For Tag Definition	*What You Get For First Headline*	*What You Get For Second Headline*
[*Headline,1]	1	2
[*Headline,A]	A	B
[*Headline,a]	a	b
[*Headline,I]	I	II
[*Headline,i]	i	ii

Ventura precedes the numbering scheme for lower level definitions with the numbering schemes for higher level definitions. Each time a paragraph tag specified in the Auto-Numbering dialog box is encountered, the numbers for all lower level paragraphs are reset to their starting number. For example, if Level 1 generates a 1. and Level 2 generates a 2., Ventura would print the Level 2 definition as 1.2., preceding the Level definition with the Level 1 definition. This, in fact, creates headings for many technical manuals. For example, if you are creating an outline with a Level 1 of capital letters and a Level 2 of Arabic numerals, Ventura would print the first level similar to this:

A. Headline

and the second level similar to this:

A.1. Headline

The final output would look similar to this:

A. Personal Computers
   A.1. Major Components
   A.2. How They Work

To suppress the printing of the previous level and to prevent the A. from printing on the lower levels and present a more traditional outline appearance, begin the definitions for the lower levels with the Suppress Previous Level characters, [-]. For example, Level 1 and 2 entries should look like this:

[*Headline, A].　　(to print capital letters)

[-][*Headline, 1].　　(to suppress the previous level and print Arabic numbers)

The output looks like this:

A. Personal Computers
    1. Major Components
    2. How They Work

Auto-Numbering automatically creates a paragraph tag for each of the 10 levels. The automatically generated tags are named Z_SECn, where n is the level number. All the attributes of these tags can be changed to control the appearance of the automatically generated numbers.

When Auto-Numbering creates the labels, they are located on the line above the associated tagged paragraph. To place the auto-number and paragraph on the same line, enter these values for the number tag and the paragraph tag.

Item to Change	*Auto-Numbering Tag*	*Text Tag*
Font	Same As Text Tag	Same As Auto-Numbering Tag
Alignment	Left	Indent relative to previous line, plus Relative Indent: On First Line: Indent In/Outdent Width: 1,00 picas and points
Spacing	Above: Normal Below: 0.000	Above: 0.000 Below: Normal
Breaks	Line Break: Before Keep with next: Yes	Line Break: After Next Y Position: Beside Last line of Previous Para
Ruling Line Above	As desired	None
Ruling Line Below	None	As desired

Text Attributes define the appearance of the generated numbers. Selecting Text Attribute places the characters <D> on the line. Substitute the characters for "D" associated with the various text attributes Ventura supports. For example, place the characters <B> in front of the paragraph numbers to make them bold and place the characters <I> in front of the paragraph numbers to make the numbers italic. The complete list of letters and attributes are described in Appendix B.

You can also add any additional text to a numbering scheme by typing it outside the left and right brackets. For example, if you want to include the word "Headline" at the beginning of the Level 1 definition, type:

    Headline [*Headline,1]

Each time Ventura encounters text marked with the Headline, it now adds

    Headline n

to the front of the text, where "n" is the paragraph number.

If you want to place periods between the level numbers in a technical document, type for Levels 1, 2, and 3:

[*Headline 1,1].
[*Headline 2,1].
[*Headline 3,1].

For a Headline 3 paragraph tag, Ventura adds a number similar to this to the front of the text:

1.1.2. How A C.P.U. Really Works

Without the periods at the end of the brackets, the headline would look like this:

112 How A C.P.U. Really Works

Section numbers are added, deleted, or changed only when a change is made in the Auto-Numbering menu.

APPLICATIONS

This command is used to automatically number sections within a technical manual or an outline. Being able to automatically number your headlines permits easy revisions when the additional text is added or deleted during editing.

You can also automatically number chapters. If your document is made up of many small sections, you could group them together into one chapter and automatically number the chapter numbers.

TYPICAL OPERATION

In this operation, you add numbering schemes to the &BOOK-P1.CHP sample chapter. The operation begins with the &BOOK-P1.CHP already open and in use.

1. Select the **Paragraph** Tool and click on the paragraph "Chapter 1."
2. Click on the **Paragraph** menu and click on **Auto-Numbering** to display the Auto-Numbering dialog box. Click **On** for Usage. The auto-numbering function is now activated.
3. Click on the **Level 1** line and click on **I,II** for inserts.
4. Press **Left Arrow** three times, and press **Backspace** enough times to erase tag name.
5. Type **Chapter #**, press **Right Arrow** to move the cursor to the end of the line, and type a period.
6. Click on the **Level 2** line, click on **Suppress Previous Level** for Inserts, then click on **i,ii**.
7. Press **Left Arrow** three times, and press **Backspace** enough times to erase tag name.

8. Type **Chapter Title,** press **Right Arrow** to move the cursor to the end of the line, and type a period. Your screen should resemble this illustration:

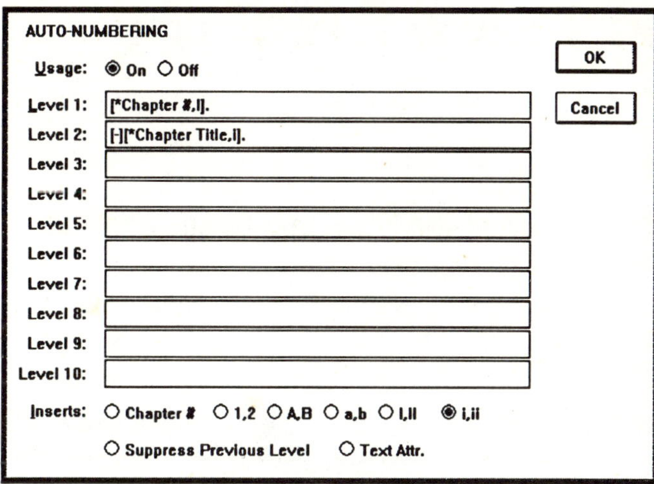

9. Click **OK**. Notice the automatically created levels are on the line above the Chapter and Chapter Title tagged paragraphs.
10. Click on the **File** menu and click on **Revert to Saved** and then click on **OK** when prompted to revert back to the last saved version.
11. Turn to Module 60 to continue the learning sequence.

Module 9
BOX CHARACTER

DESCRIPTION

The Box Character command creates square boxes. Many fonts do not provide these characters, so Ventura can create them for you.

To create a box character, Ventura must be in Text Editing mode. Position the cursor where the box character is to be created. Select Insert Special Item in the Text menu. The secondary Insert Special Item menu appears:

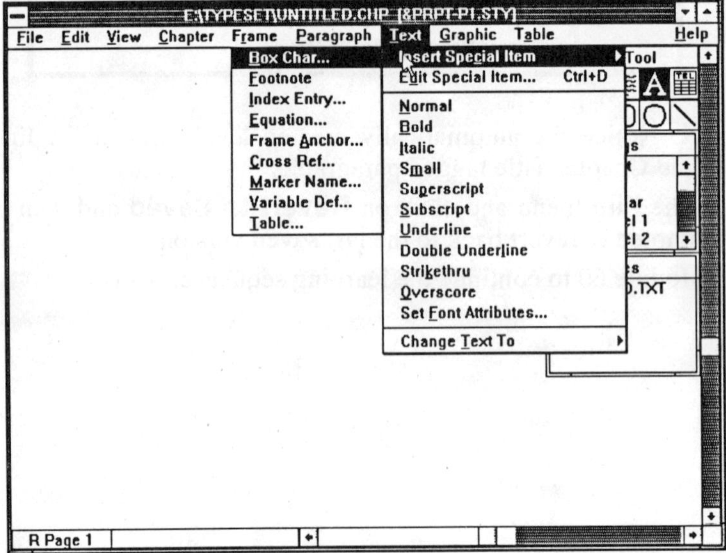

Select Box Char with the mouse from the secondary menu. The Box Char VP Alert dialog box appears:

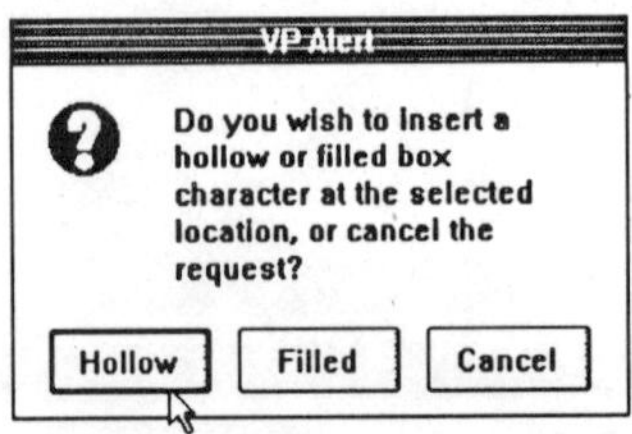

Select the type of box to be created by selecting either Hollow or Filled. Select Cancel to cancel the creation of the box character.

TIP:

Once the box character has been created, use the Text mode Set Font button to change the size of the box character, shift it up or down, or move it left or right with kerning.

After making the selection of the type of box desired, Ventura creates the box character.

APPLICATIONS

The box character is used in many different forms and to enhance the appearance of many documents. For example, a check-off type form can be created, or a box character can be placed at the beginning of a paragraph to create a different look to your document.

Without this command, the box character is not available in most fonts.

TYPICAL OPERATION

In this operation, you create a special box character. The sample chapter &LSTG-P2.CHP is used. The example begins with &LSTG-P2.CHP already in use.

1. Press **Ctrl-O** to select the Text Tool.
2. Move the mouse cursor to in front of the "E" in "Editorial Software" located in the left column. Click the mouse once.
3. Point to the **Text** menu and click on **Insert Special Item** to display the Insert Special Item dialog box.
4. Point and click on the **Box Char** in the secondary menu.
5. Select **Filled** to create a filled box.

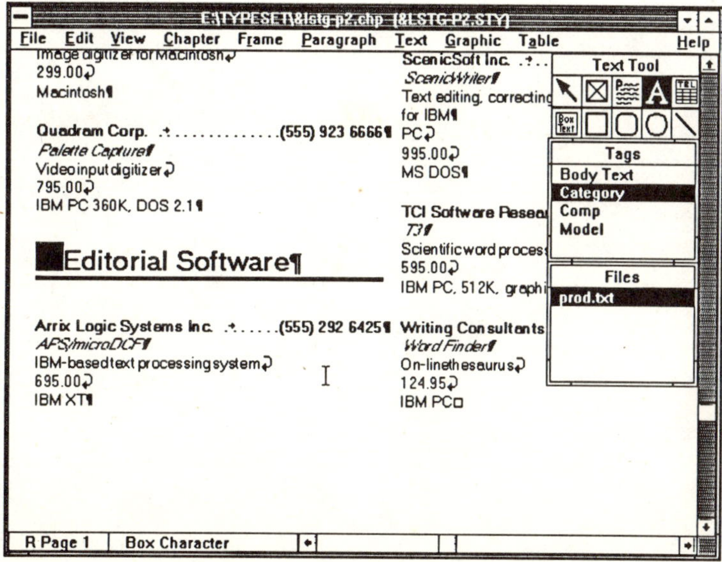

6. Notice the filled box character that has been created. Point to the **File** menu and click on **Revert to Saved**. Click on **OK** when prompted to revert back to the last saved version.
7. Turn to Module 8 to continue the learning sequence.

Module 10
BREAKS

DESCRIPTION

The Breaks command adjusts the way paragraphs are grouped and separated on a page. The command controls the flow of text between paragraphs.

Following a break, the next paragraph can begin on a new line (this is a line break), at the top of a new column (this is a column break), at the top of a new page or frame (this is a page break), or at the top of the next left or right page or frame (this is the page break before/until left/right).

A paragraph is defined as any amount of text that ends with a carriage return. A paragraph can be as short as one character, a word, a sentence; or can run many pages long. What marks the end of a paragraph is the carriage return. The carriage return is inserted into the text when you press Enter.

To select the paragraph and use the Breaks command, the Paragraph Tool must be selected. As with all other commands that control a paragraph tag, the changes you make with this command affect a particular paragraph tag. When a change is made to a paragraph tag, it affects all text marked with that paragraph tag in your document, as well as in other documents that use the same style sheet.

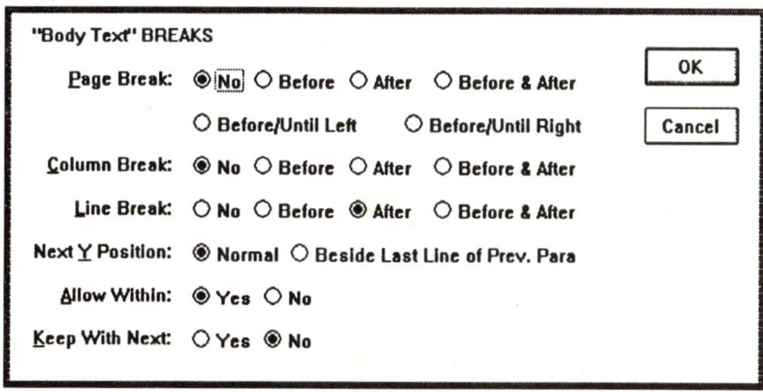

The Breaks dialog box contains these options:

Page Break — Select where the page breaks should occur in relation to the tagged paragraph. Use No if you do not want the paragraph to create a page break. Before places a page break in front of the paragraph. After places the page break following the paragraph. Before & After places a paragraph on a page by itself. Before/Until Left locates the page break at the top of right-hand pages within the document. Before/Until Right locates the page break at the top of left pages within the document.

TIP:

The Page Break Before/Until Left or Right forces the text to the next left or right page. Ventura will automatically insert a blank page if necessary.

Column Break — Select where the column breaks occur in relation to the tagged paragraphs. (This option works the same way as the Page breaks, except it forces the text to the top of the next column, rather than the next page.) Use No if you do not want the paragraph to create a break. Before places a column break in front of the paragraph. After places the column break following the paragraph. Before & After positions a paragraph in a column by itself.

Line Break — Select where the line break occurs in relation to the tagged paragraphs. Use No if you do not want the paragraph to force a line break.

NOTE

If you select No, all successive paragraphs marked with this tag will run together.

Before positions a line break in front of the paragraph. After positions a line break following the paragraph. Before & After positions the paragraph alone.

Next Y Position — Select either Normal or Beside Last Line of Prev. Para. In most cases, select Normal. The Beside Last option allows you to place the text of the next paragraph on the same line as the previous paragraph. This is useful if your layout requires columns of paragraphs.

Allow Within — Select Yes to have Ventura break paragraphs between columns or pages. Select No to keep a paragraph in one page or column. If Ventura cannot fit the paragraph into the current page or column, it pushes the entire paragraph to the top of the next page or column.

TIP:

In most cases, it is best to use Yes for Allow Within.

Keep With Next — Select Yes to keep the current paragraph and next paragraph in the same page or column. (This feature is extremely useful to keep headings with body text.) Select No if you always want Ventura to be able to break up the current paragraph and next paragraph between succeeding pages and columns.

The Breaks command is accessed by first selecting or tagging a paragraph and then selecting the Breaks command from the Paragraph menu.

APPLICATIONS

Breaks is an extremely powerful tool that will make your work with Ventura much easier. You can keep a paragraph from being split across a column or a page. Or you can allow the paragraph to be split across the column or the page.

The Breaks command also allows you to make settings that keep certain paragraphs together. This is useful for headings, caption numbers, or even bylines, where the paragraphs must be kept together to make sense in the publication. For example, you would not want the headline to appear on the bottom of the page, orphaned from the rest of the text.

The Breaks command also allows you to have certain paragraphs start at the top of a new page. For example, book chapters always start on the top of a page. Using this book as an example, suppose you create a paragraph tag called Module. You would assign Page Break Before to the tag. Then that tag would be assigned to each module heading. Ventura would automatically push the text to the top of the next page.

The Breaks command can also be used in conjunction with the Spacing commands to create a table using vertical tabs. To do so, first type the text in your word processor like this:

PART NUMBER
DESCRIPTION
PRICE

A123
Eight Inch Elastometer
$123.99
B456
Twelve Inch Hydrometer
$454.87
C789
Fourteen Inch Ohm Meter
$321.21

The paragraph tags (with proper spacing and settings) would make the text look like this:

PART NUMBER	DESCRIPTION	PRICE
A123	Eight Inch Elastometer	$123.99
B456	Twelve Inch Hydrometer	$454.87
C789	Fourteen Inch Ohm Meter	$321.21

Each category in the vertical tab table would be assigned its own paragraph tag within the style sheet. For example, there would be three paragraph tags created, one each for part number, description, and price.

In the Breaks dialog box, the Line Break settings for each paragraph tag would be:

Paragraph Tag	*Line Breaks Setting*
Part No	Before
Description	No
Price	After

To complete the vertical tab table format, you must access the Space dialog box and use the In From Left and In From Right settings. When completed, those settings should be similar to these:

Paragraph Tag	*In From Left*	*In From Right*
Part No	0	6
Description	1.5	3
Price	4	2

TYPICAL OPERATION

In this example, you use Breaks to change the attributes of Body Text within the sample chapter document called SCOOP.CHP. The example begins with SCOOP.CHP already open. Use the Open Chapter command in the File menu to retrieve and open SCOOP.CHP. Make sure that you are still in Reduced view.

1. Press **Ctrl-I** to select Paragraph Tool.
2. Click on the first paragraph in the left column. In the Tag Window, Ventura indicates this is Body Text.
3. Click on the **Paragraph** menu and click on **Breaks**. The Breaks dialog box appears.
4. Select **After** in the Page Break option.

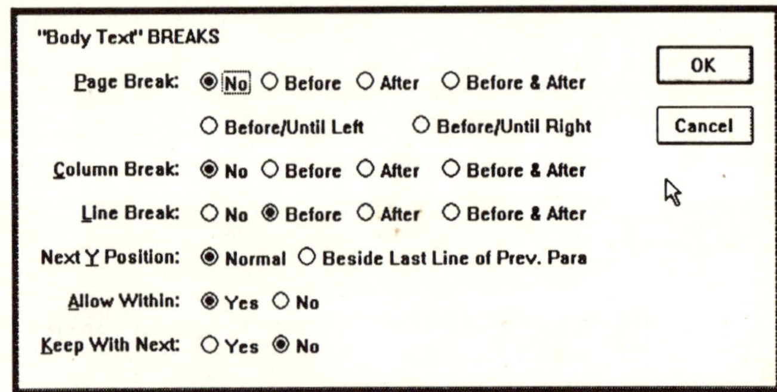

5. Click **OK**. Notice that Ventura has redrawn the screen, and the text following the selected paragraph is now on a separate page. Your screen should look like this:

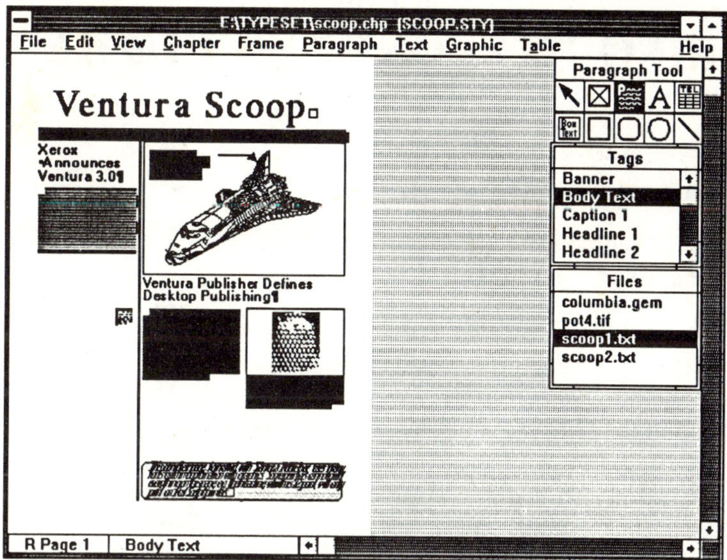

6. Click on the **Paragraph** menu and click on **Breaks**. The Breaks dialog box appears.
7. Select **No** in the Page Break option. Click **OK**. When Ventura redraws the screen, the document returns to normal.
8. Turn to Module 76 to continue the learning sequence.

Module 11
BRING TO FRONT, SEND TO BACK

DESCRIPTION

The Bring to Front and Send to Back commands allow you to change the stacking or layering of the graphics that overlay each other.

You can Bring to Front or Send to Back one graphic or multiple graphics at a time.

The Bring to Front command is accessed in the Graphic menu (you must have a Ventura created graphic selected to access it) or by pressing Ctrl-A. The Send to Back command is also accessed in the Graphic menu or by pressing Ctrl-Z.

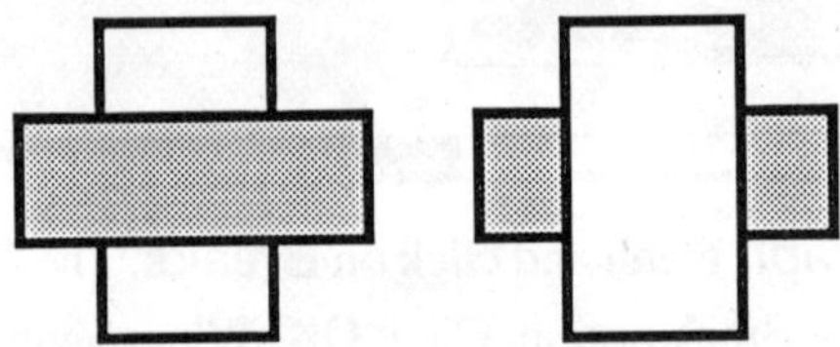

APPLICATIONS

These two commands, Bring to Front and Send to Back, are useful when you need to cover part of a graphic with another graphic.

For example, if you were drawing a simple block diagram, you could place the boxes and then connect them with a line. Then you could make the line look segmented by either bringing the blocks front, or by sending the lines back.

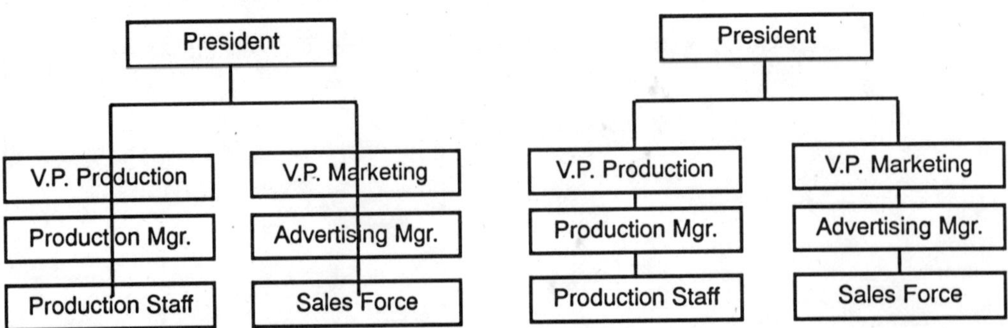

TYPICAL OPERATION

In this exercise, you create selected graphics and move them from the front to the back, and again from back to the front. Load the default style sheet into a blank page and select Normal view.

1. Click on the **File** menu and select **New**, then select **Abandon** to clear the screen.
2. Select the **Add Frame** Tool in the Toolbox.
3. Create a new frame in the middle of the page.
4. Select the **Add Circle** Tool from the Toolbox and click and drag the mouse down and to the right to create an ellipse. Release the mouse button.
5. Click on the **Graphic** menu and select **Fill Attributes**. Select the fourth pattern on the list for Pattern. Click **OK**.
6. Select the **Add Line** Tool from the Toolbox, and draw a line over the top of the circle. Your screen should resemble this illustration:

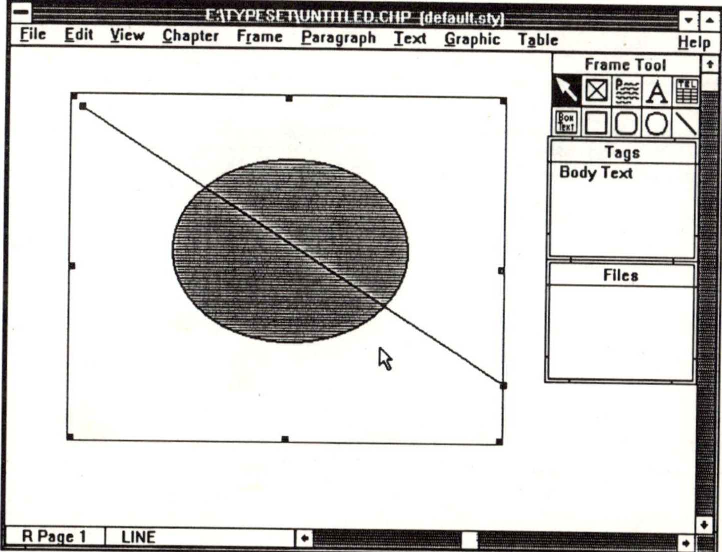

7. Click on the ellipse.
8. Press **Ctrl-A** to bring it to the front.

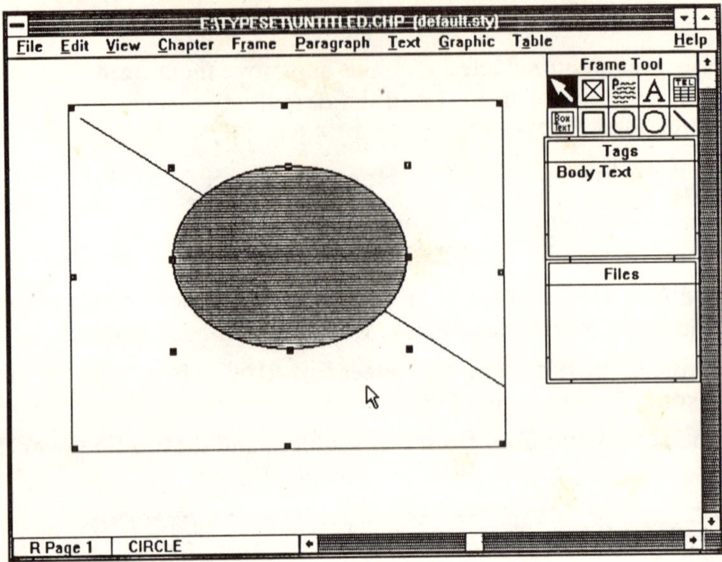

9. Press **Ctrl-Z** to send it to the back.

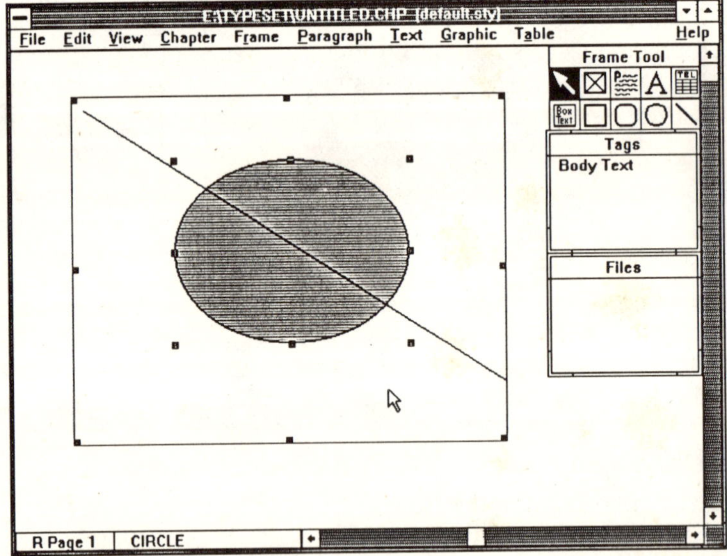

10. Click on the **File** menu and click on **New**. Click on **Abandon** when prompted to save or abandon changes to this chapter.
11. Turn to Module 18 to continue the learning sequence.

Module 12
BROWSE CHAPTER

DESCRIPTION

The Browse Chapter command retrieves a previously created and stored Ventura chapter and its related style sheet, text files, and graphic files. When using the Browse command, you cannot make any changes in the chapter.

The Browse Chapter command opens a chapter just as the Open Chapter command does.

NOTE

When a chapter has been opened using the Browse command, the word Browse appears in the title bar at the top of your computer screen.

The Browse Chapter command is available only on the Network version of Ventura. An unlimited number of users can view a chapter at the same time. If someone tries to make a change to a chapter while using the Browse Chapter command, Ventura displays an alert advising that the chapter cannot be altered while browsing.

NOTE

Although a Chapter is being browsed, other users on the network could still modify text or graphics files by using a word processor or graphics program.

Ventura allows read-only style sheets. A style sheet may be set to read-only by the DOS ATTRIB program or by other similar programs. A read-only style sheet cannot be modified within Ventura. To alert you that a read-only style sheet is in use, the letters RO appear in the Title Bar next to the style sheet name.

APPLICATIONS

The primary purpose and use of the Browse Chapter command is to allow you to view a chapter while other people on the network are working on it. This command can also be used to copy an item (text, frame, tag, graphic, table) onto the clipboard, so it can be copied into another chapter.

The Browse Chapter command is only available to those who are using Ventura on a network.

TYPICAL OPERATION

In this example, you browse a previously saved chapter. If a chapter is open on your computer screen, select Exit from the File menu. After Ventura prompts you to save the current chapter, you will return to the DOS prompt. Restart Ventura in the normal manner, and you will return to a blank screen, ready to continue with these steps:

> **NOTE**
>
> You must be operating Ventura on a network to complete this section. If you are not using Ventura on a network, turn to Module 9 to continue the learning sequence.

1. Click on the **File** menu and select **Browse Chapter**. The Browse Chapter dialog box appears.
2. Click and hold on the scroll bar until you locate SCOOP.CHP.
3. Click on **SCOOP**. The chapter SCOOP.CHP appears on your screen within a few moments.
4. Turn to Module 9 to continue the learning sequence.

Module 13
CHAPTER MENU

DESCRIPTION

The Chapter menu contains commands that control the page formatting for an entire Ventura chapter. Unlike the Frame menu's commands, which control the format for individual frames, the Chapter menu provides the commands needed to control the format of the entire chapter.

The following commands are available in the Chapter menu:

Page Size & Layout
Chapter Typography
Headers & Footers
Show Page Header
Show Page Footer
Footnote Settings
Insert/Remove Page
Go To Page

The Page Size & Layout, Chapter Typography, and Footnote Settings are stored in the style sheet. Settings created with the other commands in the Chapter menu are stored with the chapter.

NOTE

In earlier releases of Ventura, this menu was called the Page menu. In Version 2.0, the menu's name was changed to Chapter menu.

APPLICATIONS

The documents created in Ventura require a certain format. You establish or change this format with the commands available in the Chapter menu. For example, if you are planning to publish a document that is in Landscape, rather than Portrait orientation, the setting for that page orientation is set in the Page Size & Layout command, available in the Chapter menu.

TYPICAL OPERATION

In this example, you open the Chapter menu and review the commands. The example begins with SCOOP.CHP already open. If you do not have this chapter open, use the Open Chapter command in the File menu to retrieve and open SCOOP.CHP.

1. Click on **Chapter** menu. The Chapter menu drops down.
2. Review the various commands available in the menu.
3. Click outside the menu to close it.
4. Turn to Module 30 to continue the learning sequence.

Module 14
CHAPTER TYPOGRAPHY

DESCRIPTION

The Chapter Typography command controls the character and line format for the entire chapter. Any settings made in the Chapter Typography command may be overridden in a frame by using the Frame Typography command (see Module 31), or in a paragraph by using the Paragraph Typography command (see Module 56).

The Chapter Typography command is accessed in the Chapter menu. When accessed, the Chapter Typography Settings dialog box appears.

CHAPTER (DEFAULT) TYPOGRAPHY SETTINGS

Widows (Min Lines at Top):	2	OK
Orphans (Min Lines at Bottom):	2	Cancel
Column Balance:	Off	
Move Down To 1st Baseline By:	Inter-Line	
Pair Kerning:	On	
Vert. Just. Within Frame:	Feathering	
Vert. Just. Around Frame:	Moveable	
Vert. Just. Allowed:	100 %	
At Top of Frame:	0.194	Inches
At Bottom of Frame:	0.194	

The following options are available in the Chapter Typography Settings dialog box:

Widows — A widow is a single line of text at the top of a page or column which has been separated from the rest of the paragraph on the previous page or in the previous column. The Widows option increases or decreases the number of lines that can be widowed within the frame.

Orphans — An orphan is a single line of text at the bottom of a page or column which has been separated from the rest of the paragraph on the previous page or in the previous column. The Orphans option increases or decreases the number of lines that can be orphaned within the frame.

NOTE

The default setting for both Widows and Orphans is two. This setting is standard and is sufficient for most applications. This setting requires at least two lines of text be left on the previous page or column or forced to the next page or column.

Column Balance	Set Column Balance On if you want the columns within the frame to balance. This would create columns of the same length. A setting of Column Balance Off allows uneven columns within the frame.
Move Down to 1st Baseline By	Ventura provides different settings to determine where the first line of text begins within a frame. Select Move Down to 1st Baseline By Cap Height if you want the top of the column to align with the top of the tallest capital letter in the font you have chosen. Select Move Down to 1st Baseline by Inter-line if you want the first line of text to start at a distance from the top margin equal to the inter-line spacing set in the Spacing command (see Module 75).
Pair Kerning	Select either Pair Kerning Off or On for the frame.
Vert. Just. Within Frame	Vertical Justification forces text to always end at the bottom of the margin within the Frame. When turned off, no vertical justification takes place. Select Feathering to add the exact amount of space necessary to make the text reach the bottom of the column. Select Carding to add space only in multiples of Body Text inter-line spacing.

TIP:

Feathering adds space uniformly between each line but may not align the baselines of your text with each column. Carding permits vertical justification while maintaining baseline alignment.

Vert. Just. Around Frame	Vertical Justification Around Frame determines how space is added around a frame on a page. Select Fixed to keep each frame fixed in its position. Select Moveable to create space around the frame by allowing Ventura to move the frame down to create space above it.

TIP:

You should select Moveable for Vert. Just. Around Frame unless your chapter requires that frames not move at all.

Vertical Just. Allowed	The Vertical Justification Allowed option increases or decreases the amount of vertical justification allowed on each page. The normal setting for most chapters is 100%.

NOTE

This option is not available unless Vertical Justification within a frame is on.

At Top of Frame	The At Top of Frame option sets the maximum amount of space Ventura can add between the top of the frame and the text. This amount is added to any vertical padding set for that frame.
At Bottom of Frame	The At Bottom of Frame option sets the maximum amount of space Ventura can add between the bottom of the frame and the text. This amount is added to any vertical padding set for that frame.

Vertical Justification

Vertical Justification allows text to always reach the exact bottom of each column or page within a chapter. The spacing controls within the Paragraph menu cannot force text to the bottom of the page or column because the paragraph may not contain enough text to reach the bottom of the page. Other factors causing this include the Keep With Next command in the Breaks option which makes headings go to the next column or page, which creates a gap at the bottom of the current page or column. Widow and Orphan controls and page and column breaks force an artificial end to a page.

Vertical Justification should be used on any document when the text continues from one column to the next, or from one page to the next. Vertical Justification automatically adds space before and after frames, tables, paragraphs, and between each line of text, until the text reaches the bottom of the column or page. The space that Ventura adds is in this order:

- Between frames and the surrounding text, until the maximum allowed for each frame is used.
- Between paragraphs or between paragraphs and tables until the maximum amount allowed for each paragraph or table is used.
- Between lines of text until the maximum amount allowed for each paragraph is used.

TIP:

If Ventura adds Justification to your document, space is always added and never taken away.

Text is never moved across page boundaries.

Vertical justification controls appear in four options within Ventura. They are:

- Chapter Typography
- Frame Typography
- Paragraph Typography
- Insert/Edit Table

Chapter Typography sets the vertical justification on or off for the entire chapter. When on, the Chapter Typography option allows the setting of the maximum amount of space that can be added around any frame on the page.

Frame Typography is identical to Chapter Typography and allows the typography for the selected frame to be changed from the global settings to individual settings. With this option, vertical justification could be stopped within a frame, or more space could be added.

Paragraph Typography sets the maximum amount of space that could be added before and after a paragraph. This option sets the maximum amount of space to be added between lines within a paragraph. Paragraph typography permits different spacing for each paragraph tag.

Insert/Edit Table sets the maximum amount of space that can be added above and below a table. The settings can be different for each table used with a Ventura table.

Although Ventura allows you to set precisely how much space you want anywhere within a chapter, for most of your work, all you really need to do is select the Chapter Typography option and set Vertical Justification Within Frame to Feathering and Vertical Justification Around Frame to Moveable. The defaults built into each style sheet should take care of the rest of the Vertical Justification settings. Those default settings are:

- Vertical Justification Allowed (Chapter Typography option) is 100%.
- At Top of Frame (Chapter Typography) is set equal to Body Text Interline spacing.
- At Bottom of Frame (Chapter Typography) is set equal to Body Text Interline spacing.
- At Top of Paragraph is set equal to Body Text Above space in the Spacing option within the Paragraph menu.
- At Bottom of Paragraph is set equal to Body Text Below space in the Spacing option within the Paragraph menu.
- Between Line of Paragraph (Paragraph Typography) is set to zero.

On any page within a chapter, the amount of space that can be added is determined by the maximum settings in the Chapter Typography, Frame Typography, and Paragraph Typography menus. If the text would still not reach the bottom of the page after Ventura would add all this space, then no space is added, and vertical justification does not occur. This prevents the appearance of loose pages on the last page of a chapter or before a page break.

The maximum amount of space which vertical justification attempts to fill can be increased or decreased by specifying a Vertical Justification Allowed amount greater or less than 100%. For example, if Vertical Justification at Top of Paragraph is 24 points, and if you select 150%, Ventura attempts to add up to 36 points before deciding not to vertically justify a given page.

TIP:

To turn Vertical Justification off, select Vertical Justification Within Frame: Off. Do not set Vertical Justification allowed at 0%.

APPLICATIONS

The Chapter Typography command is used to define the typography of text within a chapter. This permits total control of the placement of text from column to column and from page to page. Being able to control the typography of your entire chapter permits you to change the style of documents to match your needs.

For example, you may want to use the column balance option in your document. By turning on the column balance in the Chapter Typography menu, all columns are balanced by Ventura within your chapter.

TYPICAL OPERATION

In this example, you turn off the Frame Typography and adjust the Chapter Typography for the sample chapter &LSTG-P2.CHP. This example begins with &LSTG-P2.CHP already open. To open &LSTG-P2.CHP, use the Open Chapter command in the File menu. So your view matches the screen depicted in this module, press Ctrl-R. Your screen should resemble this illustration:

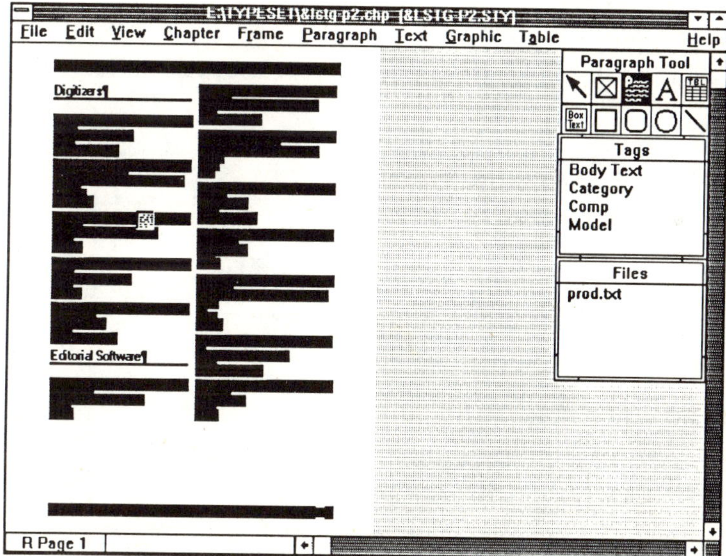

1. Click on the **Frame** Tool within the Toolbox. Click in the center of the page to select the underlying page frame.
2. Click on the **Frame** menu and click on **Frame Typography** to display the Frame Typography Settings dialog box.
3. Click on **Column Balance** and notice the Column Balance is set for **Default**. Your screen should resemble the following illustration:

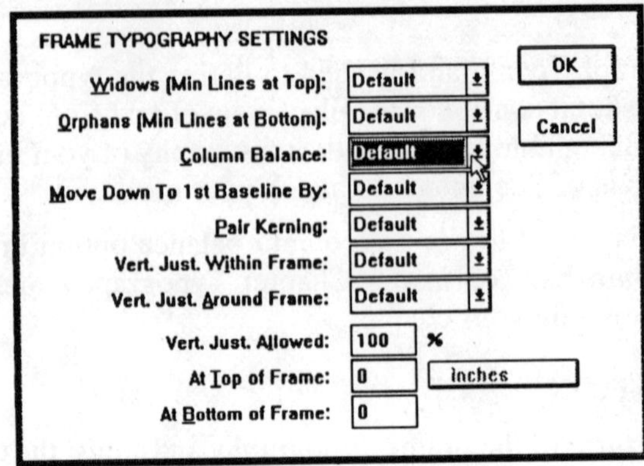

4. Click on **OK**.
5. Click on the **Chapter** menu and click on **Chapter Typography** to display the Chapter (Default) Typography Settings dialog box.
6. Click on **Column Balance**.
7. Select **Off** to turn the Column Balance off. Your screen should resemble the following illustration:

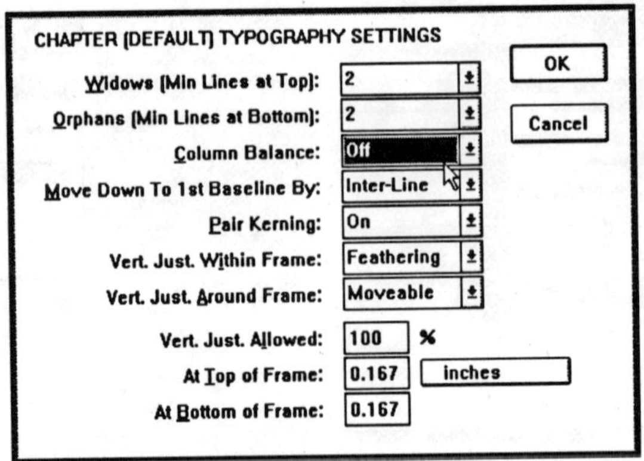

8. Click **OK**. Your screen should resemble this illustration:

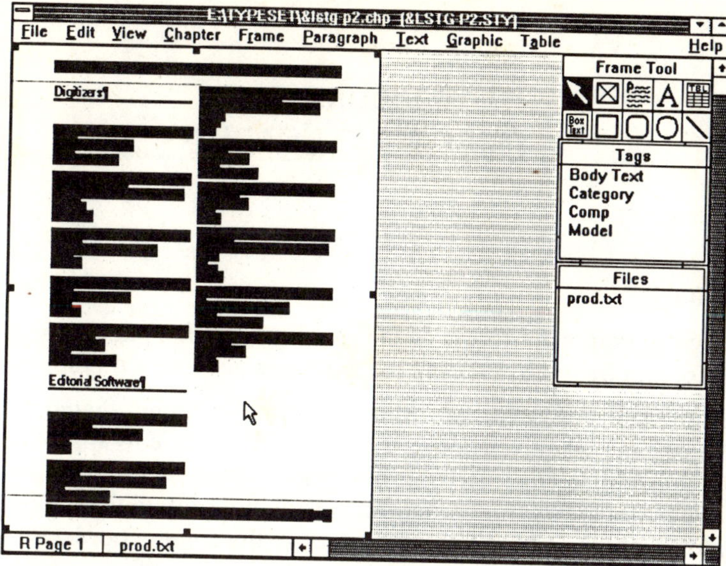

Notice the difference between the two illustrations in this section, which depicts the difference between Column Balance assigned in the Chapter Typography.

9. Click on the **Chapter** menu and click on **Chapter Typography** to display the Chapter (Default) Typography Settings dialog box.
10. Click on **Column Balance**.
11. Select **On** to turn the Column Balance on. Click on **OK**.
12. Point to the **File** menu and click on **Revert to Saved**. Click on **OK** when prompted to revert back to the last saved version.
13. Turn to Module 69 to continue the learning sequence.

Module 15
COLUMN SNAP

DESCRIPTION

The Column Snap command forces frames to align with the page's column guides. By turning the Column Snap off, you can place frames anywhere on the page.

When Column Snap is on, any new frame and previous frames that are resized snap to the edge of a column when you move the edge of the frame to approximately 1/10 of an inch from the column edge. All four borders of a new frame snap to the edge if you are close enough to the column border. Frames do not snap to the top or bottom of the column guides. Only the one or two edges snap to the column border when an existing frame is resized.

The Column Snap command is located in the View menu.

APPLICATIONS

The Column Snap On command forces pictures and text frames placed on the page to align perfectly with other text columns. When resizing, the frames are sized in one-line increments.

When the Column Snap is set to off, you can place frames anywhere on the page, without regard to any alignment.

Most Ventura users are probably better served by using the Column Snap On. The more precise alignment usually guarantees a cleaner, more professional-looking design.

TYPICAL OPERATION

In this operation, you turn Column Snap off, resize a frame, turn Column Snap on, and create another frame. The instructions begin with Ventura running and the &NEWS-P2.CHP open.

1. Press **Ctrl-U** to select the Frame Tool.
2. Click on the **View** menu and click on **Column Snap**. It should now be off. No check mark appears in the left column.

3. Click on **Add Frame**, point and click the mouse cursor in the left column, and drag the mouse slowly to the right. Your screen should resemble the following illustration:

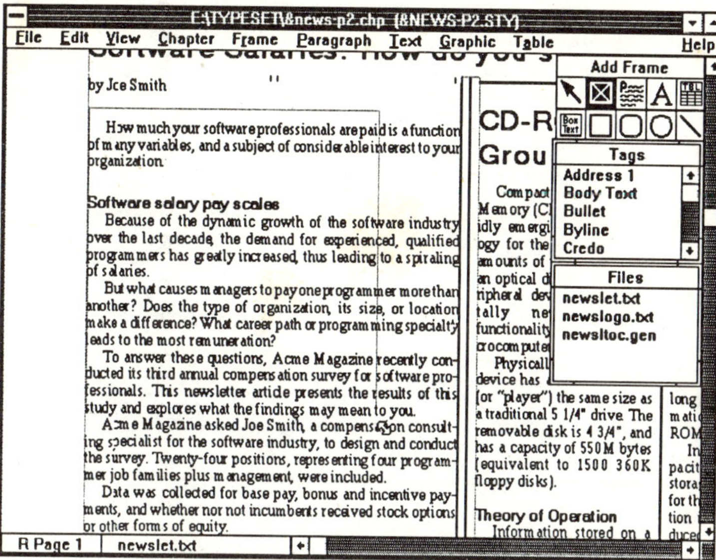

The new frame is created evenly and smoothly. Release the mouse button.

4. Press **Del** to delete the frame.
5. Click on the **View** menu and click on **Show Column Guides** to turn on the column guides (if they are not already on).
6. Click on the **View** menu and click on **Column Snap**. It should now be on. A check mark appears in the left column.
7. Click on the **Add Frame** Tool, point and click the mouse cursor in the left column, and drag the mouse slowly to the right. Be sure to draw the frame borders within 1/10 of an inch of the column guide to make the frame snap to the column. Release the mouse button. Your screen should resemble the following illustration:

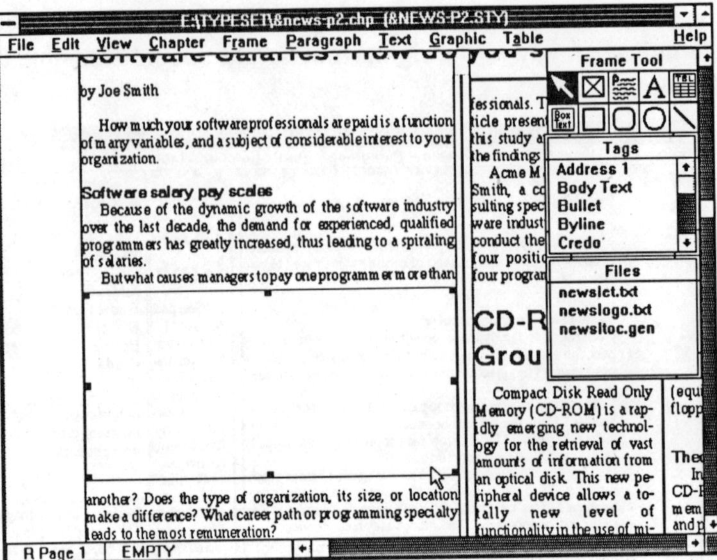

Notice how the new frame snaps to the column guides when the mouse button is released.

8. Press **Del** to delete the frame.
9. Point to the **File** menu and click on **Revert to Saved** and click **OK.**
10. Turn to Module 45 to continue the learning sequence.

Module 16
CROSS REFERENCES

DESCRIPTION

A cross reference is any reference within a Ventura document to a specific page, chapter, figure, table, caption, variable text, or section number. The cross reference feature within Ventura automatically creates a cross reference and then updates it so you do not have to keep track of where items have been moved within your document.

In a document such as a newsletter or magazine, a cross reference is created to generate a Continued On or Continued From reference within the document. This aids your reader in finding the next portion of the article. Within a manual or a book, this feature would update a reference to a figure, table, or specific pages.

To use the cross reference, you must first mark the location to which you wish to refer. You can mark either:

- A frame
- A place anywhere within the text

To insert a marker within the text, first select the Text Tool. Then move the cursor to the position where you wish to reference. The next step is to select Insert Special Item in the Text menu. When the secondary menu appears, select Marker Name from the menu. This dialog box appears:

INSERT/EDIT MARKER NAME
Marker Name:
OK
Cancel

Enter a marker name within the dialog box. The marker name can be numbers, words, or a combination of numbers and words. Case is ignored by Ventura. For example, figure 1, Figure 1, or FIGURE 1 are all treated as the same label in the cross reference.

To assign a cross reference to a frame, first select the Frame mode. Then select the frame to be cross referenced. Select Anchor & Captions from the Frame menu, and enter a name on the Anchor Name line.

Generating the Cross Reference

After all the places in the text and the frames have been marked, they can then be cross referenced. To generate the reference, a cross reference is inserted into the document. This cross reference is then used to create text when the publication is renumbered using the Manage Publication option in the File menu.

To insert a cross reference, first select the Text Tool. Move the cursor to the position within the document where you want the reference to appear. Then select Insert Special Item from the Text menu. From the secondary menu, select Cross Reference. The following dialog box appears:

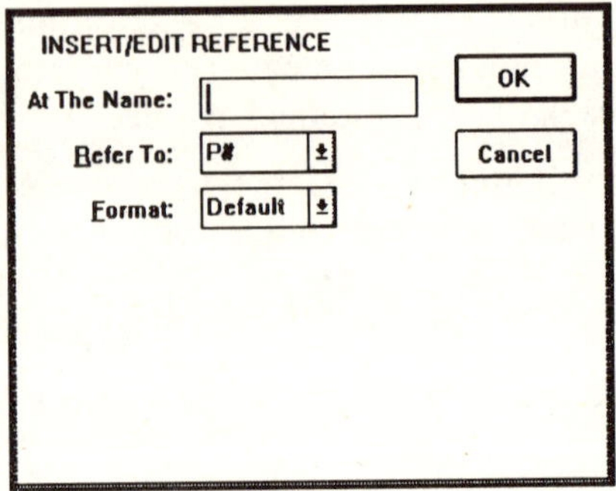

Enter the name of the frame or the name of the text label on the At The Name line within the dialog box. Then select the kind of reference to be created. The Refer To line allows you to refer to the following selections:

Page number P#	Page number of referenced item.
Chapter number C#	Chapter number of referenced item.
Figure number F#	Figure number of referenced item.
Table number T#	Table number of referenced item.
Section number S*	Section number which precedes the referenced item.
Caption text C*	Generated caption text (this is the part set by the Anchors & Caption dialog box) from the selected frame.
Variable text V*	Text defined for the referenced variable.

If you select one of the number options (#), the format for this number can be specified in the format line. Default selects the current numbering format. Finally, select OK to exit the dialog box.

NOTE

No numbers initially appear within the document.

Use the Manage Publication option located within the File menu to generate the references. First create a publication by selecting all the chapters of your document. Select Renumber to update all the cross references created within the document.

NOTE

References can be created either forward or backward within a publication. To make multiple references, such as the page number and a section number, multiple cross references must be created.

If Ventura cannot locate the name of the frame or the name of the text label, an error message appears on your screen. Ventura also creates an error file which lists all the references it could not find. This file can be reviewed by loading it into a Ventura frame or within your word processor. The information contained within this file can assist you to correct the error so the cross reference can be created.

Variable Insertion

This feature of Ventura allows documents to be customized by inserting variable text at cross reference points throughout the publication. After the publication is renumbered, the current value of the variable text is inserted at all specified locations within the publication.

NOTE

This is similar to most Search and Replace functions of a word processor.

Ventura can do many variable insertions at one time and makes the changes through all the chapters that make up the publication.

To define a variable, first select Text mode. Move the text cursor to the position within the document where the variable is to be inserted.

TIP:

To make it easier to locate and edit the variable, place the variable definition at the beginning of the first chapter in the publication.

Then select Insert Special Item in the Text menu. When the secondary menu appears, select Variable Def. with the mouse. Enter the name of the variable. (This is the name that is later referenced in the At The Name entry within the Cross Reference dialog box.) Type the text to be inserted into the cross reference and then select OK.

When Ventura runs the renumbering command in the Manage Publication option, the current definition is used for the Variable. This allows the variable definition to be changed at different locations throughout the document. Normally, the variable is only changed once, and it is best to place the variable information at the beginning of the publication.

Editing a Cross Reference

A cross reference can be edited by selecting Text mode. Select Show Tabs and Returns in the View menu to display the Cross Reference marker.

NOTE

The marker is displayed as a small round circle.

Move the text cursor to the position in front of the marker to be edited. Either Marker Name, Reference, or Variable Def. appears in the Current Selection box. The cursor arrow keys can be used to move the text cursor into position until one of these words appears within the Current Selection box.

The cross reference, variable definition, or marker name can be deleted by pressing Del. This places the item into the clipboard. Press Ins to undelete the cross reference item. The cursor can be moved and then, when Ins is pressed, the cross reference item is pasted into the new position within the text. To copy a cross reference item shown in the Current Selection box and place it in the clipboard, press Shift and Del simultaneously.

APPLICATIONS

The cross reference allows the creation of Continued to and Continued from references to help find the portion of an article. This is particularly helpful when creating newsletters, magazines, or newspapers with Ventura.

This feature can also be used to create and update references to tables, figures, pictures, or charts in books or reports.

This feature can also be used to universally insert a product or customer name within a document.

TYPICAL OPERATION

In this operation, a cross reference is inserted into the chapter &BOOK-P2.CHP. It is assumed the chapter is open.

1. Press **Ctrl-O** to select the Text Tool.
2. Click on the text in the caption on the frame containing the nozzle.
3. Click on the **Text** menu, select **Insert Special Item**, then select **Cross Ref**.
4. Type **nozzle** for At the Name and click on **OK**.
5. Turn to Module 7 to continue the learning sequence.

Module 17
CUT/COPY/PASTE

DESCRIPTION

The Cut, Copy, and Paste commands allow the deletion and duplication of text, paragraph tags, frames, graphics, and rows and columns in tables.

Cut deletes an item that has been selected and places it into a temporary holding area called a clipboard. Copy duplicates an item that has been selected and places it into the clipboard.

Paste retrieves the item from the clipboard and places it on the page. Paste places the graphics and frames on the page in the same position they were when they were cut or copied. Paste places text at the location of the insertion, determined by the position of the mouse cursor.

The clipboard is the heart of the three commands. Actually, Ventura uses Windows clipboards, which allows text to be transported in and out of Ventura. You cannot export a graphic that has been created in Ventura.

By using the Shift key, multiple frames, tags, and graphics can be cut, copied, or pasted.

Cut, Copy, and Paste are located within the Edit menu (see Module 19). Depending on which Tool has been selected and is currently being used, the Cut, Copy, and Paste commands change. For example, if text has been selected using the Paragraph Tool, the commands available are Cut Tag, Copy Tag, or Paste Tag.

Cut, Copy, and Paste are also accessed by using these keyboard commands:

Cut	Press Del
Copy	Hold Shift and press Del
Paste	Press Ins

APPLICATIONS

Cut, Copy, and Paste allows any item on the screen to be deleted, copied, or moved.

Depending on which mode is being used, these three commands assist in the manipulation of text, frames, or graphics. For example, if you are working in the Text mode, these commands can be used to move a block of text, just as Block commands are used in most word processors.

When working with graphics or frames, you might want to repeat a graphic or a frame on several pages throughout the document. By using Copy and Paste, you could reproduce the exact copy of your frame or graphic on other pages.

Being able to copy, cut, and paste paragraph tags allows you to transfer or copy a tag from one style sheet to another. By placing a paragraph tag into the clipboard and then opening another style sheet, you can easily duplicate the tag in the new style sheet.

Copying rows and columns in Ventura saves time when building or modifying tables.

TYPICAL OPERATION

In this example, you use the Cut and Paste commands. The example begins with SCOOP.CHP already open and in use. If you do not have this chapter open, use the Open Chapter command in the File menu to retrieve and open SCOOP.CHP. So your view matches the screen depicted in this book, press Ctrl-R.

1. Press **Ctrl-U** and select the frame located in the middle of the page.
2. Click on the **Edit** menu and select **Cut Frame**. Your screen should look like this:

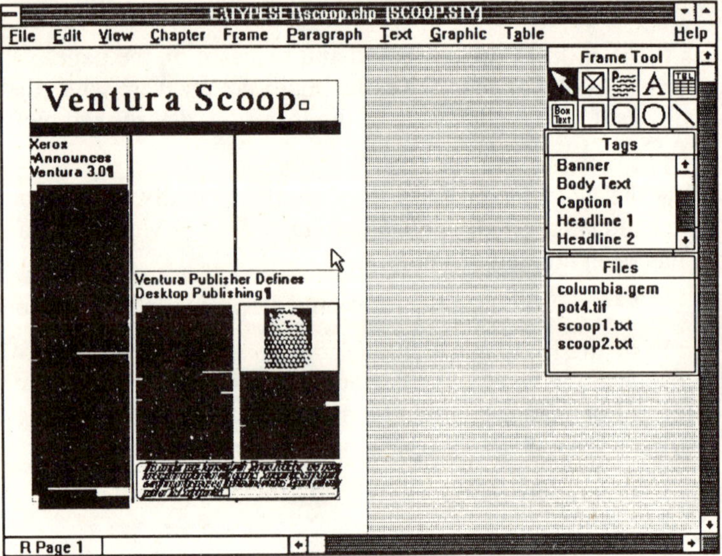

3. Retrieve the frame from the clipboard by pressing **Ins**. Your screen should now resemble this illustration:

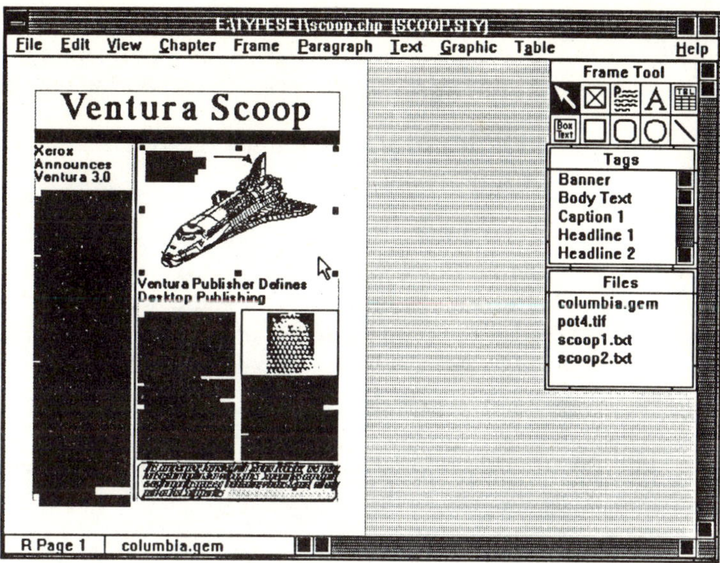

4. Turn to Module 62 to continue the learning sequence.

Module 18
DEFINE COLORS

DESCRIPTION

The Define Colors command defines colors and shades of gray. These colors can then be assigned to text, ruling lines, and graphics.

NOTE

> Ventura does not determine colors of the final printed page of your document. The printer's ink is what determines the final color of the document.

The colors and shades of gray established with the Define Colors command only determines the colors and shades displayed on your computer screen. Depending on your computer equipment, you may see actual colors or just shades of gray.

In some cases, you may be using a color PostScript printer, such as the QMS ColorScript 100. If so, your page prints in full color. Others may use a printer that converts the colors to shades of gray.

In most cases, however, you print each page to a black and white laser printer and select Color Overlays in the Print option. When this is done, a separate page is printed for each color defined and enabled. Colors are not converted to shades of gray. The commercial print shop then takes a picture of the different pages and uses them to print the different colors.

To access the Define Colors command, select the Paragraph Tool. The Define Colors command is located within the Paragraph menu. When selected, the Define Colors dialog box appears:

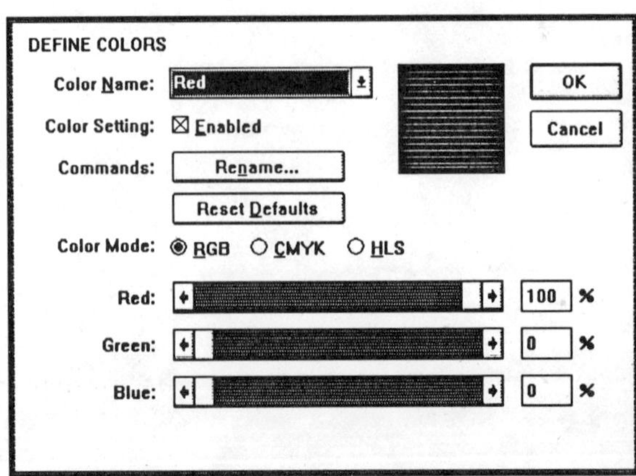

The following options are available within the Define Colors dialog box:

Color Name	Type in a color name. The color name defined is printed at the top of each page printed for that color when Spot Color Overlays is on in the To Print dialog box.
Color Setting	Select either Enable if you want to print a color separation for this color, or select Disable if you do not want to print a color separation for this color.
Commands	Click on Reset Defaults to change the colors back to their original settings.
Color Mode	Select the color mode desired for defining your colors. RGB is Red, Green, Blue. CMYK is Cyan, Magenta, Yellow, and Black. HLS is Hue, Lightness, and Saturation.
Red, Green, Blue	Define a color by mixing the colors using the scroll bars. As the color is mixed, you see the new changes in the box with the Define Colors dialog box.

For most applications, during the commercial printing process, different printing plates are made for the colors being printed on your final published document. The black and white pages being printed from the laser printer are photographed, and the people running the printing press determine the final color of your documents.

APPLICATIONS

The main purpose of the Define Color command is to define a color name that can be assigned to fonts, rules, and background patterns. A different black and white page can then be printed for each color. Different printing plates can then easily be made by a printer to allow easy creation of the color document.

If you are using a color laser printer, you can also create the desired color for your document. Over 125 million colors are possible from the settings available in the Define Colors command.

TYPICAL OPERATION

In this operation, you define the color of a paragraph tag. The sample chapter &NEWS-P2.CHP is used. The example begins with &NEWS-P2.CHP already in use.

1. Press **Ctrl-I** to select Paragraph Tool.
2. Click on "Widget World News" to select the Masthead paragraph tag.
3. Click on the **Paragraph** menu and select **Define Colors** to display the Define Colors dialog box.
4. Click on **Color Name** and select **Blue**.

NOTE

If you are printing to a black and white printer, select Shades of Gray for Screen Display.

5. Click on the left **Blue** arrow, and adjust the blue to **80%**. Your screen should resemble this illustration:

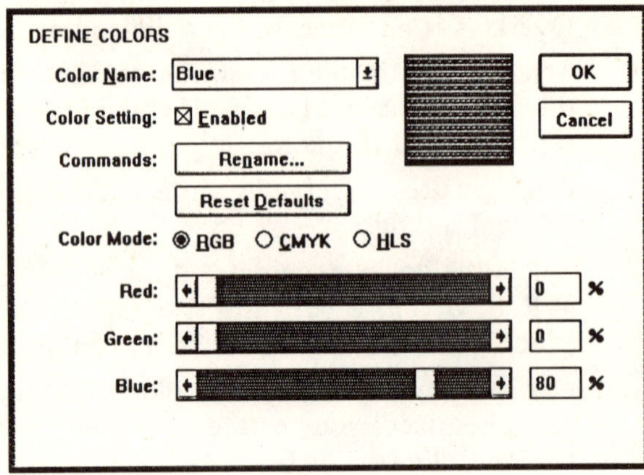

6. Click **OK**.
7. Click on **Paragraph** menu and select **Font**. Change color to **Blue** and click **OK**. Depending on your installation and computer equipment configuration, you may see the color assigned to the paragraph tag on your screen.
8. Select the **File** menu and click on **Revert to Saved** and then click on **OK** when prompted to revert back to the last saved version.
9. Turn to Module 16 to continue the learning sequence.

Module 19
EDIT MENU

DESCRIPTION

The Edit menu offers access to a variety of commands. Depending on which tool has been selected in the Toolbox, these options are available for your use:

When the Frame Tool has been chosen:

- Cut, Copy, and Paste frames, as well as their contents.

When the Add Frame Tool has been chosen:

- Cut, Copy, and Paste frames, as well as their contents.

When the Paragraph Tool has been chosen:

- Cut, Copy, and Paste paragraph tags.

When the Text Tool has been chosen:

- Cut, Copy, and Paste selected text.

When the Table Tool has been chosen:

- Cut, Copy, and Paste rows and columns.

When any one of the Graphic Tools has been chosen:

- Cut, Copy, and Paste graphics and their contents.

The Cut command removes the selected object and places it in an invisible clipboard. The Copy command places a copy of the selected object in a clipboard but does not remove it from the current chapter. The Paste command takes the last item that was cut or copied and places it:

- at the location of the mouse cursor if it is text.
- at the identical location on a new or current page if the item was a frame or graphic.
- in a current style sheet if the item was a paragraph tag.

The clipboard is shared by all Windows applications and allows the easy transfer of information from one application to another within Windows. Text and some picture files can be transported out of Ventura into other applications.

NOTE

Graphics created in Ventura cannot be exported and used in other applications. Bitmaps or pictures also cannot be exported.

The other commands available in the Edit menu allow you to update counters, re-anchor frames, renumber the chapter, and to set the preferences of how you want to work in Ventura. All of these options are explained in more detail in their own modules within this book.

APPLICATIONS

The Edit menu offers a variety of commands that are useful when working with the various tools in the Toolbox. Being able to edit—cutting, copying, or pasting—frames, text, paragraph tags, or graphics makes your use of Ventura easier and takes less time.

TYPICAL OPERATION

In this example, you access and review the Edit menu when Ventura is in both Frame and Text Editing mode. The sample chapter SCOOP.CHP is used. The example begins with SCOOP.CHP already open and in use.

1. Press **Ctrl-U**. Click on the frame containing COLUMBIA.GEM.
2. Click on the **Edit** menu and notice the available options.
3. Press **Ctrl-O**. Highlight the headline "Ventura Scoop."
4. Click on the **Edit** menu and notice the available options. The options are different than those available in step 2. If necessary, repeat steps 1 and 2 to see the difference.
5. Click on the Paragraph Tool. Click on the paragraph "Xerox Announces Ventura 3.0."
6. Click on the **Edit** menu and notice the available options. The options are different than those available in step 2.
7. Turn to Module 86 to continue the learning sequence.

Module 20
EQUATIONS

DESCRIPTION

Complex equations can be created with Ventura. Mathematical and scientific equations can be placed anywhere within the text of a Ventura document.

TIP:

> Before an equation is entered within text, make certain that Grow Inter-Line To Fit in the Paragraph Typography option is turned on. This automatically inserts vertical space to fit the equations.

To insert an equation, first select the Text Tool. The next step is to move the mouse cursor to the position just in front of where the equation is to be inserted. Then select the Insert Special Item command in the Text menu. The secondary menu box appears. Select Equation from within the secondary menu box.

The equation editing screen appears. Simply type the commands to create the formula. If you stop typing for a few seconds, the equation appears. For example, typing:

x sup 2 over y sup 2 + PI + {a sub 1~+~b sub 1} over c sub 2

would create this equation:

$$\frac{x^2}{y^2}+\Pi+\frac{a_1 + b_1}{c_2}$$

Press Ctrl-D to exit from the equation screen and to insert the equation.

A complete listing of equation commands is in Appendix F.

APPLICATION

Sometimes your documents may include complicated scientific or mathematic formulas. By using the Equations feature of Ventura, you can easily create these types of equations. By using Equations, you do not have to try to create an equation with regular text.

TYPICAL OPERATION

In this typical operation, an equation is created. Be sure to start with a new chapter.

1. Select the **Text** Tool from the Toolbox.
2. Click the mouse once in the middle of the text screen.

3. Select **Text** menu, then choose **Insert Special Item**, then **Equation**. Your screen should resemble this illustration:

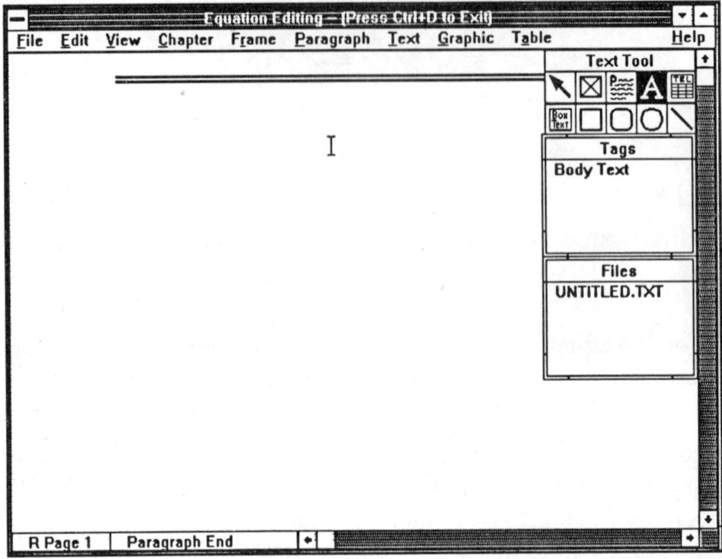

4. Type the following:

   (a+b) over pi = delta sqrt{x over b-c}-h~~sum sub 2

   Your screen should resemble this illustration:

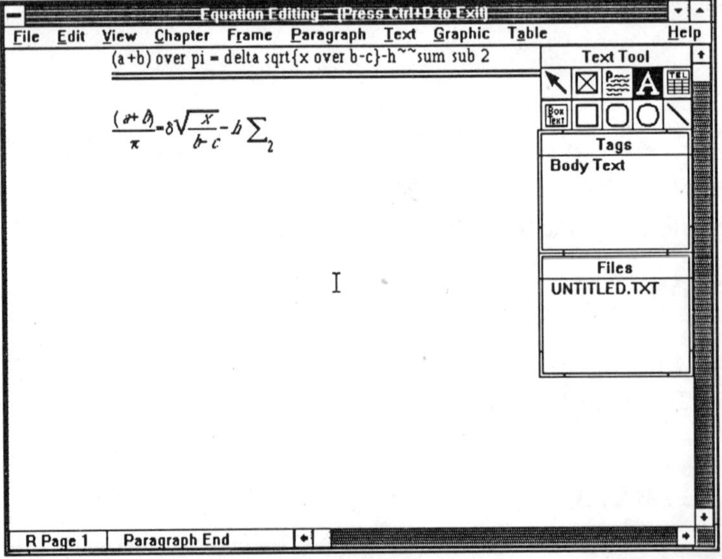

5. Press **Ctrl-D** to exit the Equation editor. Then abandon the chapter.
6. Turn to Module 28 to continue the learning sequence.

Module 21
EXIT

DESCRIPTION

The Exit command ends the current Ventura session and returns you to Windows. Exit closes all open files. If you have made any changes to any of the various Ventura documents, the program asks if you want to save the changes before Exiting.

Exit also creates the VPWIN.INF file in the VENTURA directory. The next time you start Ventura, the program uses the VPWIN.INF file to set the defaults to the way they were when you last used Ventura. The VPWIN.INF file does not reopen the last chapter file you were using.

Exit is located in the File menu.

APPLICATIONS

Exit is the command used to end a session in Ventura. You might use the command in another program, such as your word processor.

You should always use the Exit command rather than simply turning the computer power off. Exit closes all open Ventura files and provides dialog boxes to save any changes that have been made since the last time the chapter was saved.

TYPICAL OPERATION

In this example, you exit and abandon the Ventura sample chapter document SCOOP.CHP. The example begins with SCOOP.CHP already open and in use. If you do not have this chapter open, use the command Open Chapter in the File menu to retrieve and open SCOOP.CHP.

1. Click on the **Text** Tool from the Toolbox.
2. Click after the word "Ventura" in the headline and type **Latest**.

3. Click on the **File** menu and click on **Exit**. Your screen should resemble this illustration:

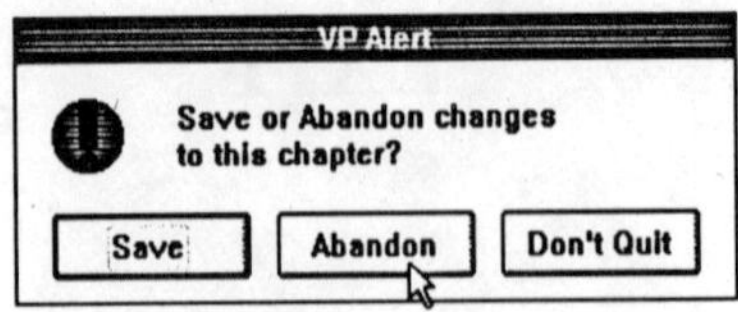

4. Click on **Abandon**. Ventura returns you to Windows.
5. Turn to Module 22 to continue the learning sequence.

Module 22
FILE MENU

DESCRIPTION

The File menu controls the flow of information and files into and out of Ventura. In addition, the File menu provides the commands to save your documents and to leave the program.

The options available in the File menu are:

New
Open Chapter
Save
Save As
Revert to Saved
Load Text/Picture
Load Diff. Style
Save Style As
Manage Width Table
Manage Publication
Printer Setup
Print
Exit

The File menu contains the commands you need to open and close a Ventura document, to print it, to load style sheets and files, and to quit the program. You can also manage the fonts. Within this menu, tables of contents, index creation, renumbering, and copying chapters can be completed.

APPLICATIONS

The File menu provides many basic functions. When you need to print a Ventura document, the command to begin the printing process is located within this menu.

The File menu offers eight basic commands. They are:

- Open or Save a Ventura document, or start a new one.
- Load text, line art, or image files into your current Ventura chapter file.
- Use a different style sheet than the one currently in use, or save a newly created style sheet.
- Print the chapter.

- Manage the usage of individual fonts.
- Generate tables of contents, indexes, and renumbering of frames and captions.
- Copy the entire chapter, and associated files, to another disk or path on your system.
- Exit Ventura by using the Exit command.

TYPICAL OPERATION

In this example, you access the File menu and review the various commands available. The Ventura sample chapter document SCOOP.CHP is used. Start Ventura and use the command Open Chapter in the File menu to retrieve and open SCOOP.CHP.

1. Select the **File** menu. Notice the various options available within this menu.
2. Turn to Module 19 to continue the learning sequence.

Module 23
FILE TYPE/RENAME

DESCRIPTION

The File Type/Rename command changes the word processor format of an existing file. The File Type/Rename command can also be used to create a new text file.

This command is accessed by first selecting either the underlying page frame or the frame holding the text file. The File/Type Rename command is accessed from the Frame menu.

FILE TYPE / RENAME

Old Name: E:\TYPESET\UNTITLED.TXT [OK]

New Name: E:\TYPESET\UNTITLED.TXT [Cancel]

Text Format: ○ Generated ○ ASCII ○ WordStar 3 ○ MultiMate
○ MS Word ○ Writer ○ WordPerfect 4 ○ WS 4.0/5.0
○ 8-Bit ASCII ○ XyWrite ○ DCA ◉ WordPerfect 5
○ PRN to Table

The File Type/Rename dialog box offers the following options:

Old Name	Type the current DOS directory path and filename that you need Ventura to process. Ventura will automatically enter the directory path and filename of the file in the selected frame or the underlying page. If desired, you can type the name of any other text file loaded into the chapter file.
New Name	Type the new directory path and the filename. Always type the file extension Ventura expects for the word processing format. For example, if the text file is XyWrite, use the .TXT extension.
Text Format	Select the type of text file you are creating. The type of file format chosen should be based upon the word processor you are using.

When the File Type/Rename command is executed, Ventura adds the name of the new text file in the Files Window. If the text file you are processing was a caption file, the new entry is displayed in the Files Window. If the file was previously loaded into Ventura with the Load Text/Picture command (see Module 47), the old filename is replaced with the new filename in the Files Window.

TIP:

You cannot convert captions into separate text files if the captions are attached to frames or box text.

Ventura does not create and save the new text file until the current chapter is saved.

APPLICATIONS

File Type/Rename is used to rename an existing text file. It is also used to create a new text file.

This command can also be used to convert text from one word processor format to another. This option allows you to use text files from several different word processors and save them in a common file format, making it easier for you to work with the text files.

The command can also be used to convert caption files to text files. This can be useful if you want to bring the caption text into a word processor for editing.

TYPICAL OPERATION

In this example, you change the ASCII text file format to WordStar format. The sample chapter document &PRPT-P1.CHP is used. The example begins with &PRPT-P1.CHP already open and in use. Use the Open Chapter command in the File menu to retrieve and open &PRPT-P1.CHP. So your view matches the screen depicted in this book, press Ctrl-R. You may need to adjust your screen using the scroll bars to make your computer look like the illustrations.

1. Press **Ctrl-U** to select the Frame Tool.
2. Click on the underlying page frame to select it.

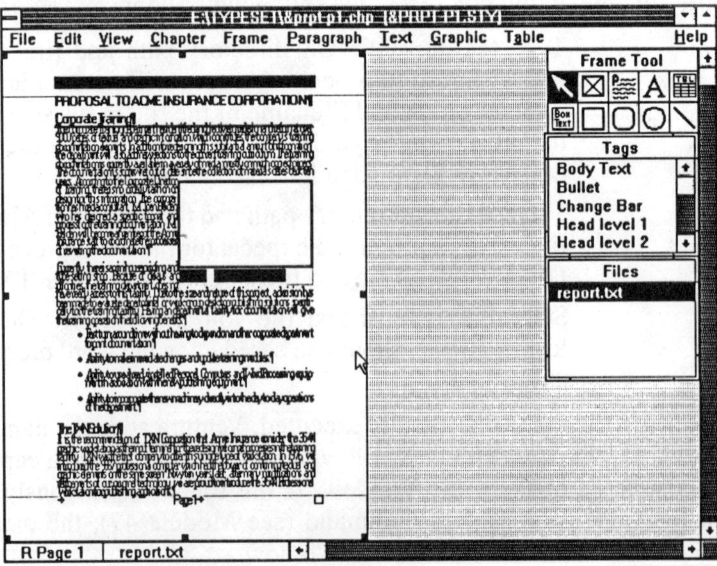

Notice that the name of the text file in the frame is displayed in the Current Selection box. Also, note the filename is displayed in the Files Window.

3. Click on the **Frame** menu and click on **File Type/Rename** to display the File Type/Rename dialog box. Your screen should resemble this illustration:

FILE TYPE / RENAME

Old Name: e:\\typeset\report.txt

New Name: e:\\typeset\report.txt

Text Format: O Generated ◉ ASCII O WordStar 3 O MultiMate

O MS Word O Writer O WordPerfect 4 O WS 4.0/5.0

O 8-Bit ASCII O XyWrite O DCA O WordPerfect 5

O PRN to Table

OK

Cancel

4. Click on the **New Name** line and press **Backspace** enough times to delete the txt extension. Type **ws** to save the file in WordStar format.

FILE TYPE / RENAME

Old Name: e:\\typeset\report.txt

New Name: e:\\typeset\report.ws

Text Format: O Generated ◉ ASCII O WordStar 3 O MultiMate

O MS Word O Writer O WordPerfect 4 O WS 4.0/5.0

O 8-Bit ASCII O XyWrite O DCA O WordPerfect 5

O PRN to Table

OK

Cancel

5. Click on **WS 4.0/5.0** and press **Enter**.

Notice that the new name of the text file in the frame is displayed in the Current Selection box and in the Files Window. The old name is no longer in the Files Window.

6. Click on the **File** menu and select **Revert to Saved**. Click on **OK** when prompted to revert back to the last saved version.
7. Turn to Module 77 to continue the learning sequence.

Module 24
FILL ATTRIBUTES

DESCRIPTION

The Fill Attributes command establishes or changes the color, background, and pattern of each Ventura graphic.

To access this command, a graphic must first be selected. To select a graphic, click on it with the Selection Tool. The Fill Attributes command is accessed from the Graphic menu or by pressing Ctrl-F. When the Fill Attributes command is accessed, the Fill Attributes dialog box appears.

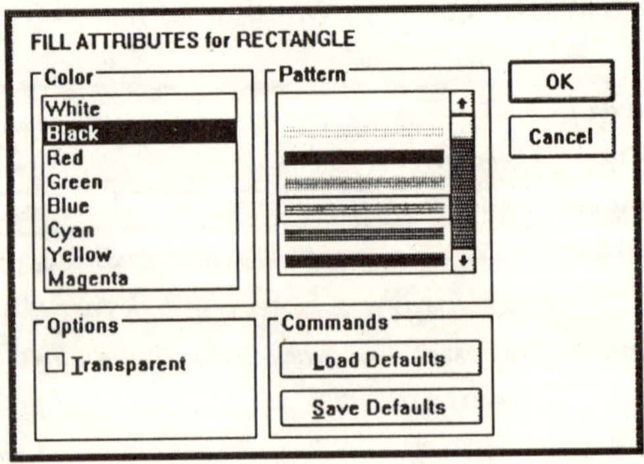

The Fill Attributes dialog box offers these options:

Color	Select a color that was previously defined.
Pattern	Select a pattern from the display.
Options	Select Transparent to show an overlapping graphic. Select Transparent for the graphic on the top, and if its fill pattern is anything other than a solid, then the graphics below shows through the graphic on top. Do not select Transparent if the graphic on the top is to block all other graphics on the stack.
Commands	Select Load Defaults to use the settings selected for another graphic, or select the Save Defaults option to make the current settings the default for other graphics of the same type.

TIP:

Not all laser printers can print transparent graphics. To determine if your laser printer can print these types of graphics, print CAPABILI.CHP located in the \TYPESET directory to determine the capabilities of your printer.

APPLICATIONS

Fill Attributes determine the background of graphics that have been created. This is an effective tool to help make more dynamic graphics. By adding a fill color or pattern, graphics can be more outstanding or more easily interpreted by the reader.

By using Fill Attributes, you can add background for cells in a table or areas within a form.

TYPICAL OPERATION

In this operation, a graphic is created and filled. The operation begins with Ventura running and a blank screen. Use the New command in the File menu to get the blank screen. Use the Load Diff. Style command and select the DEFAULT.STY style sheet.

1. Click on the **Frame** Tool.
2. Move the mouse cursor to the middle of the page and click once.
3. Click on the **Add Round Rect** Tool, and move to the middle of the page. Click and drag, to create a rounded corner box, and release the mouse button. Your screen should resemble the following illustration:

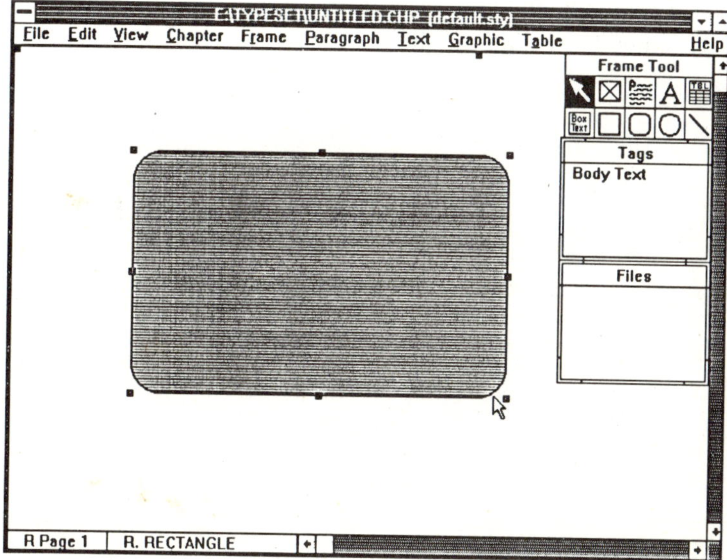

4. Click on the **Graphic** menu and click on **Fill Attributes** to display the Fill Attributes dialog box.
5. Click on the third pattern on the list for Pattern and click **OK**. Your screen should resemble the following illustration:

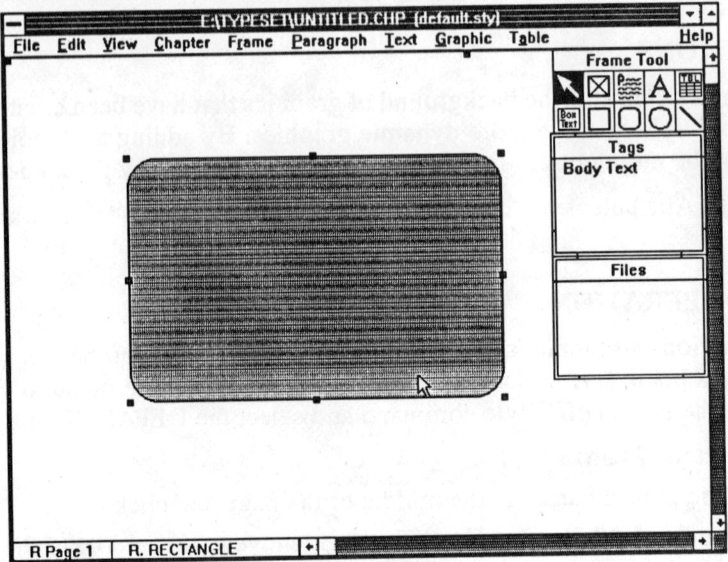

Notice the fill pattern of the rounded corner box.

6. Select the **File** menu and click on **Revert to Saved** and click on **Abandon**.
7. Turn to Module 26 to continue the learning sequence.

Module 25
FONT

DESCRIPTION

The Font command sets the typeface, size, style, and color of the type for each paragraph tag. The command also allows you to assign underlines and strike-outs to your paragraph text. This command is accessed by selecting a Paragraph Tool and then selecting the Font command from the Paragraph menu.

NOTE

Before Font can be accessed, either text or a paragraph must *first* be selected with either the Text Tool or the Paragraph Tool.

After the Font dialog box appears, select the face, size, style, and color from lists. These lists can be scrolled through to see more entries than can appear on the screen at one time.

Any changes made with this command affect the paragraph tag associated with the selected text. When a change is made to a paragraph tag, it affects all text marked with that paragraph tag in your document, as well as in other documents that use the same style sheet.

A font is a type face of a particular size and style.

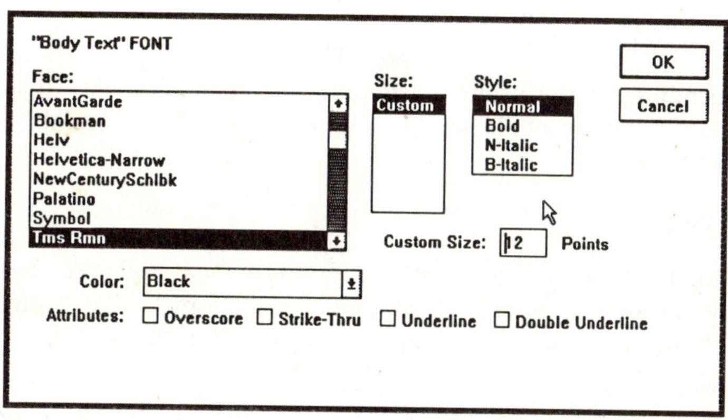

The Font dialog box contains these options:

Face	Select the typeface desired for the paragraph tag. Scroll through this list by clicking on the up and down scroll arrows. Not all typefaces are available for all printers. When a type- face is available, its name is shown in black in the Face list. If it is not available, it will be displayed in gray in the Face list.
Size	If you have an HP or dot matrix type printer, select the size of font desired from a list of available type sizes. Scroll through this list by clicking on the up and down scroll arrows. Available sizes of fonts are shown in black. Sizes not available are shown in gray. When using a PostScript printer, select a custom size by typing the size of the font in the Custom Size entry area.
Style	Select the appearance attributes desired for the font. The style list includes light, normal, bold, bold-italic, normal, normal italic, and light italic. If a particular style is not available on your printer, it is displayed in gray.
Color	Select the color desired to be assigned to the font.
Custom Size	Enter the size of type desired (if you are using a PostScript or other scalable font printer). Any size between 1 and 254 points are available.
Attributes	Overscore — Turn on if overscored type is desired. Strike-Thru — Turn on if strike-thru (sometimes called overstrike) type is desired. Underline — Turn on if underlined text is desired. Double Underline — Turn on if double underlined text is desired.

NOTE

Depending on the printer installed with your computer, not all typefaces will be available. Also, not all styles will be available for every typeface.

APPLICATIONS

The Font command allows you to select different typefaces and styles for your various paragraphs. By choosing a paragraph and assigning a font to that paragraph, you can control the style of your entire document and assure that all paragraphs will look the same.

It is usually best to limit the number of different typefaces being used in a document. Designers tell us that a maximum of two typefaces per page is ideal. However, you can use different sizes of the same typeface, and you can use different styles—bold, italic, normal—of the same font to create stimulating, appealing, and easy-to-read documents. This command allows you to assign fonts and styles to your paragraphs.

Use normal text for your body text, and use the italics and bold attributes for subheadlines and headlines within your Ventura documents. Simple designs often work best. Use care not to create documents with every possible attribute used in some form on each page.

TYPICAL OPERATION

In this example, you change the font assigned to a paragraph tag. This example uses the sample chapter &PRPT-P1.CHP. The example begins with &PRPT-P1.CHP open. Use the Open Chapter command in the File menu to retrieve and open &PRPT-P1.CHP. You may need to adjust your screen using the scroll bars to make your computer look like the illustrations.

1. Press **Ctrl-I** to select the Paragraph Tool.
2. Click on the first paragraph.
3. Click on the **Paragraph** menu and click on **Font** to display the Font dialog box.
4. Click on either **Times Roman** or **Dutch** for Face, select **Bold** for Style, **Black** for color. Enter or select **14** point for size.
5. Click on **OK**. Your screen should resemble this illustration:

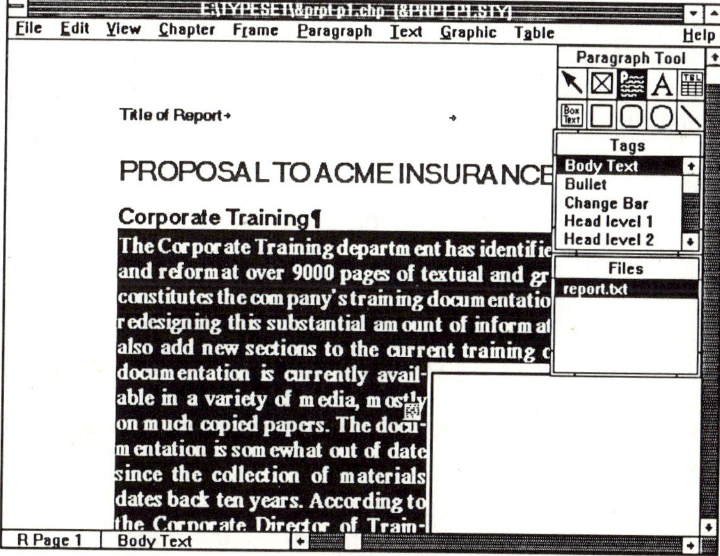

Notice the different appearance of the body text.

6. Click on the **File** menu and click on **Revert to Saved**, then click on **OK** when the message box appears asking if you want to abandon changes.
7. Turn to Module 83 to continue the learning sequence.

Module 26
FOOTNOTE

DESCRIPTION

The Footnote command positions a footnote reference at the current text cursor position and also adds a footnote at the bottom of the current page. The Footnote Settings command controls the chapter's footnote formatting, the numbering, and positioning of the footnotes. See Module 27 for more information about Footnote Settings.

Footnotes are created with the Insert Special Item: Footnote command in the Text menu. Ventura automatically adjusts the space required to place the footnotes at the bottom of the page.

To create a footnote, first select the Text Tool. Position the text cursor where you want the footnote reference to appear and then click the mouse once. Select the Insert Special Item option from the Text menu and then select Footnote from the secondary menu. Depending on the current Footnote Settings (see Module 27), a number or a character appears next to the text cursor. The same reference appears at the bottom of the current page. Move your cursor to the marker on the bottom of the current page, and type the text for your footnote.

TIP:

Footnotes that are too long to fit on the current page are automatically continued onto the next page.

To delete a footnote, place the text cursor at the footnote reference in the main body of the text (not at the reference on the bottom of the page), and then move the cursor back and forth (with the right and left arrow keys) until the Current Selection Indicator displays the word Footnote. Press Del, and both the footnote reference and the footnote are deleted.

NOTE

Footnote references must be placed in the underlying page. Ventura ignores footnotes in frames or in box text.

APPLICATIONS

The Footnote command offers the capability of adding footnotes to your documents. The most common use of footnotes is to provide quick, easy references to other information.

TYPICAL OPERATION

This operation selects the format to be used for a footnote and inserts a footnote on a page. The sample chapter <R1-P1.CHP is used. The instructions begin with the chapter open.

1. Click on the **Chapter** menu and click on **Footnote Settings** to display the Footnote Settings dialog box.
2. Select **# From Start of Chapter (1,2,3)**, type **0100** for Start With #, and click **OK**.
3. Press **Ctrl-O** to select the Text Tool.
4. Move the cursor to the word **widget** in the first sentence. Click the mouse button once.
5. Click on **Text** menu and select **Insert Special Item**, then choose **Footnote**.
6. Use the scroll bars to move to the bottom of the page.
7. Click and hold and drag the mouse button to select **Text of Footnote**. Press **Del**.
8. Type **Our Special A-199 Widgets**. Your screen should resemble this illustration:

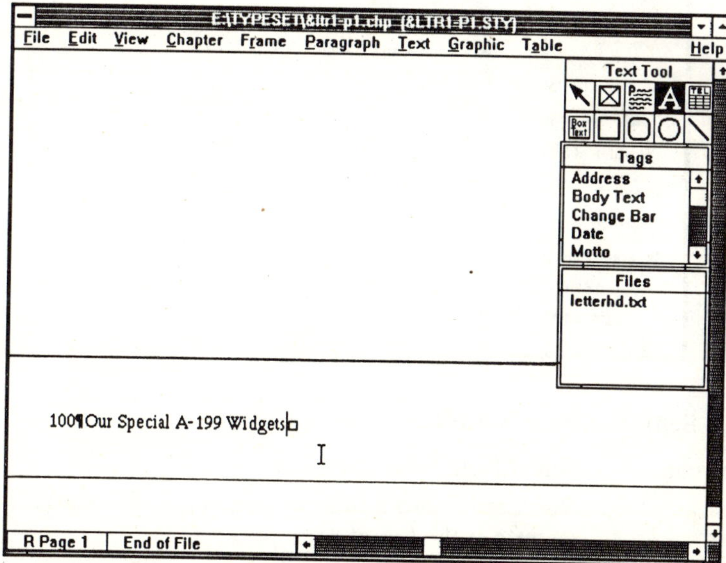

9. Turn to Module 27 to continue the learning sequence.

Module 27
FOOTNOTE SETTINGS

DESCRIPTION

The Footnote Settings command controls the chapter's footnote formatting, the numbering, and positioning of the footnotes.

Footnotes are actually created with the Insert Special Item: Footnote command in the Text menu. Ventura automatically adjusts the space required to place the footnotes at the bottom of the page.

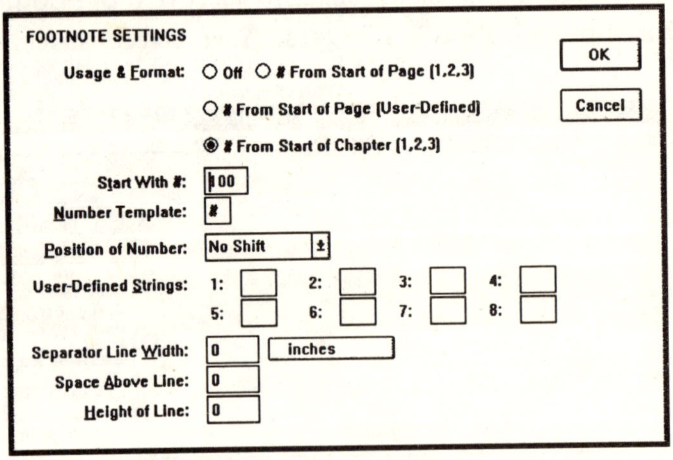

FOOTNOTE SETTINGS
Usage & Format: ○ Off ○ # From Start of Page (1,2,3)
○ # From Start of Page (User-Defined)
◉ # From Start of Chapter (1,2,3)
Start With #: 100
Number Template: #
Position of Number: No Shift ±
User-Defined Strings: 1: 2: 3: 4: 5: 6: 7: 8:
Separator Line Width: 0 inches
Space Above Line: 0
Height of Line: 0
OK
Cancel

The Footnote Settings dialog box offers these options:

Usage & Format	Select from three formats: Number (#) From Start of Page (1, 2, 3) — Arabic numbering restarts at the top of each page; Number (#) From Start of Page (User-Defined) — User-Defined designations restart at the top of each page (see User-Defined Strings below); Number (#) From Start of Chapter (1, 2, 3) — Arabic numbering starts at the beginning of the chapter and continues sequentially through the end of the chapter.
Start With #	Enter the beginning number to use when Arabic numbering is selected for the footnotes.

Number Template	Enter the style desired for printing the footnote numbers at the bottom of the page. For example, enter -#- to make the numbers begin and end with a dash such as: -1-, -2-, and -3-. The pound character (#) indicates the position of the number itself.
Position of Number	Designate where the footnote numbers are to appear: on the same level (No Shift), above (Superscript), or below (Subscript) the regular text.
User-Defined Strings	If # From Start of Page (User-Defined) for Usage & Format is selected, enter the characters to use for up to eight footnotes on a page.
Separator Line Width	Enter the length of the line desired to separate the body text from the footnote text. Enter 00.00 if no line is desired.
Space Above Line	If separator line is used, enter the amount of space between the line and the text above.
Height of Line	If a separator line is used, enter the thickness of the line.

Ventura also creates a paragraph tag of your footnotes. You can use the automatically generated paragraph tag to add other attributes to your footnotes. (For more information see the Paragraph Tagging command.) The footnote number at the bottom of the page is automatically assigned a paragraph tag called Z_FNOT#, and the footnote itself is automatically assigned a tag called Z_FNOT ENTRY.

The footnote information is stored in the chapter file.

The Footnote Setting command is located in the Chapter menu.

TIP:

Footnote references must be placed in the underlying page. Ventura ignores footnotes in frames or in box text.

APPLICATIONS

The Footnote Settings command offers the capability of adding footnotes to your documents. The common use of footnotes is to provide quick, easy references to other information.

The footnote itself is created in the Insert Footnote option within the Insert Special Item command located in the Edit menu. The Footnote Settings command controls the format of the footnote after it has been created.

TYPICAL OPERATION

This operation selects the format to be used for a footnote. The sample chapter <R1-P1.CHP is used. The instructions begin with the chapter open.

1. Click on the **Chapter** menu and click on **Footnote Settings** to display the Footnote Settings dialog box.

2. Select **# From Start of Chapter (1,2,3)**, type **0100** for Start With #, and change Position of Number to **Subscript**. Click **OK**. Your screen should resemble this illustration:

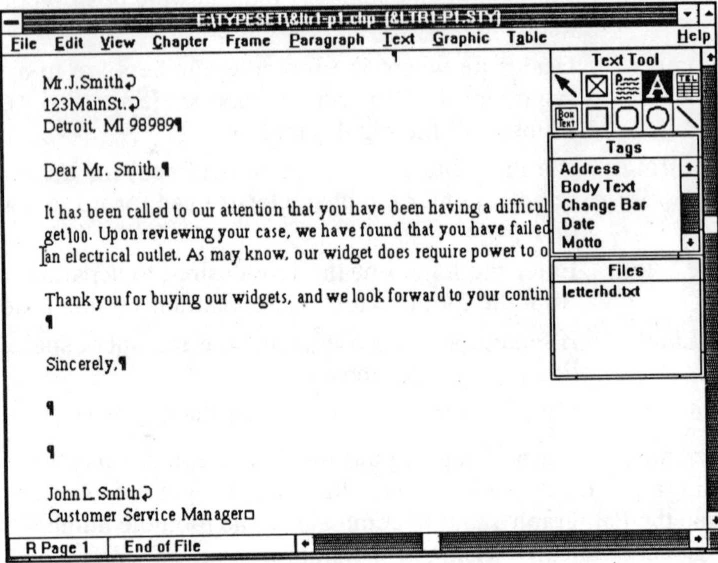

3. Click on the **File** menu, then click on **Revert to Saved** and click on **OK** when prompted to revert back to the last saved version.
4. Turn to Module 59 to continue the learning sequence.

Module 28
FRACTIONS

DESCRIPTION

Ventura allows the creation of true typographic fractions. True fractions look like this: ¼ or $\frac{3}{4}$ and not like this: 1/4 or 3/4

True typographic fractions use smaller type which is shifted up and down and separated by a special fraction bar available in the symbol font.

To insert a fraction within the text, select the Text Tool from the Toolbox Window. Place the cursor at the location of the text where a fraction is to be created. Select Insert Special Item from the Text menu. Then select Equations from the Insert Special Item dialog box. The Equation Editing screen appears:

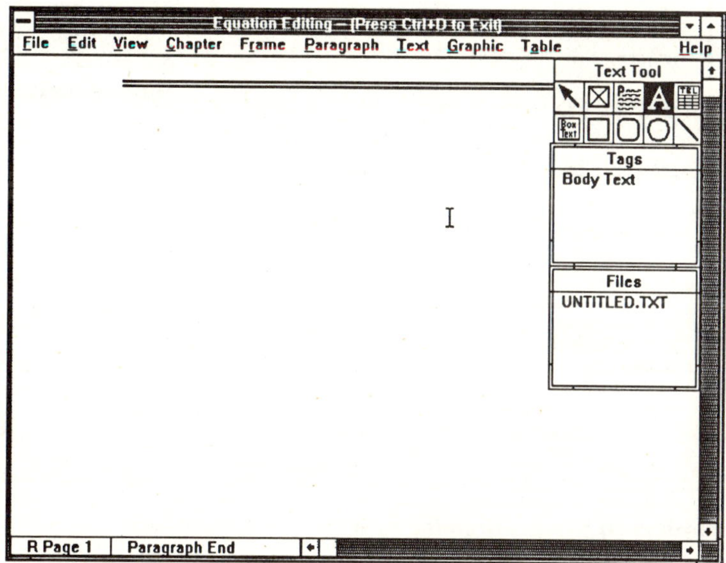

Type 1/4 to create a ¼ fraction. Or type 1 over 4 to create a $\frac{1}{4}$ fraction. Then press Ctrl-D to return to the main screen and insert the equation.

TIP:
Be sure to leave a space on either side of the word over.

APPLICATIONS

The Insert Fraction option allows the creation of typographically correct fractions without spending the time to change fonts, shift text, and insert fraction bars.

TYPICAL OPERATION

In this example, you insert a fraction in the text of the sample chapter &PRPT-P1.CHP. The example begins with &PRPT-P1.CHP open.

1. Press **Ctrl-O** to select the Text Tool.
2. Move the cursor to the middle of the second line of text. Click once.
3. Select the **Text** menu and click on **Insert Special Item**.
4. Select **Equations** from the Insert Special Item dialog box.
5. Type **1/300**.
6. Press **Ctrl-D** to return to the main screen and insert the fraction. Your screen should resemble the following illustration:

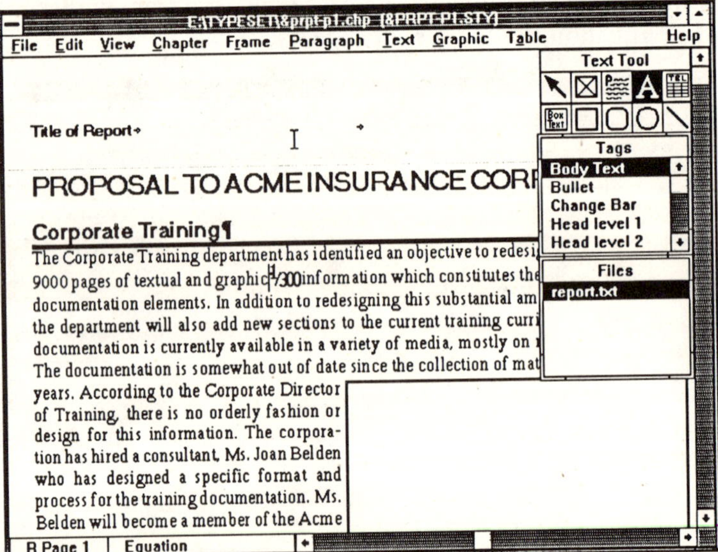

7. Select **Revert to Saved** from the **File** menu and click **OK**.
8. Turn to Module 12 to continue the learning sequence.

Module 29
FRAME BACKGROUND

DESCRIPTION

The Frame Background command allows you to create a background color and texture for each frame you create or for the underlying page frame. This command can be assigned to any frame, including those created by Ventura when you specify a caption, header, or footer.

To use this command, a frame must first be selected.

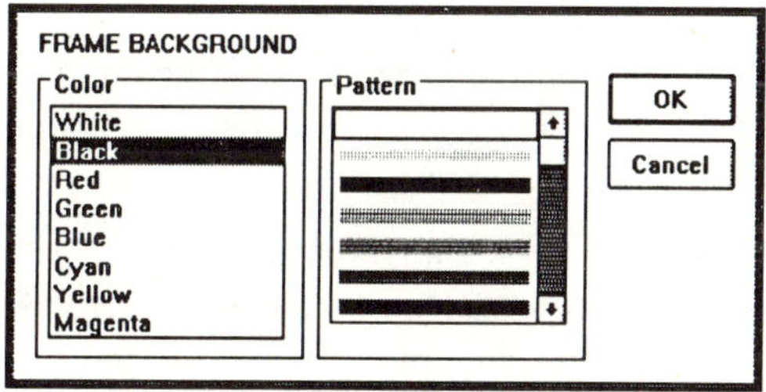

The Frame Background dialog box contains this information:

Color — A selection list is available to choose the color you want to assign to a frame's background.

TIP:
To see different colors, first define them in the Define Color dialog box. See Module 18.

Pattern — Select a pattern for the color of the Frame's background. Ventura displays several different patterns to choose from the pattern list. You can scroll through the list by using the scroll bar on the side of the pattern list.

The Frame Background command is located in the Frame menu.

APPLICATIONS

Background colors and patterns are an effective tool for highlighting or calling attention to articles or sidebars. As an example, you can create a light gray screen in a frame to call attention to it.

TIP:

Be careful not to choose a heavy screen when text is going to be placed in the frame. Choosing too dark a frame background can make your text difficult, if not impossible, to read.

You can also use color to create reverse type in your document. By choosing a solid background and white as the color of your text, you can create reverse type. (Some laser printers are not capable of printing white text on a black background.)

Remember that when you choose a color for a background, your laser printer will create only a black or gray color background. Printer's ink, and not your laser printer, determines the color of your published document. The color selection is useful in creating a color separation. (See Module 18 for more information about Define Color.)

TYPICAL OPERATION

In this example, you add a frame and assign a background color and pattern to the frame. The sample chapter document &PRPT-P1.CHP is used. The example begins with &PRPT-P1.CHP open. Use the Open Chapter command in the File menu to retrieve and open &PRPT-P1.CHP. So your view matches the screen depicted in this module, press Ctrl-R. You may need to adjust your screen using the scroll bars to make your computer look like the illustrations.

1. Click on the **Add Frame** Tool within the Toolbox.
2. Move the mouse cursor, which has changed shape to a corner of a box with the letters FR in the corner, to the upper left corner of the &PRPT-P1.CHP document.
3. Click and hold the mouse button. The cursor now changes to a double sided arrow.
4. Drag the pointer (you should still be holding the mouse button as directed in step 3) and create a frame as illustrated:

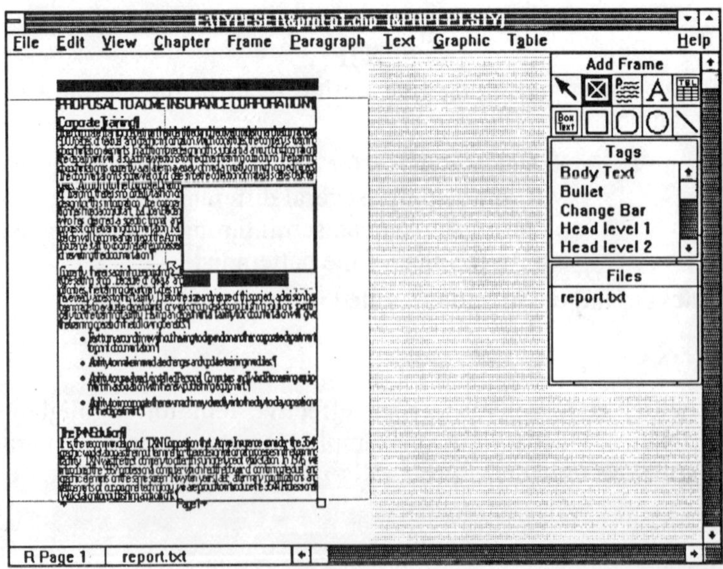

Let go of the mouse button to finish drawing the frame.

5. Select the **Frame** menu and click on **Frame Background**. Change the color to **Blue** by clicking on it in the Color menu. Change the Pattern to the last one on the Pattern list. (Use the scroll bar to access it.)
6. Click **OK**. The frame background of the frame created in steps 2 through 4 now has the new background.

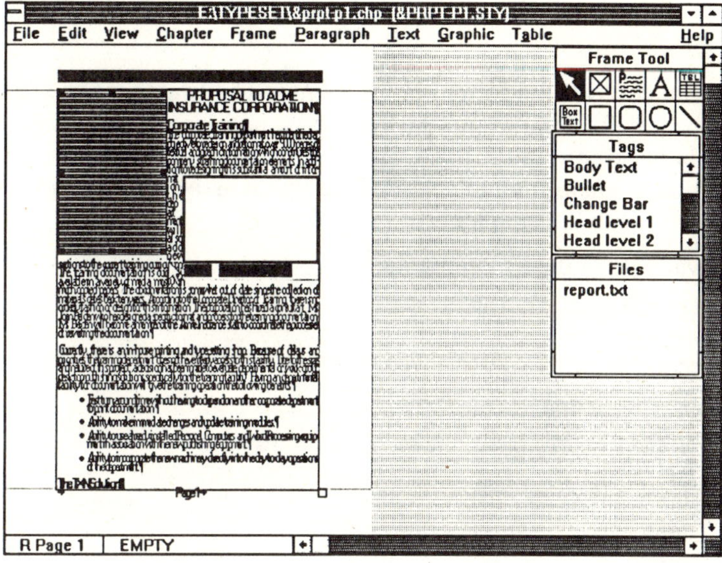

7. Press **Del** to delete the frame.
8. Click on **File** menu, click on **Revert to Saved**, and then click on **OK**.
9. Turn to Module 61 to continue the learning sequence.

Module 30
FRAME MENU

DESCRIPTION

The Frame menu controls the format of all frames. The Frame menu also controls the format of all pages. Remember that in Ventura, a page is nothing more than another frame. The only difference in the page frame is the margin and column settings. Those settings for the page's margins and columns are stored in the style sheet. All other frame settings are stored with the chapter.

The options available in the Frame menu are:

- Margins & Columns
- Sizing & Scaling
- Frame Typography
- Anchors & Captions
- Repeating Frame
- Vertical Rules
- Ruling Line Above
- Ruling Line Below
- Ruling Box Around
- Frame Background
- Remove Text/File
- File Type/Rename
- Image Settings

Changes made to any page affect all noninserted pages (see Module 40, Insert /Remove Page). Changes to each page you insert or to each frame you draw affect only that page or frame.

APPLICATIONS

Ventura's Frame menu provides you with the commands needed to maintain extensive control over all the frames that are used in a Ventura chapter.

Each frame can have its own set of formatting attributes, including its own margins and columns, captions, anchors, background, and ruling lines above, below, or around.

When producing documents with simple layouts, such as business reports, memos, or sales letters, the text is normally placed on the underlying page frame. For these types of documents, use the Frame menu to control the format of the underlying page frame.

When creating magazines, newsletters, books, manuals, and other types of publications that might include illustrations or multiple text files on the same page (just like a newspaper has more than one story on a page), you will need to use the Frame menu much more to define the settings for each frame you are placing within the document.

Remember also that frames can be layered, or stacked, on top of each other. Each frame is controlled, and its attributes are defined, in the Frame menu.

TYPICAL OPERATION

In this example, you access the Frame menu after selecting the Frame Tool, and review the various commands available within the menu. The sample chapter document SCOOP.CHP is used. The example begins with SCOOP.CHP open and in use. If you do not have this chapter open, use the Open Chapter command in the File menu to retrieve and open SCOOP.CHP.

1. Click on the **Frame** Tool within the Toolbox.
2. Press **Ctrl-R** to see the page in reduced view.
3. Move the pointer to the middle of the working area of your screen, and click the mouse cursor on top of the COLUMBIA.GEM picture. Your screen should resemble this illustration:

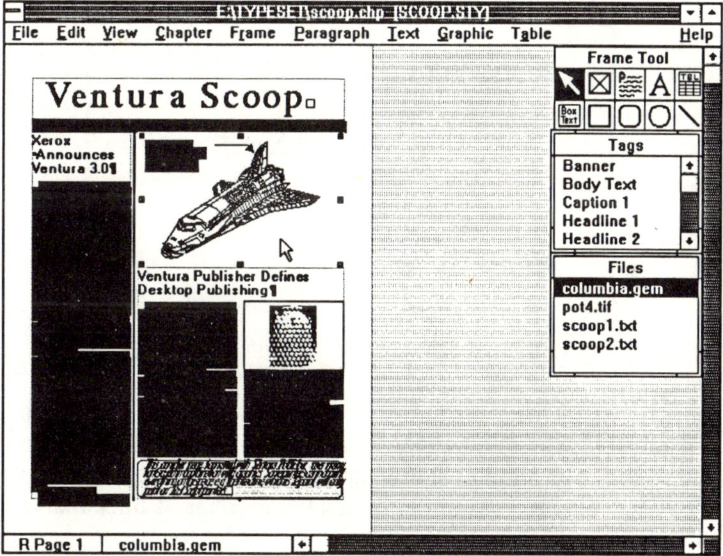

4. Click on the **Frame** menu and notice all the selections available. The Columbia frame could have any of these commands assigned to it.
5. Move the mouse outside the Frame menu and click once. The Frame menu disappears.
6. Turn to Module 54 to continue the learning sequence.

Module 31
FRAME TYPOGRAPHY

DESCRIPTION

The Frame Typography command overrides the settings defined with the Chapter Typography (see Module 14) command.

To use this command, the Frame Tool must be selected, and a frame must be chosen. The Frame Typography command can then be selected in the Frame menu. When the command is accessed, the Frame Typography Settings dialog box appears.

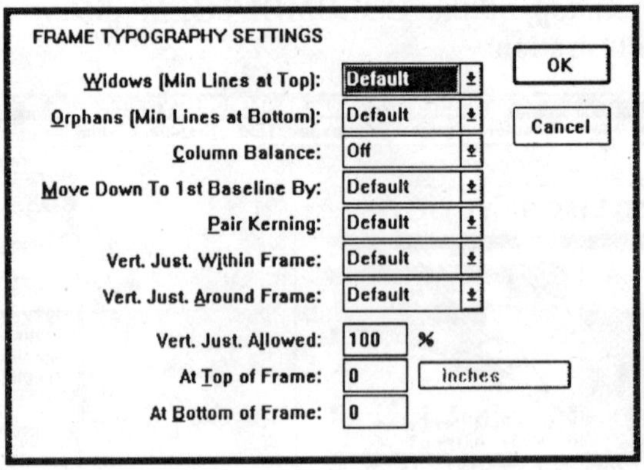

The following options are available in the Frame Typography Settings dialog box:

Widows — A widow is a single line of text at the top of a page or column which has been separated from the rest of the paragraph on the previous page or in the previous column. The Widows option increases or decreases the number of lines that can be widowed within the frame.

Orphans — An orphan is a single line of text at the bottom of a page or column which has been separated from the rest of the paragraph on the previous page or in the previous column. The Orphans option increases or decreases the number of lines that can be orphaned within the frame.

NOTE

The default setting for both Widows and Orphans is two. This setting is standard and is sufficient for most applications. This setting requires at least two lines of text be left on the previous page or column or forced to the next page or column.

Column Balance — Set the Column Balance on if you want the columns within the frame to balance. This would create all columns to be the same length. A setting of Column Balance Off will allow uneven columns within the frame.

Move Down to 1st Baseline By — Use one of these settings to determine where the first line of text will begin within a frame. Select Move Down to 1st Baseline By Cap Height if you want the top of a column to align with the top of the tallest capital letter in the font you have chosen. Select Move Down to 1st Baseline by Inter-Line if you want the first line of text to start at a distance from the top margin equal to the inter-line spacing set in the Spacing command (see Module 67).

Pair Kerning — Select either Pair Kerning Off or On for the frame.

Vert. Just Within Frame — Select Vertical Justification Within Frame on to allow vertical justification. When turned off, no vertical justification takes place. Select Feathering to place the exact amount of space to make the text reach the bottom of the column. Select Carding to add space between elements in multiples of Body Text inter-line spacing. Carding does not actually force body text to align. It maintains alignment of each paragraph if the style sheet is designed so that its spacing is an exact multiple of the Body Text's inter-line spacing.

TIP:

Feathering adds space more uniformly, but carding helps prevent misalignment between Body Text lines in side-by-side columns.

Vert. Just. Around Frame — Use Vertical Justification Around Frame to determine how space is added around a frame. Select Fixed to keep each frame in its fixed position. Additional space required for justification is allowed below the Frame. Select Moveable to allow the frame to be moved down to create space above the frame. Extra space is then added as needed, at the bottom of the frame.

TIP:

Use Moveable unless your document requires that frames cannot be moved.

Vert. Just. Allowed — Enter the amount of Vertical Justification that can be allowed within the frame when Vertical Justification Within Frame is on.

At Top of Frame — The At Top of Frame option sets the maximum amount of space that can be added between a frame and the text above it (when Vertical Just. Around Frame is on).

At Bottom of Frame — The At Bottom of Frame option sets the maximum amount of space that can be added between a frame and the text below it (when Vertical Just. Around Frame is on).

NOTE

To turn the Vertical Justification off, select Vertical Justification Within Frame: Off. Do not set Vertical Justification Allowed to 0%.

Selecting Default for any of these options forces Ventura to use the settings selected in the Chapter Typography menu (see Module 14). Selecting any other setting will override the values chosen in the Chapter Typography menu.

APPLICATIONS

The Frame Typography command is used to fine-tune the typography of text within a frame. This permits a more sophisticated layout, and provides a set of different typographical controls in a given frame from the typography used in the rest of the document.

For example, you may not want to use the column balance option in your document, but you may want to use it in a specific frame. By using the Frame Typography command, you can opt to use column balancing in a specific frame.

You can increase or decrease the maximum amount of space by specifying a Vertical Justification Allowed amount greater or less than 100%. For example, if Body Text spacing is currently set at 12 points and you specify 150%, Ventura would add up to 18 points of vertical space.

TYPICAL OPERATION

In this example, a new frame is created, and the typography of the frame is set by using the Frame Typography command. The sample chapter &PRPT-P1.CHP is used. The example begins with &PRPT-P1.CHP open. Use the Open Chapter command in the File menu to retrieve and open &PRPT-P1.CHP.

1. Select the **Add Frame** Tool from the Toolbox.
2. Draw a new frame in the middle of your page.
3. Click on the **Frame** menu and click on **Frame Typography** to display the Frame Typography Settings dialog box.
4. Change the Widows setting to **4** by accessing the pop-up menu.
5. Press **Enter**. The Frame typography for your new frame has been changed.
6. Press **Del** to remove the frame from your document.
7. Select **Revert to Saved** from the **File** menu and select **OK**.
8. Turn to Module 35 to continue the learning sequence.

Module 32
GO TO PAGE

DESCRIPTION

The Go to Page command allows you to move quickly to any specific page in your document.

The Go to Page command is accessed in the Chapter menu or by pressing Ctrl-G.

When you access the Go to Page command, the Go to Page dialog box appears. Your screen will look like this illustration:

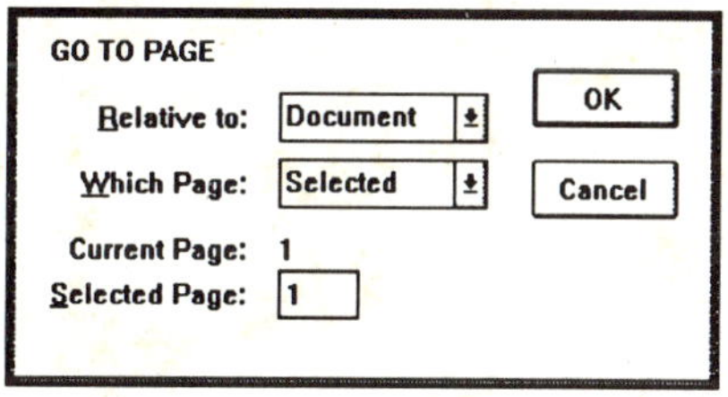

GO TO PAGE
Relative to: Document
Which Page: Selected
Current Page: 1
Selected Page: 1
OK
Cancel

The Go to Page dialog box provides these choices:

Relative To	You can select either document or file. If you choose Document, the Go to Page command takes you page by page regardless of the content of each page. If you first select a frame, then access the Go to Page command, and finally select File, the Go to Page command will only access and move you to those pages with frames containing the text file.
Which Page	Select First, Previous, Selected, Next, or Last. First will move you to the first page of your document or to the first page of your text file. Previous will move you back one page (for example, from page 7 to page 6). Selected moves you to the page you typed at the bottom of Go to Page dialog box. Next moves you forward one page (for example, from page 7 to page 8). Last moves you to the last page of the document or the last page of a text file.
Current Page	This simply displays the current page of the chapter file.
Selected Page	This displays the page being selected and shows you where Ventura will be going. You can type in a specific page number here.

Keyboard Shortcuts

There are several keyboard shortcuts to help you move around within a document. They are:

Go to:	*Use This Key:*
First	Home
Previous	PgUp
Next	PgDn
Last	End

APPLICATIONS

The Go to Page command is used to quickly move through your chapter file. This is helpful during the editing, revising, or changing of your document. You can easily go to any specified page by using this command. If you are working on page 1 in a chapter that has 50 pages, you could press the PgDn thirty times to go to page 31, or you could more easily use the Go to Page command and type 31 as the selected page. By doing so, you will save time and make your work easier.

NOTE

The Go to Page command moves you to the page within the document. To go to a specific page for a text file, select a frame holding the text file, select File for Relative to:, and then make your selection in the Which Page section of the Go to Page dialog box. This is useful for newletter and magazine layout.

TIP:

To halt a Go to command, press Esc.

TYPICAL OPERATION

In this example, you use the Go to Page command. The &PRPT-P1.CHP sample chapter is used. The example begins with &PRPT-P1.CHP open and in use. Use the Open Chapter command in the File menu to retrieve and open &PRPT-P1.CHP. Press Ctrl-N to select Normal View.

1. Click on the **Chapter** menu and click on **Go to Page**. When the Go to Page dialog box appears, click on **Which Page** and select **Last**. Your screen should now resemble the following illustration:

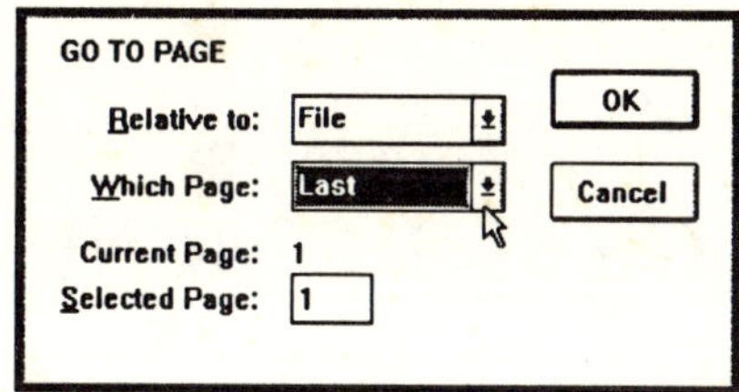

3. Select **OK**. Your screen displays the last page within the chapter.
4. Turn to Module 40 to continue the learning sequence.

Module 33
GRAPHIC MENU

DESCRIPTION

The Graphic menu allows access to commands that control selected graphics that have been created within a Ventura document. These commands affect the graphics drawn and created with the Graphics Tool.

The commands available in the Graphic menu are:

Show On All Pages
Send to Back
Bring to Front
Line Attributes
Fill Attributes
Select All
Grid Settings

To access the various commands available in the Graphic menu, you must first select a graphic that has been created. To select that graphic, you use the Frame Tool.

APPLICATIONS

The Graphic menu provides commands to make working with the graphics created within Ventura easier. The major functions of the commands are:

- Repeat the graphic on each page of a document.
- Move the graphic in front of or behind another graphic.
- Change and set the line and shading attributes.
- Create a grid so the graphics will snap to it, making positioning easier.

There are keyboard shortcuts available for some of the commands located within the Graphic menu. They are:

Ctrl-Z	Send to Back
Ctrl-A	Bring to Front
Ctrl-L	Line Attributes
Ctrl-F	Fill Attributes
Ctrl-Q	Select All

TYPICAL OPERATION

In this example, you access the Graphic menu and review the various commands available. The sample chapter SCOOP.CHP is used. The example begins with SCOOP.CHP in use. If you do not have this chapter open, use the Open Chapter command in the File menu to retrieve and open SCOOP.CHP.

1. Click on the **Frame** Tool from the Toolbox.
2. Click on the shaded rectangle box located in the lower right corner of the SCOOP.CHP chapter.
3. Click on the **Graphic** menu and notice the various options available. Your screen should resemble this illustration:

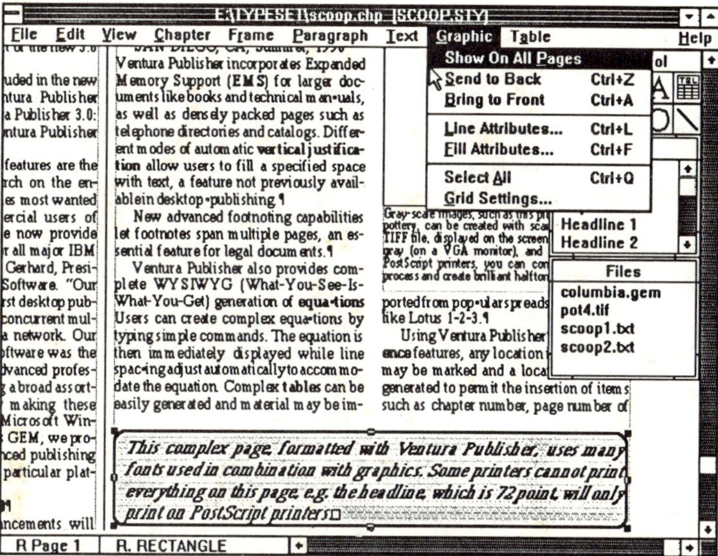

4. Click outside the menu, and the menu disappears.
5. Turn to Module 55 to continue the learning sequence.

Module 34
GRID SETTINGS

DESCRIPTION

The Grid Settings command defines the settings of a grid used during the sizing and shaping of Ventura graphics. You can turn the grid either on or off.

When the grid is on, the graphics you create or size will automatically align or "snap" to horizontal and vertical lines of the grid.

The grid lines are invisible and cannot be seen on your computer screen. The following illustration depicts the function of the Grid Settings feature in Ventura Publisher:

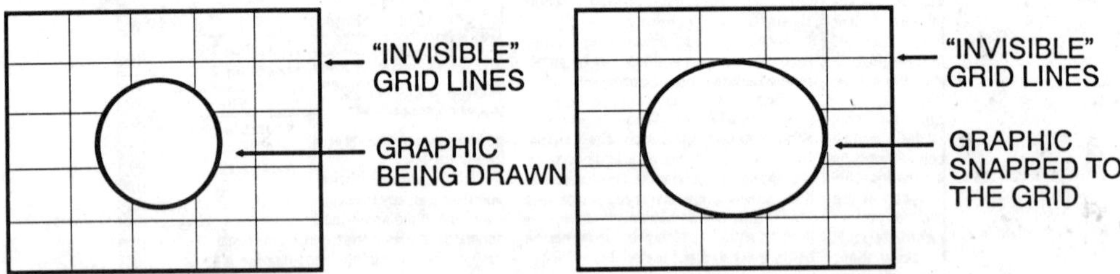

The Grid Settings is accessed in the Graphic menu. When accessed, the Grid Settings dialog box appears. Your screen will resemble this illustration:

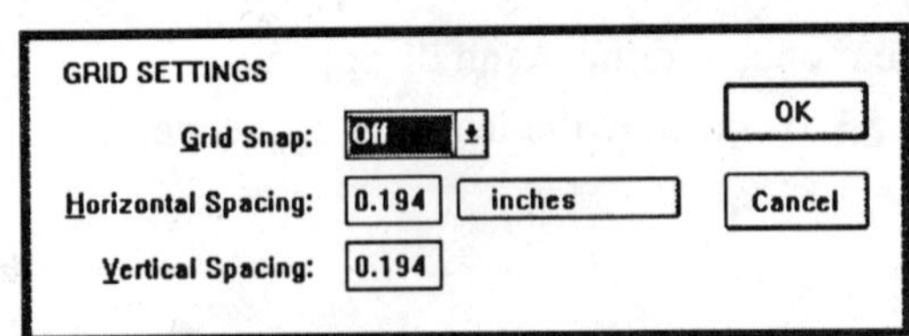

The Grid Settings dialog box provides these choices:

Grid Snap	Select either on or off to make the grid active or not active.
Horizontal Spacing	Type the amount of space desired between the horizontal lines of the grid.
Vertical Spacing	Type the amount of space desired between the vertical lines of the grid.

NOTE

The grid settings affect only the graphics associated with the selected frame. Grid settings apply only to that particular frame, not to all the graphics or frames in your document.

APPLICATIONS

The Grid Settings command allows precise creation of graphics within Ventura documents. The grid settings assure perfect vertical and horizontal alignment.

When creating forms or tables, where adjacent boxes must line up exactly, the Grid Settings command allows the precision placement to take place so precise alignment is achieved.

TYPICAL OPERATION

In this operation, you define a grid, turn it on, and draw and resize graphics. The instructions begins with the sample chapter &PRPT-P1.CHP being used. Use the Open Chapter command in the File menu to retrieve and open &PRPT-P1.CHP. You may need to adjust your screen using the scroll bars to make your computer look like the illustrations.

1. Select the **Add Frame** Tool in the Toolbox.
2. Create a new frame in the middle of the page.
3. Select the **Add Round Rect** Tool from the Toolbox.
4. Click on the **Graphics** menu and click on **Grid Settings** to display the Grid Settings dialog box.
5. Select **On** for Grid Snap, type **36.00** points for Horizontal Spacing and **24.00** points for Vertical Spacing.

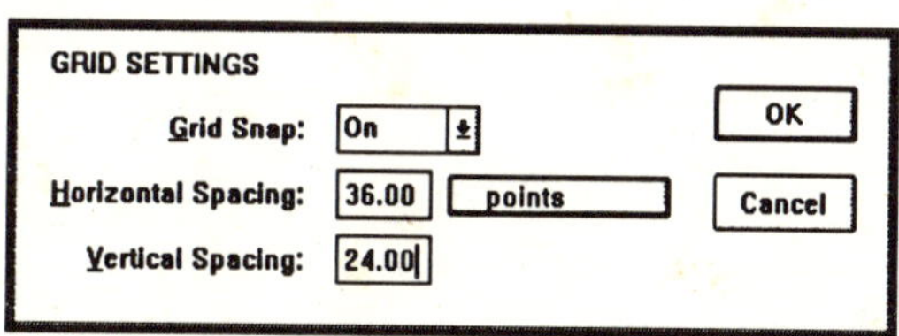

6. Press **Enter**. The Grid has been set.
7. Move the mouse cursor to the frame, and click and hold the mouse button. Drag the mouse to draw a box. Release the mouse button. Notice the frame you have just created is highlighted with small gray boxes on its edges.

8. Click on the graphic box just drawn in step 7. Click and hold on the box in the lower right corner, and drag the mouse pointer down and to the left. Your screen should resemble this illustration:

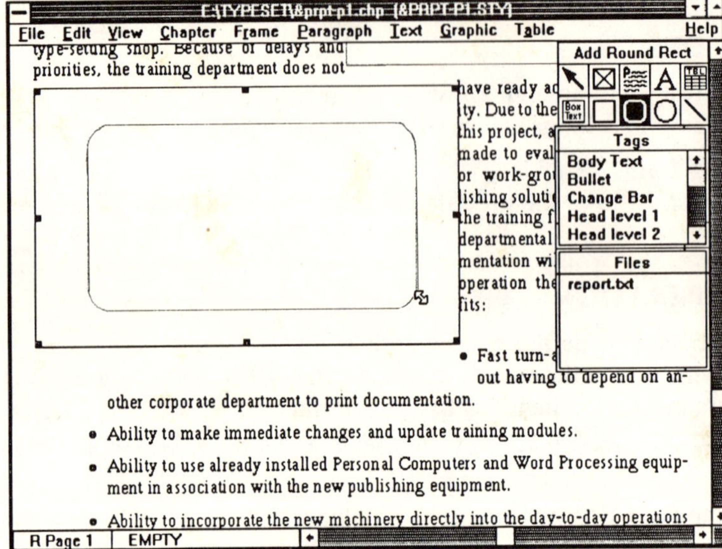

Release the mouse button. Notice how the resized graphic snaps to the invisible grid lines.

9. Click on the **File** menu, click on **Revert to Saved**, and select **OK**.
10. Turn to Module 15 to continue the learning sequence.

Module 35
HEADERS & FOOTERS

DESCRIPTION

The Headers & Footers command creates the text that is to appear at the top (headers) and bottom (footers) of every page. Different information for the headers and footers and different information for the left- and right-hand pages can be entered.

The header or footer appears on every page. The header and footer can be turned on and off for the left-hand or right-hand pages.

Each header and footer in the document consists of three separate sections: left, center, and right. Ventura automatically left aligns the left section, centers the center section, and right aligns the right section of the header and footer on the page. Each header or footer can include one or two lines of text.

Chapter number and page number can be inserted into any header or footer.

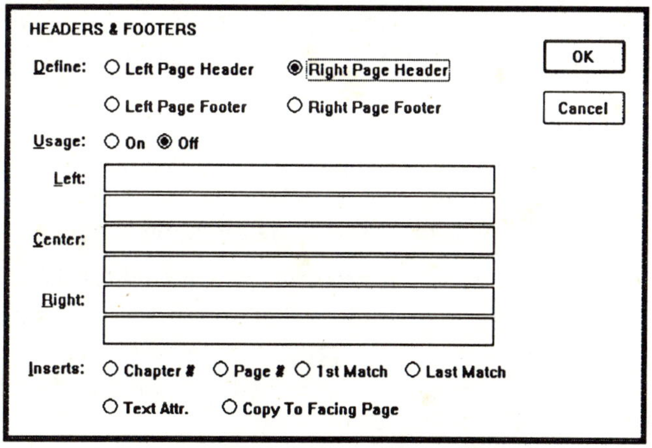

HEADERS & FOOTERS
Define: ○ Left Page Header ◉ Right Page Header
○ Left Page Footer ○ Right Page Footer
OK
Cancel
Usage: ○ On ◉ Off
Left:
Center:
Right:
Inserts: ○ Chapter # ○ Page # ○ 1st Match ○ Last Match
○ Text Attr. ○ Copy To Facing Page

The Header & Footers dialog box offers these options:

Define — Select either the Left Page Header, Right Page Header, Left Page Footer, or the Right Page Footer.

Usage — Select On to display the header or footer text that is entered. Select Off to hide the information. When the information is hidden by selecting off, it remains in the file but is not displayed on the pages. (The headers and footers on individual pages can be displayed or hidden by using the Turn Footer On/Off and the

Turn Header On/Off commands from the Chapter menu. See Module 72 for more information.)

Left	Enter the text information for the left part of the header or footer.
Center	Enter the text information for the center part of the header or footer.
Right	Enter the text information for the right part of the header or footer.
Inserts	Select Chapter #, Page #, 1st Match, Last Match, Text Attr., or Copy to Facing Page. Selecting one of these options allows Ventura to place automatically the variable information into the header or footer, define the appearance of the text, or copy the information you entered for the header or footer to the facing page.

The variable information includes the Chapter #, Page #, 1st Match, and Last Match selections.

Selecting Chapter # in the Header & Footer dialog box inserts the characters [C#] in the header or footer. Each time Ventura reads these characters in the header or the footer, it substitutes the current chapter number.

Selecting 1st Match inserts [<tag name] and selecting Last Match inserts [>tag name] in the header or footer. You must substitute the name of a paragraph tag for "tag name." For example, [<tag name] might become [<Headline 1]. In this case, each time Ventura reads these characters, it substitutes the first text marked with the Headline 1 tag on the current page. For Last Match, Ventura substitutes the last occurrence of text marked with the paragraph tag on the current page.

The appearance of the header and footer is defined by selecting Text Attribute. Selecting Text Attribute places the characters <D> in the header or footer. Other text attribute codes can be substituted for <D> character. For more information, see Appendix B.

Select Copy to Facing Page to copy the information entered for the header or footer to the facing page.

TIP:

Header information cannot be copied to a footer, and footer information cannot be copied to a header.

The options selected in the Page Layout command affect how headers and footers are used in the final printout of your publication. If Single for Sides and Right Side for Start On is selected, Ventura uses only the right page header and right page footer. If Single for Sides and Left Side for Start On is selected, Ventura uses only the left page header and left page footer. If Double for Sides is selected, Ventura will use both the left and right headers and footers.

Ventura also creates two paragraph tags automatically for your headers and footers. These tags can be accessed to add other attributes (such as font, size, color) to your headers and footers.

The header and footer information is stored in the chapter file. The Header & Footer command is accessed in the Chapter menu.

APPLICATIONS

Headers and footers make your publication easier to read. Think how difficult this book would be to use if it had no page numbers. The layout of this book is such that a footer is used on each page. The footer for this book only contains the page number.

In some books, the left page header is often used to name the book, and the right page is used to list the chapter. In this book, the left page header states the module number, and the right page contains the name of the module.

One important feature of this command is that you can have two different headers or footers. This is important to make your pages easier to read. By placing the page number in the outer corner of the pages of the book, it is easier for this book's readers to find a specific page.

TYPICAL OPERATION

In this example, you add a header to the sample chapter SCOOP.CHP. This example begins with SCOOP.CHP open and in use. If you do not have this chapter open, use the Open Chapter command in the File menu to retrieve and open SCOOP.CHP. So your view matches the screen depicted in this book, press Ctrl-N.

1. Click on the **Chapter** menu and click on **Headers & Footers** to display the Headers & Footers dialog box.
2. Click on the **Right Page Footer** for Define and **On** for Usage. Move the cursor to **Left** and click once.
3. Type **Scoop News.**
4. Move the cursor to **Right** and click once and then point and click on **Page #** for Inserts. Your screen should resemble the following illustration:

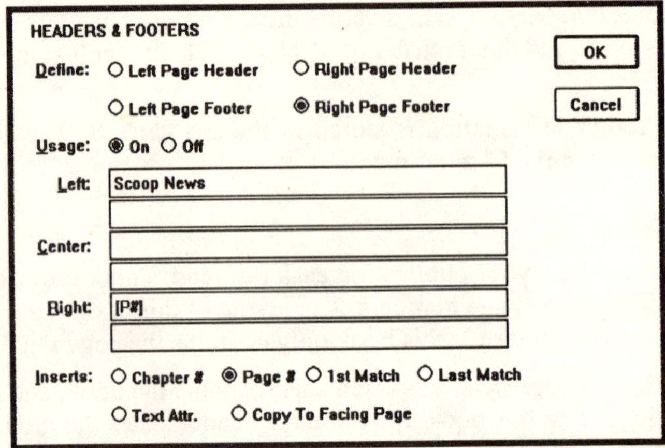

5. Click **OK**. Scroll your page down to the bottom left corner of the page. Your screen should resemble this illustration:

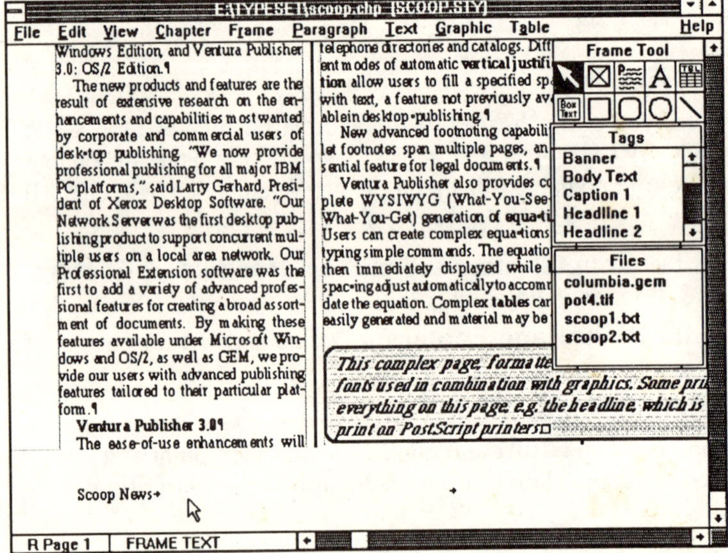

Notice the addition of the footer.

6. Click on the **File** menu and click on **Revert to Saved**. Select **OK** to confirm the Abandon when the message box appears.
7. Turn to Module 25 to continue the learning sequence.

Module 36
IMAGE SETTINGS

DESCRIPTION

The Image Setting command controls halftone (picture) processing for images which contain shades of gray. This command is only available for PostScript and TIFF images and is only available when those images contain shades of gray.

The Image Setting command only works when a PostScript or TIFF image is being sent to a PostScript printer. TIFF files that contain shades of gray will print to non-PostScript-driven printers, such as the Hewlett-Packard LaserJet Series II, but the Image Setting command will have no effect on the image.

TIP:

A gray scale image is a scanned image which has every dot in the picture as a shade of gray rather than just black. Halftoning modifies the gray scale image so that it can be printed by a device that only has the capability of producing black dots.

The Image Settings command is located in the Frame menu. To select this command, Ventura must be in Frame mode, and a frame containing a PostScript or TIFF image must be selected. After selecting the command, the Image Settings dialog box will appear:

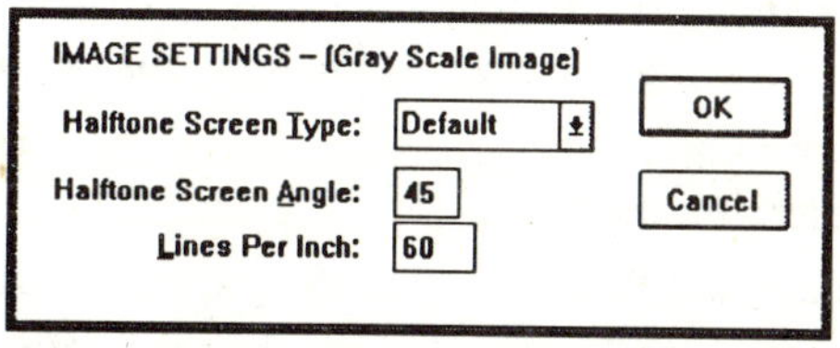

IMAGE SETTINGS – (Gray Scale Image)
Halftone Screen Type: Default ±
Halftone Screen Angle: 45
Lines Per Inch: 60
OK
Cancel

Within the Image Settings dialog box, these options are available:

Halftone Screen Type — The screen produces a regular pattern through the image. This pattern is often rotated to make the screen less noticeable. Select Default to use the standard settings for image control. The default settings are a screen angle of 45 degrees and 60 lines per inch for laser printers. Other settings can be entered if desired. For most images, these default settings will work.

Halftone Screen Angle	Select an angle of the halftone screen. Halftoning is the process of modifying the gray scale image into a form that can be printed by a device that can only produce black dots. A screen is placed on the image and usually rotated to make the dots less noticeable. A 45-degree screen angle is standard, but for some images, a special effect can be achieved by using a different screen angle.
Lines Per Inch	Select the number of lines per inch that is to be assigned to the image. Most laser printers are only capable of printing at 60 lines per inch. The lines-per-inch setting determines how many dots per inch are placed on the page.

To use this command, a PostScript or TIFF image must be available, and these are generally created with a scanner. In most cases, the image is a photograph, which is a gray-scale image. A gray-scale image is a scanned image where every dot in the picture is a shade of gray, rather than just black. The Image Settings control is only one part of a series of operations required to print a scanned image.

APPLICATIONS

The Image Settings command is used to enhance or modify the appearance of a PostScript or TIFF image within the chapter, when printed. By making adjustments to the image, a special effect or enhancement to the printed picture can be realized.

TYPICAL OPERATION

In this example, you use the Image Settings command to adjust the gray scale image. This example uses the sample chapter SCOOP.CHP. The example begins with SCOOP.CHP open and in use. So your view matches the screen depicted in this book, press Ctrl-N. You may need to adjust your screen using the scroll bars to make your computer look like the illustrations.

1. Press **Ctrl-U** to select Frame mode.
2. Click in the middle of the frame holding the jar to select the frame.
3. Point to the **Frame** menu and click on **Image Settings** to display the Image Settings dialog box.
4. Type **90** for Halftone Screen Angle and **100** for Lines Per Inch. Your screen should resemble this illustration:

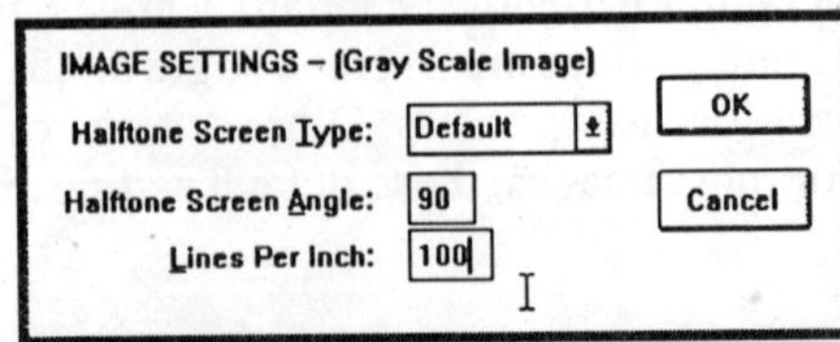

5. Click **OK**.

NOTE

Depending on your computer equipment, you may not notice any difference in the changes made on your screen image. You may want to print this document to a laser printer to see the changes. The amount of change you see will be determined by the capability of the printer you are using.

6. Turn to Module 44 to continue the learning sequence.

Module 37
INSERT/EDIT ANCHOR

DESCRIPTION

The Insert/Edit Anchor command places a frame anchor into the text file. The Insert/Edit Anchor command links a specific frame to an anchor's location within the text of a document. The frame then moves whenever this specified location in the text moves.

To insert a frame anchor within the text of a page, Ventura must be in Text mode. The next step is to position the cursor where you want to insert an anchor point and click the mouse once. Select Insert Special Item in the Edit menu and then select Frame Anchor from the Insert Special Item submenu. The Insert/Edit Anchor dialog box appears.

INSERT/EDIT ANCHOR

Frame's Anchor Name: [ ] OK

Frame's New Location: (•) Fixed, On Same Page As Anchor Cancel

( ) Relative, Below Anchor Line

( ) Relative, Above Anchor Line

( ) Relative, Automatically At Anchor

Within the Insert/Edit Anchor dialog box, the following options are available:

Frame's Anchor Name	Type the name of the frame anchor desired. The name typed in this section of the Insert/Edit Anchor dialog box *must* match the name entered for the chosen frame in the Anchors & Captions dialog box (see Module 6). It does not matter if the information is in uppercase or lowercase. If the name typed in this section does not match the name typed into the Anchors & Captions dialog box, Ventura will display an error message.
Frame's New Location	Select either Fixed, On Same Page As Anchor; Relative, Below Anchor Line; Relative, Above Anchor Line; or Relative, Automatically At Anchor.

If Relative, Above Anchor Line is selected, the bottom of the frame is moved to the line above the text line containing the anchor. If Relative, Below Anchor Line is selected, the top of the frame is moved to the line below the text line containing the anchor.

If Fixed, On Same Page As Anchor is selected, the frame's position on a new page is exactly as it was on the old page.

If Relative, Automatically At Anchor is selected, the frame automatically moves as the text moves.

TIP:

Always check each page after the Re-Anchor Frames command has been executed to make sure that the frames are properly positioned, are not pushed off the edge of the page, and do not overlap other frames.

APPLICATIONS

The purpose of Insert/Edit Anchor is to place an anchor within the text so that the illustration placed within a frame automatically moves with the text. If the text is edited, changed, or deleted, or if different attributes are assigned to the text, the text can drastically change. Illustrations intended to complement the text will no longer be positioned at the correct point. Ventura can automatically move the illustration as the text is realigned with this command.

By using Insert/Edit Anchor, the exact point in the text a frame is to be anchored to is determined. From that point on, Ventura will keep the frame in its correct position, eliminating the need to move each frame individually. This command can save hours of work, having eliminated the need to cut and paste the frames after the text has been realigned.

TYPICAL OPERATION

In this operation, you insert a frame anchor in the Ventura sample chapter SCOOP.CHP. This example begins with SCOOP.CHP open.

1. Click on the **Frame** Tool.
2. Point to the frame containing COLUMBIA.GEM and click once.
3. Click on the **Frame** menu and click on **Anchors & Captions**. The Anchors & Captions dialog box appears.
4. Type **1** for Anchor. Press **Enter**.
5. Press **Ctrl-O** to select the Text Editing mode.
6. Press **Ctrl-N** for Normal View. Move the mouse to the "t" in the word three, located in the first sentence in the third paragraph in the left column. Click once.
7. Click on the **Text** menu and select **Insert Special Item**. Select **Frame Anchor**. Your screen should resemble the following illustration:

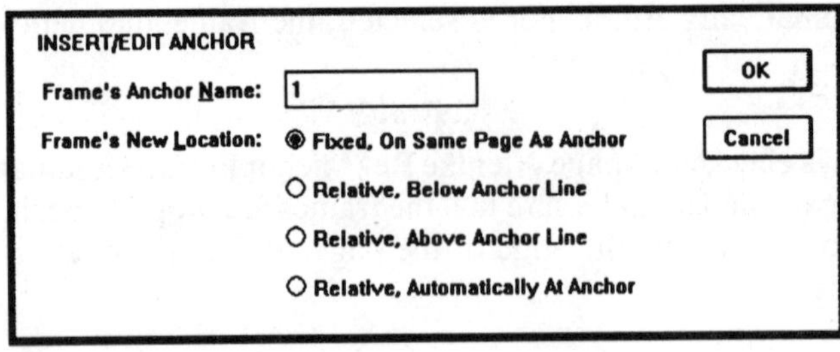

8. Type **1** for Frame's Anchor Name (if necessary).
9. Select **Relative, Automatically At Anchor** for Frame's New Location and click **OK**. Your screen should resemble this illustration:

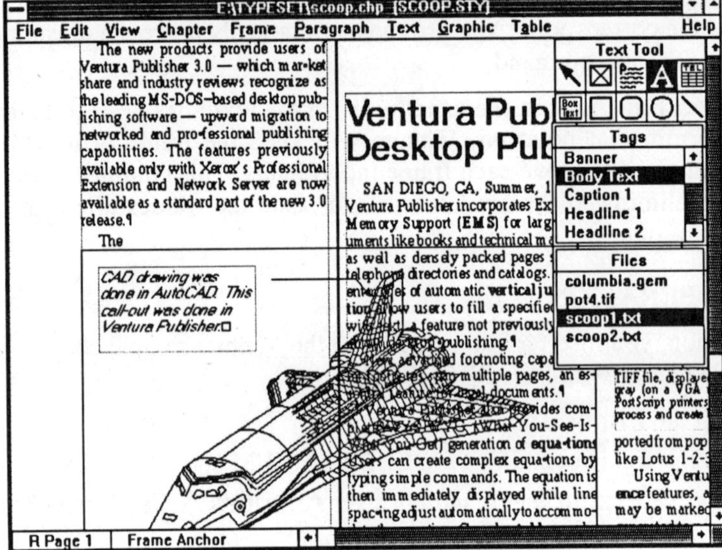

10. Click on the **File** menu and select **Revert to Saved**. Select **OK** to confirm the Abandon when the message box appears.
11. Turn to Module 58 to continue the learning sequence.

Module 38
INSERT/EDIT INDEX

DESCRIPTION

The Insert/Edit Index command creates or changes an index entry. The entry is attached to a point in the text. Once an entry is placed in the text, it remains with the same text, even if the text is cut and pasted. This permits easy updating of an index even if the sequence of paragraphs, pages, and chapters has been changed.

Ventura uses the Index option of the Manage Publication command to create an index from the various index entries. During processing, the Manage Publication command extracts the entries, along with their page numbers, sorts the entries in alphabetical order, and finally places the entries in a text file. This text file can then be loaded and formatted like any other Ventura file.

The Insert/Edit Index command creates a two-level index. This allows an index to have primary and secondary entries such as this:

Books	Primary entry
Illustrated DisplayWrite 4	Secondary entry
Illustrated Ventura 2.0	Secondary entry
Illustrated Ventura 3.0	Secondary entry
Services	Primary entry
Consulting—Applications	Secondary entry
Consulting—Training	Secondary entry

In addition, Insert/Edit Index can create "See" and "See also" references to other entries in the index. The following text shows examples of these entries:

Books	Primary entry
See also Authors	See also entry
See also Desktop Publishing	See also entry
See also Word Processing	See also entry
Using Computers	Secondary entry
Consultants	Primary entry
See Sheldon, George	See entry

Insert/Edit Index also permits the insertion of a word or phrase with one type of spelling and the sort with another type. For example, if "The Illustrated Ventura 3.0 Book" were being indexed, it would naturally sort with the T's. Obviously, it should be sorted with the I's. To do so, enter Illustrated Ventura 3.0 Book as the sort key. There can be sort keys for both primary and secondary entries.

The Insert/Edit Index command is used by inserting the text entry point at the desired position for the entry and then selecting the Index Entry option from the Insert/Special Item command in the Text menu. This command then inserts a mark at the location of the text entry point. The mark can be seen if the Show Tabs & Returns command in the Options menu has been set.

Always make sure that index entries are part of the paragraph and not in separate paragraphs of their own. If the index entry is not a part of a paragraph, your document will not format correctly.

Ventura must be in the Text mode to use this command. After selecting Insert Special Item from the Text menu, select the Index Entry option to make the Insert/Edit Index Entry dialog box appear.

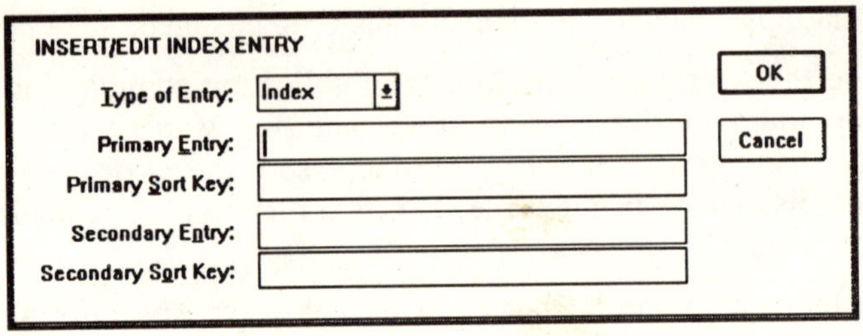

INSERT/EDIT INDEX ENTRY

Type of Entry: Index

Primary Entry:

Primary Sort Key:

Secondary Entry:

Secondary Sort Key:

OK

Cancel

The options available within the Insert/Edit Index Entry dialog box are:

Type of Entry	Select the type of entry desired. The options are Index, See, and See Also.
Primary/Secondary Entry	Type the primary or secondary entry. For a "See" or "See Also" entry, type the reference in the Secondary Entry area.
Primary/Secondary Sort Key	Type the content of the sort key.

When entries are being typed, make certain that words are spelled exactly the same each time an entry is made for the same subject. If spelling errors occur, Ventura sorts the entries differently and presents multiple entries because of the misspelling. For example, if you type "consultant" for one primary entry and "consultants" for another, Ventura will provide two entries within the index because one ends with an "s."

Ventura permits the edit of an index entry by selecting its mark in the text and selecting the Edit Special Item command from the Text menu.

However, another way to edit and, sometimes, enter index entries, is to use a word processor. Consider these examples:

<$IPrimary Entry[Sort Key]; Secondary Entry[Sort Key]>.

For a "See" entry, type:

<$SPrimary Entry[Sort Key];See Reference[Sort Key]>.

For a "See Also" entry, type:

<$APrimary Entry[Sort Key];See Also Reference[Sort Key]>.

TIP:

Placing these entries anywhere in a paragraph makes the text file nearly impossible to use. One solution to this problem is to place the index entries after the last sentence of the paragraph, but included as part of the paragraph, as shown in the following example:

The Insert/Edit Index command creates or changes an index entry. The entry is attached to a point in the text. Once an entry is placed in the text, it remains with the same text, even if the text is cut and pasted. This permits easy updating of an index even if the sequence of paragraphs, pages, and chapters have been changed. ***<$IInsert/Edit Index command;description> <$AInsert/Edit Index command;Manage Publication command>.***

If a paragraph breaks to a second page in the chapter, the index entries are for the page following the beginning of the paragraph. This can be prevented by setting Allow Within to No in the Breaks command located within the Paragraph menu (see Module 10 for more information about Breaks). This setting keeps paragraphs from breaking across the pages.

APPLICATIONS

An index enhances the quality of a document as it provides an easy way for the reader to locate information within the text. Just as you will use the index in this book to locate information about various commands, functions, and features of Ventura, readers of your documents will find them easier to use if an index is included.

Ventura will create the index automatically for you with the Insert/Edit Index command.

Perhaps the most difficult thing about creating an index for your publications is the fact that you must think like a reader, and you must remember that a reader using an index is trying to find something; that is why they are using the index. The bigger the index, the more entries, the better. And remember that all people do not think the same. For example, if your document had a section in it about the care and treatment of a lawn, some people would look under lawn to find the information, while others would look under grass, and still others would look under yard. The index should have references under grass and yard to see lawn.

Another point to consider when creating an index is remember that the index should contain as much information as possible. For example:

Lawn
    Care, 9
    Cutting, 12
    Diseases, 11

Fertilizing, 19
Insect Damage, 21
Replacing, 14

With this type of index, the reader could easily find information about fertilizing a lawn.

TYPICAL OPERATION

In this operation, you insert two index entries into the sample chapter &LSTG-P2.CHP. This operation begins with &LSTG-P2.CHP open. Use the command Open Chapter in the File menu to retrieve and open &LSTG-P2.CHP.

1. Press **Ctrl-O** to select the Text Tool.
2. Move the cursor to the "C" in Chorus Data Systems and click once.
3. Click on the **Text** menu and click on **Insert Special Item**. Select **Index Entry**.
4. Type **Chorus Data Systems** for Primary Entry and type **PC-Eye** for Secondary Entry.

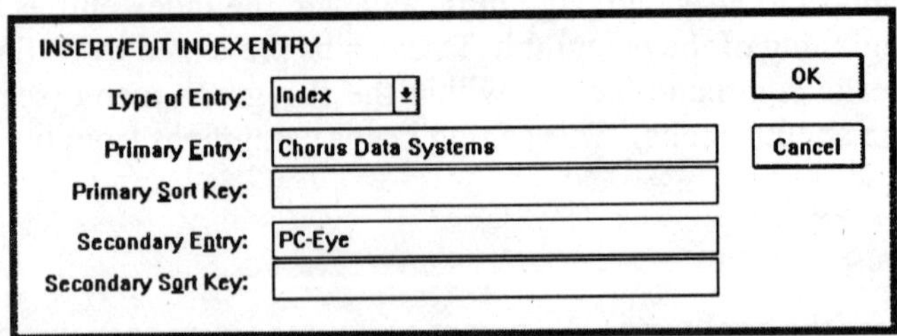

5. Press **Enter**.
6. Point to the **File** menu and click on **Revert to Saved**. Click on **OK** when prompted to revert back to the last saved version.
7. Turn to Module 85 to continue the learning sequence.

Module 39
INSERT SPECIAL ITEM

DESCRIPTION

The Insert Special Item command permits easy access to insert these special codes:

- Box Characters
- Footnotes
- Index Entries
- Equations
- Frame Anchors
- Cross References
- Marker Names
- Variable Definitions
- Tables

To insert a special item, first select the Text Tool. The next step is to move the mouse cursor to the position just in front of where the special item is to be inserted. Then select the Insert Special Item command in the Text menu. The secondary menu box appears.

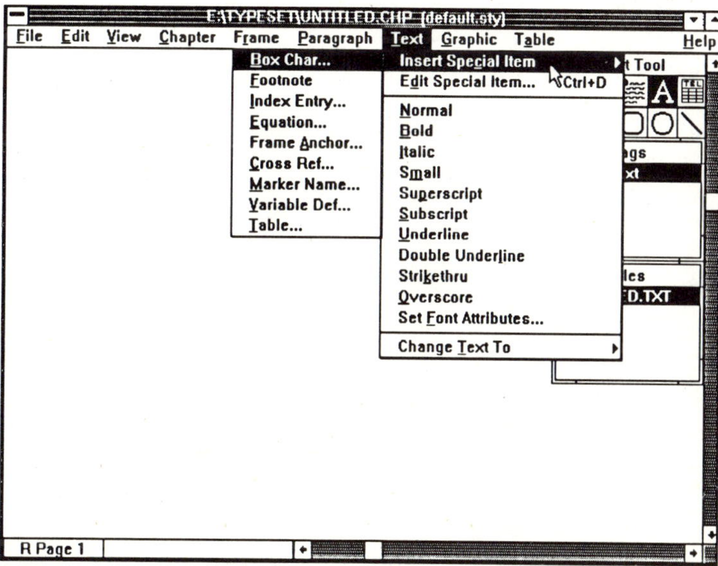

Select the special item you want to insert. The dialog box for the special item appears. Select any desired options and then select OK.

A special item can be deleted by pressing Del when the name of the special item appears in the Current Selection Box in the lower left side of the screen.

These special items are described in more detail in their own modules within this book. For more information about editing a special item, see Module 20.

The Insert Special Item command is accessed in the Text menu.

APPLICATIONS

Use the Insert Special Item command as the first step to creating box characters, footnotes, etc. in your Ventura document.

TYPICAL OPERATION

In this example, you access the Insert Special Item secondary menu and review the various commands. The sample chapter SCOOP.CHP is used. The example begins with SCOOP.CHP open and in use.

1. Press **Ctrl-O** to access the Text Tool.
2. Move the text cursor to an area in the text and click the mouse button once.
3. Click on **Insert Special Item** from the **Text** menu. Review the various options available to select.
4. Move the mouse outside the menu and click once.
5. Turn to Module 6 to continue the learning sequence.

Module 40
INSERT/REMOVE PAGE

DESCRIPTION

The Insert/Remove Page command allows the addition or deletion of pages to a chapter file. Adding a new page creates a new underlying page. Ventura will not delete a page that contains any information in the underlying page. Ventura will delete a page that contains information in other frames, but not in the underlying page frame.

The underlying page frame is part of the actual page structure. Other frames can be positioned on top of the underlying page frame. The underlying page frame contains the information for the margin settings and number of columns. This underlying page frame information is a part of the style sheet being used with each document. If the underlying page contains any other information, it cannot be deleted.

Ventura allows you to have more than one underlying page. Additional underlying pages can be added anywhere within a document. Since each underlying page operates separately from any other underlying page, additional underlying pages can be inserted in the middle of an existing group of pages. Ventura will not flow text from one underlying page to another. Text being placed onto different underlying pages must be maintained in separate text files.

The Insert/Remove Page command is accessed in the Chapter menu. When accessed, the Insert/Remove Page dialog box will appear, and your computer screen will resemble the following illustration:

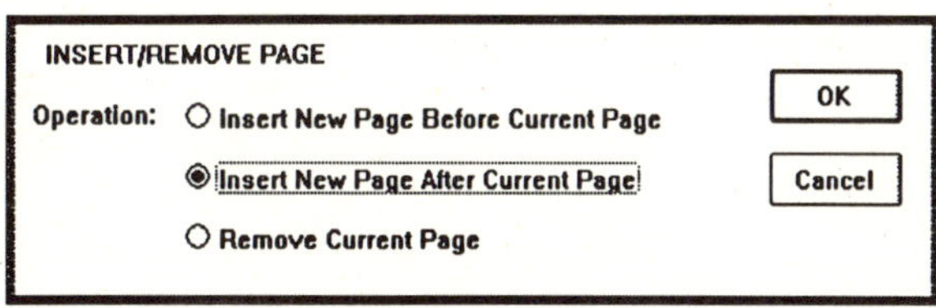

The Insert/Remove Page dialog box provides these choices:

- Insert new page before current page.
- Insert new page after current page.
- Remove current page.

APPLICATIONS

Ventura automatically creates and inserts new pages when a text file placed in the underlying page requires more than one page because of its length. Ventura removes those pages if portions of the text file are deleted.

There are times when you may want to insert a new page. For example, you might decide to add a graph, chart, or text table within a document. If so, the Insert/Remove Page command permits the addition of these types of items.

NOTE

> Ventura does not limit the number of pages that can be added. When a page is added, Ventura automatically moves to that new inserted page. When a page is removed, Ventura automatically moves to the previous page.

TYPICAL OPERATION

In this example, you insert a new page after the current page. The sample chapter &MAG-P3.CHP is used. The example begins with &MAG-P3.CHP open. Use the Open Chapter command in the File menu to retrieve and open &MAG-P3.CHP.

1. Click on the **Chapter** menu and click on **Insert/Remove Page.**
2. Select **Insert New Page After Current Page** in the Insert/Remove Page dialog box.
3. Select **OK**. Within a moment, you see the new page inserted.
4. Click on the **Chapter** menu and click on **Insert/Remove Page.**
5. Select **Remove Current Page** in the Insert/Remove Page dialog box.
6. Select **OK**. Within a moment, the page is removed and you are on page 2.
7. Select **New** from the **File** menu, then click on **Abandon** twice to clear the screen.
8. Turn to Module 50 to continue the learning sequence.

Module 41
INSERT ROW/COLUMN

DESCRIPTION

The Insert Row and Insert Column options allow you to add rows or columns to an existing table.

To add a new column or row within an existing table, select the Table Tool. Then select the location within the table where the new column or row is to appear.

NOTE

New rows are inserted below the selected row. New columns are inserted to the right of the selected column.

Select Insert Row or Insert Column in the Table menu. The dialog box appears:

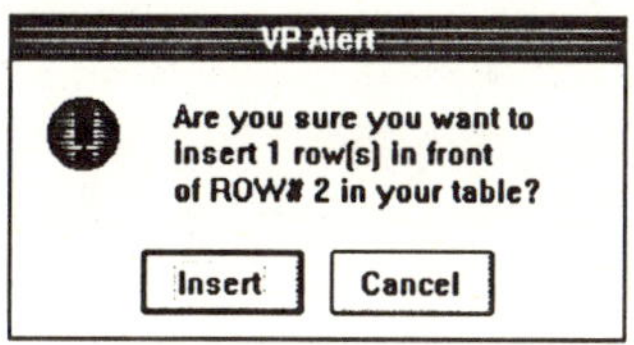

Select Insert to insert columns or rows. Ventura automatically adds the rows or columns to your table.

TIP:

To delete a row or column, select the row or column to be deleted, and use the Cut command available within the Edit menu.

APPLICATIONS

If you create a table and later desire that it be expanded, these two commands allow you to make those changes. Rather than recreate the entire table, the Insert Row and Insert Column commands allow the table to be modified by adding the additional columns and rows as needed.

TYPICAL OPERATION

In this activity, you insert a row and column within a table. This table was created in the Typical Operation of Module 42, and modified in Modules 43, 68, and 71. (If you have not created the table, you must do so before proceeding with these steps.)

1. Select the **Table** Tool in the Toolbox.
2. Move the mouse to the upper left corner of the first cell in the second row, and click and hold the mouse. While still holding the mouse button, drag the mouse to the lower right corner of the second row. Release the mouse button.
3. Click on the **Table** menu and select **Insert Row**. Your screen should resemble this illustration:

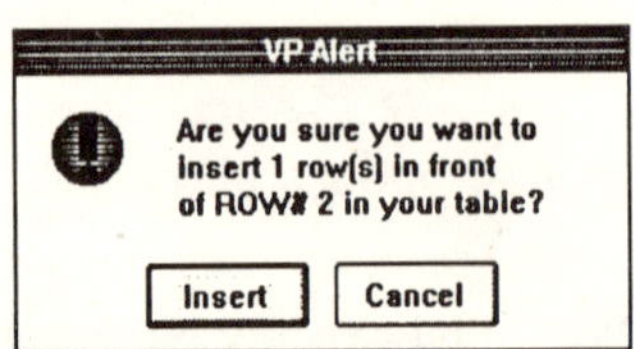

4. Click **Insert**. Your screen should now resemble this illustration:

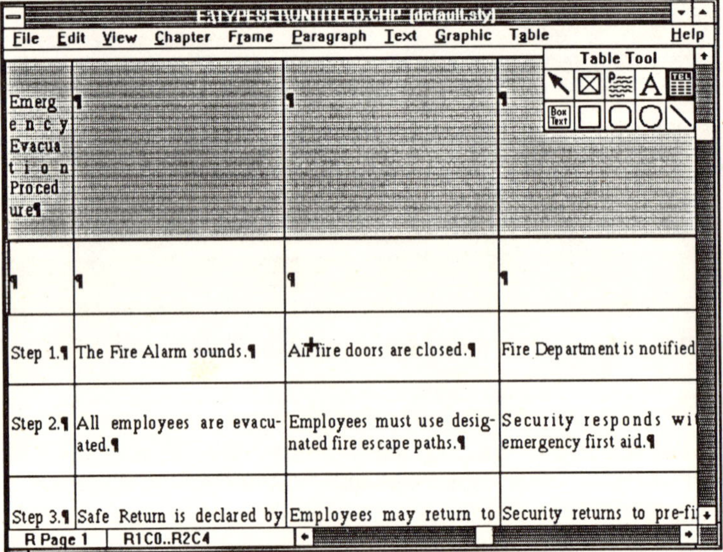

5. Move the mouse to the upper left corner of the first cell in the first row, and click and hold the mouse. While still holding the mouse button, drag the mouse to the lower right corner of the first column. Release the mouse button.
6. Click on the **Table** menu and select **Insert Column**.

7. Click **Insert**. Your screen should now resemble this illustration:

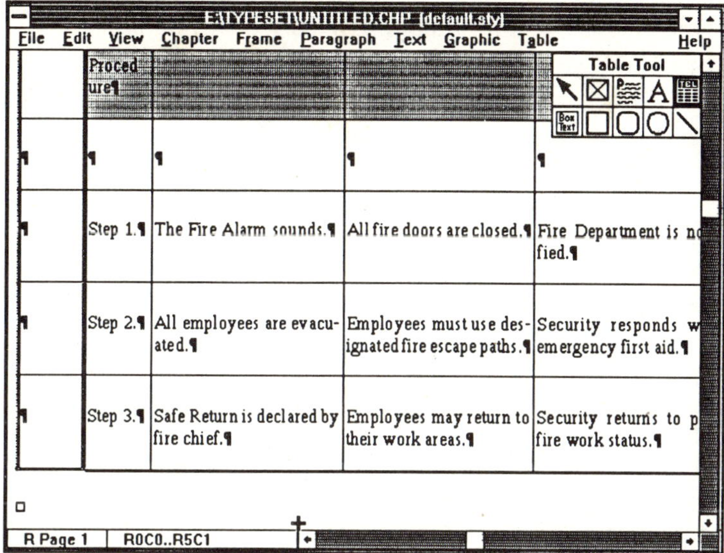

8. Click on the **File** menu, click on **Revert to Saved**, then select **OK**. This ends the learning sequence.

Module 42
INSERT TABLE

DESCRIPTION

The Insert Table function allows you to insert a table anywhere within a document. You can insert the table at the current location of the text or table cursor.

TIP:

The Insert New Table option in the Table menu performs the same operation as the Insert Special Item: Table located in the Text menu.

If a table exists, it can be edited by changing the settings within the Insert/Edit Table dialog box.

NOTE

Both Insert New Table and Change Settings use the same dialog box.

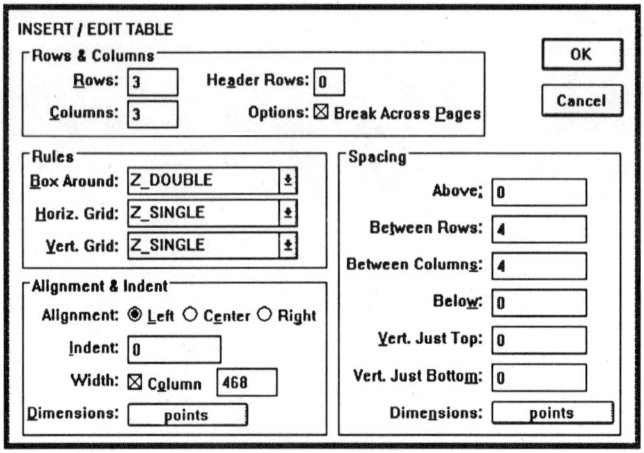

INSERT / EDIT TABLE
Rows & Columns
Rows: 3 Header Rows: 0
Columns: 3 Options: ☒ Break Across Pages
OK
Cancel
Rules
Box Around: Z_DOUBLE
Horiz. Grid: Z_SINGLE
Vert. Grid: Z_SINGLE
Alignment & Indent
Alignment: ◉ Left ○ Center ○ Right
Indent: 0
Width: ☒ Column 468
Dimensions: points
Spacing
Above: 0
Between Rows: 4
Between Columns: 4
Below: 0
Vert. Just Top: 0
Vert. Just Bottom: 0
Dimensions: points

These options are available from within the Insert/Edit Table dialog box:

Rows & Columns:

Rows, Columns, Header Rows	This option sets the numbers of rows and columns. When a table is first created, every cell within the table is assigned the same height and width. Enter the number of rows desired and the number of columns desired. Header Rows determines if a header is to be added to each table. (This is used for tables that

break across more than one page.) Select Break Across Pages if the table can be split onto more than one page.

TIP:

Once a table has been created, the numbers cannot be changed to edit the table. Rather, use the Insert Row and Column option.

Rules:

Box Around	Select Z_DOUBLE to place a double rule around the entire table. Choose another setting if desired.

TIP:

Ventura creates three generated tags: Z_Double, Z_Single, and Z_Thick. These tags can be defined within the Paragraph menu. By editing these three tags, the thickness of ruling lines can be easily adjusted.

Horizontal Grid	Select to place a ruling line between each row within the table.
Vertical Grid	Select to place a ruling line between each column in the table.

Alignment & Indent:

Alignment	This option specifies where the table should be aligned relative to the current column if Custom has been selected within the Overall Width option. Select either Left, Center, or Right. Indent permits the positioning of the table away from the left edge of the current column.
Width	This option sets the width of the table. Select Column to make the table fit into the current column, or specify any desired width.
Dimensions	Select the desired unit of measurement.

Spacing:

Above	This option adds vertical space between the beginning of the table and the bottom of the previous paragraph.
Between Rows	This option adds vertical space between each row in a table.
Between Columns	This option adds or deletes space to the left of each column. This option is used to prevent text from touching text in an adjacent cell.
Below	This option adds space between the end of the table and the top of the following paragraph.
Vert. Just Top	This option provides vertical justification control at the top of the paragraph. It allows Ventura to treat the table as a paragraph.
Vert. Just Bottom	This option provides vertical justification control at the bottom of a paragraph. It allows Ventura to treat the table as a paragraph.
Dimensions	Select the desired unit of measurement.

When you first create a table in Ventura, all cells within the table are the exact same size. The width can be changed (see Module 68). The height of each row grows automatically as text is added to a cell.

TIP:

To add rows or columns to a table that already exists, use the Insert Row or Insert Column commands in the Table menu.

APPLICATIONS

The Insert New Table command allows you to define and set the height, width, and spacing of a table. Sometimes you may want the table to align on the right margin of the table. Or you might want to change the rule around the table. This command allows you to make these changes to your preferences.

The Insert/Edit Table dialog box is used to make changes in an existing table if desired.

TYPICAL OPERATION

In this operation, you create a table. After creating the table, you enter text into its cells. This table is used in later modules within the learning sequence as you make adjustments to the table created in these steps. Start the exercise with a blank screen and the default style sheet loaded.

1. Select the **Table** Tool in the Toolbox.
2. Move the mouse to the middle of the text screen, and click once.
3. Click on the **Table** menu and select **Insert New Table**. Your screen should resemble this illustration:

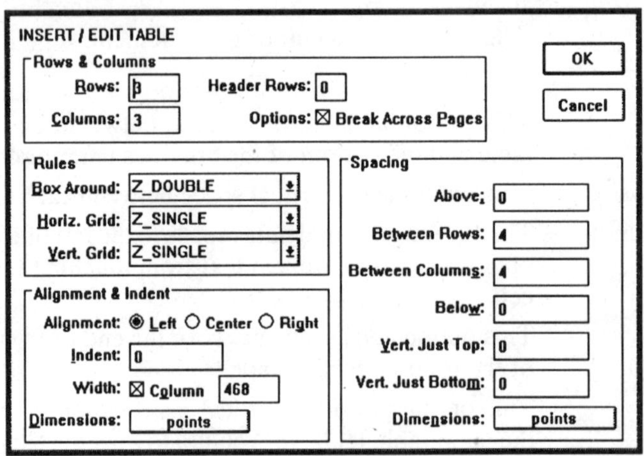

4. Change the number of rows to **4** and number of columns to **4**.

5. Click **OK**. Press **Ctrl-Y**, then **Ctrl-V** to hide the Tags List and Files List windows. Your screen should resemble this illustration:

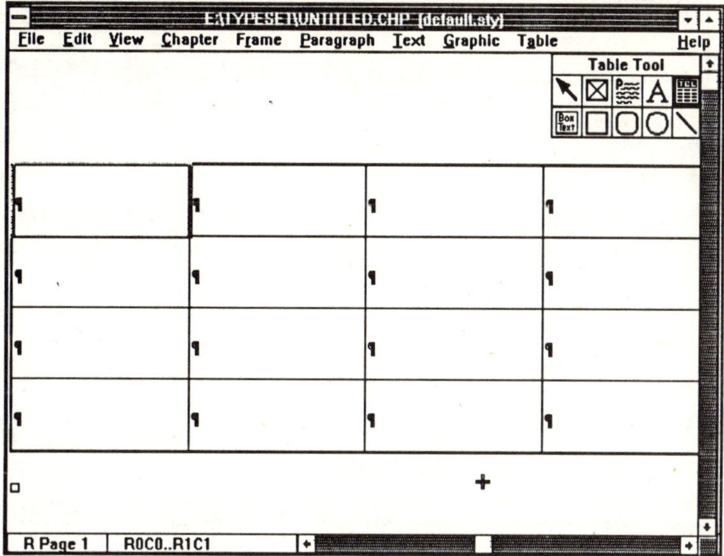

6. Select the **Text** Tool from the Toolbox.
7. Move the cursor to the first cell within the table. Type the following text within the cell:

   Emergency Evacuation Procedure

8. Press **Down Arrow** to move to the first cell in the second row.
9. Type the following text in the remaining cells:

TIP:

Make sure you move the cursor to the next cell before you begin typing.

Step 1.	**The Fire Alarm sounds.**	**All fire doors are closed.**	**Fire Department is notified.**
Step 2.	**All employees are evacuated.**	**Employees must use designated fire escape paths.**	**Security responds with emergency first aid.**
Step 3.	**Safe Return is declared by fire chief.**	**Employees may return to their work areas.**	**Security returns to pre-fire work status.**

When completed, your screen should resemble this illustration:

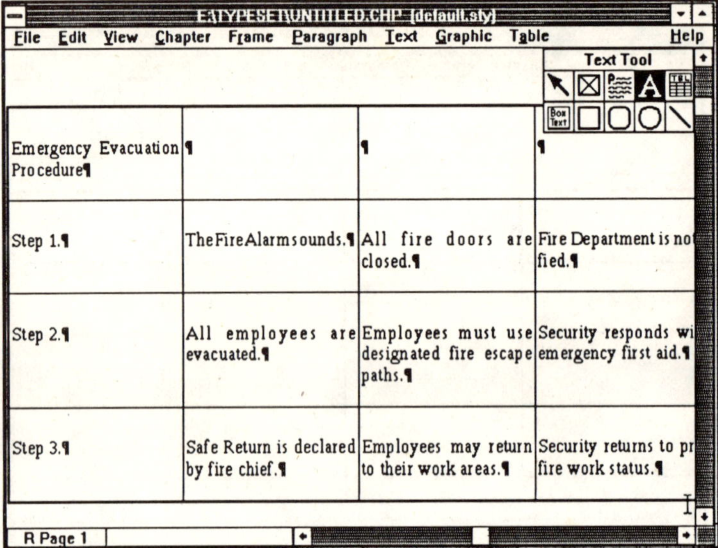

10. Print the table and review the result.
11. Turn to Module 68 to continue the learning sequence.

Module 43
JOIN/SPLIT CELLS

DESCRIPTION

The Join Cells command lets you connect adjoining cells in a table. The Split Cells command allows you to divide a cell or cells.

The following represents a typical table:

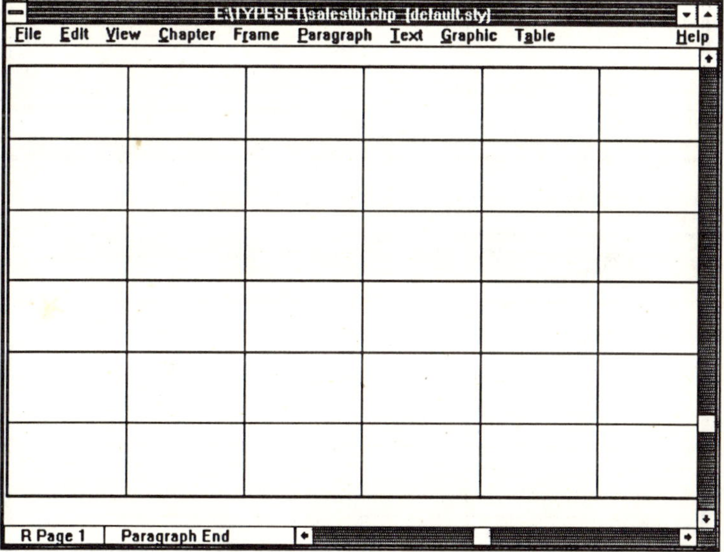

When some of the cells have been joined, this is the effect:

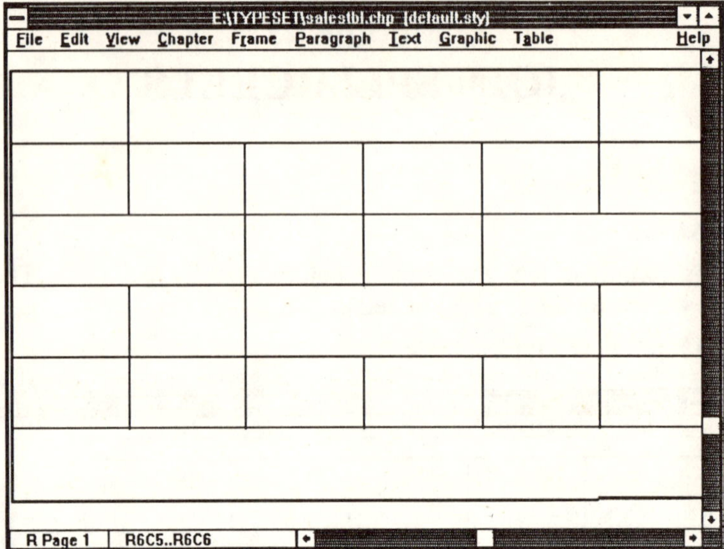

When some of the cells have been split, this is the effect:

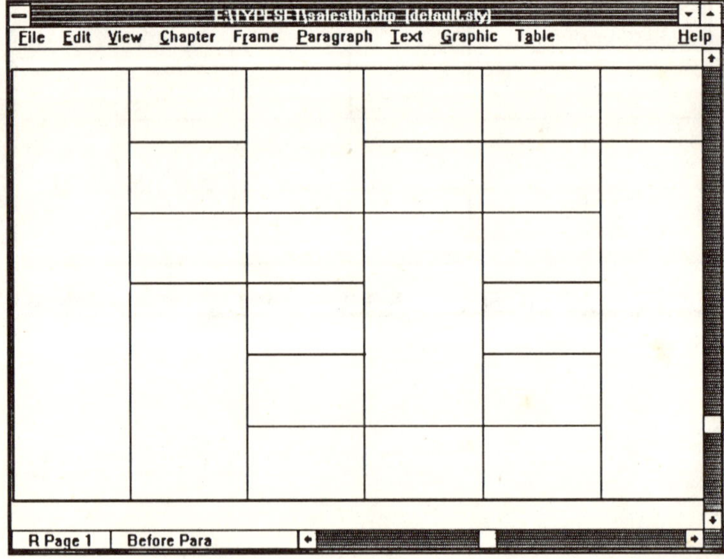

To split or join cells, use the Table Tool to select the desired cells. Then select either the Join Cells or Split Cells option in the Table menu. The cell is then either split or joined.

If text was in the cell when it was split or joined, some of the text may appear to be missing. It is actually hidden, and the table columns need to be adjusted so the text can be seen. If the table columns are not adjusted, the text is lost when the chapter is saved.

APPLICATIONS

In many tables, some cells need to be larger or smaller than other cells. These commands allow you to join cells to make then larger or divide cells to make them smaller.

One application for this command is to make a large cell across the top of the entire table to use as a headline or title.

TYPICAL OPERATION

In this activity, you join and split cells within a table. This table was created in the Typical Operation of Module 42 and modified in Modules 68 and 71. (If you have not created the table, you must do so before proceeding with these steps.)

1. Select the **Table** Tool in the Toolbox.
2. Move the mouse to the upper left corner of the first cell in the first row, and click and hold the mouse. While still holding the mouse button, drag the mouse to the lower right corner of the first row. Release the mouse button.
3. Click on the **Table** menu and select **Join Cell**. Your screen should resemble this illustration:

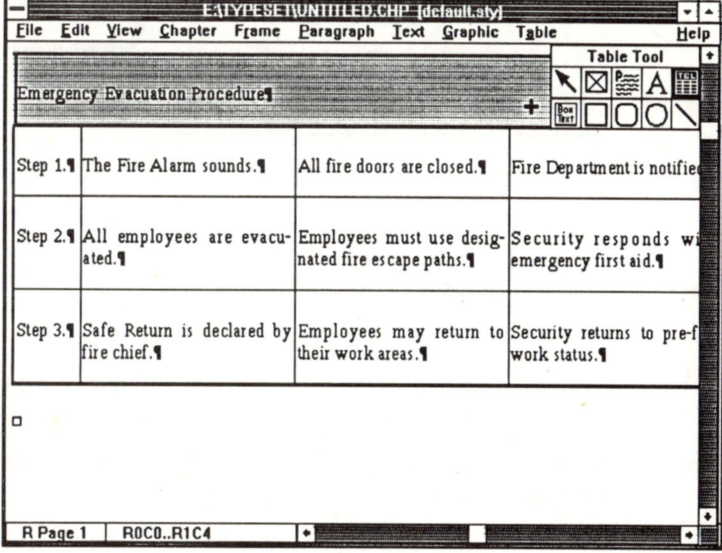

4. Click on the **Table** menu and select **Split Cell**.
5. Turn to Module 41 to continue the learning sequence.

Module 44
LINE ATTRIBUTES

DESCRIPTION

The Line Attributes command allows the selection of different types of lines created with the Graphics Drawing function. The lines created when drawing circle, box, rectangle, rounded corner rectangle, as well as straight lines can have different thicknesses and colors. A straight line can also have a different end style, such as an arrow.

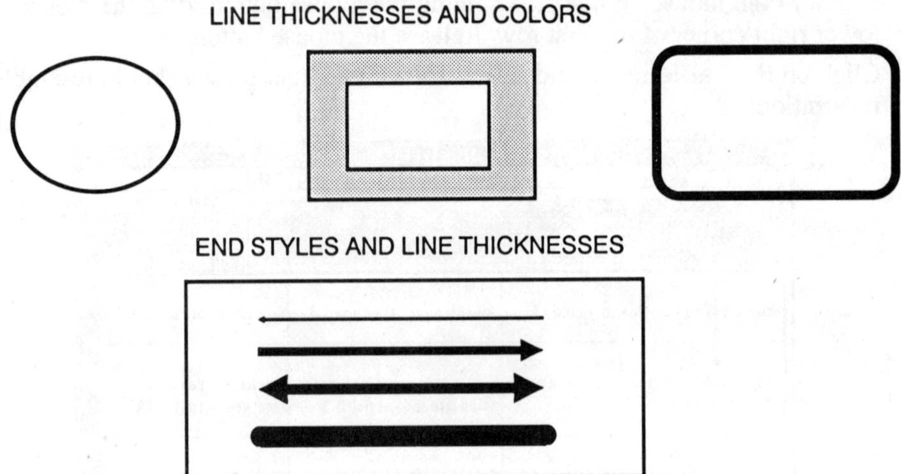

The Line Attributes command is accessed from the Graphic menu or by pressing Ctrl-L.

NOTE

Select a Graphic with the Graphics Drawing Tool before accessing Line Attributes command.

After selecting the Line Attributes command, the Line Attributes dialog box appears. Your screen should resemble the following illustration:

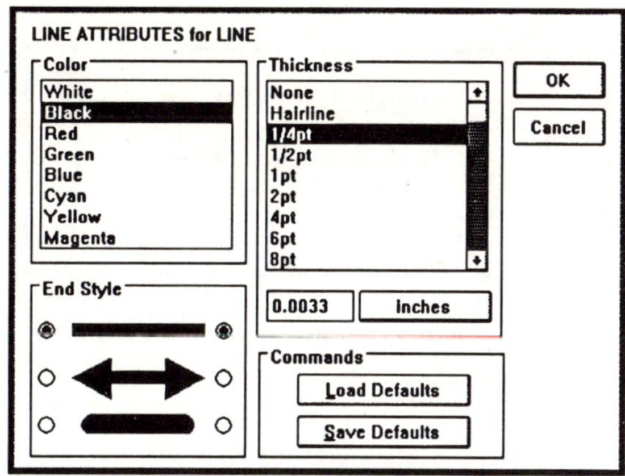

The Line Attributes dialog box provides these choices:

Thickness	Select the thickness of the line. The thickness can be none (for those boxes or circles where no border is desired) to 18pt. A custom width can also be entered. Ventura always shows the thickness of the line in the area to the left of measurement units.
Color	Select the color being assigned to the lines.
End Styles	Select the type of ends you want to place on straight lines. Ventura permits the choice of square ends, arrow-head ends, or round ends. Each end of a line can have a different end style assigned to it.
Commands	Select Load Default to use the line attributes saved for a different graphic. Select Save Defaults to use the current settings as the default for other graphics of the same kind. For example, if you select Save Defaults while creating a square, the next square you create will automatically use the same attributes as those that were just saved.
Dimensions	Select the measurement unit desired for the thicknesses of lines.

APPLICATIONS

Varying the thickness of lines offers versatility when creating graphics. By using different line sizes, many different effects can be created. For example, you might want to draw a line and use an arrow-head line end style to point to a special place on your document. You can also assign a color to a line within a document, allowing a more interesting graphic effect when reproduced.

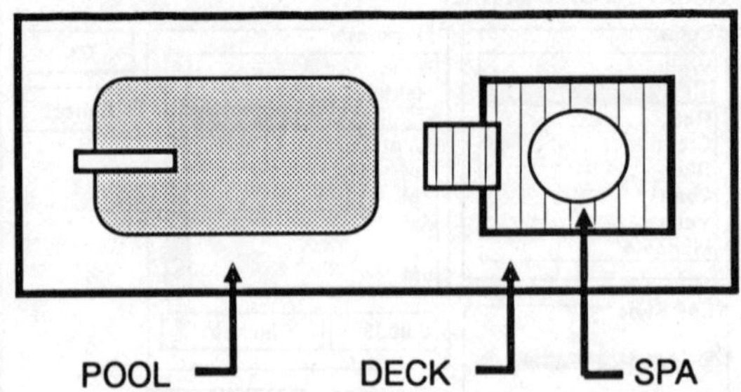

TYPICAL OPERATION

In this operation, you draw a line and change the thickness of it. The instructions begin with Ventura running and &BOOK-P1.CHP open. Press Ctrl-N to access Normal View.

1. Point and click on the **Add Frame** Tool in the Toolbox.
2. Draw a new frame on the page.
3. Click on the **Line** Tool in the Toolbox and then draw a line. Your screen should resemble this illustration:

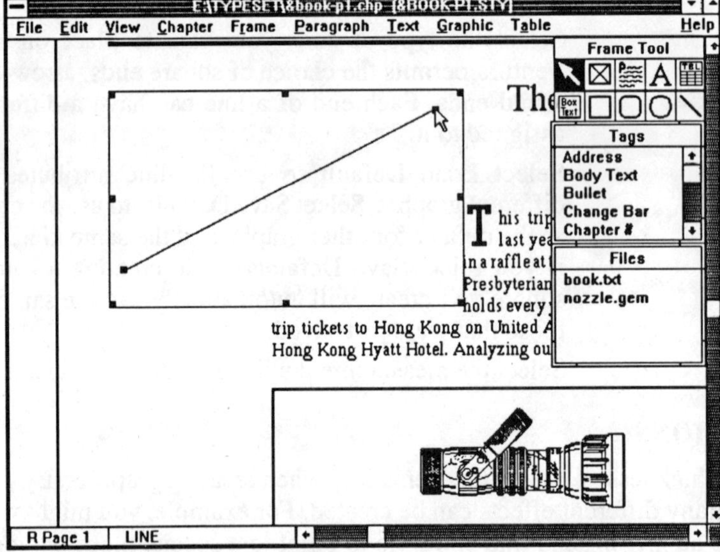

4. Click on the **Graphic** menu and click on **Line Attributes** to display the Line Attributes dialog box.
5. Select **Custom** for Thickness. Click on the measurement unit until it changes to Points. Type **15.00** for points.

6. Select **Black** for Color and click on the **Left Arrow** and the **Right Arrow** for End Styles. The dialog box should look like this:

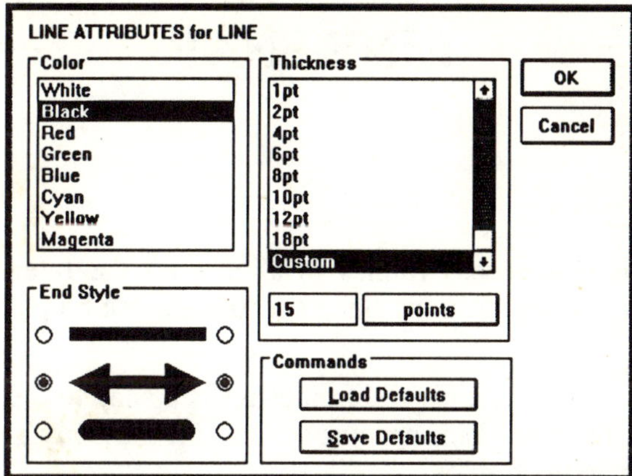

7. Click **OK**.

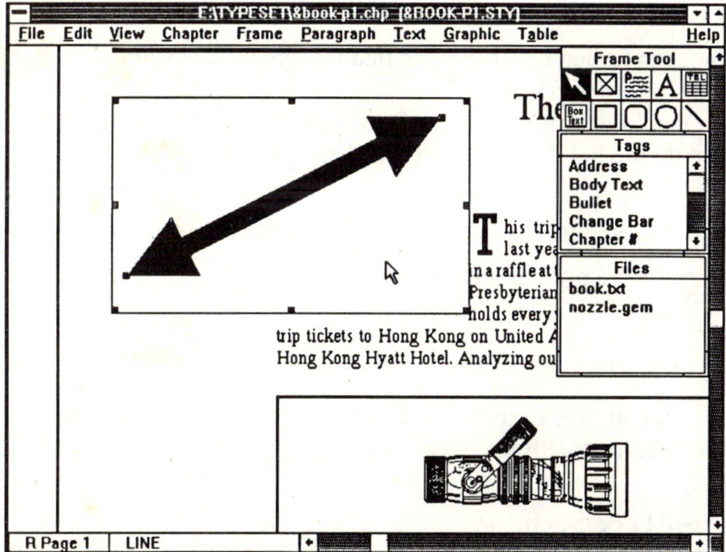

Notice the new thickness and ends of the line.

8. Click on the **File** menu and click on **Revert to Saved**. When the message box appears, click on **OK** to abandon the changes made to the chapter.
9. Turn to Module 39 to continue the learning sequence.

Module 45
LINE SNAP

DESCRIPTION

The Line Snap command forces frames to align with the Inter-Line spacing in the underlying page. By turning the Line Snap off, frames can be placed anywhere on the page.

When Line Snap is on, new frames and frames resized snap to the nearest line guide in the underlying page. The Inter-Line spacing settings for the Body Text create an invisible grid that is used to snap the frames.

The Line Snap command is located in the View menu.

APPLICATIONS

When Line Snap is turned on, it ensures that frames in adjacent columns line up exactly and forces the top of one frame to align with the bottom of the frame above it. The Line Snap On command also forces a line of text in a column to move down by exactly one line by increasing the height of a frame that has been snapped to the column.

When the Line Snap Off command is used, you can place frames anywhere on the page, without regard to any alignment of the text within the frame.

Most Ventura users are probably better served by using the Line Snap On command. The more precise alignment usually guarantees a cleaner, more professional-looking design.

TYPICAL OPERATION

In this operation, you turn Line Snap off, resize a frame, turn Line Snap on, and create another frame. The instructions begin with Ventura running and the &NEWS-P2.CHP open.

1. Press **Ctrl-U** to select the Frame Tool.
2. Click on the **View** menu and click on **Line Snap**. It should now be off. No check mark appears in the left column.

3. Click on **Add Frame**, point and click the mouse cursor in the left column, and drag the mouse slowly to the right. Your screen should resemble the following illustration:

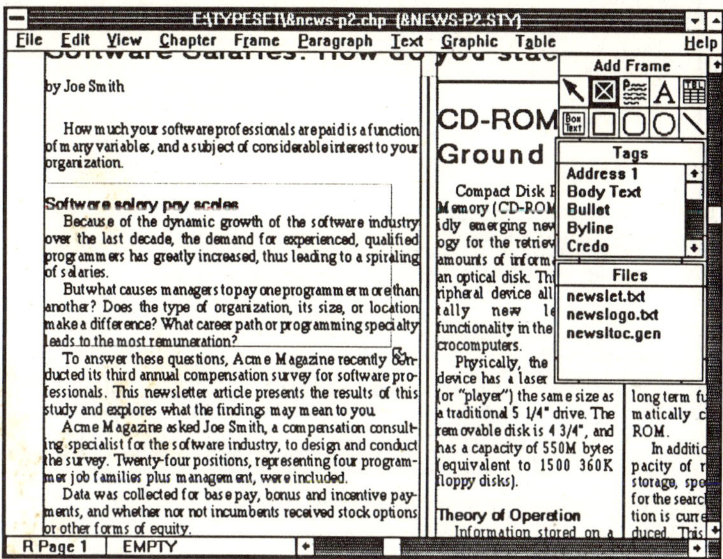

The new frame is created evenly and smoothly. Release the mouse button.

4. Press **Del** to delete the frame.
5. Click on the **View** menu and click on **Show Column Guides** to turn on the column guides (if they are not already on).
6. Click on the **View** menu and click on **Line Snap**. It should now be on. A check mark appears in the left column.
7. Click on the **Add Frame** Tool, point and click the mouse cursor in the left column, and drag the mouse slowly to the right. Be sure to draw the frame borders within 1/10 of an inch of the column guide to make the frame snap to the column.
8. Release the mouse button. Your screen should resemble the following illustration:

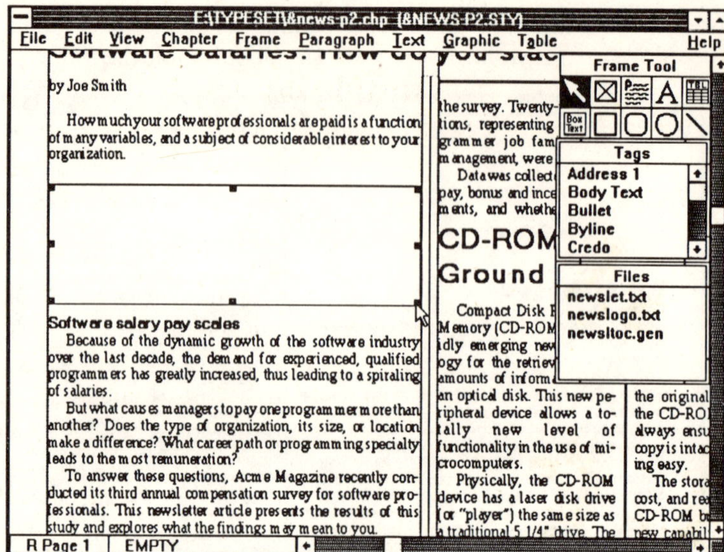

Notice how the new frame snaps to the column guides when the mouse button is released.

9. Press **Del** to delete the frame.
10. Click on the **File** menu, click on **Revert to Saved**, and click **OK**.
11. Turn to Module 24 to continue the learning sequence.

Module 46
LOAD DIFFERENT STYLE

DESCRIPTION

The Load Diff.(erent) Style command applies a different style sheet to the chapter currently being displayed on the screen. If the chapter is then saved, Ventura ignores the old style sheet and replaces it with the new style sheet. In Ventura, a style sheet is a separate file used to control the style and appearance of your final document. This style sheet is only associated with the Ventura chapter file.

NOTE

When the Open Chapter command is executed, Ventura automatically loads the style sheet assigned to that chapter.

APPLICATIONS

The Load Diff.(erent) Style command is used to retrieve an existing style sheet. It is often easier to modify an existing style sheet than to create a new one from the beginning. Loading a different style sheet, making the necessary changes, and saving it under a new name (see Module 66) is the best way to create your own set of new style sheets.

TYPICAL OPERATION

In this example, you load a new style sheet after a chapter has been opened. The sample chapter SCOOP.CHP is used. This operation begins with SCOOP.CHP open and in use. If you do not have this chapter open, use Open Chapter in the File menu to retrieve SCOOP.CHP. So your view matches the screens depicted in this module, press Ctrl-R. Your screen should resemble the following illustration:

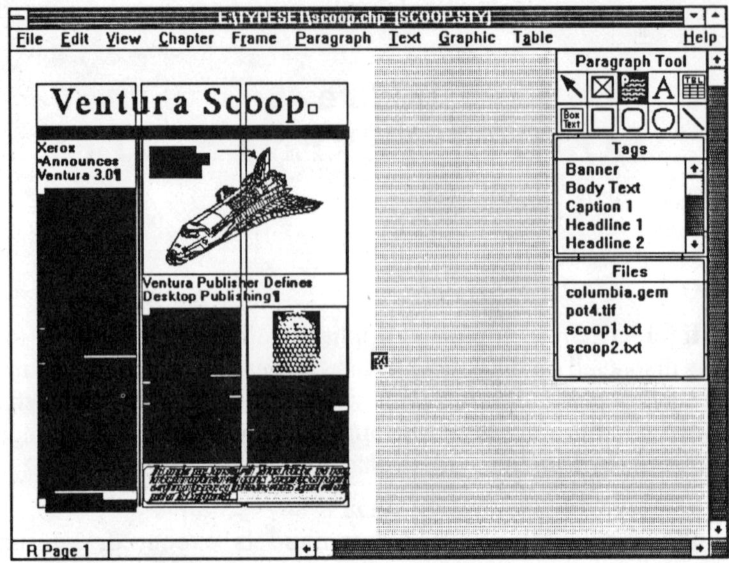

1. Click on the **File** menu and click on **Load Diff. Style** to display the Open File dialog box. Your screen should resemble this illustration:

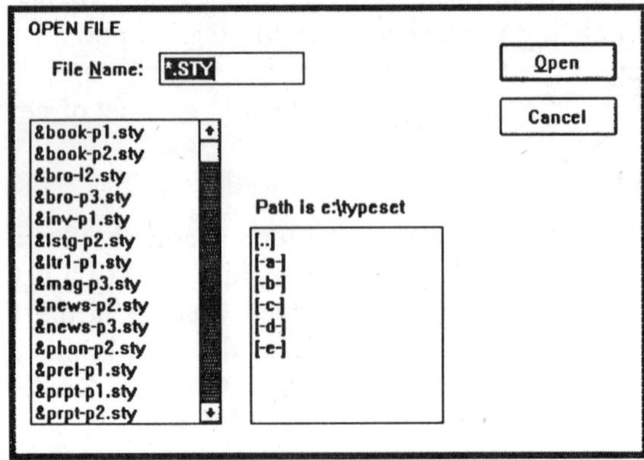

2. Double click on **&BOOK-P1.STY** to select it as the new style sheet. (Use the scroll bars to find it in the window.) Your screen should now resemble the following illustration:

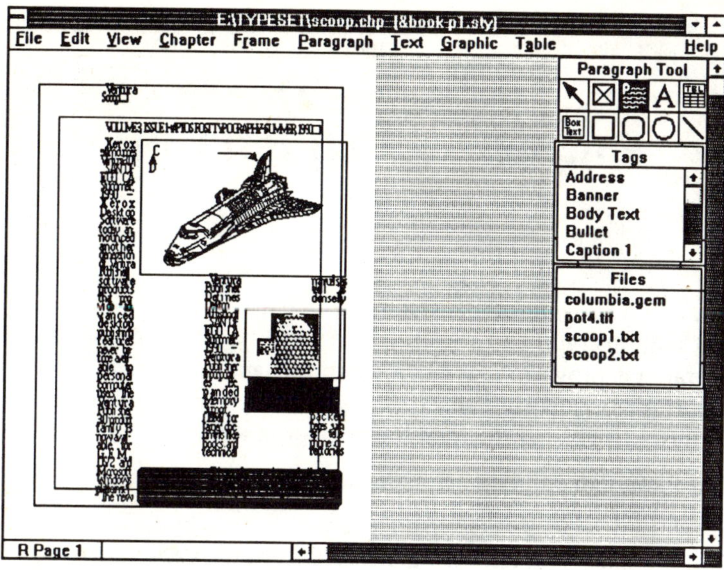

3. Click on the **File** menu and click on **Revert to Saved** and click on **OK** to revert back to the original SCOOP.CHP.
4. Turn to Module 66 to continue the learning sequence.

Module 47
LOAD TEXT/PICTURE

DESCRIPTION

The Load Text/Picture command allows you to import a text or graphics file from a word processor or graphics program into your Ventura chapter. Ventura divides graphics into two forms: Line Art or Image. The Load Text/Picture command places the files in the Files Window prior to placing them on the page or in a frame.

The Load Text/Picture dialog box offers these options:

File Type	Select the type of file you want to load: Text, Line Art, or Image. Text files are generated from the various word processors. Line art files contain "vector" type drawings, which means the graphic is stored as a series of mathematical formulas. Vector drawings are common for business or scientific graphics, maps, and mechanical-type drawings. Image files contain bit-map graphics. Usually more of an artistic type drawing, the image is stored as a series of on and off bits of information.
Format	Select the type of text file you are loading, which is determined by which word processor you are using.
Options	Select Several Files if you want to load several files of the same type at one time.
Destination	Select List of Files to send the text file to the Files Window, select Clipboard to send it to the Windows Clipboard, or select Cursor to insert the text file at the current text cursor location.

If you select Line Art or Image, the dialog box changes to show you the available Line Art or Image file formats available for importing into Ventura. When you select Line Art, a list of possible file types is displayed. Select the type of Line Art file format you are loading, which depends on the type of Line Art program you are using. As long as your graphics program produces files compatible with any of the following, you should be able to import the graphic into Ventura.

Here is the list of Line Art and Image programs/files that can be imported into Ventura:

GEM	CGM	GEM/HALO DPE
Windows Metafile	PostScript	Macintosh Paint
Autocad .SLD	HPGL	PC Paintbrush (PCX)
Lotus .PIC	VideoShow	Mac Pict
TIFF		

TIP:

Use PC Paintbrush, PostScript, or TIFF formats to load files created by a scanner.

When you select Image, a list of possible file types is displayed. Select the type of Image file format you are loading, which depends on the type of Image program you are using. As long as your graphics program produces files compatible with any of the files listed, you should be able to import the graphic into Ventura.

After selecting the type of file you wish to load, Ventura then displays the Open File Window.

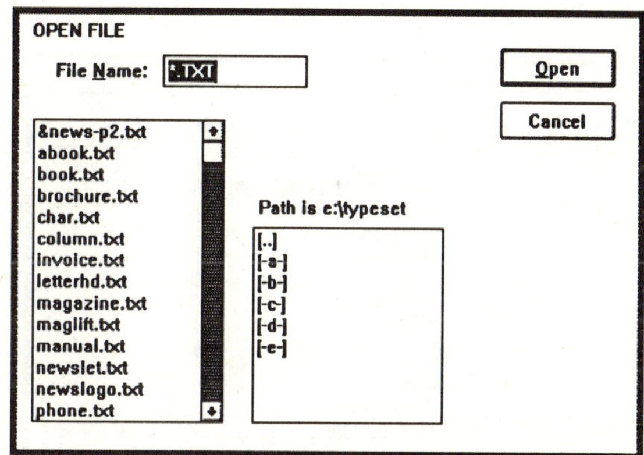

This window indicates the current path, as well as any files located. You can select another directory and change the path by pointing at the desired directory or drive. With the appropriate subdirectory and file already chosen, finally select the filename, and choose Open.

TIP:

You can double click on the desired filename to load the file to the File Window.

The Load Text/Picture command is located in the File menu.

APPLICATIONS

The Load Text/Picture command is used to build a list of text and graphics files you want to use within a Ventura document.

When a text file is loaded into Ventura, the file will be changed by Ventura if you make any changes or edits in the text. You should make a backup of a text file *before* you load the text file into Ventura.

Graphic files—both Line Art and Image—cannot be altered or changed at any time within Ventura. If you want to change the file, you must do so before the file is loaded into Ventura.

This command is used to import the text, line art, and image files that were created in other programs.

TYPICAL OPERATION

In this operation, you will load a picture file in the File Window, then place the picture on the underlying page. It is assumed Ventura is running.

1. Select **New** from the File menu.
2. Click on the **File** menu and click the mouse on **Load Text/Picture.**
3. Within a moment, the Load Text/Picture dialog box appears, and your screen resembles this illustration:

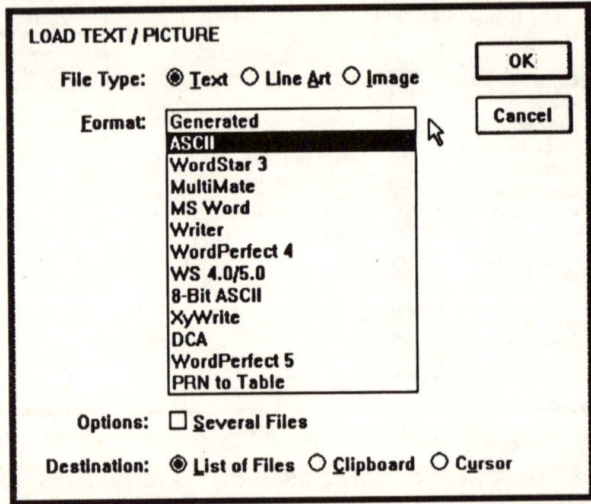

4. Click on **Line Art** for File Type, and select **GEM** as Format. Your screen should resemble this illustration:

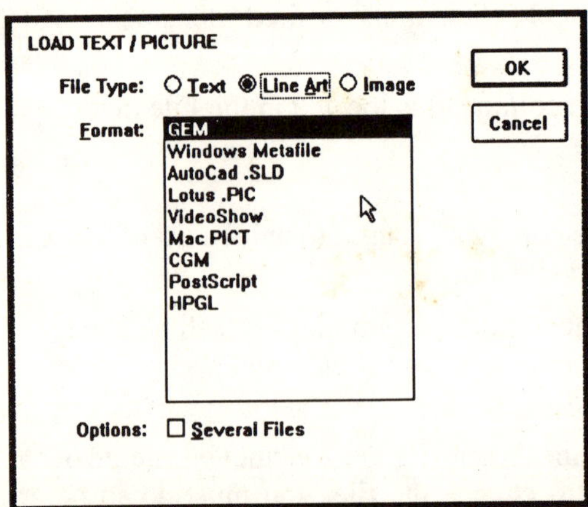

5. Click **OK** to display the File Open dialog box. Your screen should resemble this illustration:

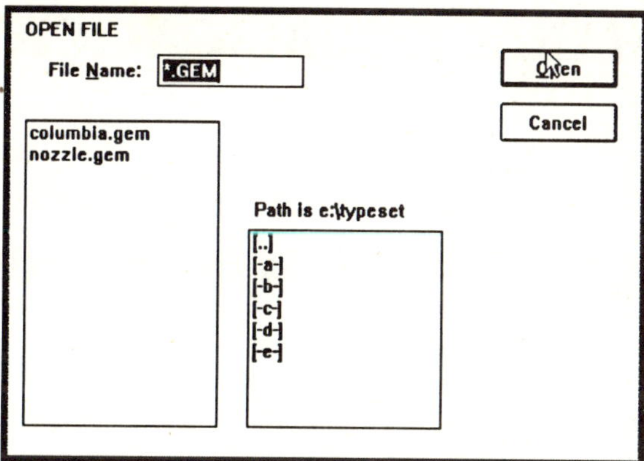

6. Double click on the **COLUMBIA.GEM** file to load the file. Within a few moments, Ventura returns to the opening screen and the file, COLUMBIA.GEM, is listed in the File Window.
7. Click once in the center of the page. Then click on **COLUMBIA.GEM** in the Files Window. Press **Ctrl-R** to see a reduced view of the page. Within a moment, your screen should resemble this illustration:

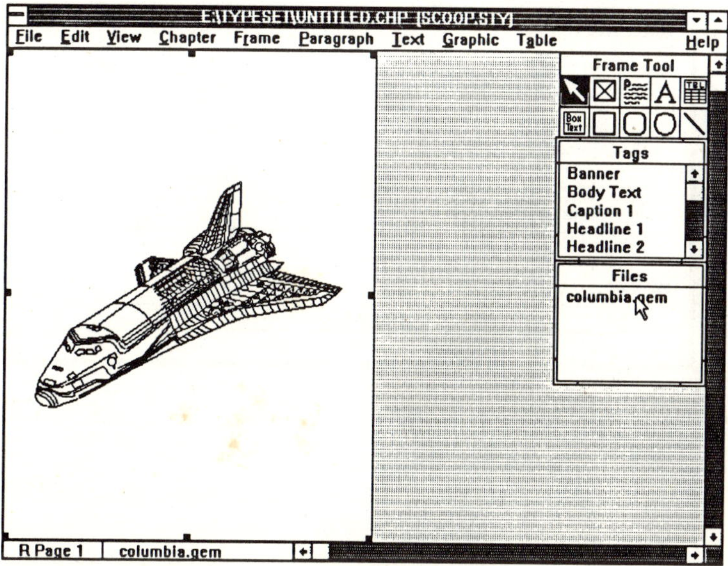

8. Point to the **File** menu and click on **New**. When the VP Alert dialog box appears, click on **Abandon** to not save the changes.
9. Turn to Module 65 to continue the learning sequence.

Module 48
MANAGE PUBLICATION

DESCRIPTION

The Manage Publication command links multiple chapter files together into a single publication. Once all the chapters are grouped, a PUB file is created which contains the list of chapter files making up the publication. Several functions can be executed on the PUB file, including the generation of a table of contents, creation of an index, renumbering of the pages within all chapters that make up the publication, and finally, printing the document.

Manage Publication also contains a file management utility option called Copy All that copies the multiple files associated with a Ventura document from one location to another.

TIP:

Do not use the DOS COPY command to make copies of your Ventura chapters. Always use Manage Publication to make any copies.

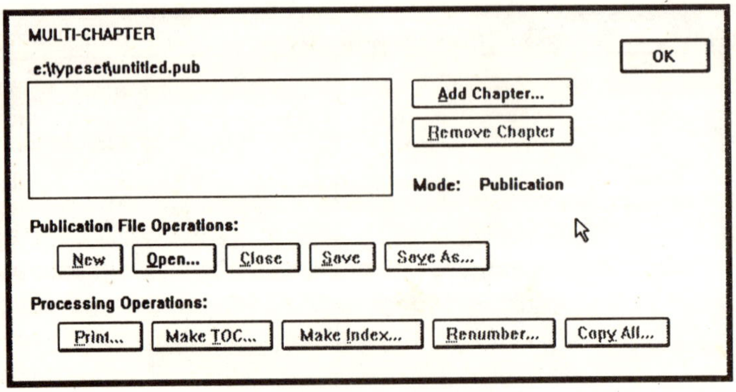

MULTI-CHAPTER
c:\typeset\untitled.pub
OK
Add Chapter...
Remove Chapter
Mode: Publication
Publication File Operations:
New | Open... | Close | Save | Save As...
Processing Operations:
Print... | Make TOC... | Make Index... | Renumber... | Copy All...

The Manage Publication dialog box offers these options:

Add Chapter — Select this option to add another chapter file to the current PUB file list. When Ventura displays the Item Selector dialog box, choose the CHP file to add to the list.

NOTE

The chapters in the PUB list can be rearranged by using the mouse. To do this, click and hold on the filename to be moved, drag it to its new position, and release the mouse button. If the name is dragged to the bottom of the displayed list, the list does not scroll up, even if other filenames are below. Leave the name at the bottom of the display, scroll the display until the name is at the top of the display, and then reselect it and drag it again.

Remove Chapter	Select a chapter file in the list, then choose this option to remove the selected file from the list.
New	Select this option to create a new PUB file. When Ventura displays the Item Selector dialog box, type the name of the new PUB file.
Open	Select this option to open an existing PUB file. When Ventura displays the Item Selector dialog box, type the PUB file to open.
Close	Select this option to close an open PUB file.
Save	Select this option to save a PUB file that has been created or changed. If a chapter file is open when the Manage Publication command is selected, the Save option creates a PUB file containing the current chapter plus any others added to the list. When Ventura displays the Item Selector dialog box, type the name of the PUB file to create. In this instance, do not use the New option to create the PUB file.

NOTE

The PUB file must be created and *saved* before an index or table of contents can be created with the Manage Publication options.

Save As	Select this option within the Manage Publication dialog box to save an existing PUB file under a new name. Ventura displays the Item Selector dialog box. Type the name of the new PUB file to create.
Print	Select this option to print the PUB file. Ventura then displays the To Print dialog box. All options in the Print dialog box are the same except for Manage Publication. Manage Publication applies when files are being printed to disk. Select Combined to send all output of the various chapter files to one print file, or select Separate to route the output of each chapter file to a new print file.

Make TOC — Select this option to create a publication-wide table of contents from paragraphs in the various chapters tagged as headlines. When selected, Ventura displays the Generate Table of Contents dialog box.

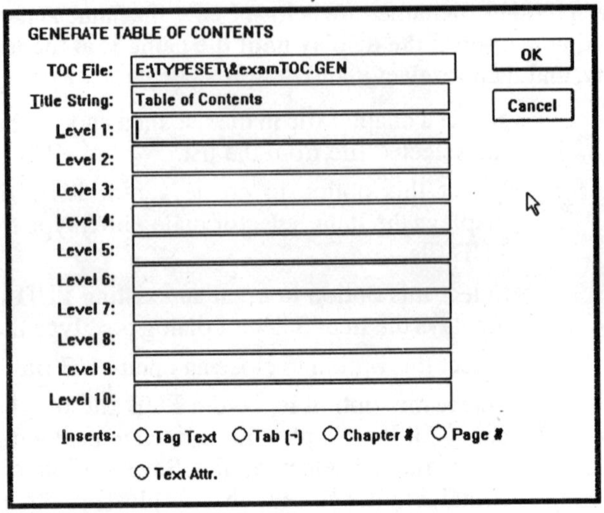

GENERATE TABLE OF CONTENTS

TOC File: E:\TYPESET\&examTOC.GEN
Title String: Table of Contents
Level 1:
Level 2:
Level 3:
Level 4:
Level 5:
Level 6:
Level 7:
Level 8:
Level 9:
Level 10:
Inserts: ○ Tag Text ○ Tab (→) ○ Chapter # ○ Page # ○ Text Attr.

OK
Cancel

The Generate Table of Contents dialog box offers these options:

TOC File — Type the directory path, filename, and extension of the file to hold the table of contents information. Use the .GEN extension since Ventura is generating the file. After the file has been created, it can be loaded into a chapter file just as any other text file can be.

Title String — Type the title name desired at the top of the table of contents.

Level 1 through 10 — Type the names of the paragraph tags to be used for each level of the table of contents. For example, Level 1 might be tag Headline 1 and Level 2 might be tag Subheadline.

Inserts — Select the type of information Ventura is to add on each level of the table of contents. Also, within this option, the appearance of the entries is defined. The information Ventura inserts into the table of contents definition is:

Item	*Inserted Characters*
Tag Text	[*tag name]
Tab	tab character (→)
Chapter #	[C#]
Page #	[P#]
Text Attr	<D>

For the [*tag name], replace "tag name" with the name of the paragraph tag being associated with the table of contents level.

For the tab character, Ventura enters a tab character.

For the [C#], Ventura substitutes the current chapter number.

For the [P#], Ventura substitutes the current page number.

For the <D>, substitute for "D" the characters associated with the various text attributes Ventura supports. For example, delete the <D> and type <193> to make an ellipse (...) appear. The letters and attributes are described in Appendix B.

Any additional text can be added to each level of the table of contents definition by typing it outside of the left and right brackets that appear on each selected level line.

Make Index — Select this option to create an index from the entries created with the Make Index command. When Make Index is selected, Ventura displays the Generate Index dialog box.

GENERATE INDEX
Index File: E:\TYPESET\&examIDX.GEN
Title String: Index
Letter Headings: On
Before #s: ¬
For Each #: [C#]-[P#] - [C#]-[P#]
Between #s: ,
After #s:
"See ": See
"See Also": See also
Inserts: ○ Tab (¬) ○ Chapter # ○ Page # ○ Text Attr.
OK
Cancel

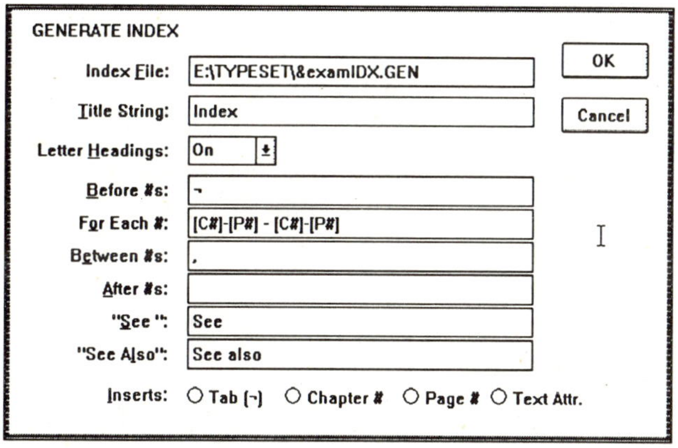

The options available in the Generate Index dialog box are:

Index File — Type the directory path, filename, and extension of the file to hold the table of contents information. Use the .GEN extension since Ventura is generating the file. After the file has been created, it can be loaded into a chapter file just as any other text file can be. If desired, use the default path and name Ventura supplies.

Title String — Type the title desired at the top of the index.

Letter Heading — Select whether or not Ventura is to place letters of the alphabet automatically at the beginning of each grouping in the index. For example, the A's listing would automatically begin with a single letter A.

Before #s

Type the character to appear after the index text and before the page number. The default is a tab. A comma followed by a space can be substituted if desired. If used, the comma and space option would produce index entries that look like this:

Books
    Illustrated DisplayWrite 4, 32
    Illustrated Ventura 2.0, 13

For Each #

Type the format desired for the same index entries that appear on multiple sequential pages. For example, the index can include both the chapter and the page number. [C#]-[P#] generates page numbers like this:

Manage Publication, 5-18

Between #s

Type the punctuation desired between each chapter and page number. The default is a command followed by a space. Typical output would look like this:

Manage Publication, 5-18, 25, 76

After #s

Type the punctuation desired for use after the last page number. The default is none, but a period or other punctuation could be added. If added, typical output would look like this:

Manage Publication, 5-18, 25, 76.

See

Type the text desired for the "see" entries. The default is See.

See Also

Type the text desired for "see also" entries. The default is See also.

Inserts

Select the formatting information desired for the index entries. The information Ventura inserts into each entry each time you click on the item is:

Item	*Inserted Characters*
Tab	tab character (→)
Chapter #	[C#]
Page Number	[P#]
Text Attr.	<D>

For Tab, Ventura enters a tab character.

For the [C#], Ventura substitutes the current chapter number.

For the [P#], Ventura substitutes the current page number.

For the <D>, substitute for "D" the characters associated with the various text attributes Ventura supports. For example, delete the <D> and type <193> to make an ellipsis (...) appear. The letters and attributes are described in Appendix B.

Renumber

Select this option to automatically renumber the chapters, page, table, and figure numbers across chapter boundaries.

TIP:

To make this feature work, use the Update Counters feature to set the initial chapter, page, table, and figure counter for each chapter to Previous Number+1.

Copy All — Select this option to automatically copy all files associated with a chapter or publication. Each type of file—style sheet, picture, text, graphics—can be copied to a different disk. Ventura will also automatically update the references and pointers in the chapter and publication files to the new drives and directories. When this option is selected, the Copy All dialog box appears.

COPY ALL

SOURCE (from this file)

OK

Cancel

PUB or CHP: E:\TYPESET\&example.pub

DESTINATION (to these directories)

PUB & CHPs: E:\&example

STYs & WIDs: E:\&example

Text Files: E:\&example

Graphic Files: E:\&example

Image Files: E:\&example

Command: Make All Directories the Same As the First

The options available in the Copy All dialog box are:

Source — Type the directory path and filename and extension of the chapter file [CHP] or publication file [PUB] to be copied. If a publication is open and no chapters are selected in the Manage Publication dialog box, Ventura automatically inserts the publication file. If a chapter is selected, this entry is automatically the chapter file.

Destination — Type the directory path where the files are to be copied. PUB & CHP, STY & WIDS, Text Files, Graphic File, and Image Files can be copied to different locations or the same location.

Command — Select Make All Directories the Same as the First option to copy all files to the same directory path as the first entry.

NOTE

In the Copy All dialog box, you must click on OK. Pressing Enter does not work. This is to eliminate starting the copying process by accidentally pressing Enter.

The Manage Publication command is accessed from the Options menu.

APPLICATIONS

The primary purpose for using the Manage Publication command is to produce extremely long documents. Ventura can easily produce documents of 1000 pages or more. Rather than trying to work with a very long document, it only makes sense to create several smaller documents, and then, using Manage Publication, make them into one publication, and finally print the publication. A good example would be a book, where each module would be created as its own chapter and then, finally, all the chapters would be printed in one publication.

Manage Publication also allows you to see every file associated with a chapter.

One of the other prime functions of the Manage Publication command is the ability to create the "front matter" and "back matter " of a book automatically. What could be a laborious job—creating an index and table of contents—Ventura does quickly with the options located within the Manage Publication command.

The Manage Publication command also permits page numbering across the boundaries of a chapter.

Manage Publication also offers the ability to copy the entire chapter or publication to another disk or directory. This is the best way to make backup copies of your chapters or publications. Trying to do so with the DOS commands can create problems. The reason is that the Ventura chapter file tells the program where to look for different files. If you do not place the files exactly where Ventura expects to find them, the chapter or publication will not open as expected.

TYPICAL OPERATION

In this operation, you create a publication file, make an index, and print the file. The instructions begin with Ventura running and the screen blank. Use Load Diff. Style Sheet from the File menu and select the DEFAULT.STY style sheet.

1. Click on the **File** menu and click on **Manage Publication** to display the Manage Publication dialog box. If any chapter titles are in the list, select **New** to remove them. When prompted about changes to your style sheet, select **Abandon**.

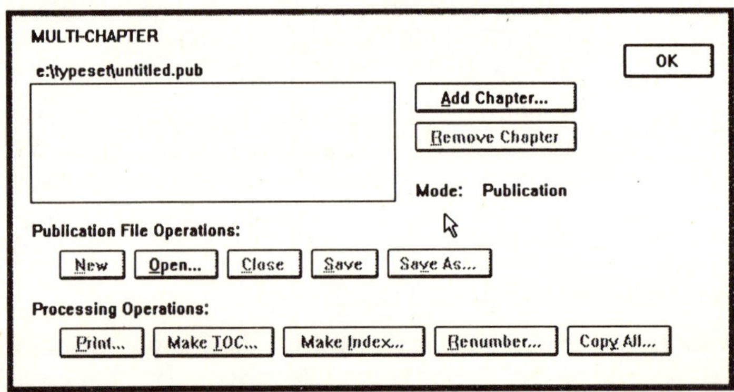

2. Click on **Add Chapter** to display the Item Selector dialog box.
3. Select **&BOOK-P1.CHP** and click **Open**.

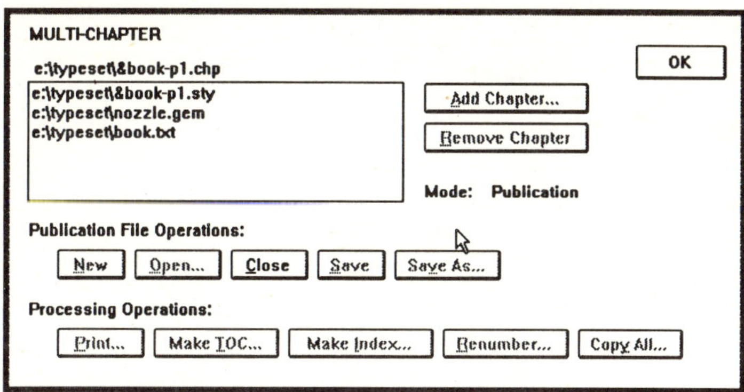

4. Click on **Add Chapter** to display the Item Selector dialog box.
5. Select **&BOOK-P2.CHP** and click **Open**.
6. Click on **Add Chapter** to display the Item Selector dialog box.
7. Select **&LSTG-P2.CHP** and click **OPEN**.
8. Click on **Save As** to display the Save File As dialog box. Type **MYPUB1** for selection and press **Enter**.
9. Click on **&LSTG-P2.CHP** once to remove the highlighting.
10. Click **Make Index** to display the Generate Index dialog box.

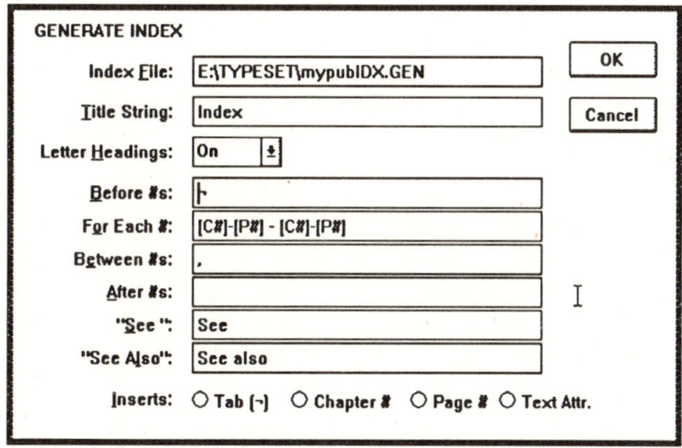

11. Click **OK**.
12. Click **Print** to display the Print dialog box. Press **Enter**. Within a few moments, the various chapters print as a publication.
13. Click **OK**.
14. Turn to Module 23 to continue the learning sequence.

Module 49
MANAGE WIDTH TABLE

DESCRIPTION

The Manage Width Table command adds or removes additional printer fonts to the Ventura fonts file (width table). In most cases, this command is used to add fonts.

NOTE

Before fonts are added for use in Ventura, the fonts file must be loaded onto your computer by following the instructions provided with Microsoft Windows for adding new fonts.

To use this command, select Manage Width Table from the File menu.

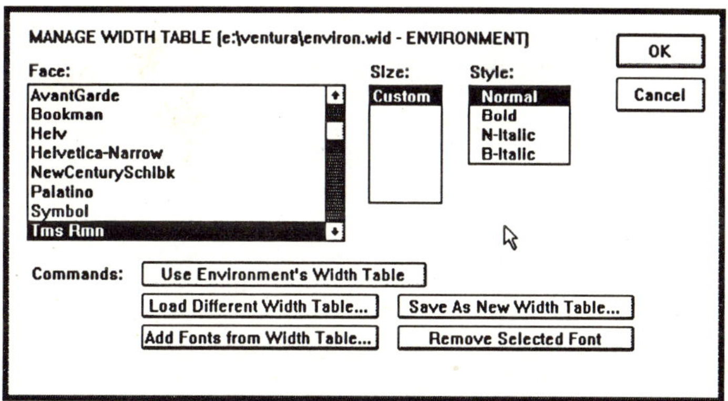

The Manage Width Table dialog box provides these options:

NOTE

The typefaces, sizes, and styles in the Manage Width Table dialog box will vary, depending on your hardware.

Face	Select the typeface to either remove from the fonts file or add or remove from being automatically downloaded to the printer.
Size	Select the size of each typeface to either remove from the fonts file or add or remove from being automatically downloaded to the printer.
Style	Select the style of each typeface to either remove from the fonts file or add or remove from being automatically downloaded to the printer. If the word Resident appears at the bottom of the

Style box, the currently selected typeface, size, and style of font are already loaded in the printer. If the word Download appears at the bottom of the Style box, the currently selected typeface, size, and style of font must be downloaded to the printer from Ventura at print time. The download status of a selected face, size, and style can be changed by clicking on the words Download or Resident. However, Ventura automatically establishes the correct download status for each font when the program is installed.

Commands

Select the function needed to process your fonts.

Select Merge Width Tables to add new fonts to an existing fonts file (width table). Before doing this, use the Save As New Width Table to save the current fonts file under a new name in case something goes wrong when the new fonts are being added. Ventura displays the Item Selector dialog box where the name of the new fonts file to be created is typed.

NOTE

When two width tables are merged together, they must both be for the same printer.

Select Remove Selected Font to remove the selected face, size, and style from the fonts file.

If you buy additional fonts to use with your copy of Ventura, make sure you read the installation directions thoroughly *before* trying to load the fonts. There are roughly ten different steps, from making the fonts, to installing them in Ventura and merging the width tables. If you are going to undertake the task of loading fonts, be sure to read and follow the directions carefully. Doing so will eliminate hours of frustration and aggravation.

TIP:

Always merge a new width table into a width table that already exists. Do not load the new width table using the Load Different Width Table command.

APPLICATIONS

The Manage Width Table command allows additional fonts to be added for your use when running Ventura. New typefaces are being developed and released by software developers each month. By adding additional fonts to your computer, you can create more dynamic, interesting documents.

You can also use this command to remove fonts, particularly if you find you have loaded a font series that you are never using and need additional disk space.

Finally, this command can be used to automatically download fonts to your printer. You can decrease printer time when using either an HP LaserJet or a PostScript driven printer by eliminating automatic downloading. To do this, you must first download the fonts into your printer and make them permanent before running Ventura. For more information, see your printer manual and read the information about making fonts resident.

TYPICAL OPERATION

In this operation, the current fonts are saved under a new name and then a font is deleted. (These instructions assume you are using an HP LaserJet Series II laser printer. If you are using another printer, select another face, size, and style to delete.) The instructions begin with Ventura running.

1. Point to the **File** menu and select **Manage Width Table** to display the Manage Width Table dialog box.
2. Select **Save As New Width Table** for Command to display the Item Selector dialog box.
3. Type **FONTTEST** for selection and press **Enter** to create the new fonts file.
4. Select **Tms Rmn** for Face, **14** for Size, and **Bold** for Style when the Manage Width Table dialog box reappears.

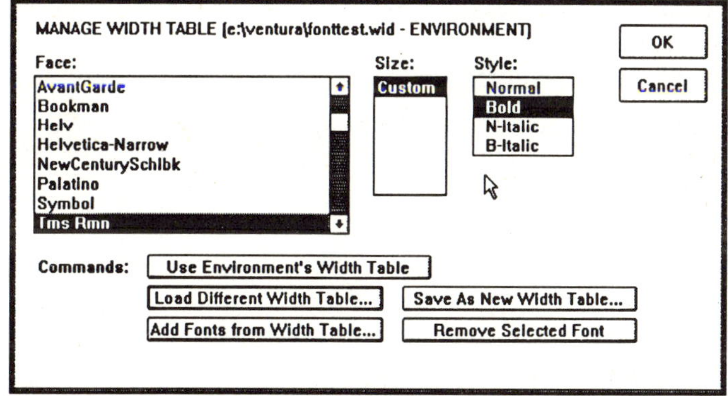

NOTE

The next step causes the Tms Rmn 14 point Bold font to be removed. Do not complete the next step unless you want to remove the font. If you want to stop, click Cancel.

5. Select **Remove Selected Font** for Command. Notice that Tms Rmn 14 point Bold is now gray and no longer available for use.
6. Click **OK** to exit.
7. Turn to Module 73 to continue the learning sequence.

Module 50
MARGINS & COLUMNS

DESCRIPTION

The Margins & Columns command establishes the number and sizes of the columns in each frame or in the underlying page frame. This command also sets the margins and columns in those frames that are automatically generated by Ventura, such as those used to establish the headers, footers, and captions.

For the underlying page frame or any other frame, the Margins & Columns command sets:

- The top, bottom, left, and right margins
- The number of columns (The maximum number of columns permitted in any frame is 8.)
- The width of each column, and the amount of spacing between each column.

All underlying pages will have the same margins and same number of columns. Of course, the left page and the right page can have a different number of columns and a different margin setting. But *all* right pages will have the same margins and the same number of columns. And all left pages will also have the same margin and column settings. To create different margins and columns for the left and right pages, you must be working within a double-sided publication.

The Margins & Columns command is available in the Frame menu. To access this command, you must be in Frame mode and select a frame. After selecting the command, the Margins & Columns dialog box appears.

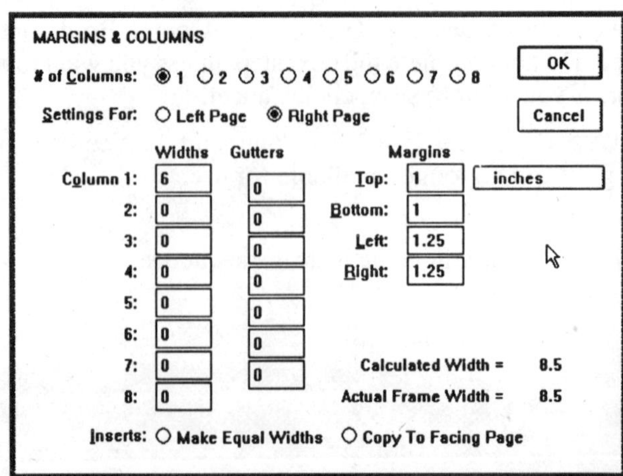

The Margins & Columns dialog box contains these options:

# of Columns	Select the number of columns needed for the frame or the underlying page.
Settings For	Select either the Left or Right Page.
Column Widths & Gutters	Type the width and gutter for each column selected in the # of columns.
Margins	Type the margin for the Top, Bottom, Left, and Right side of the frame or underlying page.
Inserts	Select Make Equal Widths if you want all the columns to have the same width. Ventura will automatically compute the width for you. Select Copy To Facing Page if you want the information entered in the dialog box copied to the other page. Of course, this command only works if you are preparing a two-sided document as established in the Page Size & Layout command.
Calculated Width	This shows you the amount of space you have selected and used. This data is used to compare against the Actual Frame Width, which Ventura displays for comparison. Since you have control over the width of your columns, Ventura will not readjust your settings for you.
Actual Frame Width	This shows you the actual width of the frame. Before selecting OK, always make sure the Calculated Width is less than or equal to the amount shown in the Actual Frame Width.

TIP:

If the margin and column appearance on your computer screen does not match what you specified, check to make certain that the Calculated Width equals the Actual Frame Width. If not, make the necessary changes within your column widths and gutter dimensions.

APPLICATIONS

The obvious application of the Margins & Columns command is to set margins and columns for each frame. This command allows you to establish a different margin for the left and right pages. This is extremely valuable when creating a report, book, or magazine that will be bound. Because the binding will take additional space, you will need a larger margin on the inside portion of the left and right pages. (For a left page, the right margin should be larger, and for a right page, the left margin should be larger to accommodate the binding.)

You may also be adding frames on top of other frames, and by doing so you may want to add columns within the new frames. This is often effective in newsletter or newspaper type documents. This allows a three-column newsletter, for example, to have another frame added and have additional columns inserted for a complementary text article.

Finally, this command is also used to add "white space" around a graphic placed in a frame. By doing so, the graphic will not run right against text, which would make the text difficult to read.

TYPICAL OPERATION

In this example, you add a new frame and assign margins and columns to that frame. The example begins with a blank screen and the DEFAULT.STY style sheet being used. Use the Load Diff. Style command from the File menu and select DEFAULT.STY.

1. Press **Ctrl-R** to see a reduced view of the page if your screen is not in Reduced View. Press **Ctrl-U** to select the Frame Tool if the Frame Tool is not selected.
2. Click on the **View** menu and click on **Show Column Guides** to turn on the column guides if they are not already on. If they are on, ignore this step.
3. Move the mouse cursor somewhere in the middle of the page, and click once.
4. Click on the **Frame** menu and click on **Margins & Columns**. The Margins & Columns dialog box appears.
5. Select **3** for **# of Columns**.
6. Type the following values:

	Widths	Gutters
Column 1:	**1.00**	**.50**
Column 2:	**2.25**	**.50**
Column 3:	**2.00**	

Your screen should resemble this illustration:

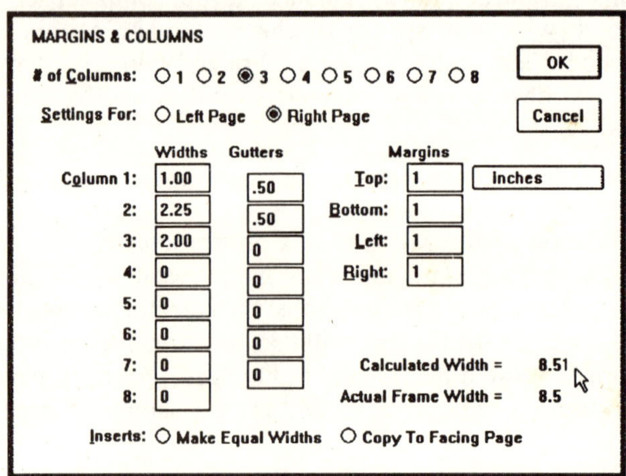

Notice that the calculated width is 8.51 inches. The actual frame width should be 8.5 inches.

7. Select **OK**. Your screen should now resemble this illustration:

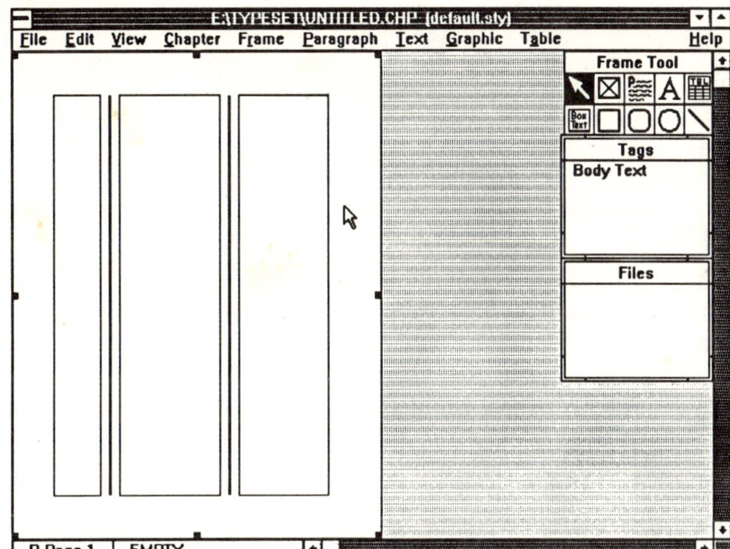

Notice the columns created within the frame.

8. Click on **File** menu and select **Revert to Saved,** then click on **Abandon** twice to clear the screen.
9. Turn to Module 56 to continue the learning sequence.

Module 51
NEW

DESCRIPTION

The New command removes the current chapter from your computer's memory and creates a blank chapter file. It is the same as starting with a blank sheet of paper. If another chapter is currently open, Ventura closes that chapter and gives you the opportunity to save it before creating the new file. The new chapter being created with the New command uses the last style sheet and defaults. New is accessed without specifying the name of a new file. When a filename is not specified, Ventura creates a new blank file.

New is located in the File menu.

APPLICATIONS

New provides a quick, easy way of creating a new file with Ventura. The obvious application for this command is to simply start composing a brand new chapter.

The New command can also be used to create various smaller chapters that can later be joined into one larger publication (see Module 48).

Finally, this command can also be used to simply start over when everything seems to have gone wrong from the very beginning. (This happens not only to beginners, but sometimes even to experienced users!) Using New provides you with a fresh start.

TYPICAL OPERATION

In this example, you use New to start another chapter. The sample chapter document SCOOP2.CHP, which was created in Module 65, is used. The example begins with SCOOP2.CHP already open and in use.

1. Click on the **File** menu and click on the **New** command.
2. Respond to the dialog box asking if you want to save or abandon the changes.

> **NOTE**
> This dialog box will appear only if you have made changes in the current chapter. If you have not made any changes, the dialog box will not appear.

3. Turn to Module 53 to continue the learning sequence.

Module 52
OPEN CHAPTER

DESCRIPTION

The Open Chapter command retrieves a previously stored chapter, as well as its related files, including the style sheet, text files, and graphic files.

Only one chapter can be open at a time in Ventura. If another chapter is currently open, Ventura will prompt you to save the existing chapter. Select either Save to save your changes, or Revert to Saved to throw away your changes.

To open a Ventura chapter, the filename *must* have the extension CHP. Ventura will not open a chapter unless the filename extension is CHP.

While Ventura is opening a chapter file, different messages may appear on your screen. This is a normal operation. Ventura places all possible hyphenation points in the text to increase the reformatting speed each time you make any change within the text.

The Open Chapter command is located in the File menu.

APPLICATIONS

The Open Chapter command opens a previously saved chapter file. The reason for opening a previously created and saved chapter file is to edit it in some way.

You could also use a previously saved chapter file as a template for another similar document. By opening a chapter and then using the Save As command (see Module 65) to create a new version of the publication, you can use the previously saved chapter as a template or guide for the next version of a document.

TYPICAL OPERATION

In this example, you will open a previously saved chapter. If a chapter is open on your computer screen, select Exit from the File menu. You will return to the Windows Program Manager. Restart Ventura in the normal manner, and you will return to a blank screen, ready to continue with these steps:

1. Select **Open Chapter** from the **File** menu. The Open File dialog box appears. Your screen should resemble this illustration:

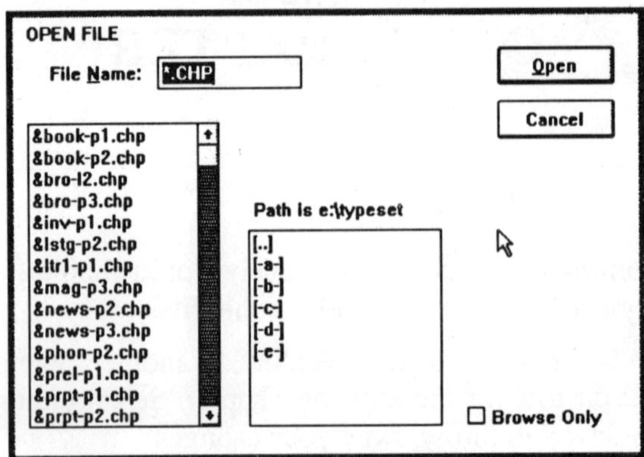

2. Click and hold on the scroll bar until you locate SCOOP.CHP.
3. Double click on **SCOOP.CHP**. The chapter SCOOP.CHP appears on your screen within a few moments.

4. Turn to Module 64 to continue the learning sequence.

Module 53
PAGE SIZE & LAYOUT

DESCRIPTION

The Page Size & Layout command assigns the physical size of the paper used in the printing, the printing orientation, and the selection of either single- or double-sided formatting.

TIP:

Only one set of sizes and layout specifications is permitted per chapter.

The Page Size & Layout dialog box provides you with these options:

Orientation
Paper Type & Dimension
Sides
Start On

Each of these options provides a drop-down list box to permit additional selections. The selections available are:

Orientation	Select either Landscape or Portrait printing. The difference is:
	Portrait / Landscape
Paper Type & Dimension	Select the physical size of the paper on which your chapter is to be printed. Remember that smaller page sizes can be printed on printers that handle only one size of paper if you decrease the page's height and width in the Frame menu Sizing and Scaling option.
Sides	Select either Single-sided or Double-sided formatting. The Facing pages option in the View menu only works when you have selected the Double-sided option.
Start On	Select either Right or Left side.

NOTE

You must select Sides: Double to allow different headers & footers, margins, column widths, vertical rules, and tag spacing settings for left and right pages.

The settings selected with the Page Size & Layout command are stored in the style sheet.

The Page Size & Layout command is located in the Chapter menu.

APPLICATIONS

The Page Size & Layout command is used to change between portrait and landscape printing. This command allows you to decide the appearance of your finished, printed page.

For most of your documents, you use the standard 8 1/2" x 11" paper size. However, you could need to use a larger size piece of paper, such as 11" x 17" or Broadsheet. These options allow you to print in a shrink or overlap mode and can be used to create larger, oversized documents, such as a newspaper or poster.

The other main application of this command is that it permits you to use different formatting on the left and right pages of your documents. This is important for most double-sided documents. Consider this book you are reading. The page numbers on a left page are in a different position than the page numbers on a right page. This type of common format can be established with the Page Size Layout command.

TYPICAL OPERATION

In this example, you change the page orientation of the sample chapter SCOOP.CHP. This example begins with SCOOP.CHP already open. Use the Open Chapter command in the File menu to retrieve and open SCOOP.CHP.

1. Click on the **Chapter** menu and click on **Page Size & Layout** to display the Page Layout dialog box.

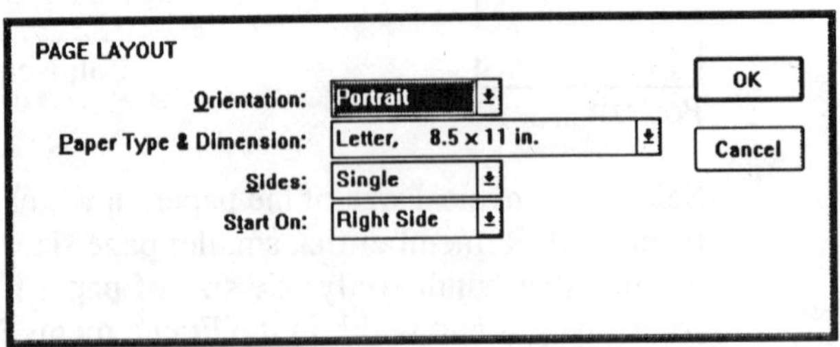

2. Click on **Orientation** and select **Landscape**.

3. Click on **OK**. Your screen should now resemble the following illustration:

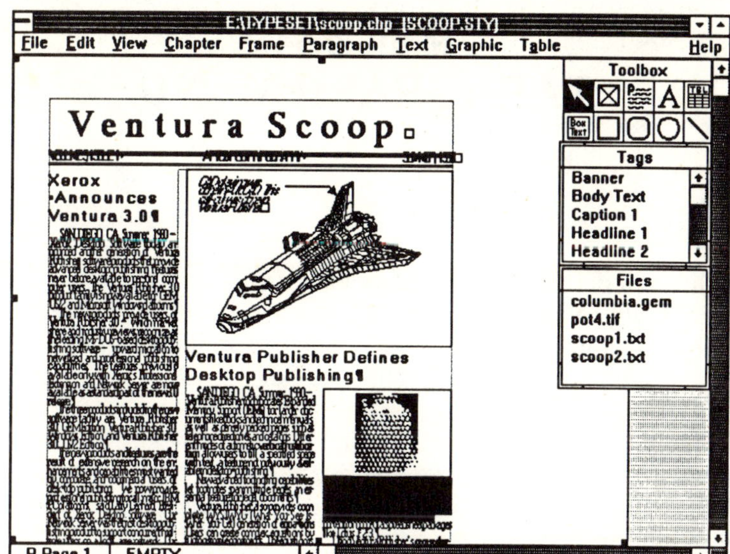

Notice the new layout of the page.

NOTE

So your screen matches the illustrations in this book when following the learning sequence, change the page orientation back to Portrait from the Chapter menu with the Page Size & Layout command.

4. Click on **File** menu, select **Revert to Saved**, and then click **OK**.
5. Turn to Module 32 to continue the learning sequence.

Module 54
PARAGRAPH MENU

DESCRIPTION

The Paragraph menu defines the individual paragraph tags (the format assigned to the paragraphs within your Ventura document) contained in the style sheet. These tags are used to change the text format for each paragraph in a Ventura chapter.

The options available in the Paragraph menu are:

Font
Alignment
Spacing
Breaks
Tab Settings
Special Effects
Attribute Overrides
Paragraph Typography
Ruling Line Above
Ruling Line Below
Ruling Box Around
Auto-Numbering
Define Colors
Add New Tag
Update Tag List

With the exception of Auto-Numbering and Define Colors, before any option in the Paragraph menu can be selected, the Paragraph mode must be selected. The Paragraph mode can be selected by clicking on the Paragraph Tool in the Toolbox or by pressing Ctrl-I. After selecting Paragraph mode, only Add New Tag and Update Tag List are available, in addition to Auto-Numbering and Define Colors. You must first click on a paragraph before all options in the Paragraph menu are available.

Although you will not need to use all of the commands in the Paragraph menu for each document you produce, you will be using the first three commands—Font, Alignment, and Spacing—many times to control the appearance of your paragraphs.

APPLICATIONS

As a desktop publisher, your most important task and goal is to convey a written message to a reader by communicating with the printed word. Although Ventura provides you with many tools to meet that goal, perhaps none are as important as the commands found in the Paragraph menu. These commands provide the control over the computer-generated typesetting process.

TYPICAL OPERATION

In this operation, you access the Paragraph menu and review the various commands located within the menu. The sample chapter document SCOOP.CHP is used. The example begins with SCOOP.CHP open. If you do not have this chapter open, use the command Open Chapter in the File menu to retrieve and open SCOOP.CHP.

1. Press **Ctrl-I** to change to the Paragraph mode.
2. Move the pointer to the middle of the working area of your screen, and click on a paragraph on the page.
3. Click on the **Paragraph** menu, and notice the various commands available within the menu.
4. Move the mouse to any area outside of the Paragraph menu and click once. The Paragraph menu disappears.
5. Turn to Module 80 to continue the learning sequence.

Module 55
PARAGRAPH TAGGING

DESCRIPTION

Ventura's Paragraph Tagging function assigns attributes to the paragraphs within your document. With the Paragraph Tagging Tool, you assign a paragraph tag from the current style sheet. The tags that are available to assign to a paragraph are selected from the Tags Window. The attributes of each available paragraph tag are changed by using the options or commands available in the Paragraph menu.

Ventura contains two types of tags. They are user-defined tags, which you create, and Ventura-generated tags, which Ventura automatically creates when you use certain commands, such as Headers & Footers or Auto-Numbering.

Tags can be changed, assigned, or even deleted. By using tags, you can create special styled paragraphs, such as those with bullets, or large first letters, or with a unique indent or outdent.

The real power of using a tag is that whatever attribute is assigned to a tag, all paragraphs within the document that have the same tag will have the same attributes. For example, if you set the tag called Headline to be centered, 24 point Dutch, then all paragraphs in your document tagged as Headline—whether they are on page 1, 19, or 99—would be set in 24 point Dutch type, and they would be centered.

NOTE

Body Text is located in each style sheet, and although you can change the attributes of this tag, it cannot be deleted.

Tags can be assigned to any paragraph, but not to an individual word or sentence within a paragraph. To Ventura, a paragraph is any group of characters, words or sentences that end with a required carriage return (created by pressing Enter). A paragraph can be as short as a word, or can run many pages long.

Tags are saved in a Ventura file called a style sheet.

The Paragraph Tagging mode is enabled by pressing Ctrl-I or by selecting the Paragraph Tool from the Toolbox.

APPLICATIONS

Ventura makes setting text easier by using the Paragraph Tagging feature. Because each tag can be set to assign a different style to a paragraph, you are able to take advantage of design freedom. And since more than one paragraph can be assigned with the same tag, you assure a uniform appearance throughout the document.

For example, you can assign attributes to each level of headline, subheading, and caption throughout the document. Then, whatever text is chosen as the headline, it will be set with the correct attributes and will always be the same throughout the entire document.

All text not assigned a tag will automatically be assigned Body Text by Ventura. Whatever the attributes for Body Text, all body text paragraphs throughout the document will look alike.

Paragraph tags enforce a consistent appearance of text throughout the entire document. Because the paragraph tags are saved in a style sheet, you can use the same style sheet with other text documents, and by assigning paragraph tags, each publication will look the same.

TIP:

You can apply the same tag to multiple paragraphs by pressing Shift before clicking on the desired paragraphs.

TYPICAL OPERATION

In this example, you use the Paragraph Tool and select a paragraph. Then, you assign another paragraph tag to the paragraph. The sample chapter SCOOP.CHP is used. The example begins with SCOOP.CHP open and in use. Use the command Open Chapter in the File menu to retrieve and open SCOOP.CHP. So your view matches the screens depicted in this book, press Ctrl-N. You may need to adjust your screen using the scroll bars to make your computer look like the illustrations.

1. Press **Ctrl-I** to select the Paragraph Tool. The mouse cursor changes shape. It looks like the corner of a box with lines of text inside of it.
2. Click on the words "SAN DIEGO, CA, Summer 1990." Notice that Ventura reverses the color of the entire selected paragraph text.
3. Point and click on **Headline 2** in the Tags Window. Notice that the words in the selected paragraph now appear on your screen with the same attributes and appearance as the other Headline 2 text. Your screen should resemble the following illustration:

Also notice that the Current Selection Box shows the name of the tag (Headline 2) assigned to this paragraph.

4. Point and click on **Body Text** in the Tags Window. The paragraph reverts to its normal size.
5. Turn to Module 87 to continue the learning sequence.

Module 56
PARAGRAPH TYPOGRAPHY

DESCRIPTION

The Paragraph Typography command controls the typographic attributes for each paragraph tag, including kerning, letterspacing, spacing between words, and spacing between lines.

"Body Text" TYPOGRAPHY SETTINGS

Automatic Pair Kerning:	Off		OK
Letter Spacing:	On	Up to: 0.1 Ems	Cancel
Tracking:	Looser	0 Ems	
Grow Inter-Line To Fit:	On		
Minimum Space Width:	0.6	* (space width) = 0.150 Ems	
Normal Space Width:	1	* (space width) = 0.250 Ems	
Maximum Space Width:	2	* (space width) = 0.500 Ems	
Vert. Just. At Top of Para:	0.194	inches	
At Bottom of Para:	0.194		
Between Lines of Para:	0		

The options available within the Paragraph Typography Settings dialog box are:

Automatic Pair Kerning
Letter Spacing
Tracking
Grow Inter-Line to Fit
Minimum Space Width
Normal Space Width
Maximum Space Width
Vert. Just. At Top of Para
At Bottom of Para
Between Line of Para

Within each option, different settings are available, offering an array of powerful typographic controls to your individual paragraph tags.

For example, in automatic kerning, Ventura will automatically kern letter pairs. There are over 30,000 possible pairs of characters, but only 100 to 500 (depending on the style of your font) need to be kerned. Kerning permits the characters to be squeezed together, making the type characters easier to read. A classic example is the combination of A and W. Ventura will automatically kern these letters for you when used in combination.

Automatic kerning is turned on or off for the entire chapter in the Chapter Typography (see Module 14) option. If it is turned on for the entire chapter, kerning can be turned on or off for any specific paragraph tag within the Paragraph Typography Settings dialog box.

To turn Automatic Pair Kerning for a particular paragraph tag on or off, simply access the Paragraph Typography Settings dialog box and, using the drop-down list box, select either on or off. Ventura will take care of the kerning for you automatically, and for most applications, that will be sufficient.

TIP:

> To see the effect of the automatic kerning on your computer screen, you must turn on On-Screen Kerning in the Set Preferences command in the Edit menu.

One of the other options available within the Paragraph Typography Settings dialog box includes Letter Spacing. When Ventura justifies a line of text, space is added and subtracted between each word until the last character on a line reaches the right column. Letterspacing attempts to control the appearance of a line of text by adding additional space between the characters of each word. By doing so, not as much white space is required between the words. If letterspacing is turned on, additional spaces are added between letters until the space between words is equal to or less than the amount specified in the Maximum Space Width.

To use Letter Spacing, you must first set the horizontal alignment to Justified in the Alignment dialog box, turn Letter Spacing on in the Paragraph Typography Settings dialog box, and set the Minimum Space Width to less than the Normal Space Width. A typical number would be 0.700 (70% of the Normal Space Width). Remember that values above the normal space width would have no effect. The Minimum Space Width is the smallest amount of space that can appear between words in a justified line. Set the Normal Space Width to 1.000, and set the Maximum Space Width to the largest space allowable between words during justification. A typical value is 2.000 (double the Normal Space Width). Finally, set the maximum space allowed between letters during letterspacing in the Up to area. A typical amount is 0.100 Em.

Ventura calculates the space character's width and shows it in Ems, a typographic measurement equal to the width of the capital M in the current font and point size being used and assigned to the paragraph tag.

Tracking increases or decreases the space between every letter in a paragraph. To use the Tracking control, select Looser to increase the space, and select Tighter to decrease the amount of space. Then enter, on the Tracking line, the amount of space to add or subtract between individual letters. The amount of tracking is also set in Ems.

Grow Inter-Line To Fit allows larger type sizes to fit within a line. For example, you might want to use a large size typeface for one or two words within a paragraph of text. If the Grow Inter-Line is turned off, the words with the bigger size text, assigned in the Set Font function within the Text Editing mode, will overlap the previous line of text. If Grow Inter-Line is turned on, the amount of spacing between lines of the paragraph will be increased so as to prevent the larger text overlapping the previous line of text.

NOTE

These controls available to set the paragraph typography are powerful tools. However, they can easily be abused. It is recommended that a conservative approach be taken when making adjustments within this dialog box. Be careful not to use too much or too little spacing, because either can make your text impossible to read.

The Paragraph Typography Settings dialog box is located within the Paragraph menu. The Paragraph Tag Tool must be enabled and a paragraph selected to access this command.

The Vert. Just. At Top of Para and At Bottom of Para options within the Paragraph Typography dialog box allow you to set the maximum amount that can be added above and below a paragraph during vertical justification.

The Between Line of Para option is used to add space between lines in each paragraph, if needed. Space is added between lines within a paragraph only if the text does not reach the exact bottom of the column.

TIP:

If Between Lines of Paragraph is set at zero, then no space is added between lines for paragraphs tagged with the tag.

APPLICATIONS

Automatic pair kerning makes headlines easier to read and more attractive by placing individual letters closer together. Kerning also reduces the amount of space needed for some text.

The Grow Inter-Line To Fit option automatically increases the space between lines. This command is also available for creating local overrides to the Paragraph font settings instead of creating a new tag. For example, if you wish to change a paragraph's font but do not need to change the alignment or space between paragraphs, you should select the entire paragraph in Text mode and then change the font with the Set Font command in the Text menu. The Inter-line spacing will automatically adjust if Grow Inter-Line To Fit is turned on. This procedure eliminates the need for another paragraph tag.

Letter Spacing reduces the number of lines that would have too much white space (called loose lines) between words by adding space between the letters in the words on the line.

Tracking is used to expand or contract headlines to fit a given space or, if used in the body text, the entire document can be expanded or reduced in size with only a minor, subtle change in the overall appearance.

The Vertical Justification options within the menu automatically add space between paragraphs and between lines within paragraph to make text exactly reach the bottom of a column. This is often used in newsletters or newspaper-type column layouts, where additional space is needed to fill a column.

TYPICAL OPERATION

In this example, you adjust the Paragraph Typography of a paragraph in a chapter. The sample chapter SCOOP.CHP is used. The example begins with SCOOP.CHP open and in use. Change the view size to Normal view. Use the Open Chapter command in the File menu to retrieve and open SCOOP.CHP.

1. Press **Ctrl-I** to select the Paragraph Tool.
2. Point to and select the first paragraph of text in the left column of your screen.
3. Click on the **Paragraph** menu and click on the **Paragraph Typography** option.
4. Type **0.500** to change the Tracking. Your screen should resemble the following illustration:

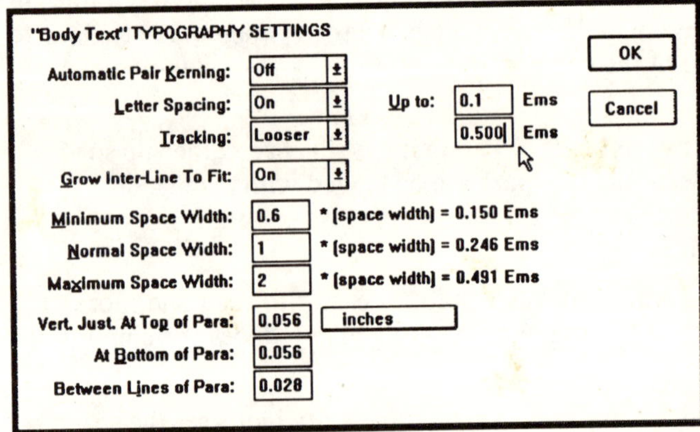

5. Select **OK**. Then click on a white area outside the paragraph. Your screen should resemble the following illustration:

Notice the exaggerated word spacing now being shown.

6. Abandon the changes by pointing to the **File** menu and clicking on **Revert to Saved**. Confirm the abandon command in the dialog box.
7. Turn to Module 57 to continue the learning sequence.

Module 57
PRINT

DESCRIPTION

The Print command prints a Ventura document to the printer or to a disk. Before printing, you can select which pages to print, the number of copies to print, and which order to print the pages of your document. Crop marks can also be added before the printing process is started.

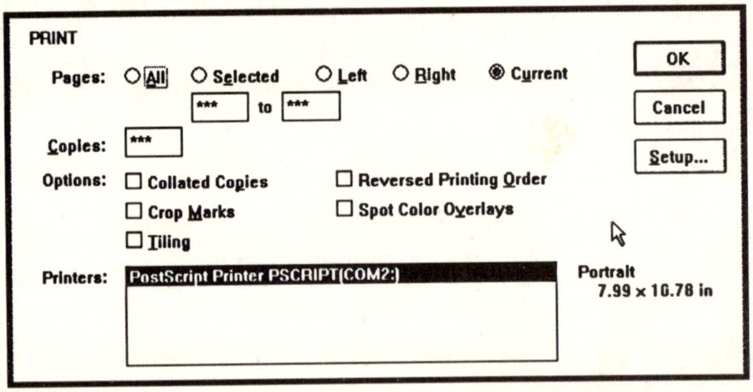

PRINT
Pages: ○ All ○ Selected ○ Left ○ Right ◉ Current
*** to ***
Copies: ***
Options: ☐ Collated Copies ☐ Reversed Printing Order
☐ Crop Marks ☐ Spot Color Overlays
☐ Tiling
Printers: PostScript Printer PSCRIPT(COM2:)
Portrait
7.99 x 10.78 in
OK
Cancel
Setup...

The Print command presents the Print dialog box. The options available are:

Pages
Copies
Collated Copies
Reversed Printing Order
Crop Marks
Spot Color Overlays
Tiling
Printers

There are many different possible selections available within the Print dialog box. These include:

Pages	To print only a part of the chapter, click on the Selected button. Then type the first page to be printed in the first box, and type the last page to be printed in the other box.
	To print only the current page, click on the Current button.
	To print the entire chapter, click on the All button.

Select Left or Right to print only left pages or right pages.

Copies — Type the number of copies you need to print.

Select Collated Copies if you want all copies to print in page sequence. Turn the Collated Copies button off if you want all the copies of each page to print together. (This setting greatly increases the speed of your printing process.)

Select Reversed Printing Order to print the pages last to first.

Select Crop Marks to place camera crop marks exactly at the edge of a page. (Depending on your laser printer, this feature may not work as many laser printers cannot print to the edge of the paper.)

Select Spot Color Overlays On to generate a separate page for each color enabled in the Define Colors command (see Module 18).

Select Tiling to print large page sizes on multiple pages.

You must set up your printer correctly in the Windows Set Up before attempting to print in Ventura. If your printer information is not correctly set up in Windows, Ventura is not able to print properly. It is extremely important that your configuration be precisely identified.

Use the Windows setup to select a different printer, to select a different paper tray (if necessary), to scale the page larger or smaller (if your printer can support this option), or to print to a file.

TIP:

Always select the printer in Windows Set Up before you access Print.

To print a document to a file, first select Options in the Set Up menu within the Print menu. Select Print To: Filename. Enter the name of the file to which you wish to print. Then Select Ok to return to the Print menu.

If you have selected oversize page dimensions in the Page Layout dialog box, another dialog box appears as soon as you have selected OK in the Print Information dialog box. This dialog box offers three choices:

Shrink
Overlap
Nothing

Choose Shrink if you want to reduce the 11" x 17" page to fit an 8 1/2" x 11" sheet of paper (this option will only work if you are using a PostScript printer). Choose Overlap if you want to print four 8 1/2" x 11" pages which can be pasted together to form one 11" x 17" page. Choose nothing if your printer can actually handle an 11 x 17 sheet of paper.

TIP:

If you need to stop the printing when it is in progress, press Esc. The printing will stop *after* the current page is printed. This will not be an instant stop for most laser printers.

To access the Print command, select the File menu.

APPLICATIONS

The application of this command is obvious: this command generates the printed pages of your document. The command also allows you to tailor your printed output.

For example, suppose you are working on a 30-page document and decide to change only page 22. The document is already printed, but you need just one copy of the new page 22. This command allows you to print just page 22.

This command also allows you to print to a file, so the file can be sent to a commercial typesetter. This is an important function available in Ventura for those who need truly professional output. By sending a Ventura file to a typesetter, your finished output has a higher resolution than that which is available from today's laser printers.

TYPICAL OPERATION

In this example, the sample chapter document SCOOP.CHP is printed. The example begins with SCOOP.CHP open and in use.

1. Click on the **File** menu and click on **Print**.
2. Select **All** for Pages and click on **OK**. Within several minutes, the printer will generate the pages.
3. Turn to Module 46 to continue the learning sequence.

Module 58
RE-ANCHOR FRAMES

DESCRIPTION

The Re-Anchor Frames command moves each frame in the chapter to the page where its anchor appears. For information about anchors, see Module 6.

This command moves only those frames that have both an anchor name and a text anchor in the same page.

The anchor is established under the Anchors & Captions command, located within the Frame menu. However, the Re-Anchor Frames command is located in the Edit menu.

After selecting the command, Ventura will move the frames to their anchor points within the text. If the anchored frames are at a point in the text where the text is currently at the top or bottom of a page, the Re-Anchor command will move those frames to the upper and lower margins. Those frames must then be relocated manually by selecting the Frame mode and then moving them with the mouse.

TIP:

Whenever using this command, it is always a good idea to check each anchored frame within your chapter. Many times, minor adjustments must be made for optimum appearance.

If the anchor name in the text does not match the anchor names assigned to a frame, Ventura displays a message on the computer screen during the Re-Anchor command's execution. You may then correct the name of the anchor in the text before the reanchor process continues.

APPLICATIONS

This command is used to move frames to anchor points within your text. Frames that contain charts, diagrams, or pictures associated with certain text need to be kept with the text. During the editing and moving text processes, the frames could be no longer near the associated text. By using the Re-Anchor Frames command, the frames would be moved to that text.

TYPICAL OPERATION

In this example, you reanchor the frames within the sample chapter SCOOP.CHP. The example begins with SCOOP.CHP already in use.

1. Click on the **Edit** menu and select **Re-Anchor Frames**. A message box appears asking if you wish to reanchor this page's frames, all frames, or cancel.
2. Select **All Pages** in the chapter to be reanchored.

NOTE

After using this command, you should check each page within the chapter to fine-tune or adjust any frame.

3. Turn to Module 38 to continue the learning sequence.

Module 59
REMOVE TEXT/FILE

DESCRIPTION

The Remove Text/File command completely deletes a file and its contents from a frame or underlying page frame or from the Files Window. The file is *not* deleted from the disk. To delete a file from the disk, use the Windows File Manager commands.

To access the Remove Text/File command, the frame or underlying page frame must be selected. Use the Frame Tool to select the desired frame. The Remove Text/File command can then be accessed from the Frame menu. When selected, the Remove File dialog box appears.

The Remove File dialog box offers these options:

File Name	Type the name of the file as it appears in the Files Window. Ventura will automatically enter the name of the file in the selected frame or underlying page frame.
Remove from	Select either List of Files or Frame. If you select Frame, the file will be removed from the frame, but will remain in the Files Window. If you select List of Files, the file will be removed from the frame and the Files Window.

TIP:

Any unused file should be removed from the Files Window. By doing so, you will speed up the operation of Ventura. All text files included in the Files Window are loaded into your computer's memory, whether or not they are placed anywhere in the chapter. Removing unnecessary files eliminates this use of the computer memory.

APPLICATIONS

The Remove Text/File command is used to remove files from a frame or from the Files Window. Removing unwanted files from the Files Window speeds the amount of time it takes for Ventura to open a chapter file for you. Removing a file from a frame is useful when a frame has been copied for its attributes, such as rules, margins, columns, background pattern, but the text file within the frame is not wanted.

TYPICAL OPERATION

In this operation, a frame is drawn, a text file is loaded in the frame, the text file is removed from the frame, and finally the frame is deleted. The sample chapter document &PRPT-P1.CHP is used. The example begins with &PRPT-P1.CHP already open and in use. Use the Open Chapter command in the File menu to retrieve and open &PRPT-P1.CHP. Press Ctrl-R to change to Reduced view.

1. Click on the **Add Frame** Tool in the Toolbox.
2. Move to the middle of the page and draw a new frame. Your screen should resemble this illustration:

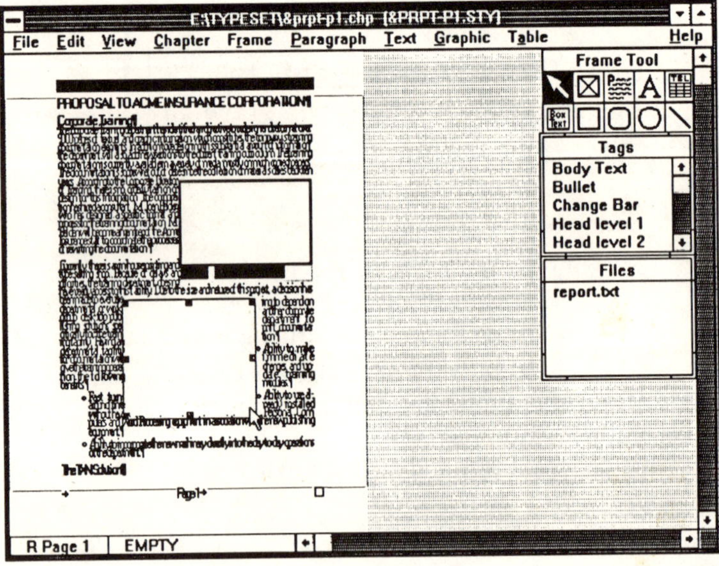

3. Click on the **File** menu and click on **Load Text/Picture**. Select **Text** for type of file and **ASCII** for Text Format. Click on **OK**.

4. Double click on **REPORT.TXT**. Your screen should resemble this illustration:

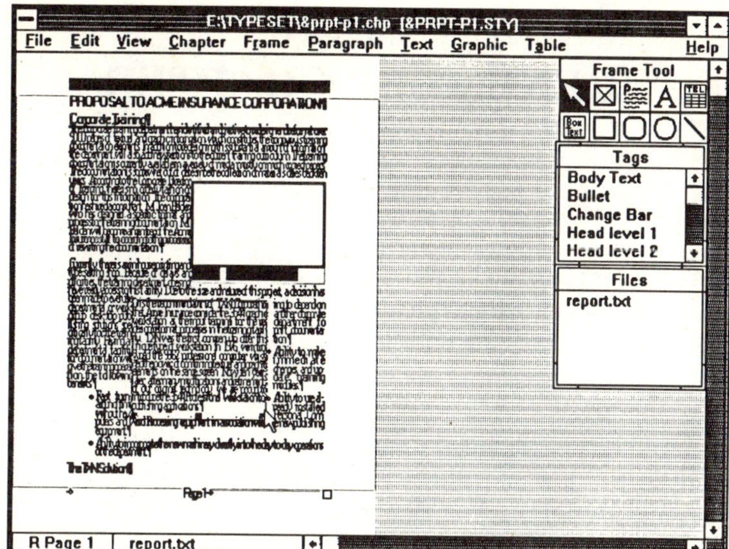

Notice that REPORT.TXT also appears in the Files Window.

5. Click on the **File** menu and select **Remove Text/File** to display the Remove File dialog box.
6. Type **REPORT.TXT** for File Name and select **Frame** for Remove from.
7. Click **OK**. Notice the file has been removed from the frame.
8. Press **Del**. The frame is deleted.
9. Turn to Module 10 to continue the learning sequence.

Module 60
RENUMBER CHAPTER

DESCRIPTION

The Renumber Chapter command updates the numbering of paragraphs defined with the Auto-Numbering command. Paragraphs must first be automatically numbered with the Auto-Numbering command (see Module 8 for more information about Auto-Numbering).

TIP:

When you tag paragraphs or modify text with the Text Tool, section numbers are not added, deleted, or modified. Select Renumber Chapter to update section numbers.

Use Renumber Chapter anytime you want to update numbering in the currently open chapter.

The Renumber Chapter command is located in the Edit menu. It can also be accessed by using the keyboard command Ctrl-B. The entire chapter is then renumbered.

APPLICATIONS

The Auto-Numbering command will not change the paragraph numbers automatically each time a paragraph is added or deleted. When paragraphs are edited, changed, moved, deleted, or added, the Renumber Chapter command must be accessed to renumber the paragraphs.

TYPICAL OPERATION

In this example, you renumber the sample chapter &TDOC-P1.CHP. The example begins with &TDOC-P1.CHP open and in use. Use the Open Chapter command in the File menu to retrieve and open &TDOC-P1.CHP.

1. Press **Ctrl-O** to access the Text Tool, place the text cursor to the left of "K" in "Keyboard Keys" (Section 1.1.1) and press **Return** to add a new paragraph.
2. Press **Up Arrow** and type **Computer Command Keys**.
3. Click on the **Edit** menu and select **Renumber Chapter**. The entire chapter has been renumbered.
4. Click on the **File** menu and click on **Revert to Saved**. Click on **OK** when prompted to revert back to the last saved version.
5. Turn to Module 49 to continue the learning sequence.

Module 61
REPEATING FRAME

DESCRIPTION

The Repeating Frame command duplicates a frame on every page of your Ventura chapter. All attributes assigned to the frame—its ruling lines, background, and contents—are also copied onto each chapter page.

A repeating frame can also be hidden on selected pages within your chapter. For example, you could have a repeating frame and its contents appear on all pages within your document except the first page.

NOTE
Repeating frames cannot have captions.

Repeating frames can be sized and positioned on a page, but they cannot be cut, copied, or pasted. Any change made to a repeating frame *changes* all reoccurrences of the repeating frames on each page. In other words, the repeating frame will be *exactly* the same throughout the entire chapter.

When a repeating frame is selected, it is displayed in gray, rather than black, to alert you that the frame is a repeating frame, and not a regular frame.

To use the Repeating Frame command, first create the frame that you wish repeated on each page within your document. Then, while in the Frame mode, access the Frame menu and select the Repeating Frame command.

REPEATING FRAME
For All Pages: ◉ Off ○ Left ○ Right ○ Left & Right
On Current Page: ○ Show This Repeating Frame
○ Hide This Repeating Frame
Show All Hidden Frames
OK
Cancel

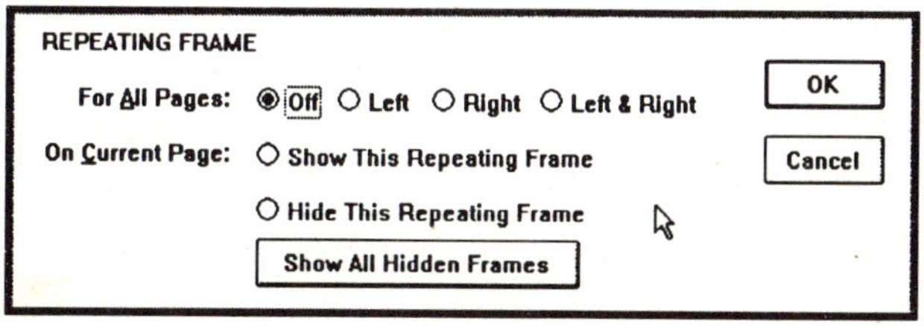

When the Repeating Frame dialog box appears, the following commands are available:

For All Pages: Select Off, Left, Right, or Left & Right. Select Left if you want the repeating frame to appear only on the left pages; select Right if you want the repeating frame to appear only on the right pages; select Left & Right if you want the repeating frame to appear on both left and right pages. Select Off if you want to remove the repeating frame from all other pages within the chapter.

On Current Page: Select Show This Repeating Frame, Hide This Repeating Frame, or Show All Hidden Frames. Select Hide This Repeating Frame to remove a repeating frame from a page. To restore a hidden frame, select Show This Repeating Frame. If you have selected another frame and then return to the hidden repeating frame, select Show All Hidden Frames.

APPLICATIONS

This command is used to place text or graphics on every page within your document. For example, you might want to produce a document that has a company letterhead or logo on each page. The Repeating Frame command allows you to position the text or graphics on each page automatically. This eliminates the necessity to position the text and logo on each page. Rather, the Repeating Frame command will routinely repeat on each page for you.

This command can also be used to create headers and footers larger than those generated by Ventura.

TYPICAL OPERATION

In this operation, a repeating frame is created. The sample chapter document &PRPT-P1.CHP is used. The example begins with &PRPT-P1.CHP open.

1. Select the **Add Frame** Tool from the Toolbox.
2. Move to the center of the page. Click and hold the mouse, and draw a medium-size frame.
3. Click on the **Frame** menu and click on **Frame Background**. Select a **Solid** for pattern and click on **OK**. Your screen should resemble this illustration:

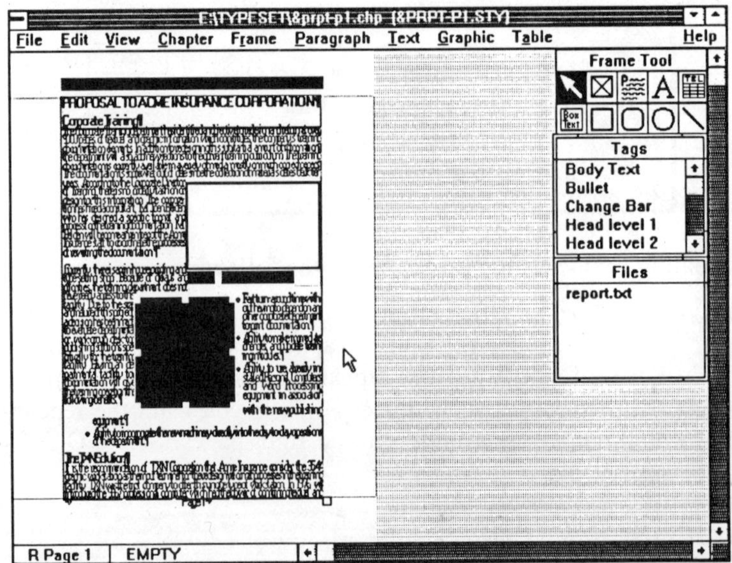

4. Click on the **Frame** menu and click on **Repeating Frame**. Click on **Left & Right**, and click on **OK**.
5. Click on the **Chapter** menu and click on **Insert/Remove** page. Click on **Insert New Page After Current Page**. Select **OK**. Your screen should resemble this illustration:

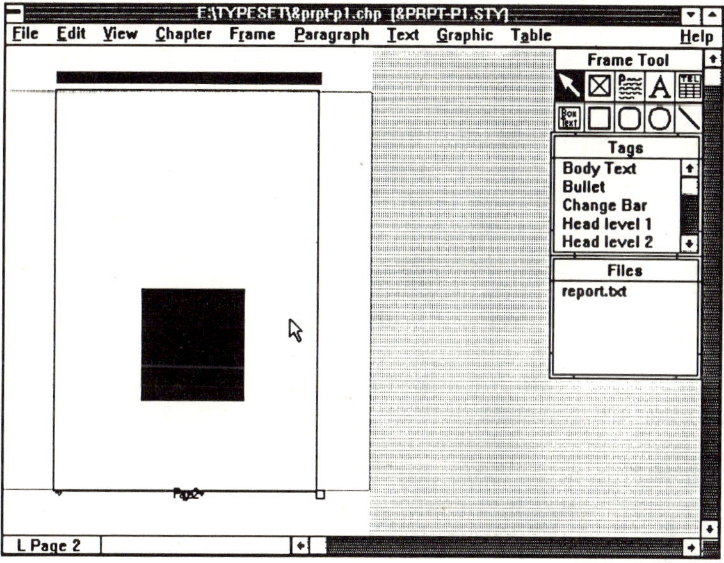

Notice the repeating frame.

6. Press **PgDn** to view the other pages. Notice the repeating frame.
7. Click on the **File** menu and select **Revert to Saved**. Confirm the Abandon in the confirmation block.
8. Turn to Module 63 to continue the learning sequence.

Module 62
REVERT TO SAVED

DESCRIPTION

The Revert to Saved command allows you to revert to the last, most recently saved version of your document. It abandons any changes made during the current session. Revert to Saved returns to the last saved version of the document, the currently active style sheet, and any external graphic files. You cannot change graphic files in Ventura.

The Revert to Saved command is located in the File menu.

TIP:

By using the Save command often (press Ctrl-S or select it in the File menu), Revert to Saved is more effective and can be used to recover from a mistake or error.

APPLICATIONS

Revert to Saved is a useful tool when you choose, for any reason, not to save changes you have made. For example, you might use Revert to Saved if you accidentally removed a page.

You may also want to use Revert to Saved when you are experimenting with a new design on a document. If you do not like your new design, select Revert to Saved to revert back to the original version of your document.

TYPICAL OPERATION

In this example, you make a change to the sample chapter document SCOOP.CHP, then Revert to Saved. The example begins with SCOOP.CHP open and in use. If you do not have this chapter open, use the Open Chapter command in the File menu to retrieve and open SCOOP.CHP. Press Ctrl-N to show the file in Normal View.

1. Click on the **Text** Tool to select that tool.
2. Select the word "Ventura" in the second headline that reads "Ventura Publisher Defines Desktop Publishing" by clicking and dragging the mouse cursor across the word. Your screen should look like the following:

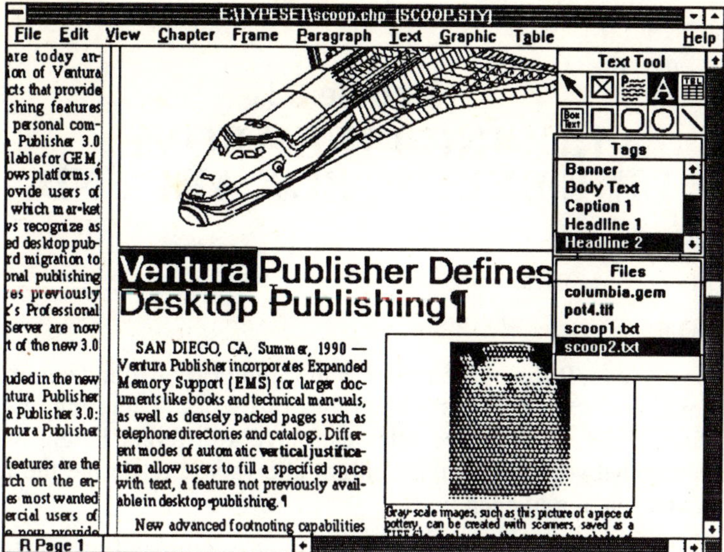

3. Press **Del**.
4. Select the **File** menu and click on **Revert to Saved**. A dialog box appears asking if you want to revert to the last saved version.
5. Click **OK** to restore the file. Notice that the word "Ventura" now appears.
6. Turn to Module 47 to continue the learning sequence.

Module 63
RULING LINE ABOVE, LINE BELOW, BOX AROUND

DESCRIPTION

The Ruling Line Above, Ruling Line Below, and Ruling Box Around commands position ruler lines above, below, and around paragraphs or frames. There may be one, two, or three ruling lines. Each of the three rules can have a different height and a different amount of spacing between each rule. Ventura allows you to define the location, size, color, texture, and spacing of each line.

A display area in the Ruling Line dialog box of each command previews the size and spacing of the ruling lines. This allows you to design your rules more easily.

When a ruling line is desired above, below, or around a paragraph, the commands are selected with the paragraph tag. After selecting the Paragraph mode, select the command from the Paragraph menu. The changes made with these commands affect the paragraph tag associated with the selected text. When a change is made to a paragraph tag, it affects all text marked with that paragraph tag in your current document, as well as in other documents that use the same style sheet.

When a ruling line is desired above, below, or around a frame, the commands are selected with the Frame Tool. First select the Frame mode, then select the command from the Frame menu. A Ruling Line Above, Below, or Around command can be assigned to any frame, including the underlying page frame.

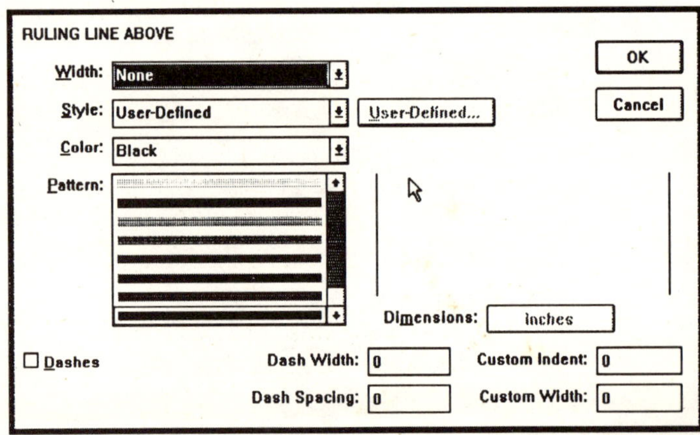

The dialog boxes for all three commands contain these options:

Width — Select the overall width of the rule or box. The available options are the width of the paragraph's text, the frame's margins, the current column in the frame, or the width of the frame itself. A custom width can also be specified by selecting Custom, then typing the width in the Custom Width entry area.

Style — You can select a predefined line style from the style menu. Or, you can select User-Defined to define your own lines. If you select User-Defined, the User-Defined Ruling Style dialog box appears.

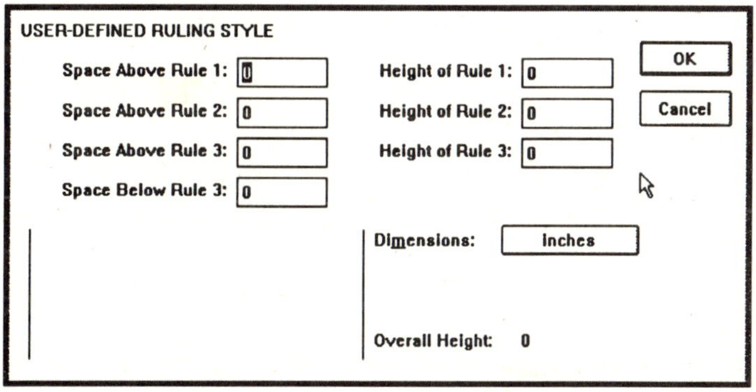

USER-DEFINED RULING STYLE

Space Above Rule 1: 0
Space Above Rule 2: 0
Space Above Rule 3: 0
Space Below Rule 3: 0
Height of Rule 1: 0
Height of Rule 2: 0
Height of Rule 3: 0
OK
Cancel
Dimensions: Inches
Overall Height: 0

These options are available within the User-Defined Ruling Style dialog box:

Space Above Rule 1/2/3 — Type the white space needed above the line.

Height of Rule 1/2/3 — Type the width or thickness of each line.

Space Below Rule 3 — Type the white space needed below each line.

Overall Height — Ventura calculates the height of the rules and displays it.

The result of your custom lines is displayed in the display area, located in the lower left corner of the User-Defined Ruling Style dialog box. Select OK or cancel to dismiss the dialog box.

Color — Assign a color to the ruling line(s) if desired.

Pattern — Select the pattern of the ruling lines. Select the solid pattern for a continuous black line. The same pattern will be used for all lines in the ruling.

Dashes — Click on or off the Dashes option to make the ruling lines above, below, or around into dashes. If a dashed line is chosen, type the dash length and space between dashes in the Dash Width and Dash Spacing entry areas.

Custom Indent — If Custom was specified for width of a paragraph tag, type the amount of offset desired for the line length. If subtracting from the length, type a – (minus) with the number.

Custom Width — If Custom was specified for width of a paragraph tag, type the width desired for the line.

TIP:

Some laser printers cannot support extremely thin ruling lines, often referred to as hairlines. If your printer does not print a thin ruling line, enlarge the width of the ruling line.

APPLICATIONS

Ruling lines above, below, or around text or frames are used to emphasize or isolate text or pictures. The reason for doing so will depend on your publication. For example, you might be creating an advertisement that contains a discount coupon. You may want to use the Ruling Box Around command—with dashes—to emphasize the coupon, and for the consumer to use as a guide to cut out the coupon from the rest of the advertisement.

Adding rules above or below text usually adds design and style to a document. What would first appear as bland or dull is often a bright and dazzling document when these simple rules are added.

Perhaps one of the best ways to learn how to effectively use ruling lines is to look through and study magazines, books, and newspapers. Notice the way other graphic designers use these simple techniques to make their layout more interesting and to attract your attention.

TYPICAL OPERATION

In this example, you add a new frame and use the Ruling Box Around command. The sample chapter document &PRPT-P1.CHP is used. The example begins with &PRPT-P1.CHP open.

1. Press **Ctrl-N** to view the page in Normal View.
2. Select the **Add Frame** Tool from the Toolbox.
3. Move the cursor to the middle of the page and draw a new frame. Your screen should resemble the following illustration:

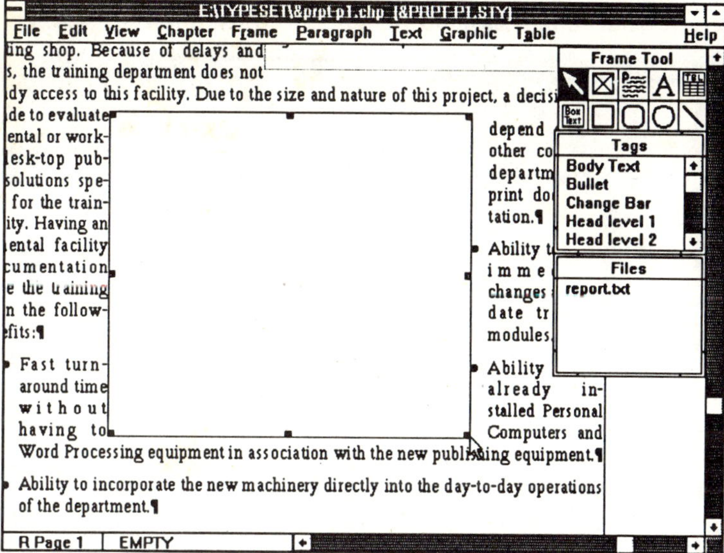

4. Click on the **Frame** menu and click on **Ruling Box Around** to display the Ruling Box Around dialog box.
5. Select **Frame** for Width, select **8 point** for Style, **Black** for Color, and the last pattern on the Pattern list for Pattern.

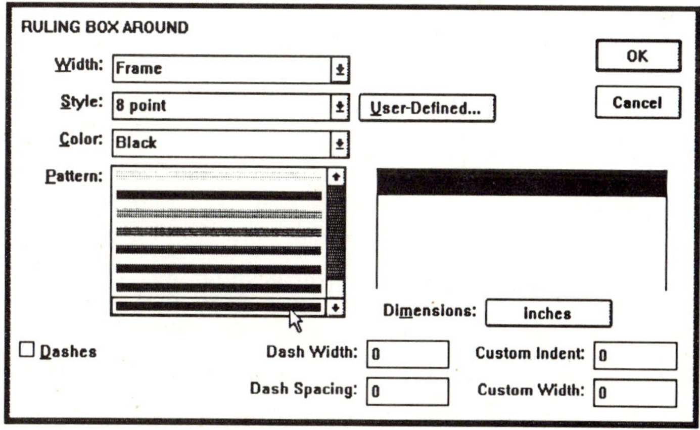

6. Press **Enter**. Your screen should resemble this illustration:

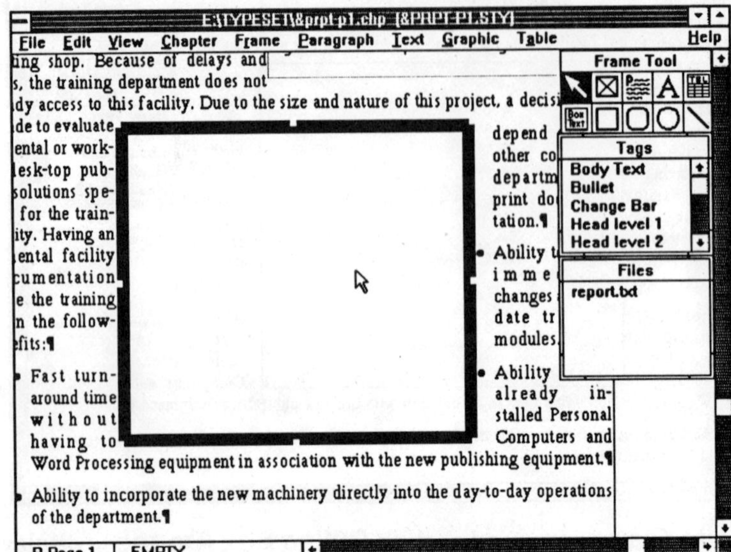

7. Press **Del** to delete this new frame.
8. Select the **Add Frame** Tool from the Toolbox.
9. Move the cursor to the middle of the page and draw a new frame.
10. Click on the **Frame** menu and click on **Ruling Line Above** to display the Ruling Line Above dialog box.
11. Select **Frame** for Width. Select **picas & points** for Dimensions. Click on **User-Defined**, and the User-Defined dialog box appears. Type **0,06** for Space Above Rule 1, **0,10** for Height of Rule 1, **1,03** for Space Above Rule 2, and **1,07** for Height of Rule 2.

NOTE

All of these settings are in picas and points.

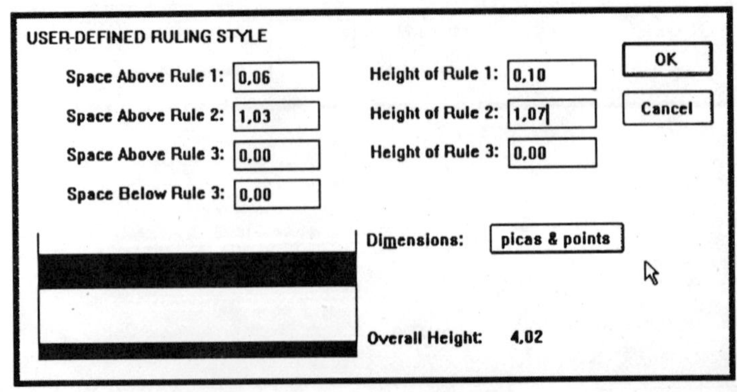

12. Select **OK** twice. Your screen should resemble this illustration:

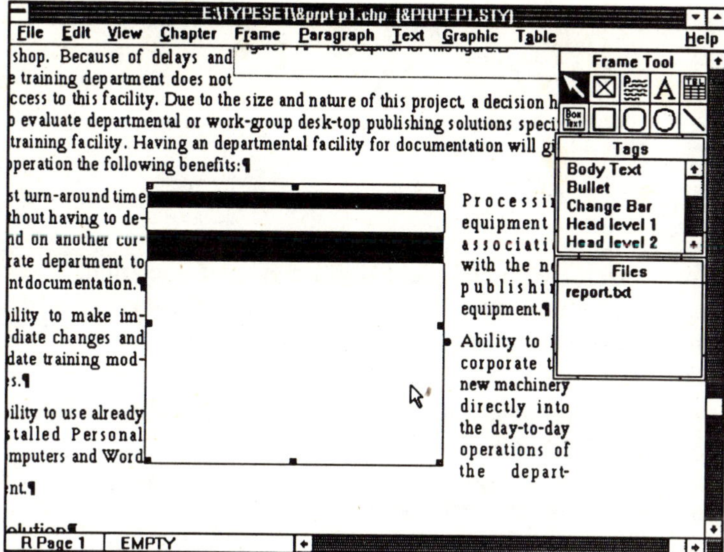

13. Press **Del** to delete this new frame.
14. Click on **File** menu, click on **Revert to Saved**, and then click **OK**.
15. Turn to Module 75 to continue the learning sequence.

Module 64
SAVE

DESCRIPTION

The Save command stores your complete Ventura chapter document in several files on your floppy diskette or hard drive. The chapter will be saved under the filename shown in the Title Bar on your computer screen. The style sheet and each text file are also saved if they have been changed.

When the Save command is executed, Ventura also saves all captions, internal graphics (the ones you draw in Ventura), and chapter information in separate files. Ventura creates files with the same filename as your chapter, but uses extensions CAP for captions, VGR for graphics, and CIF for chapter information.

If you have set Ventura to create backup copies (See Module 69, Set Preferences), when the Save command is executed, the backup files are also created. The backup files are recognized by the inclusion of $ in the first position in the extension (for example, .$HP).

The Save command is accessed in the File menu. It can also be accessed by pressing Ctrl-S.

NOTE

> When Save is executed, the style sheet, including any changes, is saved. If you are using the style sheets supplied with Ventura, it is best to first select the Save As New Style option to save the style sheet under a new name prior to saving the chapter. By doing so, you will always have the original style sheets in their original configuration.

Save should not be confused with Save As (see Module 65). Save As allows you to save the document under a new name, where Save retains the document under the name displayed in the Title Bar.

APPLICATIONS

The Save command protects you against losing your work. You should get into the habit of using this command often. By saving your changes under an existing filename, you can always retrieve your work. This protects you should your computer lose power and an accidental erasure occur. It also protects you against a major mistake.

Should the power to your computer go off, you can restart the computer and reopen your document. If you make a major mistake, you can use Revert to Saved (Module 62) to automatically revert to a previously saved version of the chapter.

TIP:

You cannot overuse Save. Although it is not necessary to keep an alarm clock at your computer, you should use Save every 10 to 20 minutes and before you attempt any major revisions. The more you use Save, the more likely you can recover from any unexpected problem that might occur with your work.

TYPICAL OPERATION

In this operation, you use Save to save the chapter. This Typical Operation begins with SCOOP.CHP open and on your screen. Refer to Module 52 for the steps to open this Ventura chapter.

1. Click on the **File** menu and click on **Save**.
2. Press **Ctrl-S**. Once again, Ventura saves the files for you. As you can see, you can Save as often as you want.
3. Turn to Module 21 to continue the learning sequence.

Module 65
SAVE AS

DESCRIPTION

The Save As command allows you to save your Ventura chapter file under a new name. This actually creates a duplicate copy of your chapter file. You can use the Save As command to make the duplicate copy by using another filename or another DOS path or both.

The style sheet and each associated text file are also saved—if they have been changed in any way. Save As creates only a copy of the Ventura chapter file.

The Save As command is located in the File menu.

APPLICATIONS

Save As is used to create a duplicate copy of a Ventura chapter file. Use Save As so you do not make changes to a style sheet or a text file that is still used in an original chapter file. This is used when you want to keep the original chapter file intact, but require changes. For example, suppose you had to change a business report proposal. Rather than alter the original proposal, you would simply copy it by using Save As, then make changes to the new chapter file. By doing so, you could still publish the first proposal, even though you altered it to produce the second draft or proposal.

NOTE

Do *not* use Save As for making a backup copy of your documents to a floppy diskette. When you use the Save As command, Ventura only creates a copy of the Ventura chapter file, but not your text and graphics files. To make a backup copy of your complete Ventura documents, use the Copy All command. (See Module 48, Manage Publication for more information.)

TYPICAL OPERATION

In this operation, you use the Save As command. The sample chapter SCOOP.CHP is used. The example begins with SCOOP.CHP open and in use. Use the Open Chapter command in the File menu to retrieve and open SCOOP.CHP.

1. Click on the **File** menu and click on **Save As** to display the Save File As dialog box.

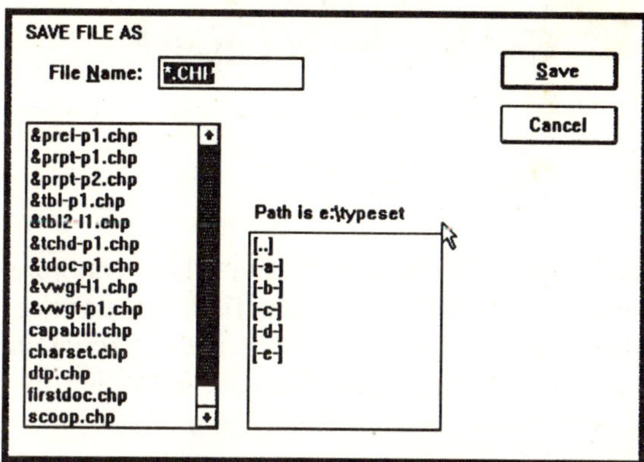

The Save File As dialog box should be set to the TYPESET directory on the C drive and contain files with the .CHP extension.

2. Type **SCOOP2.CHP** in the Selection entry area and press **Enter**. Within a moment, Ventura displays a message that the chapter is being saved, and you are returned to the regular screen area. Notice the Title Bar. The document has been renamed to SCOOP2.CHP.
3. Turn to Module 51 to continue the learning sequence.

Module 66
SAVE STYLE AS

DESCRIPTION

The Save Style As command saves the current style sheet under a new name. The style sheet contains information used to control the final appearance of your document. Ventura uses a separate computer file, called a style sheet, to contain the information that controls the style of your document. These files are identified by the .STY extension. Each Ventura chapter uses a style sheet.

The Save Style As command not only saves the current style sheet under a new name, but it also modifies an existing style sheet.

NOTE

> Saving a Ventura chapter after modifying a style sheet or saving a modified style sheet under its original name changes the appearance and style of other chapters using that same style sheet. *Always save modifications to current style sheets under a new name with this command.* If you don't, your modifications will affect the other chapters.

The Save Style As command is located in the File menu.

APPLICATIONS

The main purpose of this command is to create new style sheets. It is generally a good idea to create a new style sheet for each kind of document. Remember that style sheets are separate files and control the general appearance and style of your final document. One style sheet can be associated with many different chapters. If you were to change the style sheet that has been associated with many different chapters, then all chapters would reflect those changes.

This is a powerful feature: all documents using the style sheet will look the same. Of course, if you don't want all documents to look the same, you need to create a new style sheet with the Save Style As command.

TYPICAL OPERATION

In this example, you save the &NEWS-P2 style sheet as a new style sheet. The sample chapter &NEWS-P2.CHP is used. The example begins with &NEWS-P2.CHP open and in use. Use the command Open Chapter in the File menu to retrieve and open &NEWS-P2.CHP.

1. Click on the **File** menu and click on **Save Style As** to display the Save File As dialog box.

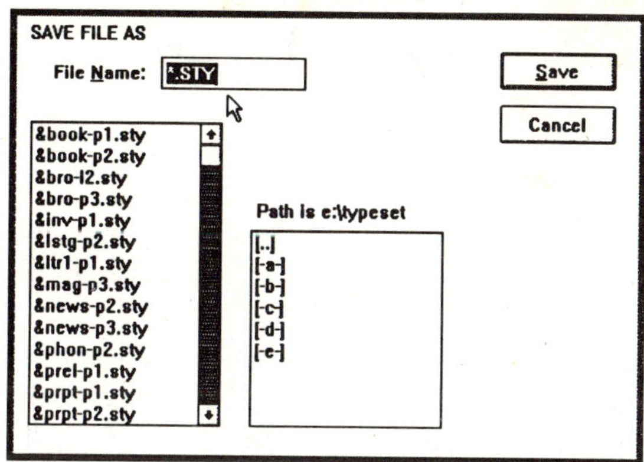

2. Type **TESTSAVE** for Selection and press **Enter** to save the new style sheet. Notice that the style sheet name in the title bar has changed to (TESTSAVE.STY).
3. Click on the **File** menu, click on **Load Diff. Style**, and double click on **&NEWS-P2.STY** to eliminate using this new style sheet.
4. Turn to Module 5 to continue the learning sequence.

Module 67
SELECT ALL

DESCRIPTION

The Select All command selects every graphic associated with the currently selected frame.

After all the graphics have been selected, all the graphics can be moved, copied, cut and pasted, or deleted. The Select All command can also be used to change the attributes for all the graphics associated with a particular frame.

To access the Select All command, first select the Frame Tool, and then a frame must be selected. The Select All command can then be accessed in the Graphic menu or by pressing Ctrl-Q. Once all graphics are selected, they can then be moved, copied, cut, deleted, pasted, or have their attributes changed.

TIP:

A graphic can be unselected from the Select All command by holding the Shift key and clicking on the graphic.

To move all the graphics selected, move the mouse cursor to the center of any one of the selected graphics and then press and hold the mouse button. Within a moment, the mouse cursor changes shape; still holding the mouse button, move the graphics to the new location.

APPLICATIONS

The Select All command can be used to move every graphic associated with a specific frame to a new location. The Select All command can also be used to change the attributes of all graphics. For example, the line thickness of all graphics can be changed by first selecting all the graphics and then assigning a different line thickness.

This command also shows which graphics are associated with a specific frame.

TYPICAL OPERATION

In this example, you use Select All to select all the graphics and then assign a common line thickness. Finally, you delete all the selected graphics. The sample chapter document SCOOP.CHP is used. The operation begins with SCOOP.CHP open and in use.

1. Click on the **Chapter** menu and select **Insert/Remove Page** to display the Insert/Remove Page dialog box. Select **Insert New Page After Current Page** and click on **OK**.

2. Click on the **Frame** Tool from the Toolbox. Point to the middle of the page and click once.
3. Select the **Add Rectangle** Tool and draw three boxes within the middle of the page. When completed, your screen should look like this illustration:

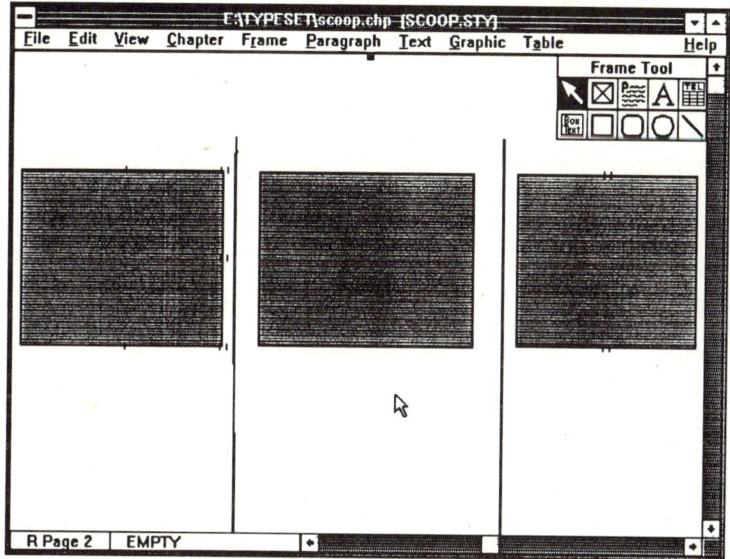

4. Press **Ctrl-Q** to activate Select All. Notice that the three boxes are now selected.
5. Click on the **Graphic** menu and click on **Line Attributes** to display the Line Attributes dialog box.
6. Select **Custom** for Thickness and type **12.00** for points. Click **OK**.

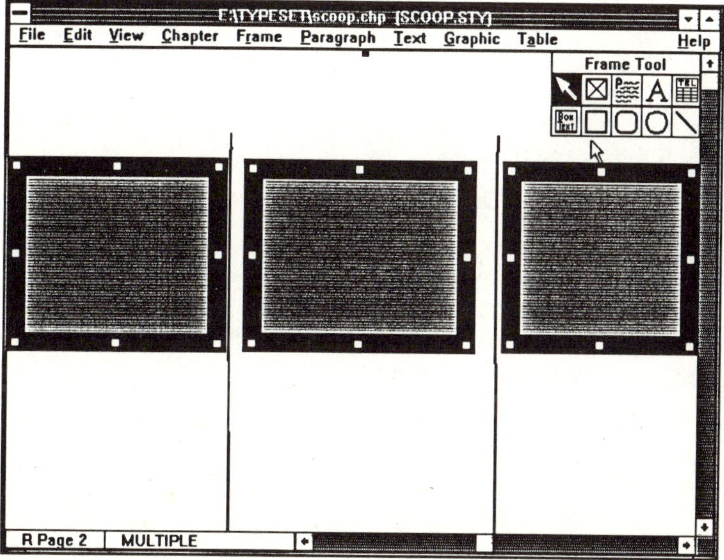

Notice the new line thickness for all the boxes.

7. Press **Del**. Notice that all the boxes disappeared.
8. Click on the **File** menu and click on **Revert to Saved**. Click on **OK** when prompted to revert back to the last saved version.
9. Turn to Module 11 to continue the learning sequence

Module 68
SET COLUMN WIDTH

DESCRIPTION

The Set Column Width option allows you to precisely define the width of any column within a table.

The width of any column within a table can be adjusted in two ways. One method provides precise adjustment, while the second method is useful when extreme exactness is not required.

The first method of setting the column width in a table is with the use of a dialog box:

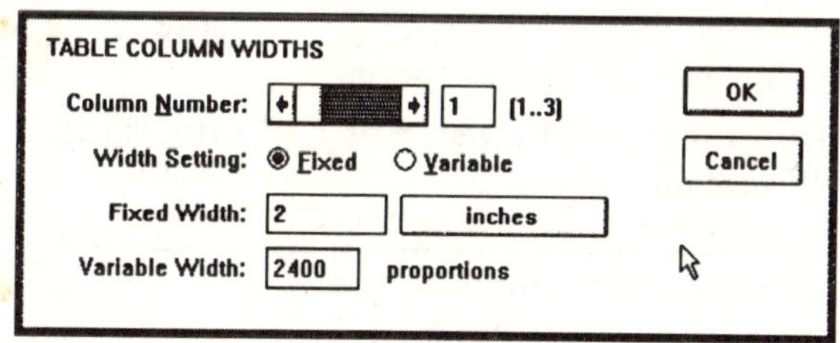

When displayed, select the column number that you want to adjust.

TIP:

You can change any column number by selecting the arrow on either side of the Column Number.

Next, choose a width setting of either fixed or variable width. A fixed width column sets the width entered on the Fixed Width line within the Column Width dialog box. Select Variable Width Setting if the columns can be adjusted automatically.

TIP:

If all columns are to have the exact same width, set the Variable Width setting to 1.

When finished, select OK.

The second method of adjusting the width of a column is by using the Alt. Press and hold Alt, then move the mouse cursor to the middle of the column you want to change. Then press and hold the mouse button, and move the right column to the new width. Finally, release the mouse button, then Alt.

APPLICATIONS

When you create a table in Ventura, it may be necessary to adjust the width of the columns. This is particularly true if you want to have uneven or different widths for your columns.

The Set Column Width command allows you to determine precisely how wide the columns should be, or you can use Alt and the mouse to adjust the columns visually.

This command allows you to adjust the width of your columns easily so the text contained within the columns is easier to read or interpret.

TYPICAL OPERATION

In this activity, you set the column width of a table. This table was created in the Typical Operation of Module 42. (If you have not created the table, you must do so before proceeding with these steps.)

1. Select to the **Table** Tool in the Toolbox.
2. Move the mouse to the upper left corner of the table, and click and hold the mouse. While still holding the mouse button, drag the mouse to the lower right corner of the first column. Release the mouse button.
3. Click on the **Table** menu and select **Set Column Width**. Your screen should resemble this illustration:

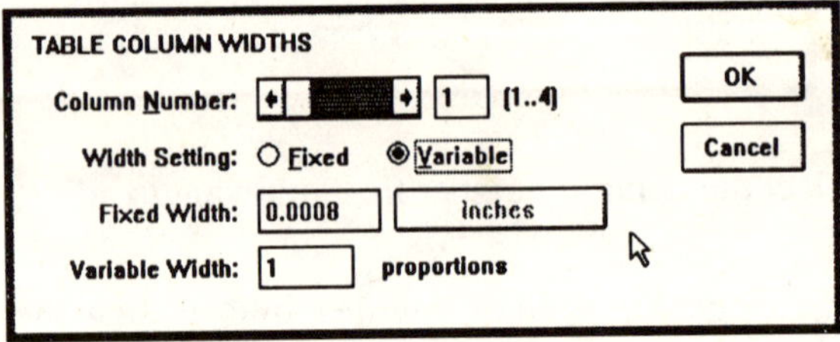

4. Click on **Fixed** for Width Setting.
5. Change the Fixed Width to **3,08** picas. Click **OK**. Your screen should resemble the following illustration:

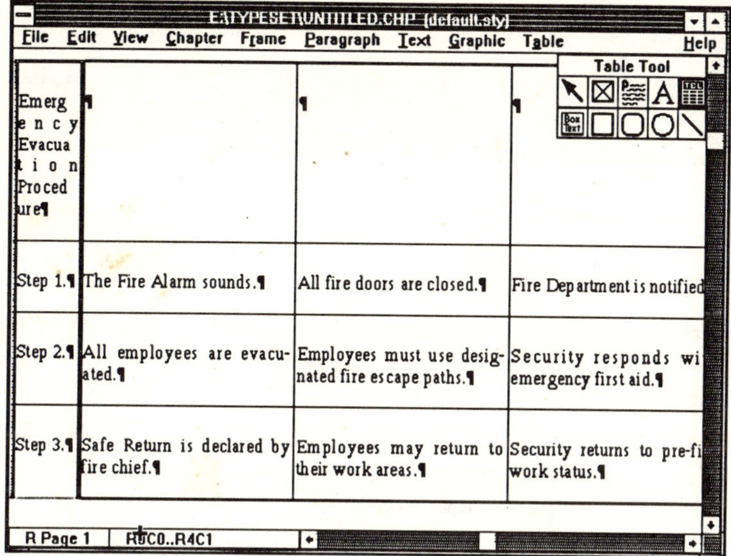

6. Turn to Module 71 to continue the learning sequence.

Module 69
SET PREFERENCES

DESCRIPTION

The Set Preferences command sets miscellaneous features which affect the appearance of the Ventura screen and the basic performance of the software. All the preferences are entered by selecting options or typing information in the Set Preferences dialog box.

SET PREFERENCES

Generated Tags: Hidden

Text to Greek: 6

Keep Backup Files: No

On-Screen Kerning: All

Auto-Adjustments: Styles

Decimal Tab Char: 46 (ASCII)

OK

Cancel

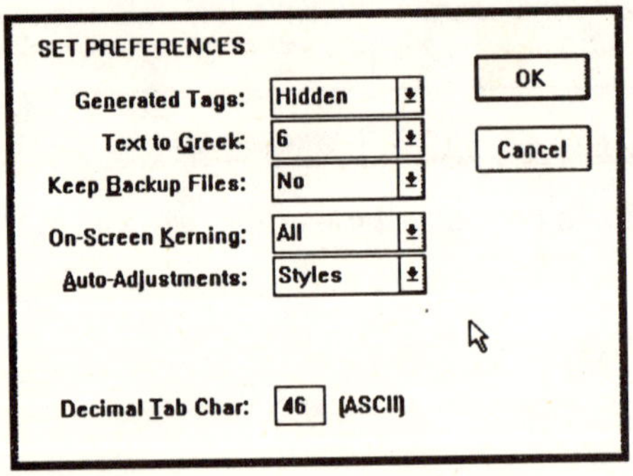

The options in the Set Preferences dialog box are:

Generated Tags — Select whether you want Ventura to show or hide the generated paragraph tags. Ventura automatically generates these tags when you use commands to create headers, footers, footnotes, and auto-numbering schemes.

Text to Greek — Select the amount of greeking you want to use with the Reduced View or Facing Pages View commands. Greeking speeds up the performance of Ventura. With greeking, Ventura changes the text of specified sizes to a series of lines. Greeked text displays the general appearance of the page. Select All to greek all of the text. Select None to prevent any text from being greeked. The numbers between All and None specify the type size to be greeked when you are looking at the screen with the Reduced View or Facing Pages View.

Keep Backup Files — Select Yes to create backup files each time the current files are saved. If you select Yes, Ventura saves copies of the chapter, caption text, and style sheet files when you use the Save or Save As commands. Ventura designates the backup files by changing the first letter of the file extension to $. The backup file for

	TESTDOC.CHP is TESTDOC.$HP. Select No if you do not want to create backup files.
On-Screen Kerning	Select the smallest type size to show kerning on the screen. Select All if you want to kern all text on screen. Select None if you do not want to kern any text. The numbers between All and None specify the type size in points where Ventura begins on-screen kerning. For example, if you select 18, Ventura kerns all the text that is 18 points in size or larger. Ventura runs faster when it displays a screen without kerning than one with all of the characters kerned.
Auto-Adjustments	Select Styles to adjust automatically the space between lines when you change point sizes in the Font dialog box. Select None to keep the line spacing the same no matter what the point size. Select " and - - to allow Ventura to convert typewriter-style quotes and dashes to typeset styles. Select Both if you want both the typographic and style conversions.
Decimal Tab Char	Type the decimal value of the ASCII character used for decimal points. The default is 046 for a period. Ventura uses this ASCII character for aligning the decimal point column of decimal tabs. (See the Tab Setting command for more information on decimal tabs.)

The Set Preferences command is located in the Edit menu.

APPLICATIONS

Preferences are nothing more than your choices of how you want to run Ventura. They have little effect on the final appearance of your printed document. Preferences do affect the way Ventura is used and the way the program is operated.

The list of tag names in the Tag Window can be made smaller by hiding the generated tag names.

Maximum speed performance is available from Ventura by selecting All for Text to Greek and None for On-Screen Kerning. Both of these preferences reduce the amount of time Ventura requires to create an image on your screen.

It is a good work habit to create a backup copy of your Ventura files. The backup files can save a lot of time if you make a major mistake. Simply rename the backup files to those of the working files and continue working.

If a character other than a period is used for a decimal point (sometimes a comma is used in other parts of the world), type the decimal value of the character in Decimal Tab Character.

Auto-Adjustments affect the appearance of the printed page. Normally, Ventura automatically adjusts the space between lines when point sizes of the text are changed. The fonts are normally designed with the correct amount of space above and below the characters to provide an appealing appearance. You may want to overrule automatic line adjustment if you are using different type sizes but need all lines spaced the same, regardless of the type size. Converting typewriter style quotes and dashes to true typesetting symbols improves the professional appearance of your finished documents.

TYPICAL OPERATION

In this operation, you change the preference for greeking text, and you observe how it affects the performance of Ventura. The instructions begin with SCOOP.CHP open.

1. Click on the **Edit** menu and click on **Set Preferences** to display the Set Preferences dialog box.
2. Select **2** for Text to Greek. Click on **OK**. Notice that none of the words are greeked, and watch how long it takes Ventura to draw the screen.

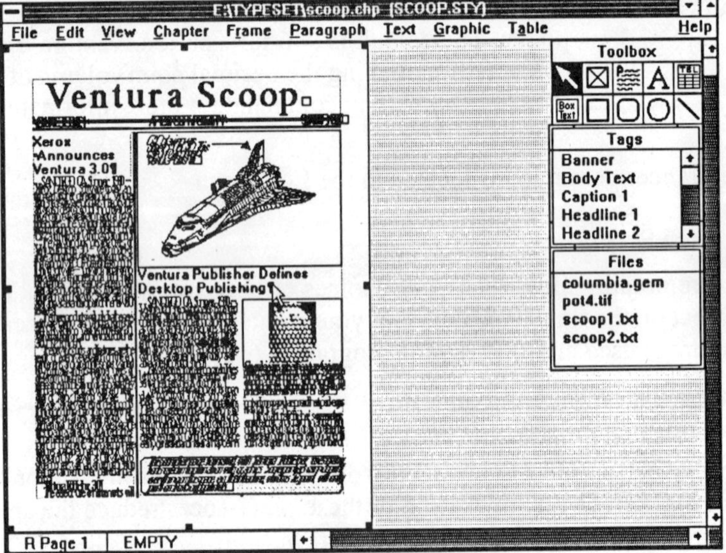

3. Click on the **Edit** menu and click on **Set Preferences** to display the Set Preferences dialog box.
4. Select **All** for Text to Greek. Click on **OK**. Notice that all the words are greeked, and watch how much faster Ventura draws the screen.

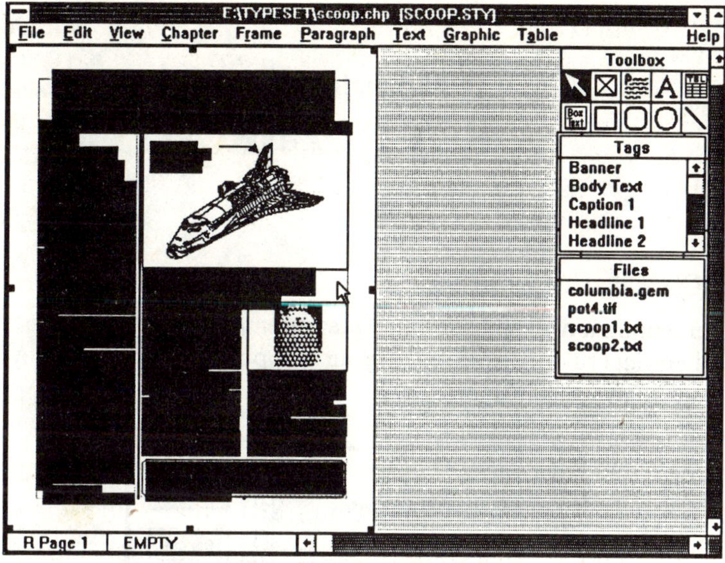

5. Return the Text to Greek setting to 6.
6. Turn to Module 36 to continue the learning sequence.

Module 70
SET RULER

DESCRIPTION

The Set Ruler command establishes the measurement units and zero points of the horizontal and vertical rulers displayed on your computer screen. The Show/Hide Rulers command also displays or hides the rulers.

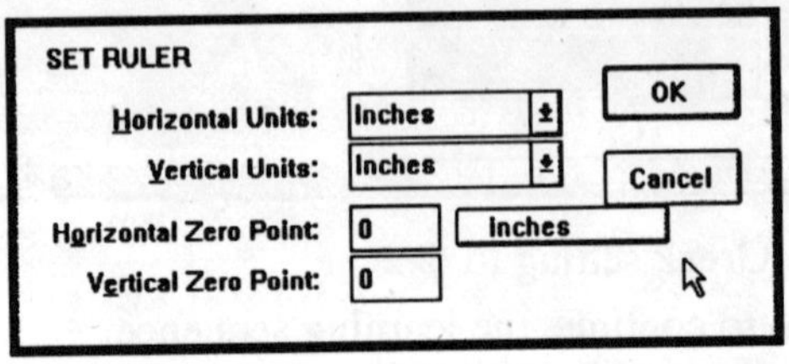

SET RULER
Horizontal Units: Inches
Vertical Units: Inches
Horizontal Zero Point: 0 Inches
Vertical Zero Point: 0
OK
Cancel

The measurement units available on the rulers are inches, centimeters, and picas.

Inches and centimeters are common units of measure found on rulers. Picas are a standard measurement unit used by printers and used in the typesetting industry. A pica is approximately one sixth of an inch, so there are six picas to an inch. Each pica contains 12 smaller units, called points. Points are standard measurement units used to measure type sizes.

The Set Ruler command also establishes the zero point for the horizontal and vertical rulers displayed on the screen. When the zero point is set to something other than the upper left corner of the page, the ruler displays measurement units for both before and after zero.

The zero point can be positioned by typing the Horizontal Zero Point and the Vertical Zero Point within the Set Ruler dialog box. The zero point can also be set by simply using the mouse. A zero point is nothing more or less than picking up the ruler and moving where the zero of the ruler begins. To move the zero point, click and hold on the 0,0 box, located in the screen where the horizontal and vertical rulers intersect. Drag the pointer to the new position of the zero points and release the mouse button. (Ventura generates cross hairs while resetting the zero point to help make the placement more accurate.) To reset the zero points to the upper left corner of the page, click the mouse once inside the 0,0 box.

The Set Ruler command is accessed in the View menu.

APPLICATIONS

The Set Ruler command allows you to use any standard unit of measurement while working with your documents. In the beginning, you will probably work with inches, only because that will be the most comfortable for you. However, it is suggested that you work with picas and points. The reason is clear: by doing so, you are using the same measurement used to determine the size of the type. At first, working with points and picas may be uncomfortable, but when you master working with this measurement system, you will find working with measurements in your Ventura documents much easier.

Remember these values:

6 picas to an inch
12 points to a pica
72 points to an inch

Being able to move the zero point is similar to picking up a ruler and repositioning it as you work on your desk. By being able to reposition the zero point, you are doing nothing more than moving the ruler, even though Ventura will continue to display it in the same position on the computer screen.

TYPICAL OPERATION

In this example, you set the ruler and move the zero point of the rulers. The sample chapter SCOOP.CHP is used. The example begins with SCOOP.CHP open. Use the command Open Chapter in the File menu to retrieve and open SCOOP.CHP. Change view to Normal by pressing Ctrl-N, and if not already on, select Show Rulers from the View menu.

1. Click on the **View** menu and select **Set Ruler** to display the Set Ruler dialog box.
2. Click on **Picas** for both the Horizontal Units and Vertical Units.
3. Click **OK**. Notice the rulers are now displayed in picas, and what was a one-inch mark is now a six-pica mark.
4. Click and hold on the **0,0** box where the horizontal and vertical rulers intersect.
5. Drag the mouse cursor to 12 picas vertical and 12 picas horizontal. Your screen should resemble the following illustration:

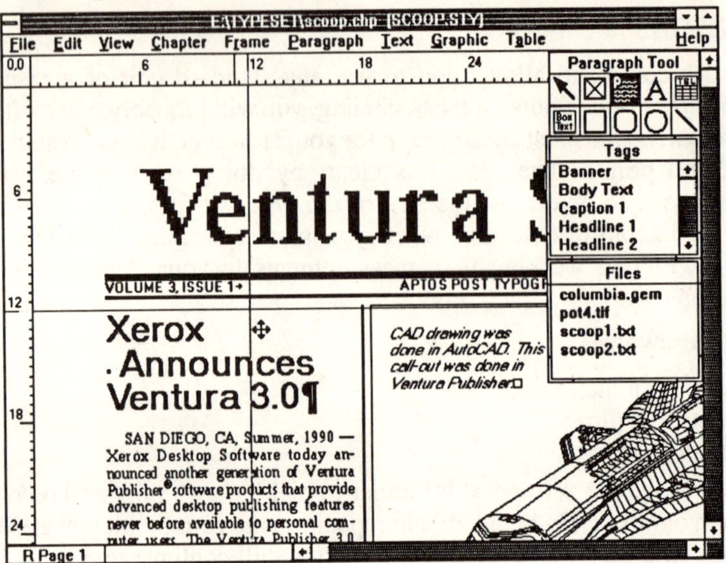

6. Release the mouse button. Notice the new zero points for the vertical and horizontal rulers.
7. Click on the **View** menu and click on **Show Rulers** to hide the Rulers.
8. Turn to Module 31 to continue the learning sequence.

Module 71
SET TINT

DESCRIPTION

The Set Tint command is used to add a background color to selected cells within a table. The Define Colors command (see Module 18) sets the colors which can be applied to any cell within the table.

TIP:

> If you want to assign a shade of gray to cells within your table, set Cyan, Magenta, and Yellow to 0% and then select the percentage of black necessary to make the desired shade of gray.

To set the tint within a table, first select the Table Tool. Then select or highlight the cells to be tinted. Next, select Set Tint from the Table menu.

Select any of the colors or patterns being displayed and then select OK. The selected color and pattern is then assigned to the selected cells within the table.

APPLICATIONS

When creating a table, you may want to tint certain cells. By doing so, you can add emphasis to certain parts of your table.

TYPICAL OPERATION

In this activity, you set tint within a table. This table was created in the Typical Operation of Module 42 and modified in Module 68. (If you have not created the table, you must do so before proceeding with these steps.)

1. Select the **Table** Tool in the Toolbox.
2. Move the mouse to the upper left corner of the table, and click and hold the mouse. While still holding the mouse button, drag the mouse to the lower right corner of the first row. Release the mouse button.

3. Click on the **Table** menu and select **Set Tint**. Your screen should resemble this illustration:

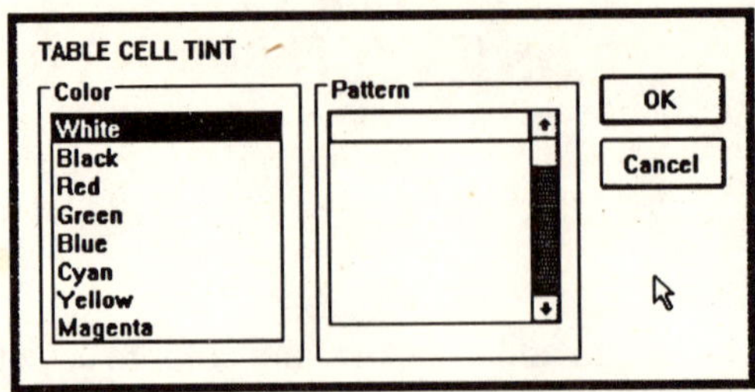

4. Choose color **Black** and the third pattern on the list. Click **OK**.
5. Print the table and review the result.
6. Turn to Module 43 to continue the learning sequence.

Module 72
SHOW/HIDE PICTURES, SHOW RULERS, COLUMN GUIDES, TABS & RETURNS, LOOSE LINES, HEADER & FOOTER

DESCRIPTION

The various Show commands set how the screen looks. Some of these commands also offer tools to increase the speed of the program. Some of the other commands assist in locating formatting errors.

Most of the Show commands are located in the View menu. They are:

Show/Hide All Pictures	This command displays pictures in the frames or replaces the pictures with a shaded, gray box the size of the frame.
Show Rulers	This command displays and hides both the vertical and horizontal rulers on the screen.
Show Column Guides	This command displays and removes the dotted lines that show the position of columns on the underlying page in the chapter.
Show Tabs & Returns	This command displays and removes those special text characters that show the position of tabs, carriage returns, nonbreak spaces, line breaks, index marks, frame anchors, discretionary hyphens, and end-of-file markers. This command can be accessed within the View menu or by pressing Ctrl-T.
Show Loose Lines	This command displays and removes the highlighting of lines that contain more space between words than the Maximum Space width settings in the Paragraph Typography dialog box.

When any of the commands have been selected, Ventura places a check mark in front of the option within the menu, with the exception of Hide or Show All Pictures.

The Show Page Header and the Show Page Footer commands show or hide the text placed in the header or the footer. These commands display or hide the header or footer text on specific pages.

This information about displaying or hiding the header or footer is stored in the current page within the chapter. When the header or footer is turned off, the header or footer space remains on your page. The header or footer text is hidden, and it does not print.

The Show Page Header and the Show Page Footer commands are accessed in the Chapter menu.

APPLICATIONS

Showing the rulers gives you an excellent guideline for drawing and placing frames and graphics. A moving dotted line in each ruler displays the exact location of the mouse. Hiding the rulers provides a slightly larger area to see your document on your screen.

Showing the column guides provide a guideline for drawing and placing frames and graphics in relation to the columns on the underlying page. Hiding the column guides removes the dotted lines, making the page look more like it will appear when actually printed.

Showing the pictures allows you to see how each picture will look on the page. By seeing the pictures that will appear in your document, you can better design the overall appearance of your documents. Showing the pictures, however, dramatically slows down the speed of Ventura. This is because Ventura must redraw or repaint the picture each time the screen is adjusted. Hiding the pictures replaces the actual picture with a gray box, and Ventura can redraw the screen much faster. When the pictures are hidden, they can still be printed in the normal manner. Because of how much this command speeds up Ventura, it is suggested that the pictures be hidden except when you are actually working with them.

Showing the tabs and returns allows you to see the positions of important hidden characters with the text. This is helpful when editing a document because you can make sure the special control characters are in the correct places. For example, if you are creating a columnar table with tabs but it is not aligning correctly, by showing the tabs, you can determine what position they are in and how and where they can be moved. Hiding the tabs and returns eliminates the display of all the special control characters (similar to Codes in the word processors), making the document easier to read and review.

Showing the loose lines allows you to see the lines in which the word spacing is too wide. This permits you to fix these lines by using a discretionary hyphen in the first word below the loose line. Hiding the loose lines prevents reverse video lines on your computer screen.

Headers and footers can be turned off or removed from specific pages within your documents. For example, where a chapter or module starts on a new page, the header can be turned off.

Being able to turn off the header or footer is also used in publications where full-page advertisements or artwork is used (such as magazines).

TYPICAL OPERATION

In this example, you turn off the footer, hide and show tabs and returns, the rulers, the column guides, and the pictures in the sample chapter &NEWS-P2.CHP. The operation begins with &NEWS- P2.CHP open. Use the command Open Chapter in the File menu to retrieve and open &NEWS-P2.CHP. You may need to adjust your screen using the scroll bars to make your computer look like the illustrations.

1. Click on the **Chapter** menu and click on **Show Page Footer**. Notice that the footer is now hidden.
2. Press **Ctrl-T** to Hide Tabs & Returns.

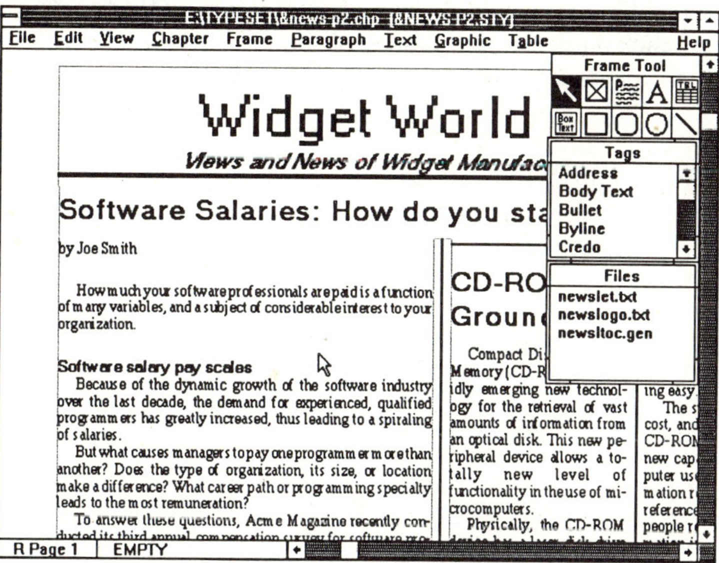

3. Press **Ctrl-T** to Show Tabs & Returns.
4. Click on the **View** menu and click on **Show Rulers**.

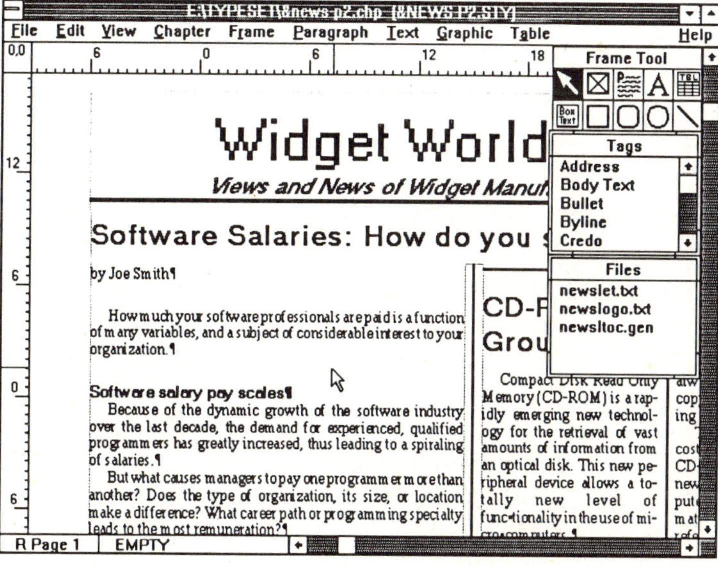

5. Click on the **View** menu and click on **Show Rulers**.
6. Click on the **View** menu and click on **Show Loose Lines**. Click on the **View** menu and click on **Show Loose Lines**.
7. Click on the **View** menu and click on **Show Column Guides**. Click on the **View** menu and click on **Show Column Guides**.
8. Turn to Module 84 to continue the learning sequence.

Module 73
SHOW ON ALL PAGES

DESCRIPTION

The Show On All Pages option causes a graphic created by Ventura to print on every page within the document.

Once a graphic has been created within Ventura, you can then select Show On All Pages from the Graphics menu. Ventura will then show the graphic on every page within your document.

If you want to stop a graphic from repeating on every page throughout your chapter, select this option. The graphic is then displayed only on the current page.

Graphics repeat or are shown in the same position on each page, regardless of whether or not it is a right or left page. Many times, you may want the graphic on every page, but in a different position on the right page than on the left page.

To make a graphic appear differently on all right and all left pages: Go to any left page, then select the Add Frame Tool from the Toolbox. Add a small new frame in the margin of your document. The placement of this frame is not important, as long as it does not interfere with any text on the page. Make sure the frame you just drew is still selected and then draw the graphic. Select the Repeating Frame option from the Frame menu, and make this frame a repeating frame on the left page only. Repeat these steps to place the graphic on right page only. See Module 61 for more information about the Repeating Frames.

APPLICATIONS

This command is useful when you need to place a graphic on every page within your document. For example, you may want to place a graphic line across the top of every page. You may also want to create custom column guides, or perhaps crop marks, on every page within your document. You may also want to place a graphic box at the top of every page.

Whenever a graphic must be placed on every page throughout the document, use Show On All Pages.

TYPICAL OPERATION

In this exercise, you create a graphic and then make it show on all pages. Load the default style sheet and select Normal view.

1. Click on the **Add Frame** Tool in the Toolbox.
2. Create a new frame in the middle of the page.
3. Select the **Circle** Tool from the Toolbox and click and drag the mouse down and to the right to create an ellipse. Release the mouse button. Your screen should resemble this illustration:

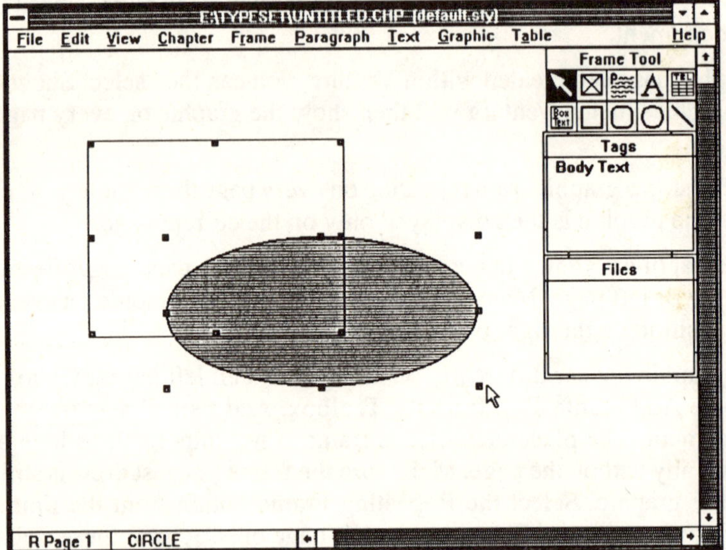

4. Click on the **Graphic** menu and select **Show On All Pages.**
5. Click on the **Chapter** menu and select **Insert/Remove Page.**
6. Select the **Insert New Page Before Current Page** from the dialog box, and then click on **OK.**
7. Notice the graphic created in step 3 now appears on page 1.
8. Select the **File** menu and click on **Revert to Saved.** Click on **OK** when prompted to revert back to the last saved version.
9. Turn to Module 78 to continue the learning sequence.

Module 74
SIZING & SCALING

DESCRIPTION

The Sizing & Scaling command controls the size, shape, and location of frames. The Sizing & Scaling command precisely controls the size and placement of a frame. It also allows you to exactly control the picture reduction or enlargement within a frame. Sizing & Scaling also controls the way text is formatted and flowed around a frame.

TIP:

When a new frame is created, Ventura automatically causes the text in your document to flow around it.

Use this command by first selecting the Frame mode. Then select a frame with the mouse cursor and select the Sizing & Scaling command from the Frame menu.

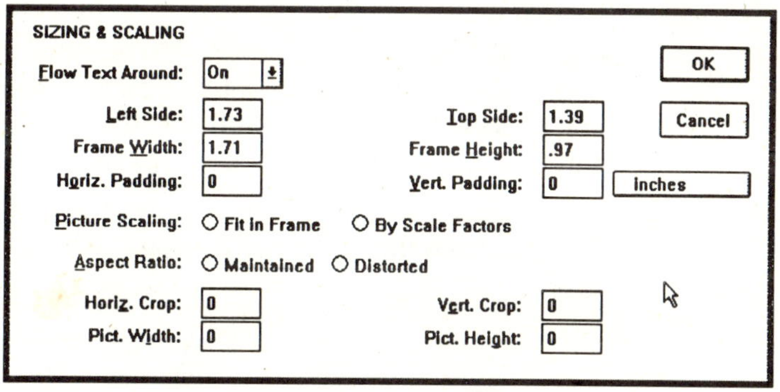

SIZING & SCALING

Flow Text Around: On | OK

Left Side: 1.73 | Top Side: 1.39 | Cancel

Frame Width: 1.71 | Frame Height: .97

Horiz. Padding: 0 | Vert. Padding: 0 | inches

Picture Scaling: ○ Fit in Frame ○ By Scale Factors

Aspect Ratio: ○ Maintained ○ Distorted

Horiz. Crop: 0 | Vert. Crop: 0

Pict. Width: 0 | Pict. Height: 0

The options in the Sizing & Scaling dialog box are:

Flow Text Around	Select whether or not the text is to flow around the frame. Selecting Off allows the text to flow under or behind the frame.
Left Side	Type the distance desired from the left edge of the page to the upper left corner of the frame.
Frame Width	Type the desired width of the frame.
Horizontal Padding	Type the distance between the left and right edges of the frame and the text that flows around the frame.
Top Side	Type the distance from the top edge of the page to the upper left corner of the frame.
Frame Height	Type the height of the frame.

Vertical Padding — Type the distance between the top and bottom edges of the frame and any text that flows around the frame.

Picture Scaling — Select Fit in Frame to alter the graphic both horizontally and vertically so it fits within the borders of the frame. If the frame proportions are different from those of the picture and if Aspect Ratio is set to Distorted, using this option distorts the picture to fill the frame, both on screen and when printed. If Aspect Ratio is set to Maintained, the picture fills the frame as much as possible without changing its vertical or horizontal proportions. Select By Scale Factors to precisely control the vertical and horizontal proportions of the graphic. Set the size of the picture by using Scale Width and Scale Height (see the illustration in the Typical Operation section). If the picture is scaled by factors, you can crop the picture by moving the graphic within the frame with the X Crop Offset and Y Crop Offset options.

NOTE

Use the mouse for cropping a picture with By Scale Factors for Picture Scaling. To do this, press and hold Alt, click and hold on the picture, move the picture within the frame to the desired cropping location, and release both the Alt key and the mouse button.

Aspect Ratio — Select Maintained to keep the horizontal and vertical proportions of an imported graphic equal to those of the original graphic. Select Distorted to fill the frame with the picture, regardless of how this distorts the proportions of the graphic.

A Ventura frame can be precisely placed on a page. For example, you could position a 3 x 2.50 inch frame exactly 2 inches from the top of the page and 2 inches from the left edge of the paper.

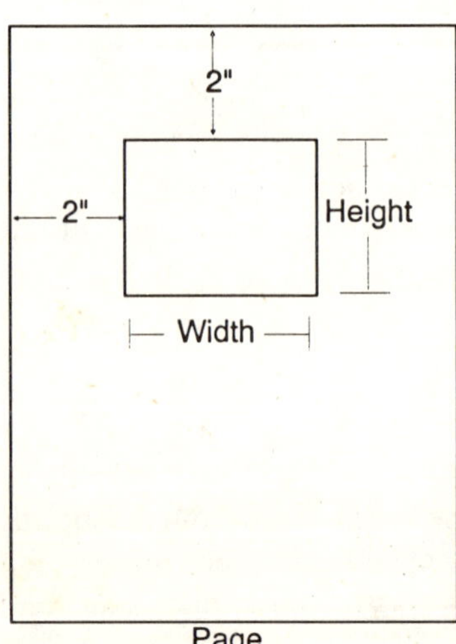

Horizontal Crop	Type the distance to move the graphic horizontally within the frame.
Picture Width	Type the exact width desired for the graphic if By Scale Factors for Picture Scaling has been selected.
Vertical Crop	Type the distance to move the graphic vertically within the frame.
Picture Height	Type the exact height for the graphic if By Scale Factors for Picture Scaling has been selected.

NOTE

To be sure that your scanned images are always scaled correctly, select Picture Scaling: By Scale Factors and Aspect Ratio: Maintained. Select OK, and your picture will print exactly as scanned.

APPLICATIONS

The Sizing & Scaling command is used to place frames and pictures in a precise location within your document. You specify in inches or picas and points the exact location where the frame is to be located on your page.

This command also allows you to superimpose text on pictures. This is a design technique that will allow you to have the text flow under your pictures.

The Sizing & Scaling command also allows you to crop pictures, as well as scale them, either in a maintained or distorted format.

TYPICAL OPERATION

In this operation, you adjust the sizing and scaling of a graphic picture and use your mouse to crop the picture. You work with maintaining and distorting its original size. The instructions begin with SCOOP.CHP open.

1. Press **Ctrl-U** to select the Frame Tool.
2. Click on the frame on the page that contains the COLUMBIA.GEM drawing. Your screen should resemble the following illustration:

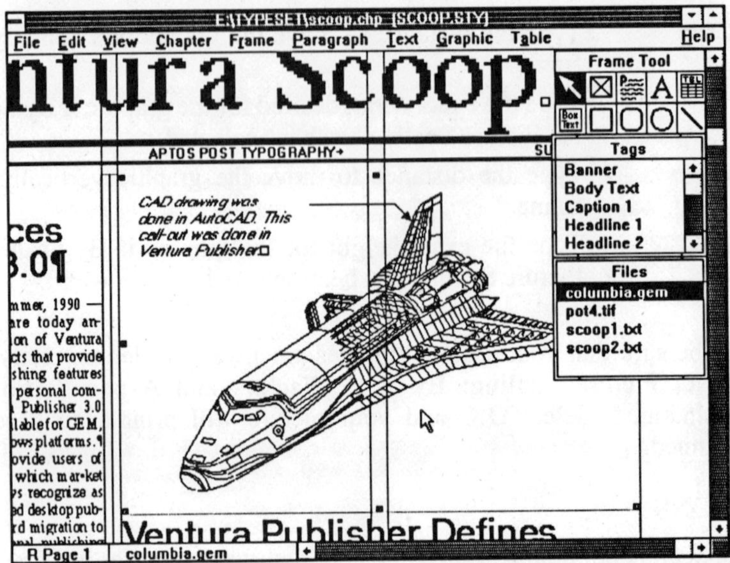

3. Click on the **Frame** menu and click on **Sizing & Scaling** to display the Sizing & Scaling dialog box.
4. Select **By Scale Factors** for Picture Scaling and **Maintained** for Aspect Ratio. Your screen should resemble this illustration:

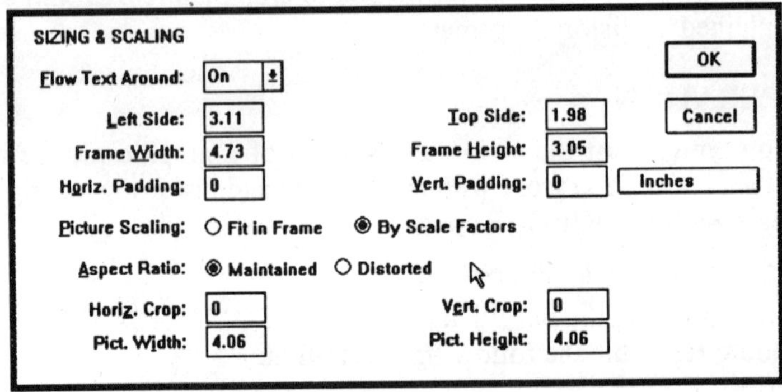

5. Click **OK**. Your screen should resemble the following illustration:

6. Click on the **Frame** menu and click on **Sizing & Scaling** to display the Sizing & Scaling dialog box.
7. Select **By Scale Factors** for Picture Scaling and **Distorted** for Aspect Ration. Click **OK**. Your screen should resemble this illustration:

8. Point to the middle of the frame. Press and hold **Alt** and click and hold on the left mouse button. The mouse pointer will change shape. Move the picture to crop it. Your screen should resemble the following illustration:

9. Release **Alt** and the mouse button.
10. Click on the **File** menu, select **Revert to Saved**, then click **OK** to ignore the changes.
11. Turn to Module 29 to continue the learning sequence.

Module 75
SPACING

DESCRIPTION

The Spacing command controls the space between lines of text and paragraphs and also sets temporary margins. The amount of space between lines—called leading (pronounced led-ding)—is adjusted and set with this command.

The amount of space entered, as well as the temporary margins, are for only the left or the right pages in the chapter. The settings for the spacing must be copied to the facing page if you want the paragraph style to be the exact same on both pages.

To access this command, the Paragraph Tool must be selected, and a paragraph must be selected. The Spacing command can then be accessed in the Paragraph menu. The changes made with this command affect the paragraph tag assigned to the selected paragraph. When a change is made to a paragraph tag, it affects all text marked with that paragraph tag in the document, as well as in other documents that use the same style sheet.

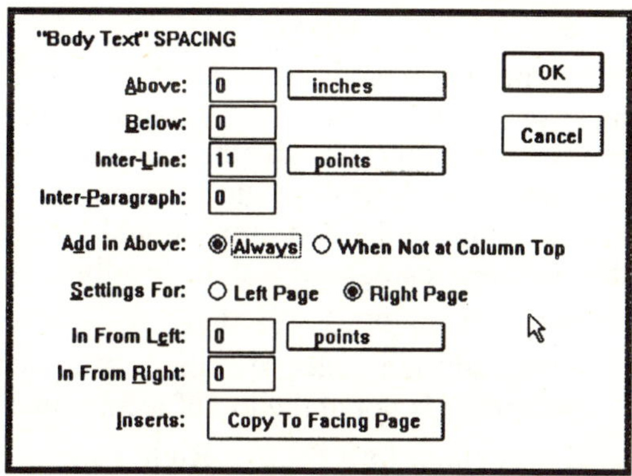

The Spacing dialog box offers these options:

Above	Enter the amount of space to insert above a paragraph.
Below	Enter the amount of space to insert below a paragraph.

TIP:

The Above and Below commands only insert the space you specify between different paragraphs. For example, if your entire document were nothing but Body Text, the amounts entered in Above and Below would have no effect. But the space would be added between two different paragraph tags, such as Body Text and Headline.

Inter-Line	Enter the amount of space required between the baseline of the characters on one line and the baseline of the characters on the next line (this is the leading).

TIP:

Typography experts agree that the correct line spacing should be the amount of the type size and approximately 20% additional space. For example, for 10 point type, set the line spacing (Inter-Line) to 12 point.

NOTE

Ventura automatically creates adequate and proper interline spacing based on the size of the type chosen. For most publications, this interline spacing inserted by Ventura will be adequate.

Inter-Paragraph	Enter the amount of space desired between paragraphs, but only if both paragraph tags have the identical Inter-Paragraph space setting.

NOTE

The Inter-Paragraph command is useful for those paragraphs where you want the space between similar paragraphs to be greater than the space between the paragraph and other paragraphs. This setting is extremely helpful in such applications as business reports, where the paragraphs making up the body text should be spaced further apart than the body text paragraph and the headline.

Add In Above	Select either Always or When Not at Column Top. Ventura will either add the space specified at all times, or only when the paragraph is not at the top of a column or page.
Settings For	Select either Left Page or Right Page.
In From Left	A temporary margin can be created by entering the amount of offset desired in this option. Enter the amount of offset desired for the left paragraph margin.
In From Right	Just like the In From Left option, In From Right sets a temporary right margin for a paragraph. Enter the amount of offset desired for the right paragraph margin.
Inserts	Select Copy to Facing Page to copy the specifications to the facing page.

The Spacing command provides a lot of typographical control. Do not overlead or underlead your paragraphs. Too much or too little space between paragraphs can make your text very difficult to read.

APPLICATIONS

Paragraph spacing is important to make your documents easy to read. Too little space between lines can make the text impossible to read, especially with computer-generated type on a laser printer.

Adding space between paragraphs is an important design tool. For some documents, you will want additional space between paragraphs, while in other documents, you will not want much space between paragraphs. With the Spacing command, you are able to precisely determine how much space is desired or required between your text lines and paragraphs.

TYPICAL OPERATION

In this operation, you adjust the spacing in the Body Text. The sample chapter &NEWS-P2.CHP is used. The example begins with &NEWS-P2.CHP open. Use the Open Chapter command in the File menu to open &NEWS-P2.CHP. You may need to adjust your screen using the scroll bars to make your computer look like the illustrations.

1. Press **Ctrl-I** to select the Paragraph Tool.
2. Click on the third paragraph in the left column.
3. Click on the **Paragraph** menu and click on **Spacing** to display the Spacing dialog box.
4. Type **22.00** points for Inter-Line and press **Enter**. Your screen should resemble this illustration:

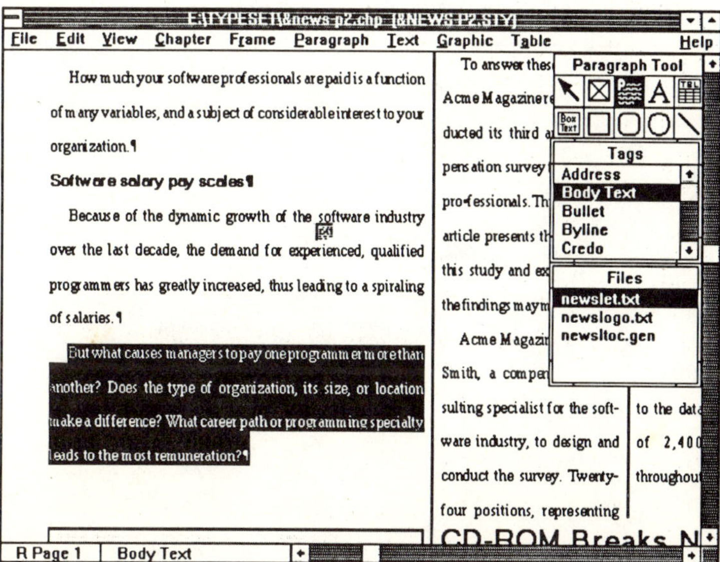

Notice how difficult this text would be to read with the excessive interline spacing added (leading).

5. Click on the **Paragraph** menu and click on **Spacing** to display the Spacing dialog box.
6. Type **07.00** points for Inter-Line and press **Enter**. Your screen should resemble this illustration:

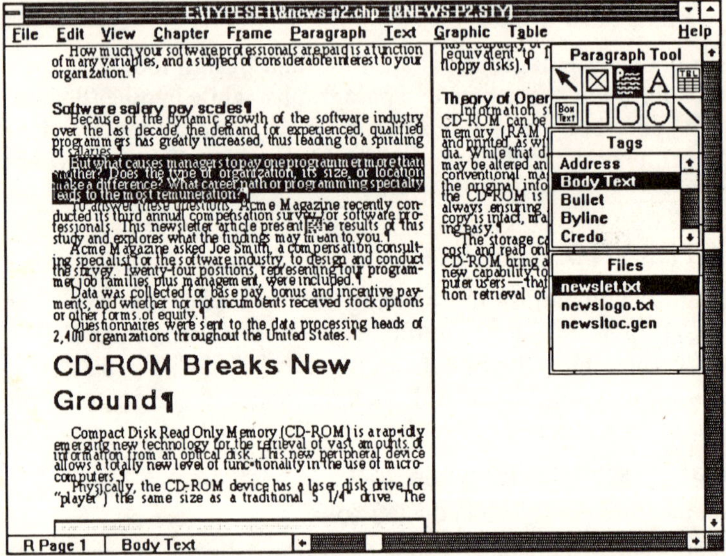

Notice how it is nearly impossible to read the text due to insufficient leading.

7. Click on the **File** menu and click on **Revert to Saved** and click on **OK** when prompted to revert back to the last saved version.
8. Turn to Module 70 to continue the learning sequence.

Module 76
SPECIAL EFFECTS

DESCRIPTION

The Special Effects command allows the addition of a big first character (also sometimes called a drop cap or dropped capital) at the beginning of a paragraph. This command can also establish a bullet at the beginning of a paragraph. The font used for the bullet or the big first character can be selected independently from the rest of the paragraph.

The Special Effects command is located in the Paragraph menu. Before it can be accessed, you must be using the Paragraph Tool and a paragraph must be selected. The changes made with this command affect all paragraphs marked with that paragraph tag in the document, as well as any other chapters using the same style sheet.

The big first character is normally used at the beginning of an article or chapter in such publications as magazines, newsletters, books, or newspapers. Only the first paragraph contains the large first character. To create this special effect, select the first paragraph (normally Body Text) and then select Add New Tag from the Paragraph menu. Then call the new tag First Paragraph, and finally, add the special effects to the new tag.

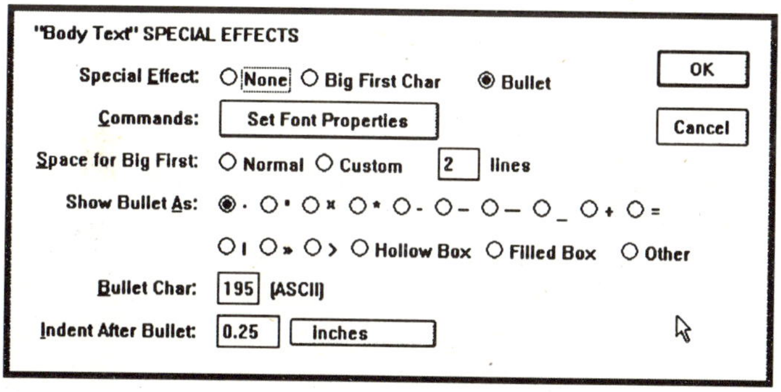

"Body Text" SPECIAL EFFECTS
Special Effect: None / Big First Char / Bullet — OK
Commands: Set Font Properties — Cancel
Space for Big First: Normal / Custom 2 lines
Show Bullet As: · • × * - – — _ + = | » › Hollow Box / Filled Box / Other
Bullet Char: 195 (ASCII)
Indent After Bullet: 0.25 inches

The Special Effects dialog box offers these options:

- Special Effect
- Commands
- Space For Big First
- Show Bullet As
- Bullet Character
- Indent After Bullet

Each of these options provides the following settings:

Special Effect — Select either None, Big First Char, or Bullet. Select Big First Char to add a big first character or drop capital to the front of your paragraph. Select Bullet to add a bullet to the front of the paragraph. Select None to remove an existing special effect from a paragraph tag.

Commands — Select Set Font Properties to display the Fonts Settings dialog box. The fonts selection available will depend on the equipment you are using. Select the typeface, size, style, color, and shift up or down (Zero Shift usually works best).

Space for Big First — Select either Normal or Custom. This command determines how many lines of text the first character will occupy. Normal allows Ventura to create the number of lines automatically. Custom allows you to select the number of lines the Big First Character will occupy.

Show Bullet As — Select the character to be used as your bullet from those displayed. If you want to use your own special character, select Other.

Bullet Char — If you chose Other in the Show Bullet As selection, you can specify a number for the ASCII character you want to use as your bullet. For a list of the ASCII characters and their decimal number equivalents, see Appendix E.

Indent After Bullet — Enter the amount of space between the bullet and the text following the bullet. If you do not specify some space, the bullet will overlap the first word in your paragraph.

APPLICATIONS

Drop caps and bullets draw attention to the beginning of a paragraph. They are used to enhance the appearance of a document.

Bullets are used to help make items on lists stand out. By using Ventura's Special Effects command, you do not need to use "typewriter style" bullets, such as *. Being able to use real typographic bullets, such as those used throughout this book, allows you to add impact to your documents.

TYPICAL OPERATION

In this example, you create a new paragraph tag and assign a special effect to the paragraph. The sample chapter &NEWS-P2.CHP is used. The example begins with &NEWS-P2.CHP open. Press Ctrl-N.

1. Press **Ctrl-I** to select the Paragraph Tool.
2. Press **Ctrl-2** to display the Add New Tag dialog box.
3. Type **First Paragr** for Name to Add and press **Enter**.

4. Click on the first paragraph. Click on **First Paragr** in the Tags Window to assign this tag to the selected paragraph.
5. Click on the **Paragraph** menu and click on **Special Effects** to display the Special Effects dialog box.
6. Select **Big First Char** for the Special Effect.
7. Select **Set Font Properties** for Commands to display the Font dialog box.
8. Click on **Swiss** for Face, **18** for Size, **Bold** for Style, and **Black** for Color. (Depending on your printer, you may need to select a different typeface.)
9. Press **Enter** to return to the Special Effects dialog box. Then press **Enter** to see the page. Click outside the margin to remove the highlight. Your screen should resemble this illustration:

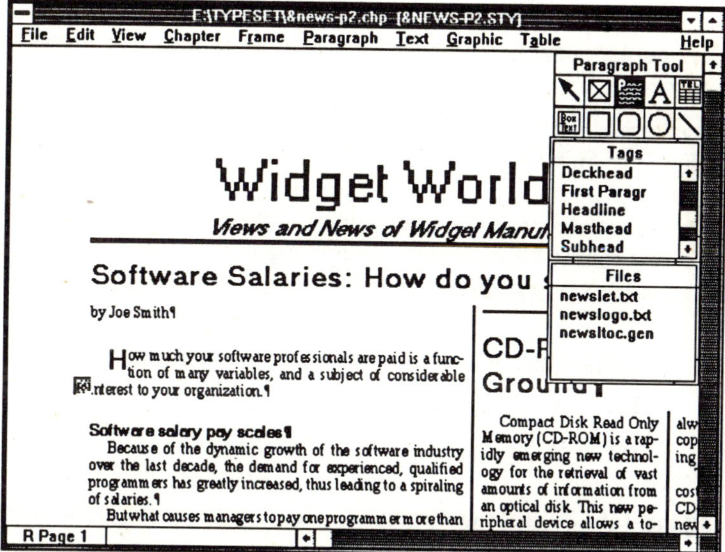

10. Click on the **File** menu and select **Revert to Saved**. Then click on **OK** when the message box appears asking if you want to save or abandon the changes.
11. Turn to Module 67 to continue the learning sequence.

Module 77
TAB SETTINGS

DESCRIPTION

The Tabs Setting command establishes the position, type, and number of horizontal tabs for a paragraph tag. A total of 16 tabs can be set for one tag. Tabs can be left-aligned, centered, right-aligned, or decimal.

TIP:

Ventura places each tab relative to the left column, and **not** the left edge of the page.

The Tab Settings command is employed by first selecting a paragraph and then selecting the Tabs Settings command from the Paragraph menu. Ventura must be in Paragraph mode before a paragraph can be selected. The changes made with this command affect the paragraph tag associated with the selected text. When a change is made to a paragraph tag, it affects all text marked with that paragraph tag in the document, as well as in other documents that use the same style sheet.

TIP:

A line of tabs must end with a carriage return or line break (press Ctrl-Enter for a line break).

A leader character can also be assigned to fill the blank space created in the front of each tab.

After selecting the Tabs Settings command, the Tab Settings dialog box appears.

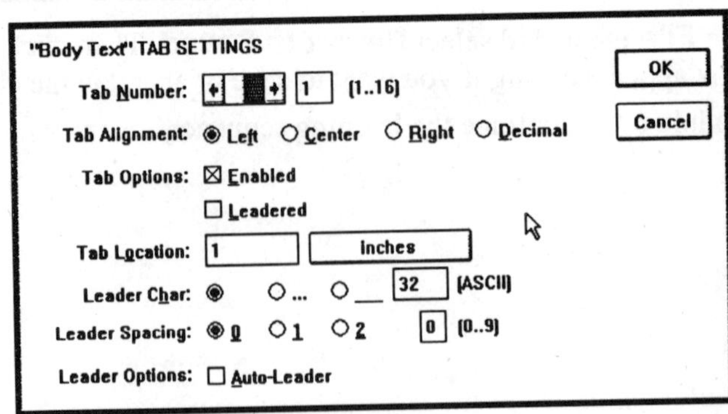

The Tabs Settings dialog box provides these options:

Tab Number	Select the number of the tab to be set. Use the arrows to scroll through the tab numbers. Up to 16 tabs can be operative at one time. Each tab can be selectively turned on or off. For example, tabs 1, 3, 4 could be on and tabs 2, and 8 through 16 could be off.
Tab Alignment	Select the alignment of the current tab being set to either Left, Center, Right, or Decimal. Left, Center, and Right align the tabbed text at the left, center, and right of the current tab. Decimal aligns numbers at the decimal character in the number. The default decimal character is a period. To change the character, use the Set Preferences command (see Module 69).

TIP:

Justification overrides tab settings. Therefore, tabs do not work when the paragraph has been tagged with justified alignment. To change the alignment of a justified paragraph so a tab can be set, use the Alignment command located in the Paragraph menu.

Tab Options	Select Enabled if the tab is to be used. Select Leadered if a leader is to be placed by the tab setting. This text demonstrates tabs without leader characters and tabs with leader characters. Without leaders One Two Three With leaders One....................Two....................Three
Tab Location	Enter the distance from the left-hand margin to the position of current tab. This is not the distance between tabs, but always the distance from the left margin to the tab.
Dimensions	Select the preferred unit of measurement.
Leader Char	Select a leader character or define one of your own. The options are spaces, periods (....) or underlines (______). Define your own leaders by selecting Other and typing the decimal value for the ASCII character to use. For a list of ASCII characters and their decimal equivalents see Appendix E. This text demonstrates a leader character of . separated by no spaces and separated by two spaces. No Spaces..............One...................Two...................Three Two Spaces . . . . . . One. . . . . Two. . . . . .Three

Leader Spacing — Select the number of spaces (0 to 9) desired between the leader characters.

Leader Options — Select Auto-leader to turn the auto-leader on. Auto-leader automatically places the selected leader characters from the end of the last line in the paragraph to the right margin. This is useful when creating forms, such as:

Name: ________________________________

Address: ______________________________

City, State, Zip: ________________________

The auto-leader would automatically include the lines.

NOTE

To create paragraph indents or outdents, use the Alignment command located within the Paragraph menu. Do not use the Tab Setting command to create indents or outdents, because tabs in a paragraph disable the automatic word wrap function of Ventura. In addition, a tab line cannot wrap to a second line.

The Tabs Setting command can also be used to format simple equations. To do so, set a center tab for the position on the page where the center of the equation is to appear. Then, press Tab and type the equation. The equation will automatically center itself at the tab stop.

APPLICATIONS

Tabs in Ventura work much like tabs in a word processor or a typewriter. Tab settings are used to align text or numbers for simple tables. Whenever a horizontal tab character is encountered within the text, Ventura positions the next character at the next tab location. By doing so, simple tables can easily be created.

Text in a table can be aligned to the right, left, or center of a tab position. In addition, numbers can be aligned on a decimal.

Tabs with dot leaders are used to create simple forms and questionnaires.

When using proportionally spaced fonts, Ventura tables cannot be formatted by using spaces between entries. This is particularly important if the text has been imported into Ventura from a spreadsheet. You must use tabs to make the text align properly.

TYPICAL OPERATION

In this operation, you create a table using tabs and then save the file. The instructions begin with a blank screen. Use the DEFAULT.STY style sheet. If necessary, use both the New command and Load Diff. Style command in the File menu. Change view to Normal.

1. Click on the **Add Frame** Tool.
2. Draw a frame that is the width of the column.

3. Press **Ctrl-O** to select the Text Tool. Click in the frame and type the following information. (Press **Tab** each time you see <Tab> and press **Enter** each time you see <Enter>.)

   Seminar<Tab>**Location**<Tab>**# of Participants**<Enter>
   Desktop Publishing Overview<Tab>**Philadelphia**<Tab>**22**<Enter>
   Introduction to Ventura<Tab>**Washington, DC**<Tab>**31**<Enter>
   Advanced Ventura Training<Tab>**New Orleans**<Tab>**19**<Enter>
   The Desktop Publishing Operations<Tab>**San Jose**<Tab>**26**<Enter>

When you are finished, your screen should resemble this illustration:

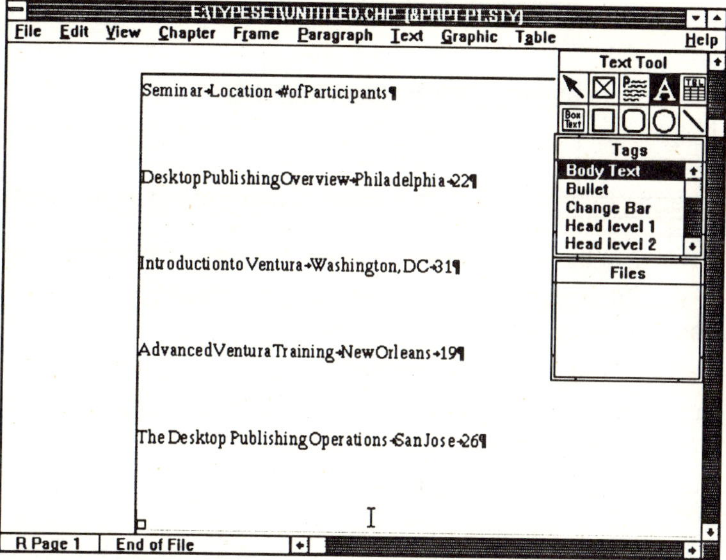

Notice that the tabs are represented by right arrows. If they are not visible, select Show Tabs & Returns in the View menu.

4. Press **Ctrl-S** to display the Save File As dialog box. Type **tabs1** and press **Enter**.
5. Click on the **File** menu and click on **Save Style As**. Type **tabs** and press **Enter**.
6. Press **Ctrl-I** to select the Paragraph Tool.
7. Click on **Add New Tag** in the Paragraph menu to display the Add New Tag dialog box.
8. Type **Tabs** for Tag Name to Add and press **Enter**.
9. Press and hold **Shift** and click on each line of text.

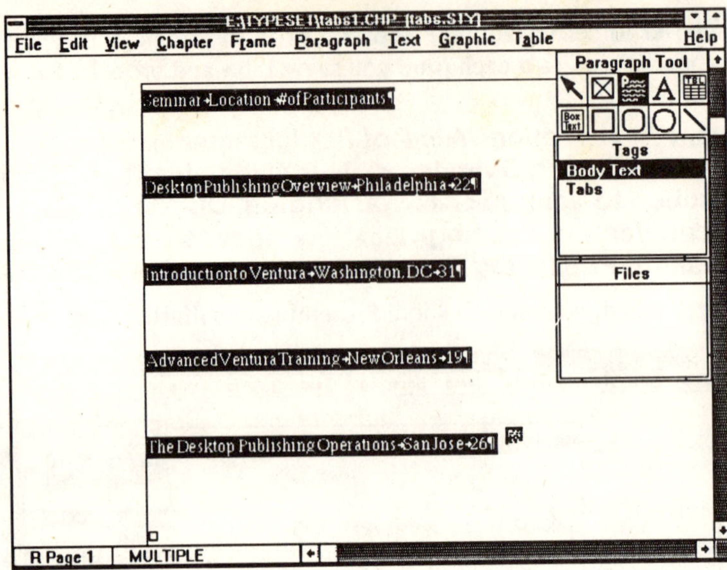

10. Click on **Tabs** in the Tag Window to assign the tag to the selected paragraphs.
11. Click on the **Paragraph** menu and select **Alignment** to display the Alignment dialog box.
12. Select **Left** for Alignment and click **OK**.
13. Click on the **Paragraph** menu and select **Font** to display the Font dialog box. Change the size of the font to **8** points. Click **OK**.
14. Point to the **Paragraph** menu and select **Tab Settings** to display the Tab Settings dialog box.
15. Select **1** for Tab Number, **Left** for Tab Type, and **2** (inches) for Tab Location.
16. Select **2** for Tab Number, **Left** for Tab Type, and **3.5** (inches) for Tab Location.
17. Press **Enter**. Notice the words have aligned.
18. Click on a white area outside the paragraphs. Your screen should resemble the following illustration:

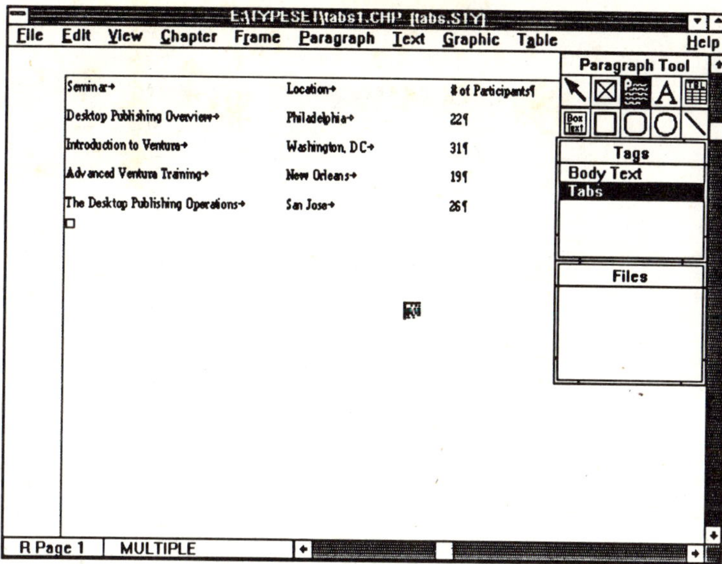

19. Click on the **File** menu and click on **Save**.
20. Turn to Module 14 to continue the learning sequence.

Module 78
TABLE MENU

DESCRIPTION

A table is any text that is formatted in rows and columns. A cell is the intersection of a row and a column. The following represents a table with three rows, three columns, and nine cells.

	Column 1	Column 2	Column 3
Row 1			
Row 2			
Row 3			

Spreadsheets are an example of row and column formatting. One major difference between Ventura and the common spreadsheet is the ability of Ventura to have more than one line of text within a cell. In addition, Ventura allows the cells to be formatted in a different style. Ruling lines can also be placed above, below, or around a cell or group of cells.

Sales Volume Breakdown By Divisions		
Division	Last Year	This Year
Northern	$554,001.00	$667,127.87
Southern	$589,241.06	$1,991,812.84
Eastern	$785,549.54	$1,354,458.65
Western	$209,812.19	$654,331.12

NOTE

Whenever a table is created in Ventura, a text file is created. The information for the table is stored in the text file.

The Table menu offers these command options:

Insert Row
Insert Column
Join Cells
Split Cells
Set Tint
Set Column Width
Normal Rules
Custom Rules
Insert New Table
Change Settings

Creating a Table

Ventura's Toolbox includes a tool called the Table Tool. This tool permits the insertion and editing of tables.

A table can be inserted between paragraphs. A table cannot be placed within a paragraph. After a table is created, text can be inserted into the table by using the regular Text Tool. Once a table has been created, the structure of the table can be changed by switching back to the Table Edit menu.

To create a table, first select the Table Tool. Place the table cursor between the two paragraphs where the table is to be inserted.

NOTE

The location of a table is marked within a document by a short horizontal line.

Next, select Insert New Table from the Table menu. The Insert/Edit Table dialog box appears:

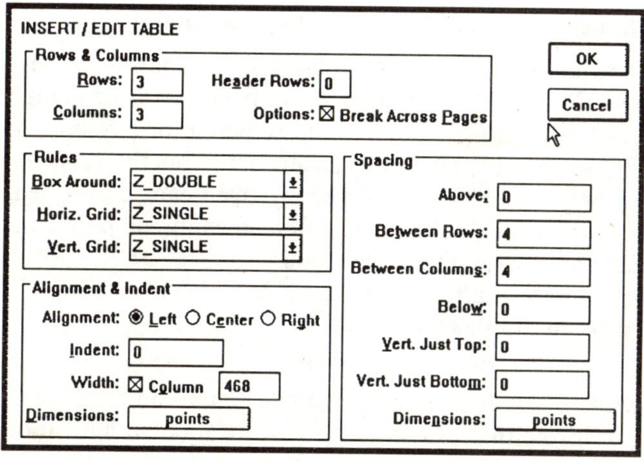

NOTE

A table can also be inserted when in the Text mode. After positioning the cursor before or after a paragraph—never within it—select Insert Special Item in the Text menu. Select Table from the secondary menu. The Insert/Edit Table dialog box appears.

For more information about this dialog box, see Module 42.

Entering Text in a Table

To enter text into a table, first change to the Text mode. After positioning the text cursor, simply type the information for the table. As text is added, new lines are automatically created and row height increases to accommodate these new lines.

TIP:

Ventura allows only one paragraph per cell within a table. Use line breaks (Ctrl-Enter) to create additional lines of text within a cell.

Text can be cut, copied, and pasted within a table just as it can anywhere else in Ventura. The cursor movement keys can be used to move the text cursor anywhere within the table.

Editing a Table

To edit a table, first select the Table Tool. Then move the Table Edit cursor to the first cell of the table. This is the cell in the upper left of the table. The next step is to press and hold the mouse button and then move the mouse to the lower right-hand corner of the cell at the end of the portion of the table you wish to select. When the mouse button is released, the selected portion of the table appears outlined in gray.

By following this procedure, any horizontal or vertical line between cells in the table, any single cell, any continuous group of cells, or the entire table can be selected for editing.

TIP:

Only one group of cells can be selected at any one time.

Once the table has been selected for editing, it can be modified to:

- Add a new column or row. Move the table cursor to the desired position, click, and then select Ins Row or Ins Column from the Table menu.
- Apply cell attributes. Following the selection of any horizontal line, vertical line, cell, or group of cells, apply an attribute from the Table menu. For example, cells can be joined together, or a background can be assigned.
- Change all the cells in the table. After selecting the portion of the table, select Edit Table Settings in the Table menu.
- Change column width. After the cells have been selected, choose Set Column Width from the Table menu.

TIP:

The width of a column can be changed by pressing and holding Alt while dragging the column to the new location with the mouse.

- Cut, copy, or paste rows or columns. The entire table could also be deleted.

- Tag a cell. A tag can be applied to text anywhere within a cell. The attributes of the tag (spacing, special effects, leader characters, color, alignment, etc.) can then be assigned to the text within the table.

APPLICATIONS

Ventura's Table commands make it easy to create charts, forms, and tables. These items are used to make information easier to interpret. By using the Table Tool, you can instantly create any table or chart.

These charts are used to display information neatly and uniformly. They can be used to create catalog price sheets or detailed information.

Tables help to enhance the appearance of information.

They can also be used to create complicated or simple forms. For example, tables could be used to create attendance sheets, purchase orders, or invoices.

TYPICAL OPERATION

In this activity, you examine the contents of the Table menu.

1. Point to the **Table** Tool in the Toolbox and click once.
2. Point to the **Table** menu and click once. Your screen should resemble this illustration:

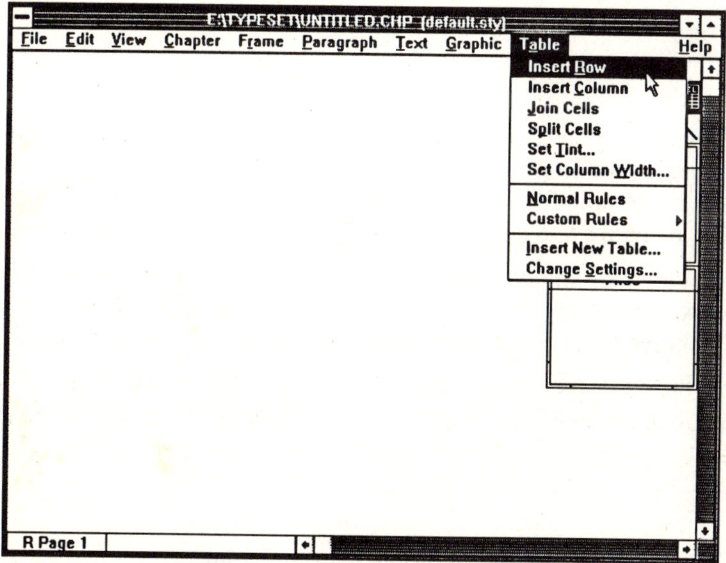

3. Examine the various options available within the Table menu.
4. Move the mouse anywhere outside of the Table menu and click once to dismiss the Table menu.
5. Turn to Module 42 to continue the learning sequence.

Module 79
TEXT EDITING

DESCRIPTION

The Text Editing feature in Ventura works like a word processor. It is a limited word processor and does not have the power to perform complicated functions like other regular word processors.

Text Editing allows you to create, edit, and delete text. With this function, you can change the text attributes. The attributes that can be changed include:

Normal
Bold
Italic
Overscore
Small Caps
Subscript
Superscript
Strike-thru
Underline and Double Underline

NOTE

When using the Text Tool, changes for the text attributes and fonts can be made to a single character or to blocks of text. In contrast, the Paragraph Tool changes *all* attributes, including line spacing, for *the entire paragraph.*

In addition to changing the attributes of text, the Text Tool allows the kerning of text, inserting index references, frame anchors, and footnotes. Tabs, carriage returns, line breaks, and nonbreak spaces can also be edited.

To edit when the Text Tool is selected, simply move the mouse cursor to the item you need to edit. Click and hold the mouse button, and drag the mouse to the right. Release the mouse button when the item has been selected. The area selected will be highlighted. You can then edit or change the selected text.

TIP:

To mark a block of text, you can also move the mouse cursor to the beginning of the text you want to select and press and release the mouse button. Move the mouse cursor to the end of the text to be selected, press and hold the Shift key, and then click the mouse button.

When selecting text, you cannot select text across page or frame boundaries.

Although you can create text files directly with this function, it is advisable to use an external word processor, such as WordPerfect, Microsoft Word, DisplayWrite 4, or WordStar, to create your text files. Such word processors make the preparation of text much easier than using Ventura's limited word processing functions. For example, the lack of search and replace, spell checking, and block movement functions in Ventura makes it an unlikely choice to prepare text. Remember that Ventura is primarily a page composition program, and not a word processor.

The Text Tool is accessed by selecting it in the Toolbox. It can also be accessed by pressing Ctrl-O.

APPLICATIONS

Text editing is used to change the attributes of your prepared text. For example, if you typed a headline in uppercase and lowercase but now decide it would look better in all uppercase, you can select the text and choose uppercase to change the text. In the same way, the text could be underlined, bolded, or italicized.

TIP:

Selecting Normal in the Text menu clears all attributes within the selected text and returns the text to the attributes established by the paragraph tag.

Text Editing also permits a font change of text within a paragraph. Sometimes, for emphasis, you may want to change a type font within a sentence. To make the change, Text Editing is used and Set Font is chosen from the Text menu.

You can assign as many attributes as you desire to text that has been selected. The list of possible attributes available are displayed in the Text menu.

NOTE

When you edit a text file with Ventura's Text Editing function, the text file is changed by Ventura. If you were to delete a block of text with Ventura, it would delete the entire block of text from your text file. When the text attributes are changed, Ventura places markers within the text file. For this reason, you should always make a backup copy of the text file *before* importing it into Ventura.

TYPICAL OPERATION

In this operation, you edit text by adding words, deleting, and changing the appearance of the text in the <R1-P1.CHP chapter. The instructions begin with the chapter open. Use the Open Chapter command located in the File menu to retrieve the <R1- P1.CHP. Press Ctrl-N to select Normal view. Use the scroll bars to adjust your computer screen to match the illustrations.

1. Press **Ctrl-O** to select the Text Editing mode.
2. Move the cursor to the "w" in the word "widget" in the first sentence. Click once.
3. Type **Super-Charged** and press **Spacebar**.

4. Move the cursor to the "f" in the word "found" in the second sentence.
5. Click and drag the mouse to highlight the word "found" and then press **Del**.
6. Type **determined**. Your screen should resemble the following illustration:

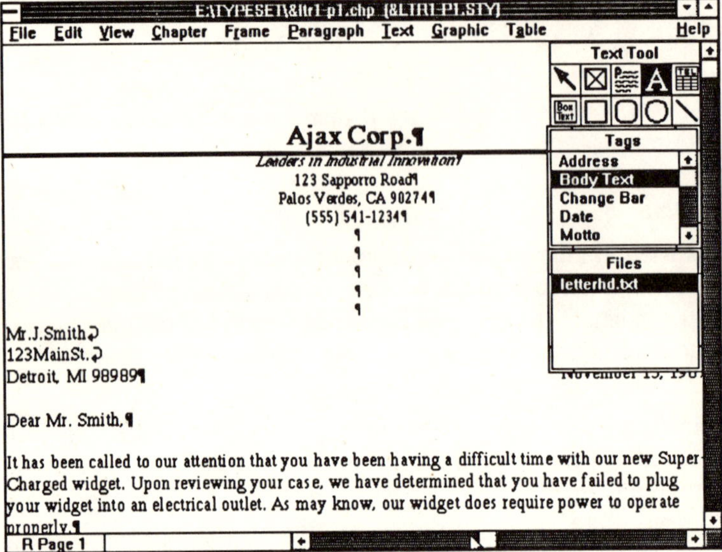

7. Scroll down to the "J" in John Smith, and click once. Point the cursor after the "r" in Manager, press and hold **Shift**, and click the mouse button.
8. Click on **Bold** in the Text menu. Your screen should resemble the following illustration:

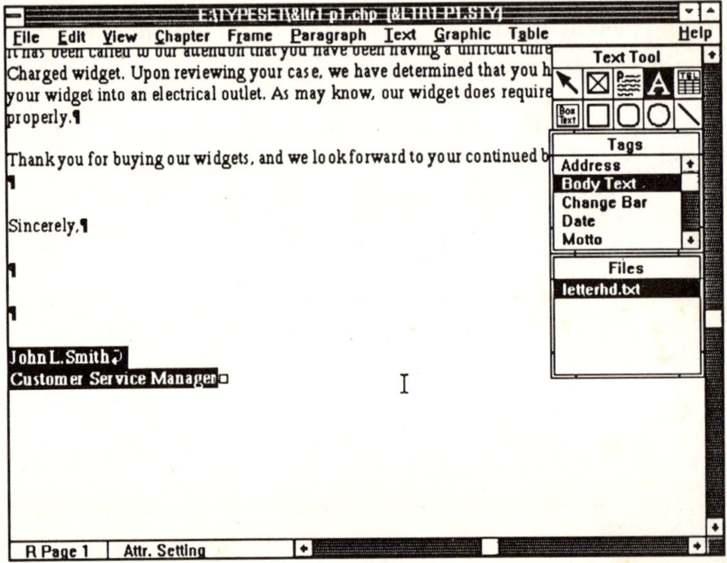

9. Click on the **File** menu and select **Revert to Saved**. Click on **OK** to Abandon.
10. Turn to Module 17 to continue the learning sequence.

Module 80
TEXT MENU

DESCRIPTION

The Text menu allows you to change the attributes or characteristics of text. The characteristics of text that can be changed include such things as bold, italic, underline, and font changes.

The Text menu also allows you to Insert Special Items, which include Box Characters, Footnotes, Index Entry, Equations, Frame Anchors, Cross References, Marker Names, Variable Defs, and Tables.

The options available in the Text menu are:

Insert Special Item	Subscript
Edit Special Item	Underline
Normal	Double Underline
Bold	Strikethru
Italic	Overscore
Small	Set Font Attributes
Superscript	Change Text To

To access the items available in the Text menu, you must first select the Text Tool in the Toolbox. To select the Text Tool, click on it with the mouse, or press Ctrl-O. Then you must select some text in order to access the options within the Text menu.

To select text, move the mouse cursor to the desired text, and click and hold the mouse button, then move the mouse to highlight the text. Release the mouse button to complete the text selection.

APPLICATIONS

The Text menu provides you with the commands needed to maintain extensive control over pieces of text that are used in a Ventura chapter.

Each section of text can have its own set of formatting attributes, including its own appearance of underlines, bolding, or italics.

By using the Insert Special Item option within the Text menu, you can also create true typographic symbols, such as box characters and fractions.

The options available within the Text menu allow you to enhance the appearance of your documents by adding attributes as needed. For example, you might be creating a newsletter and want to bold someone's name. By using the Text Tool to highlight or select the text, then accessing the Text menu to select Bold, you can easily apply the bold attribute to the text.

TYPICAL OPERATION

In this example, you access the Text menu, after selecting Text mode, and review the various commands available within the menu. The sample chapter document SCOOP.CHP is used. The example begins with SCOOP.CHP open and in use. If you do not have this chapter open, use the Open Chapter command in the File menu to retrieve and open SCOOP.CHP.

1. Click on the **Text** Tool within the Toolbox.
2. Press **Ctrl-N** to see the page in normal view.
3. Adjust your screen, by using the scroll bars, to position the page so you can see the lower right corner of the first page. Your screen should resemble this illustration:

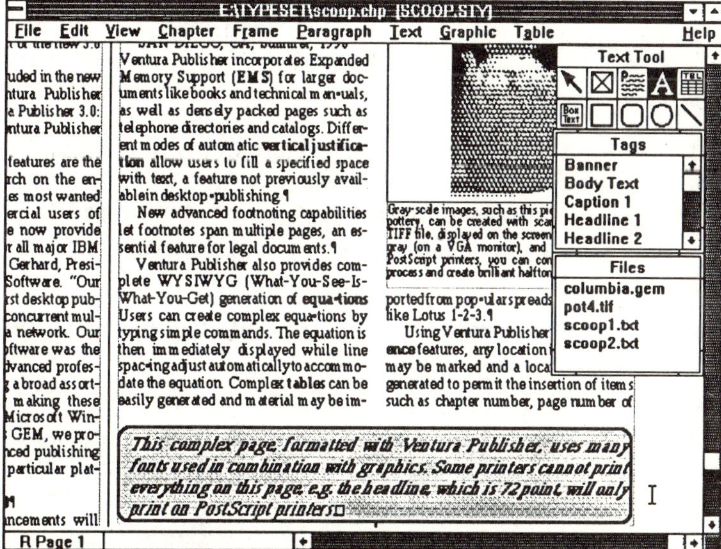

4. Click and drag your mouse anywhere within the text being displayed on your screen. Some of the text is now selected.
5. Click on the **Text** menu and notice the selections available. The text selected or highlighted could have any of these attributes assigned to it.
6. Move the mouse anywhere outside the Text menu and click once. The Text menu disappears.
7. Turn to Module 33 to continue the learning sequence.

Module 81
TOOLBOX

DESCRIPTION

The Toolbox is the key to creating a Ventura document. There are ten tools available in the Toolbox.

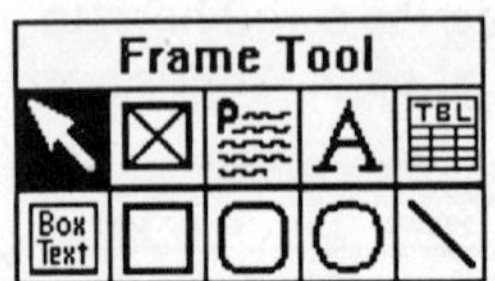

The use of each of these ten tools are:

Selection Tool	This tool lets you select any frame or graphic. It allows you to place text or pictures into any frame or onto any page. This tool is also used to cut, copy, or paste frames and graphics.
Add Frame	This tool is used to create new frames.

NOTE

Once a frame is created with this tool, the Frame Tool is automatically selected by Ventura.

Paragraph Tool	This tool allows the creation of page layout and typographical attributes of selected paragraphs. This tool is used to create style sheets and to assign attributes to a paragraph from the Tag List.
Text Tool	This tool is used to add, delete, and copy text. It can also be used to select text attributes (such as size and appearance).
Table Tool	This tool allows the creation and editing of Ventura Tables.
Box Text Tool	This tool creates box text, which is associated with Ventura's Graphic feature.
Rectangle Tool	This tool creates a graphic box.
Rounded Rectangle Tool	This tool creates a graphic box with rounded corners.
Ellipse Tool	This tool creates graphic circles and ellipses.
Line Tool	This tool creates graphic lines.

Each of these operations and uses of the various tools are explained in detail in this module.

To select and enable a tool for use that is located in the Ventura Publisher Toolbox, point the mouse cursor at the desired tool and click once. The background of the selected tool changes from white to black. The icon of the tool with the black background is the current or selected tool. The name of the tool is also displayed above the icons.

NOTE

The menu options available to you in Ventura will depend on which tool is selected. For example, the options in the Paragraph menu will only be available if you have selected the Paragraph Tool.

Selection Tool

The Selection Tool is used for many different operations in Ventura. They include:

- Placing files into a selected frame from the File List.
- Selecting, moving, resizing, copying, and deleting frames.
- Selecting, moving, resizing, copying, and deleting graphics.
- Removing text or graphic files from selected frames or from the Files List.
- Changing a frame's attributes, which includes the column balance, margins and columns, ruling lines, captions, and background patterns.
- Changing the attributes of graphics, which includes line thicknesses or fill patterns.
- Creating frames that repeat on each page of the Ventura document.

Add Frame Tool

The Add Frame Tool allows you to create or design the areas within your Ventura documents that are used to hold text or graphics.

NOTE

Only one file — text or graphic — can be assigned or placed in an individual frame. You cannot place more than one file in any single frame.

One of the things many beginners find confusing about using Ventura Publisher is its use of frames. And perhaps one of the most confusing issues is the use of the *underlying page frame*. The thing to remember is that each page in Ventura is nothing more than a frame. The underlying page frame is common to *all* pages and is a permanent part of the style sheet.

Ventura's frames are always rectangular. Frames can hold either graphics or text, but only one type of a file at one time. The text placed in a frame is most often imported from a file created with a word processor, but text created directly in Ventura can also be placed in a frame. Graphics must come from an external graphics program, such as AutoCad or PC Paintbrush. Either the underlying page frame, or frames you create, can contain either text or graphics files, but once again, not both at the same time.

The underlying page frame and the frames you create are different in several ways. Consider this table:

Underlying Page Frame	*Created Frame*
The underlying page frame cannot be moved.	The frame can be moved with the mouse.
The underlying page frame cannot be deleted.	The frame can be deleted.
The underlying page frame creates the same basic layout for each page in the Ventura document.	Frames permit each page to have a different basic layout or design.
The underlying page frame is standard to all pages.	Frames are unique to each page.
The underlying page frame cannot be sized with the mouse.	Frames can be resized with a mouse.
There is only one underlying page frame to a Ventura document page.	Multiple frames per page are permitted.

Each time you create a new frame, Ventura places it "on top" of any other frame. Of course, you must physically position or place the frame on the page.

Frames can be made to "push away" text included in the underlying page frame or in another frame. In this illustration, notice how the new frame causes the text to be pushed away from the margin:

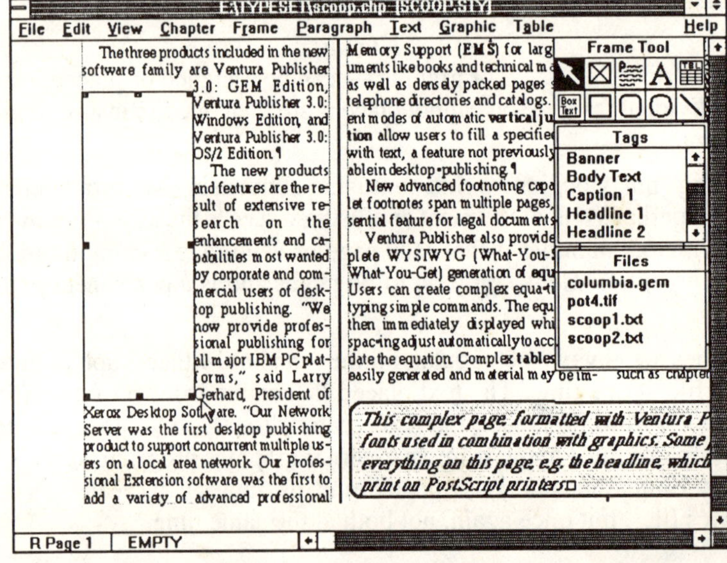

As you can see, this causes the text in one frame (in this case, the underlying page frame) to wrap around the added frame.

Text can also flow from one frame to another. This is an important concept when working with newspaper-type columns often found in newsletters. You can, for example, place three frames on a page, load the same text file into each frame, and Ventura will flow the text from the first frame you added, or the bottom one, to the top frame. The frame's position can be changed in the bottom-to-top sequence by cutting and pasting. When cut and pasted, the frame moves to the top of the sequence. The underlying page frame sequence, however, cannot be changed.

Frames can be sized, changed, or moved.

NOTE

> Frames cannot be dragged from one page to another. To move a frame from one page to another, use Cut/Copy/Paste (see Module 17).

The Add Frame Tool is located in the Toolbox. It is accessed by pointing and clicking on it.

To add a new frame, select the Add Frame Tool. Then move the mouse cursor to the point on the page where you want to position the upper left corner of the frame. Press and hold the mouse button, and pull or drag the mouse to the desired location of the lower right-hand corner of the frame. Then release the mouse button.

Text that is already on the page is pushed around the new frame. As soon as you release the mouse button, Ventura automatically switches to the Frame Tool.

NOTE

> To prevent Ventura from switching from the Add Frame Tool to the Frame Tool, press Shift before drawing the frame. This technique allows you to add multiple frames without having to reselect the Add Frame Tool each time.

Paragraph Tool

Ventura's Paragraph Tool allows you to design, create, change, and assign attributes to the paragraphs within your document. When using the Paragraph Tool, you can assign a tag from the style sheet. Those tags available are selected from the Tag List Window. The tag attributes are changed by using the options or commands available in the Paragraph menu.

The Paragraph Tool is enabled by pressing Ctrl-I or by clicking on the tool with the mouse.

Text Tool

The Text Tool allows Ventura to work much like a word processor. With the Text Tool, you can create, edit, and delete text. You can also change the text attributes, such as adding bold or underlining.

For more information about using the Text Tool and editing text, see Module 79.

The Text Tool is accessed by selecting it in the Toolbox. It can also be accessed in the View menu or by pressing Ctrl-O.

Graphic Tools

The Graphic Tools allow you to create squares, circles, square-cornered rectangles, lines, ellipses, round-cornered boxes, and rectangles. Once you have drawn these graphics, you can assign line or fill attributes to them.

To cut, copy, or paste a Ventura graphic, use the Frame Tool.

TIP:

> Graphics are always attached to a Ventura frame. They can be attached to the underlying page frame or to a specific frame. If you attach a graphic to a frame, the graphic moves or is deleted when the frame is moved or deleted. To attach a graphic to a frame, use the Frame Tool to select the desired frame.

To draw with one of the five Graphic Tools, select one from the bottom row of the Toolbox. Then move the mouse cursor to the location where you want to begin drawing. Press and hold the mouse button, and the cursor changes shape. Continue pressing and holding the mouse button, and then move or drag the mouse to create the size and shape of the graphic. Finally, release the mouse button.

As soon as you release the mouse button, Ventura automatically switches to the Frame Tool.

NOTE

> To prevent Ventura from switching from the selected Graphic Tool to the Frame Tool, press Shift before drawing the graphic. This technique allows you to create multiple graphics without having to reselect the desired Graphic Tool each time.

Box Text allows you to place text anywhere on the page. Unlike placing text in frames, Box Text is formatted in a single column and can overlap any picture or text on the page.

Table Tool

A Ventura table is any text that is formatted in a row and column format. A cell is the intersection of a row and column.

This is an example of a Ventura Table:

Sales Volume Breakdown By Divisions		
Division	Last Year	This Year
Northern	$554,001.00	$667,127.87
Southern	$589,241.06	$1,991,812.84
Eastern	$785,549.54	$1,354,458.65
Western	$209,812.19	$654,331.12

The Table Tool allows you to create a Ventura Table. Complete step-by-step instructions of setting up a table are presented in Module 42.

APPLICATIONS

The Ventura Toolbox allows you to select different tools so you can do different operations. For example, the Frame Tool allows you to select a frame, so it can be moved, deleted, or resized.

The Add Frame Tool allows you to create new frames. Frames—both the underlying page frame and the frames you draw—establish the overall design and appearance of your publications. The underlying page frame forces a consistent design on each page of your document. Frames you draw can be moved, sized, or deleted, allowing unique designs to your documents. Frames you draw can enhance the appearance of your documents by allowing you to add charts, tables, pictures, line art, or computer-created images.

Frames can also add "white space" to your documents. Since they can "push" text out of the way, you can use them for a variety of reasons, such as adding advertisements, pictures, or another text file.

Ventura makes setting text easier by using the Paragraph Tag Tool. Because each tag can be set to assign a different style to a paragraph, you are able to take advantage of design freedom. And since more than one paragraph can be assigned with the same tag, you assure a uniform appearance throughout the document.

For example, you can assign attributes to each level of headline, subheading, and caption throughout the document. Then, whatever text is chosen as the headline, it will be set with the correct attributes and will always be the same throughout the entire document.

All text not assigned a tag will automatically be assigned Body Text by Ventura. Whatever the attributes for Body Text, all Body Text paragraphs throughout the document will look alike.

Paragraph tags enforce a consistent appearance of text throughout the entire document. Because the paragraph tags are saved in a style sheet, you can use the same style sheet with other text documents, and by assigning paragraph tags, each publication will look the same.

The Text Tool is used to edit or change the attributes of your prepared text. For example, if you typed a headline in uppercase and lowercase, but now decide it would look better in all uppercase, you can select the text and choose uppercase to change the text. In the same way, the text could be underlined, bold, or italic.

TIP:

> Selecting Normal in the Text menu clears all attributes within the selected text and returns the text to the attributes established by the paragraph tag.

The Text Tool also permits a font change within a paragraph. Sometimes, for emphasis, you may want to change a type font within a sentence. To make the change, the Text Tool is used, and Set Font is chosen from the Text menu.

You can assign as many attributes as you desire to text that has been selected. The list of possible attributes available is displayed in the Text menu.

NOTE

> When you edit a text file with Ventura's Text Tool, the text file is changed by Ventura. If you were to delete a block of text, then Ventura would delete the entire block of text in your text file. When the text attributes are changed, Ventura places markers within the text file. For this reason, you should always make a backup copy of the text file *before* importing it into Ventura.

The Graphic Tools are used to create graphics directly in Ventura. This allows you to create squares, boxes, circles, graphic lines, and box text to enhance the graphic design of your documents.

The Table Tool allows you to create extensive tables in Ventura. Tables are used to display text in a neat, orderly fashion. They are often used for catalogs, reports, and charts.

TYPICAL OPERATION

In this example, you use the Paragraph mode and select a paragraph. Then, you assign another paragraph tag to the paragraph. You edit text by adding words, deleting, and changing the appearance of the text. You also add and size frames. The Ventura sample chapter &NEWS-P2.CHP is used. The example begins with Ventura open. You may need to adjust your screen using the scroll bars to make your computer look like the illustrations.

1. Select the **File** menu and click on **Open Chapter**.
2. Click on **&NEWS-P2.CHP** and click on **Open** or press **Enter**.
3. Press **Ctrl-O** to select the Text Editing mode.
4. Move the cursor to the "s" in the word "software" in the first paragraph. Click once.
5. Type **current** and press **Spacebar**.
6. Point to the "s" in the word "subject" in the first paragraph, second line.
7. Click and drag the mouse to highlight the word "subject" and then press **Del**.
8. Type **matter**. Your screen should resemble the following illustration:

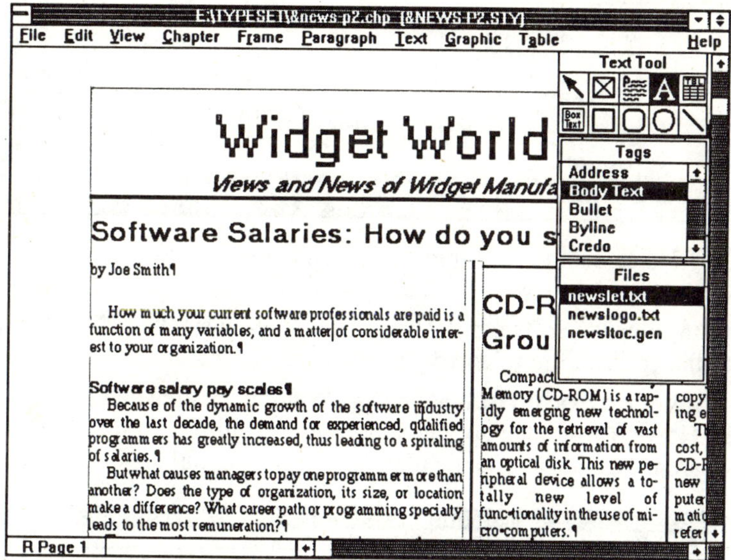

9. Point to the "y" in the second your, and click once. Point to the last "n" in organization, press and hold **Shift**, and click the mouse button.
10. Click on **Italic** in the **Text** menu. Click once anywhere in the margin to remove the highlight from the selected text. Your screen should resemble the following illustration:

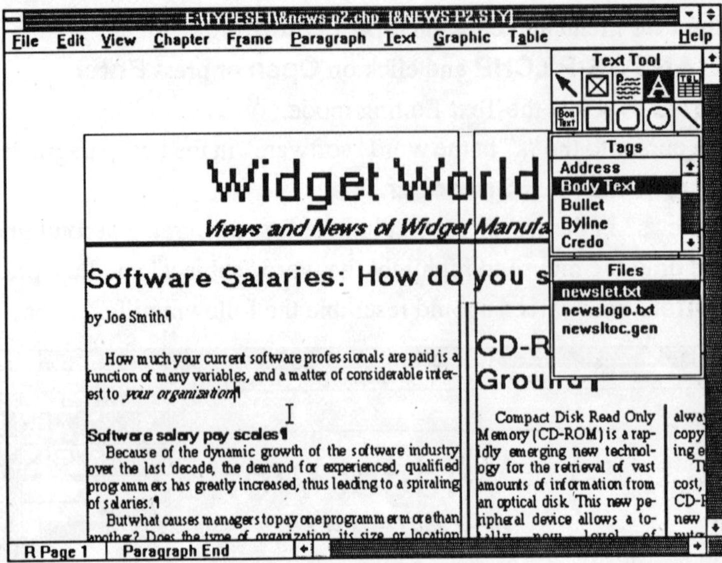

11. Press **Ctrl-I** to select the Paragraph Tool. The mouse cursor changes shape. It looks like the corner of a box with lines of text inside of it.
12. Click on the words "Software Salaries: How do you stack up?" Notice that Ventura reverses the color of the selected paragraph text.
13. Point and click on **Body Text** in the Tags Window. Notice that the words "Software Salaries: How do you stack up?" now appear on your screen with the same attributes and appearance as the other body text. Your screen should resemble this illustration:

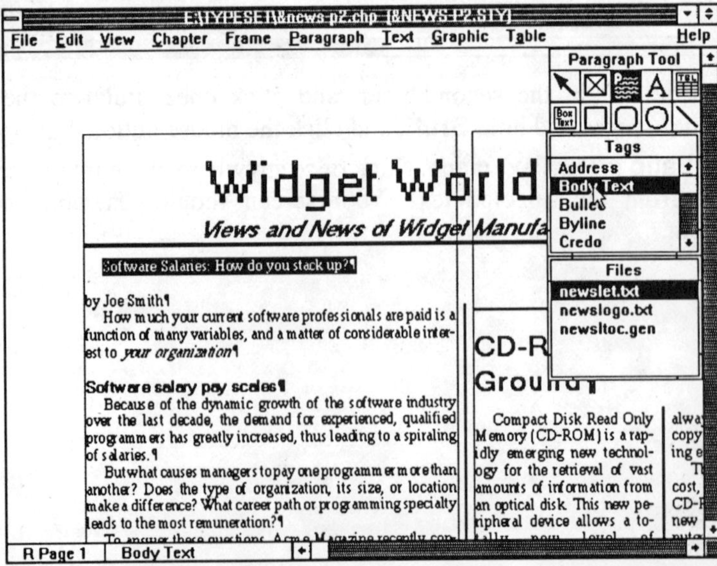

Also notice that the Current Selection Box shows the name of the tag (Body Text) assigned to this paragraph.

14. Point and click on **Headline** in the Tags Window. The words "Software Salaries: How do you stack up?" once again revert to their normal size.
15. Click on the **Add Frame** Tool.
16. Click and hold the mouse button.

TIP:
Always drag the mouse down and to the right to create a new frame.

17. Drag the pointer and release the mouse button to create a frame as illustrated:

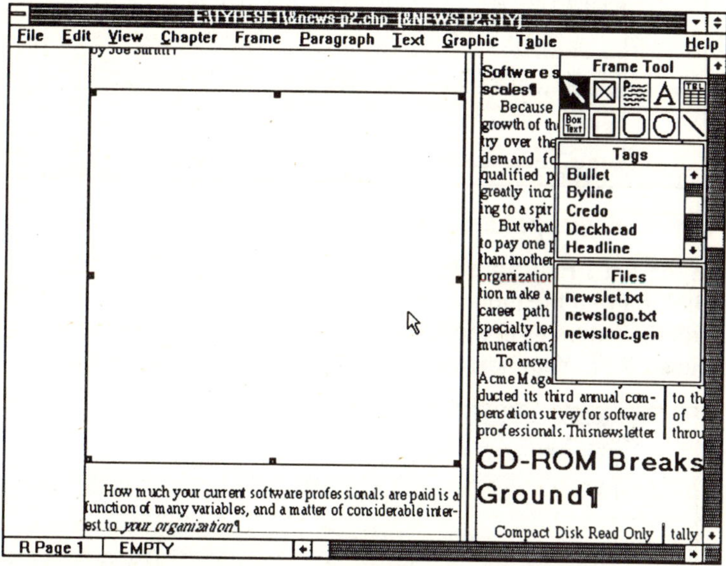

Notice that the text has been moved, and you could now load a text or graphic file into this frame. The Add Frame Tool is no longer selected. The Frame Tool is now selected. The Current Selection Box, located on the bottom of your screen, also says "EMPTY" since no text or graphic has been placed in the frame you have just drawn.

18. Move the mouse cursor to the lower right box in the frame you just created. Click and hold the mouse button and "push" the frame up to make it approximately half the size it was. Your screen should now resemble the following illustration:

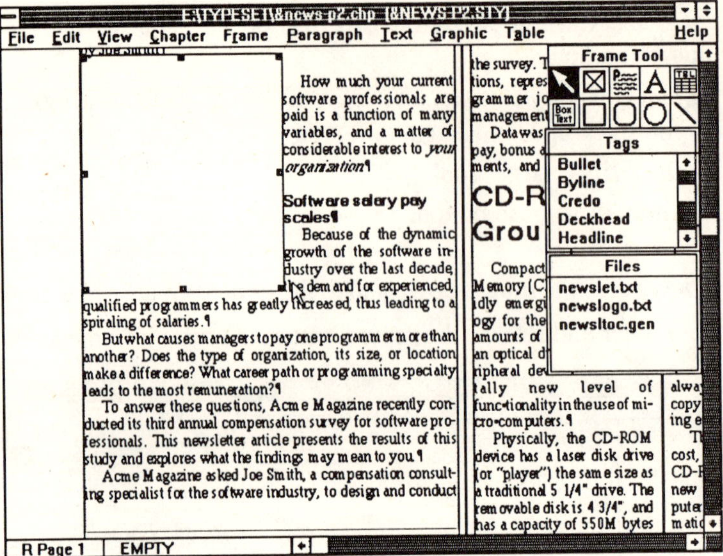

Notice how the text rewrapped around the new, smaller size frame.

19. Click on the **Add Frame** Tool again. Ventura automatically changes the tool to a reverse color. Point the mouse cursor, which again has changed shape to a corner of a box with the letters Fr in the corner, to the upper left corner of the other frame you created in step 17. Your screen should resemble this illustration:

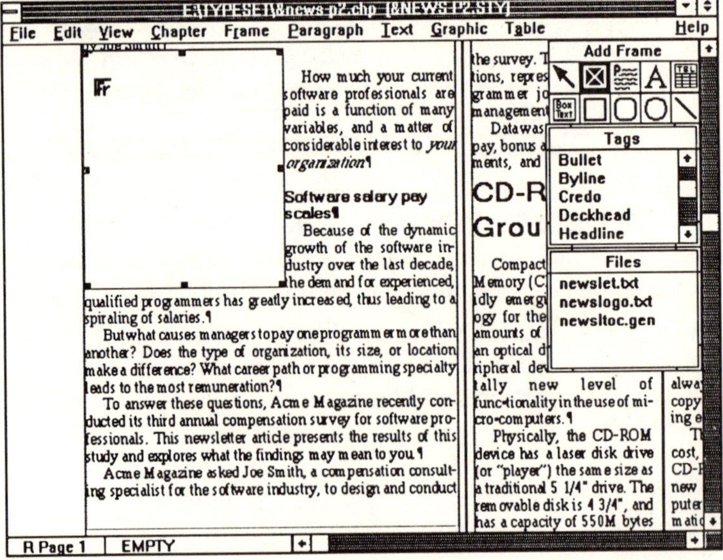

20. Click and hold the mouse button and create another frame. Create an oblong-type frame, as illustrated:

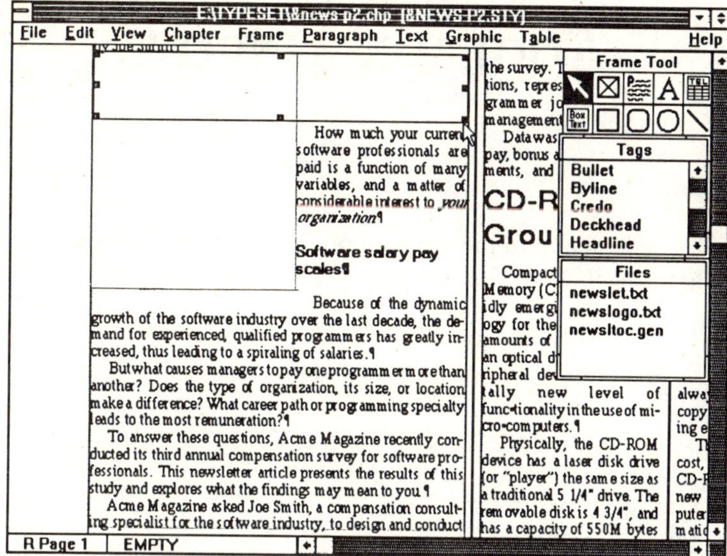

Once again, notice how the text has been pushed away by the new frame.

21. Press **Del** to delete the frame.
22. Point and click on the remaining frame. After it has been selected, press **Del** to delete that frame.
23. Turn to Module 82 to continue the learning sequence.

Module 82
TOOLBOX WINDOW

DESCRIPTION

The Toolbox is fundamental to the creation of all documents within Ventura Publisher. There are ten tools available within the Toolbox Window. They are:

Selection Tool
Add Frame Tool
Paragraph Tool
Text Tool
Table Tool
Box Text Tool
Rectangle Tool
Rounded Rectangle Tool
Ellipse Tool
Line Tool

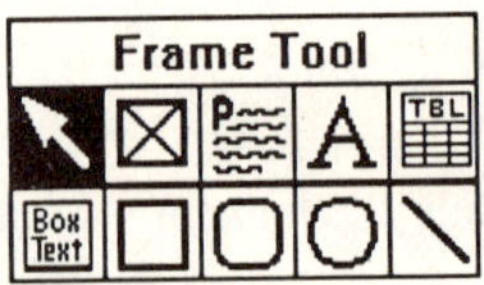

The Selection Tool is used to select any frame or graphic. It is also used to place text or pictures onto the Ventura chapter pages or within any frame. The Selection Tool is used to cut, copy, or paste frames or graphics.

The Add Frame Tool is used to create new frames anywhere within a Ventura chapter.

NOTE

Once a new frame is created, Ventura automatically switches to the Frame Tool.

The Paragraph Tool is used to apply attributes to an entire paragraph (or a group of paragraphs). After selecting the desired paragraph with the Paragraph Tool, paragraph tags are then assigned from the Tag Window. The Paragraph Tool is also used to create and modify Ventura style sheets.

The Text Tool is similar to a text editor or word processor and allows you to add, edit, delete, or copy text. It also allows you to assign special characteristics to your text, such as underlines or bold.

The Table Tool is used to create and edit Ventura Tables.

The Graphic Tools—Box Text, Rectangle, Rounded Rectangle, Ellipse, and Line Tool—are used to create graphics within a Ventura chapter.

To select a tool within the Toolbox, simply point the mouse cursor on the desired tool and click. The selected tool is then displayed with a dark or black background.

The Toolbox Window can be moved to any convenient location on your screen. To do so, simply click and hold the mouse button on the word "Toolbox" in Toolbox Window. Then, still holding the mouse button, move the window to any new location and release the mouse. The Toolbox Window appears in the new location.

The Toolbox Window can be hidden or displayed at any time. To hide or to show the Toolbox Window, press Ctrl-W.

APPLICATIONS

The Toolbox Window allows you to access various Ventura commands and options. For example, if you wanted to move, resize, copy, or delete a frame, the Frame Tool is used. By choosing the Frame Tool, you can then select the desired frame to move, resize, copy, or delete.

If you want to add a graphic to your Ventura document, you must select one of the graphic tools located within the Toolbox Window.

Text can be changed, edited, deleted, or its appearance changed by first selecting the Text Tool, and then highlighting the text to be changed or altered.

If a Table is desired anywhere within a Ventura chapter, the Table Tool must first be selected.

All the various Ventura tools are selected and chosen from the Toolbox Window.

TYPICAL OPERATION

In this operation, you select different tools and then hide and show the Toolbox Window.

1. Move the mouse to the **Table** Tool within the Toolbox Window and click once. Notice the shape of the mouse cursor.
2. Move the mouse to the **Rectangle** Tool within the Toolbox Window and click once. Notice the shape of the mouse cursor.
3. Press **Ctrl-W** once. The Toolbox Window is hidden.
4. Move the mouse to **View** menu and select **ToolBox Window**. The Toolbox Window is now displayed.
5. Turn to Module 52 to continue the learning sequence.

Module 83
UPDATE COUNTER

DESCRIPTION

This feature resets the figure, page, table, or chapter counters at any point in the chapter. This command allows the automatic linking of page, table, or figure counter across chapter boundaries.

To use this feature of Ventura, access the Update Counters command located in the Edit menu. Not only can the counters be reset, but the numbering style can also be selected. The styles of numbering available are:

1,2
A,B
a,b
I,II
i,ii
One,Two
ONE,TWO
one,two

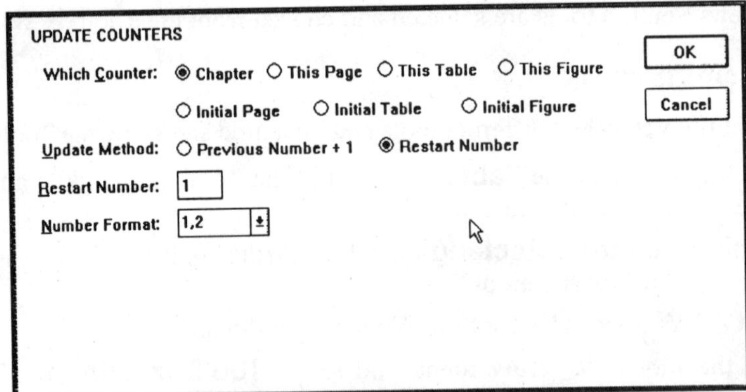

Within the Update Counters dialog box, the following options are available:

Which Counter	Select either Chapter, This Page, This Table, This Figure, Initial Page, Initial Table, or Initial Figure. These options allow you to choose what you want counted within the chapter.

Update Method	Select either Previous Number+1 or Restart Number to tell Ventura which number to use when counting.
Restart Number	Enter a number if you desire any number other than one to begin the counting.
Number Format	Select one of the numbering format styles available.

TIP:

When starting a counter for the first time, the initial default settings are Arabic format (1,2) and start at the number 1. If these are your desired settings, you need only select the counter from the Update Counters dialog box.

Counters can be changed two ways. The counter for the chapter, initial page, initial table, or initial figure can be set. This is done to link the chapter with a previous chapter (see Module 48 for more information about Manage Publication). The counter for this page, table, or figure can also be reset, and this is done when you need to change the numbering sequence within a chapter.

APPLICATIONS

Being able to number pages, tables, and figures automatically will enhance your publications. It is most important when creating longer reports, books, technical manuals, or business documents that require extensive use of tables, figures, or even appendices.

The Update Counter dialog box allows the consecutive numbering of pages, figures, or tables across chapters. This allows you to work with smaller chapters and still be able to produce logically numbered pages.

The commands also permit the override of automatically generated numbers for a given page, table, or figure.

Being able to choose which style of counting desired is also another useful benefit of this command.

TYPICAL OPERATION

In this example, you begin counting figures in the sample chapter called &BOOK-P2.CHP. This example begins with &BOOK-P2.CHP open and in use. If you do not have this chapter open, use the Open Chapter command in the File menu to retrieve and open &BOOK-P2.CHP.

1. Press **Ctrl-U** to select the Frame Tool.
2. Click in the middle of the frame holding the nozzle picture.
3. Click on the **Edit** menu and select **Update Counters** to display the Update Counters dialog box.
4. Select **This Figure** in Which Counter, **Restart Number** in Update Method.

5. Type **12** for Restart Number.

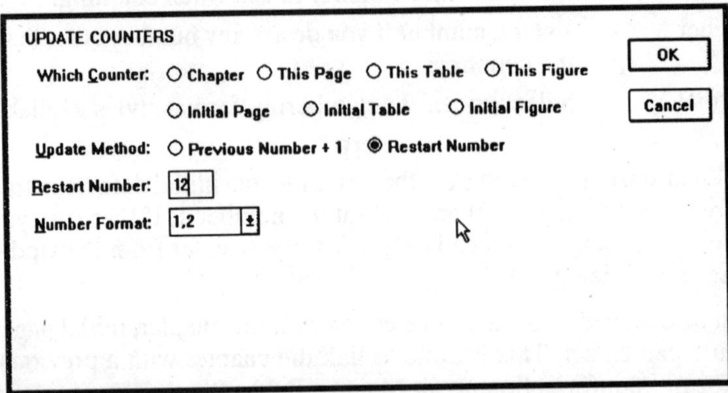

6. Click **OK**. Notice the figure number change.
7. Click on the **File** menu and click on **Revert to Saved** and click on **OK** when prompted to revert back to the last saved version.
8. Turn to Module 72 to continue the learning sequence.

Module 84

UPDATE TAG LIST

DESCRIPTION

The Update Tag List command provides several options to help manage the paragraph tags that are stored in a style sheet. These options are:

Delete Tag
Save As New Stylesheet
Rename Tag
Assign Function Keys
Add Tag
Print Stylesheet

When the Update Tag List command is accessed from the Paragraph menu, the Update Tag List dialog box appears. A list of all the tags associated with the current style sheet is displayed.

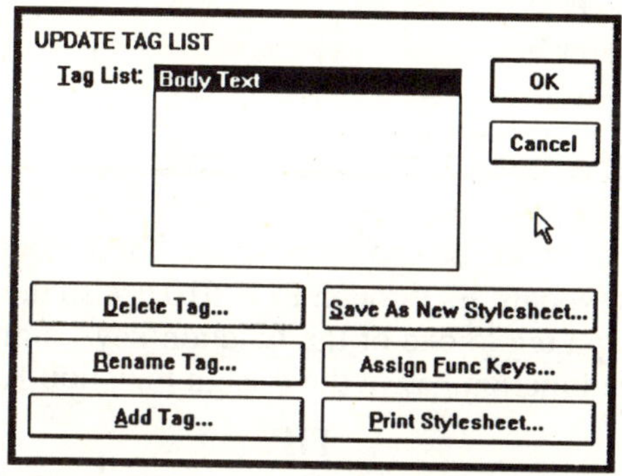

There are six commands that can be chosen. They are:

Delete Tag	Select this command to delete an existing tag from the current style sheet.
Save As New Stylesheet	Select this command to save the style sheet under a new name. By doing so, you can keep the old style sheet from being changed or modified.
Rename Tag	Select this command to rename a selected tag. Simply enter the new name of the tag.

Assign Function Keys — The Assign Function Keys command allows you to assign your paragraph tags to 10 function keys on your computer.

TIP:

The Update Tag List command is accessed in the Paragraph menu or by pressing Ctrl-K. When selecting the Assign Function Key option, it is not necessary to select text first.

Assign Function Keys does not change paragraphs or the predefined tags in the style sheet. This command only affects the style sheet. Using this command affects the style sheet for your current document and any other document that uses the current style sheet.

When you select Assign Function Keys from the Update Tag List dialog box or by pressing Ctrl-K, the Assign Function Keys dialog box appears. Your screen should look like this illustration:

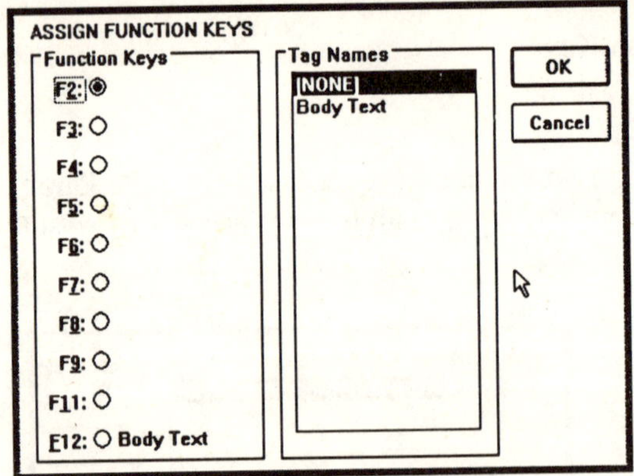

The Assign Function keys dialog box contains spaces for naming 10 paragraph tags to the function keys on your keyboard F2 through F12. F10 is also the default of the Body Text tag. To assign a paragraph tag to one of the function keys, simply type the name of the paragraph tag beside the function key in the Assign Function Keys dialog box.

TIP:

F1 and F10 cannot be assigned to a paragraph tag. F1 is reserved for Help. F10 is reserved for Body Text.

Add Tag — Select this command to add a new tag to the style sheet. When the Add New Tag dialog box appears, enter the name of the new tag. You can select which tag to copy from.

Print Stylesheet — Select this command to print the contents of the current style sheet. Ventura will copy the file and create a file with the same name as the style sheet, adding a .GEN extension. This file can then be imported into Ventura with the Load Text/Picture command, using the Generated Text format. The style sheet can then be printed.

After the Delete Tag command has been selected, the Delete Tag dialog box appears. Your screen should resemble this illustration:

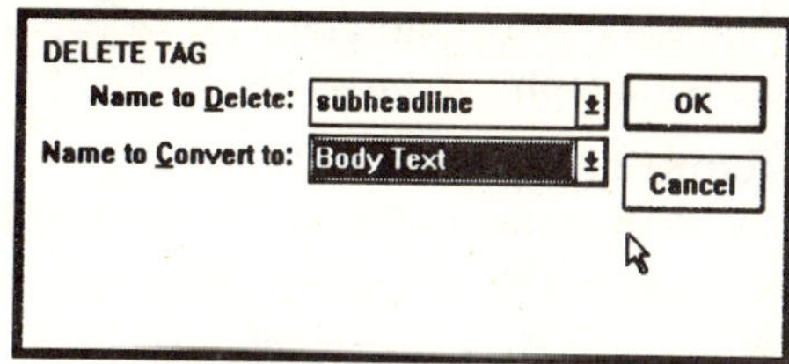

Before a tag is removed, you must assign another tag to take its place. For example, you might decide to remove the paragraph tag called subheadline and reassign all paragraphs tagged as subheadline with the headline paragraph tag. After completing the execution of this command, all the paragraphs tagged as subheadline in your document will now be reassigned and have the headline tag assigned. The paragraphs will also now assume the attributes assigned to the headline tag.

The options available in the Delete Tag dialog box are:

Name to Delete	Type the name of the paragraph tag to be removed. If a paragraph has been tagged before selecting the Delete Tag command, the name of the paragraph assigned to the selected paragraph is displayed in this section of the dialog box.
Name to Convert to	Type the name of the paragraph tag that is to be assigned to the paragraph tags being removed.

TIP:

Use the Save As New Style sheet command each time a paragraph tag is renamed or removed. This eliminates changing the format of other documents that use the same style sheet.

APPLICATIONS

This command allows you to remove tags that are no longer being used. By doing so, you will speed up Ventura. It is always preferable to eliminate any unused paragraph tags from a style sheet.

This command can also be used to make it easy to find the paragraph tags within the assignment sheet. By eliminating unused or unneeded tags, it will be easier to find the other used paragraph tags.

The command also makes it possible to document any style sheets you have created or changed. By using the Print Style sheet command, you can document the contents of a style sheet.

When you have assigned paragraph tags to your function keys, you can tag or retag your paragraphs from both the Paragraph Tagging and the Text Editing modes. This is an extremely useful command that increases the speed at which you can tag your paragraphs.

For example, suppose you created a paragraph tag called Italic Body and assigned the F6 key to that tag. Now, as you scroll through your text, you can remain in the Text Editing mode. As you select text to edit, delete, or change, you can do so in the normal manner. When you want to assign the Italic Body paragraph tag to your text, simply click the text cursor anywhere within the paragraph and press F6.

You can also change the format of any text you are adding to a document. For example, if you wanted to add a new paragraph in the Italic Body format, you would position the cursor, press F1, and begin typing. The new text would be formatted in accordance with the attributes you assigned to Italic Body paragraph tag.

NOTE

When using the Assign Function Keys command, if you type a paragraph tag name that does not exist, Ventura will display a message box and will ignore the paragraph tag name you typed.

TYPICAL OPERATION

In this operation, the tag list is updated by changing the name of a paragraph tag and by assigning a function key to the paragraph tag. The sample chapter document &NEWS-P2.CHP is used. The example begins with &NEWS-P2.CHP open.

1. Press **Ctrl-I** to select Paragraph mode. Click on the **Paragraph** menu and click on **Update Tag List** to display the Update Tag List dialog box.
2. Click on **Rename Tag** to display the Rename Tag dialog box.
3. Move the cursor to the Old Tag Name line and select the tag name **Address** from the drop-down list box.
4. Type **Address 1** for the New Tag Name line and press **Enter**.
5. Click on **OK** in the Update Tag List dialog box. A message box appears asking if you want to Save, Save As, or Abandon changes to the style sheet.
6. Click on **Save As**, type **TESTWIN.STY**, and click **OK**. Notice the new tag name in the Files Window.
7. Click on the **Paragraph** menu and click on **Update Tag List** to display the Update Tag List dialog box. Click on **Save** when the message box appears asking if you want to Save or Abandon changes.
8. Click on **Assign Func Keys** to display the Assign Function Keys dialog box.
9. Click on the **F3** button and select **Address 1**. Select **OK** twice. A message box appears, asking if you want to Save, Save As, or Abandon changes to the style sheet.
10. Click on **Abandon**.
11. Click on the **File** menu and click on **Revert to Saved** and click on **OK** when prompted to revert back to the last saved version.
12. Select **New** from the **File** menu and click on **OK** to clear the screen.
13. Turn to Module 48 to continue the learning sequence.

Module 85
VERTICAL RULES

DESCRIPTION

The Vertical Rules command sets ruling lines running between the top and bottom of the page in each frame or on the underlying page. A frame or underlying page may have a rule between each of its columns, plus two additional vertical rules. Ventura automatically positions the rules between the columns based on the columns defined with the Margins & Columns command.

The positions and widths of the other two vertical rules can be set as needed or desired. This command applies to all underlying pages and frames, even those frames that Ventura creates for its headers, footers, captions, and footnotes.

Different vertical rules for the left and right pages can be specified if a double-sided publication is being created. The left and right pages can be complementary to each other, a complete reversal, or they can be totally different from each other.

This command is accessed by selecting a frame or the underlying page with the Frame Tool and then selecting Vertical Rules from the Frame menu. The Vertical Rules dialog box then appears.

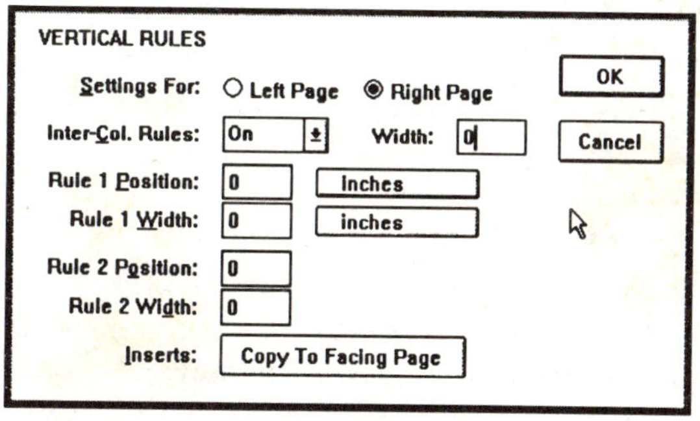

The Vertical Rules dialog box contains this information:

Settings For	Select either the Left Page or Right Page. Whichever page you were on when you selected the Vertical Rules command will automatically be selected.
Inter-Col. Rules	Select Inter-Col. Rules to be on or off. This command will direct Ventura to place rules between each column in the frame or underlying page. If On is selected, type the width of the column in the Width area.

Rule 1/Rule 2 Position	Type the distance from the left edge of the page (not the edge of the frame) where each rule is to appear. If no rule is desired, type 00.00.
Rule 1/Rule 2 Width	Type the width of the rule.
Inserts	Select Copy to Facing Page to automatically copy the information in the dialog box to the facing page. Doing this transfers the width of the inter-column rules and reverses the positions of the rules setup in the dialog box. Copy to Facing Page works only if preparing a two-sided document as established in the Page Size & Layout command. If creating complementary pages, enter the information separately for each page.

TIP:

If you do not see a vertical rule within a frame, the frame may be in the wrong position relative to the vertical rule set in the Vertical Rules dialog box.

Frame-wide paragraphs will interrupt vertical rules on the page. Column-wide paragraphs do not interrupt the vertical rule. To set the alignment of the paragraph, see Module 5.

APPLICATIONS

The Vertical Rules command places rules between text columns and places rules elsewhere on the page. By adding rules to your document, the overall design is often improved. Adding rules between text columns (what Ventura calls gutters) not only enhances the design of the document, but will also help the reader see the article or text. This is commonly used in newsletter and newspaper design.

Rules help create sections and are often used to prevent the reader's eyes flowing from one column to another.

TYPICAL OPERATION

In this example, a vertical rule is added to the sample chapter &LSTG-P2.CHP. The operation begins with &LSTG-P2.CHP open. Use the command Open Chapter in the File menu to retrieve and open &LSTG-P2.CHP. You may need to adjust your screen using the scroll bars to make your computer look like the illustrations.

1. Press **Ctrl-U** to select the Frame Tool.
2. Click on the underlying page.
3. Click on the **View** menu and click on **Show Tabs & Returns**.
4. Click on **Show Column Guides** from the **View** menu to turn the column guides off.

5. Click on the **Frame** menu and click on **Vertical Rules.**
6. Click **On** for Inter-Col. Rules, and type **0.014** inches as the width. Click **OK**. Your screen should resemble this illustration:

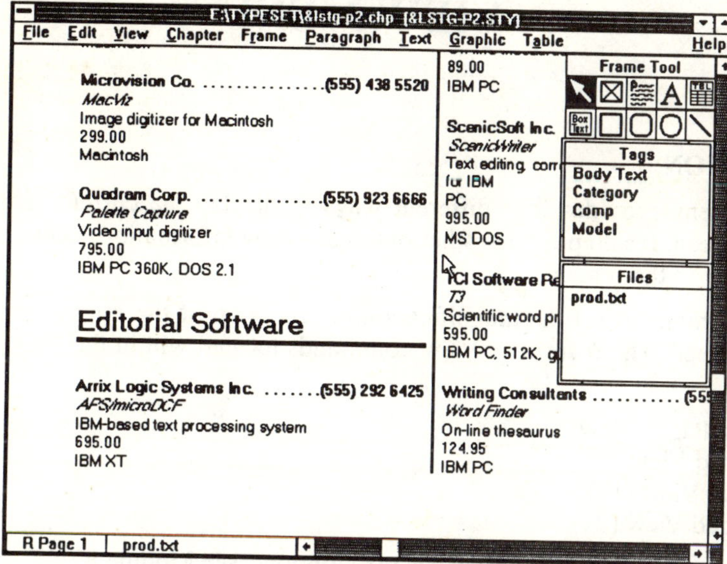

Notice the addition of the vertical rule between the columns.

7. Click on the **File** menu and click on **Revert to Saved**. Click on **OK** when prompted to revert back to the last saved version.
8. Turn to Module 34 to continue the learning sequence.

Module 86
VIEW MENU

DESCRIPTION

The View menu provides four different ways to display the current chapter on your computer screen. It also provides other options of how information, items, and windows are displayed on the screen.

The View commands set the magnification or reduction of the image area seen on the computer screen. There are four View commands located within the View menu. They are:

Facing Pages View
Reduced View
Normal View (1x)
Enlarged View (2x)

For more information about using these view options, see Module 87.

Other options are also available within the View menu. They are:

Hide/Show All Pictures
Set Ruler
Show Rulers
Show Column Guides
Show Tabs & Returns
Show Loose Lines
Column Snap
Line Snap
Toolbox Window
Tag List Window
File List Window

The Hide/Show All Pictures option displays or hides the graphics or pictures on your computer screen. For example, if you select Show All Pictures, pictures are displayed on your screen. If they are displayed, you can hide them by selecting Hide All Pictures.

Show Rulers, Show Column Guides, Show Tabs & Returns, and Show Loose Lines are displayed if a check mark is placed in front of each item in the menu. To hide any of these items, click on the item in the menu to remove the check mark. When there is no check mark, the item is not displayed on your screen.

If you choose to Show Tabs & Returns, the following symbols are displayed on your screen:

Tab	Discretionary Hyphen	Nonbreaking and other fixed spaces	Line Break	Paragraph	End of File

The Toolbox Window, Tag List Window, and File List Window can be hidden or shown by selecting the item on the View window. By hiding them when not needed, more of your document is visible on your computer screen. Each of these three commands can also be executed with the following keystroke commands:

Ctrl-W	Toolbox Window
Ctrl-V	Tag List Window
Ctrl-Y	File List Window

When working with the View menu, you can tell if an item has been selected. If a check mark is displayed to the left of the menu command, the item is currently selected.

APPLICATIONS

These commands offer you different ways of working within Ventura. For example, when in the Reduced View, you can see the layout of the entire page. You can see where to place frames, graphics, and text, and have a good idea how your finished page will look when printed. Normal View allows you to see as close as possible how your printed page will appear. Enlarged View permits precise adjustments and placements within your document. Facing Pages View allows you to see how the document's design compliments each facing page.

The purpose of the Facing Pages View command is to permit you to see and change the general layout of a two-page spread. You will be able to see how your frames, graphics, rules, text, and other page elements will appear when a document is finally published. This command allows you to make adjustments to the overall design of your facing pages to create a complimentary effect.

NOTE

> If you have chosen to start your document with a right-hand page, the Facing Page View command will show only one page when you are viewing page 1 of your document.

The keyboard commands listed in this module offer another way of executing a command and often save time.

The View menu also allows you to adjust your computer screen so you can work with Ventura as you prefer. For example, you can choose to display the column guides and rulers, but hide all pictures. By accessing the View menu, you can change the appearance of your screen by selecting different options.

TYPICAL OPERATION

In this example, you change the views of the sample chapter SCOOP.CHP. The example begins with SCOOP.CHP open and in use. If you do not have this chapter open, use the Open Chapter command in the File menu to retrieve and open SCOOP.CHP.

1. Click on the **View** menu and click on **Reduced View**. Notice the full view of the page you can now see on your screen:

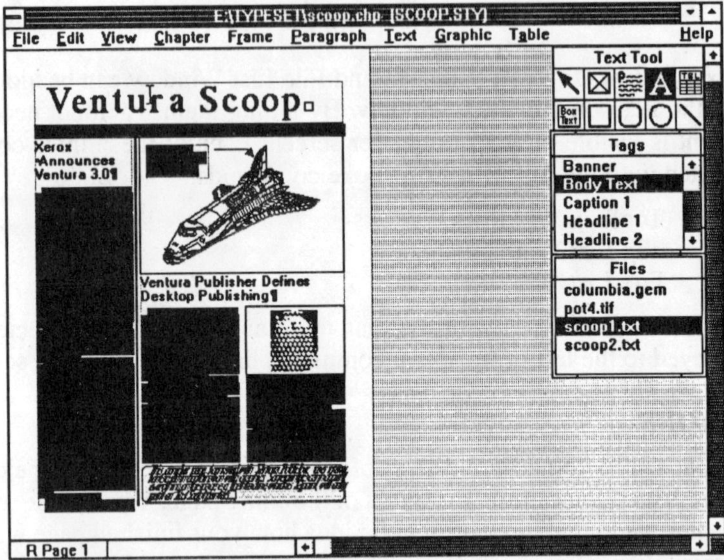

2. Position the mouse cursor in the middle of your computer screen and press **Ctrl-E**. Your screen should now resemble this illustration:

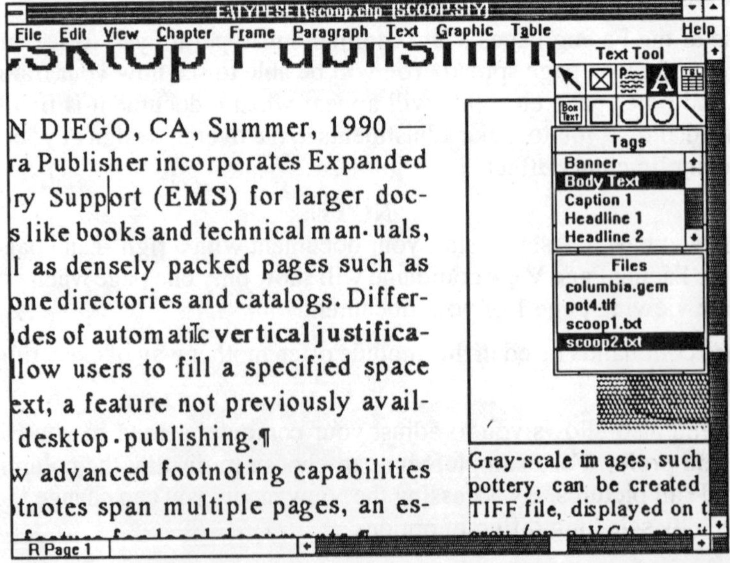

Notice that the enlarged view on your computer screen is in the portion of the page where you placed the mouse cursor before pressing Ctrl-E.

3. Click on the **View** menu and click on **Normal View**. Notice the actual size view on your computer screen.
4. Notice the other commands available within the View menu.
5. Turn to Module 13 to continue the learning sequence.

Module 87
VIEWS

DESCRIPTION

The View commands set the magnification or reduction of the image area seen on the computer screen. There are four View commands located within the View menu. They are:

Facing Pages View
Reduced View
Normal View (1x)
Enlarged View (2x)

Reduced View shrinks the size of the image until the entire page can be seen. Depending on the options selected in the Set Preferences command (see Module 69), Ventura will "greek" all or most of the text on the computer screen. Reduced View is selected from the View menu or by pressing Ctrl-R.

Normal View displays the image nearly the way it looks when it is printed. When in Normal View, you only see a portion of your document (unless you are creating an extremely small document of only a few inches in size). To see more of your document, use the scroll bars. Normal View is selected from View menu or by pressing Ctrl-N.

Enlarged View doubles the size of the image shown in the Normal View. Once again, only a portion of your document will be seen when in the Enlarged View. Enlarged View is selected from the View menu or by pressing Ctrl-E.

TIP:

By placing the pointer at a specific spot on the working part of the screen and pressing Ctrl-E, Ventura positions the selected area in the upper left corner of the enlarged screen.

Facing Pages View shrinks the size of the image until both pages, left and right, can be seen on your computer screen. Facing Pages View is accessed in the View menu. There is no keyboard shortcut to use to select this view. When in Facing Pages View, you cannot drag frames across pages.

TIP:

You can only use Facing Pages View if you have a document that has facing pages. If your document is only one or two pages in length, Facing Pages view is not available. However, if you have a three-page document, you could use Facing Pages view to see pages 2 and 3.

In addition to the Ventura keyboard commands, you can also use the Windows keyboard commands:

View	*Windows Key*	*Ventura Key*
Enlarged View	Alt-V-E	Ctrl-E
Facing Page View	Alt-V-F	None
Normal View	Alt-V-N	Ctrl-N
Reduced View	Alt-V-R	Ctrl-R

You can increase your view of the screen by hiding the Toolbox, Tag List and File List Windows. To hide or display any of these windows, you can use the View menu or these keystroke commands:

Ctrl-W	Toolbox Window
Ctrl-V	Tag List Window
Ctrl-Y	File List Window

APPLICATIONS

These commands offer you different ways of working within Ventura. For example, when in the Reduced View, you can see the layout of the entire page. You can see where to place frames, graphics, and text, and have a good idea how your finished page will look when printed. Normal View allows you to see as close as possible how your printed page will appear. Enlarged View permits precise adjustments and placements within your document. Facing Pages View allows you to see how the document's design compliments each facing page.

The purpose of the Facing Pages View command is to permit you to see and change the general layout of a two-page spread. You will be able to see how your frames, graphics, rules, text, and other page elements will appear when a document is finally published. This command allows you to make adjustments to the overall design of your facing pages to create a complimentary effect.

NOTE

> If you have chosen to start your document with a right-hand page, the Facing Page View command will show only one page when you are viewing page 1 of your document.

The Toolbox, Tag List, or File List Windows can be hidden to reduce amount of clutter on your screen when viewing the document. When the windows are hidden, accessing the View menu allows you to display the hidden Toolbox, Tag List, or File List Windows.

Each of the keyboard commands in this module offer another way of executing a command and often save time.

TYPICAL OPERATION

In this example, you change the views of the sample chapter SCOOP.CHP. The example begins with SCOOP.CHP open and in use. If you do not have this chapter open, use the Open Chapter command in the File menu to retrieve and open SCOOP.CHP.

1. Select the **View** menu and click on **Reduced View**. Notice the full view of the page you can now see on your screen:

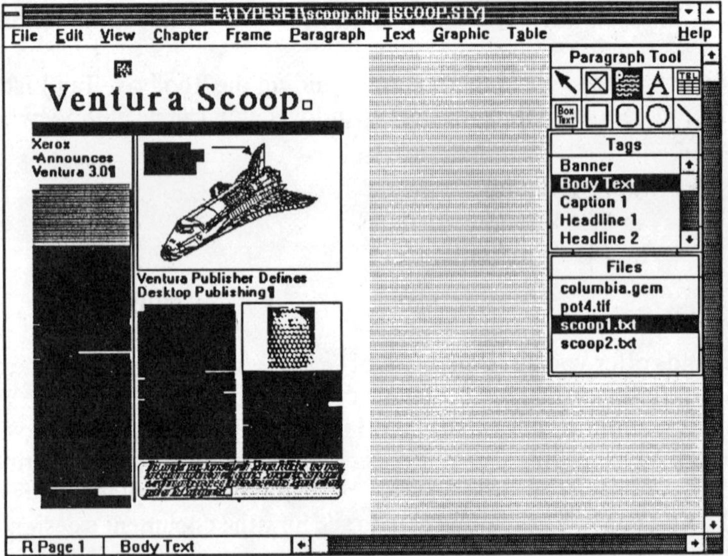

2. Position the mouse cursor in the middle of your computer screen and press **Ctrl-E**. Your screen should now resemble this illustration:

Notice that the enlarged view on your computer screen is in the portion of the page where you placed the mouse cursor before pressing Ctrl-E.

3. Point to the **View** menu and click on **Normal View**. Your screen should resemble the following illustration:

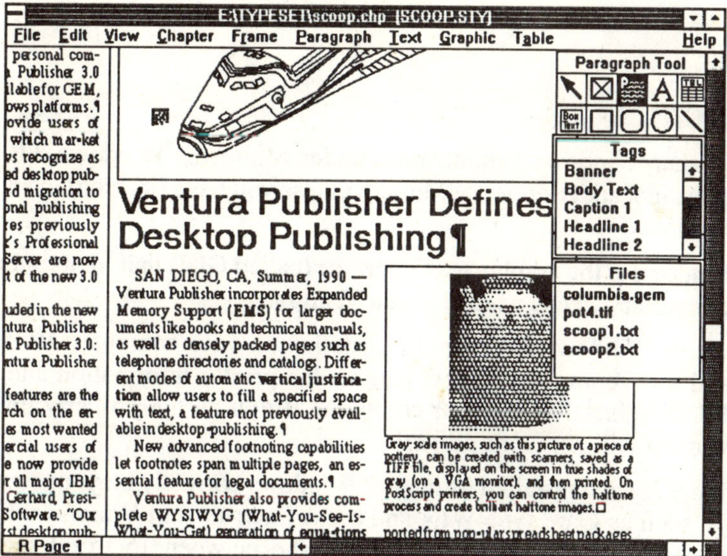

Notice the actual size view on your computer screen.

4. Press **Ctrl-R** to change to Reduced View.
5. Press **Ctrl-W** to hide the Toolbox Window. Press **Ctrl-W** to display the Toolbox Window.
6. Press **Ctrl-V** to hide the Tag List Window. Press **Ctrl-V** to display the Tag List Window.
7. Click on **File** menu, click on **Revert to Saved**, and then click **OK**.
8. Turn to Module 79 to continue the learning sequence.

Module 88
WINDOWS

DESCRIPTION

Ventura Publisher Windows Edition runs under Microsoft Windows 3.0 (or a higher version). You cannot start or operate Ventura unless you have first started and are running Microsoft Windows.

Microsoft Windows is the graphic user interface (called GUI) that Ventura Publisher uses to create the familiar screens needed to run Ventura.

You should have Windows 3.0 properly installed on your computer. Within Microsoft Windows, and not Ventura Publisher, you set the printer information and the graphics screens and drivers installed on your computer. If you do not properly install or set up Windows, Ventura will not work properly.

Assuming that you have installed Microsoft Windows correctly on your computer, at any DOS prompt, such as C:\>, type WIN and press Enter to start Windows. Depending on your computer and its configuration, it may take between 15 to 60 seconds to start Windows. You will see a large Microsoft Windows screen on your computer almost instantly, which is displayed as Windows is loaded into your computer's memory.

When Windows is finally loaded, your screen should resemble this illustration:

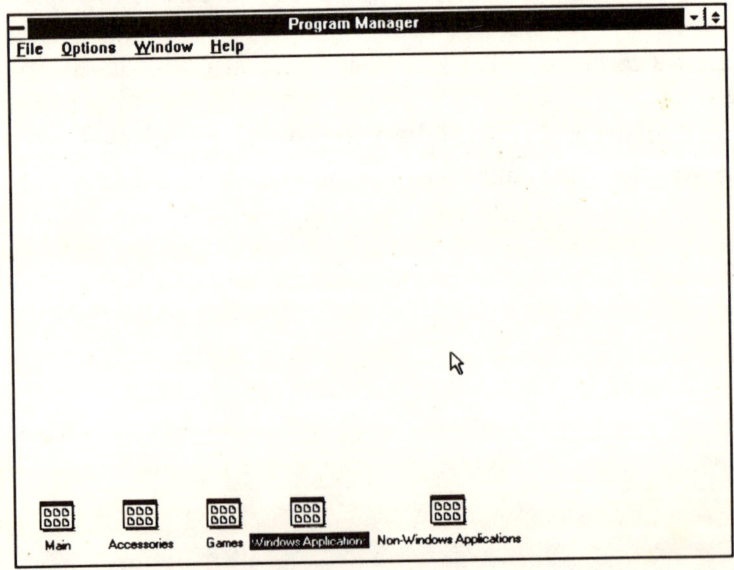

A typical Window within Windows contains a Control-menu box, menu bar, Title bar, scroll bars, and minimize and maximize buttons. Windows use icons, which are small pictures, to help you select which program you want to run under Windows. For example, Ventura Publisher's icon is:

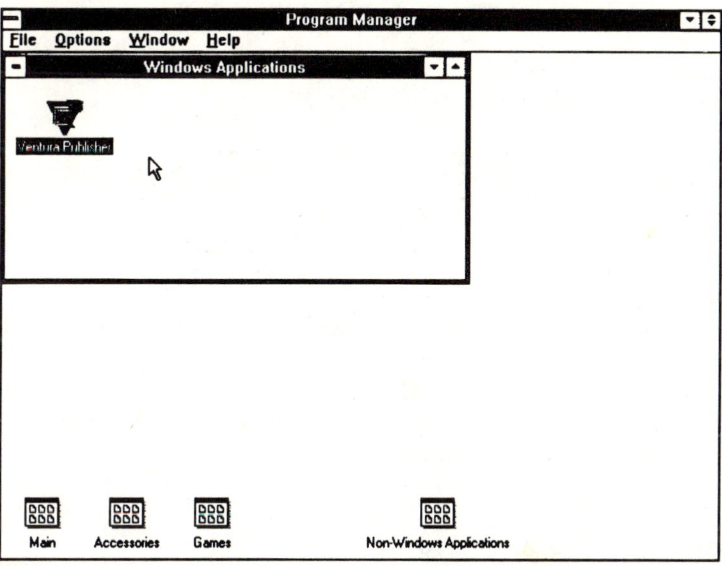

It is this icon that you must locate to start Ventura. The icon will be located in Windows Applications. To open Windows Applications, double click on the Windows Applications icon. When the Windows Applications box opens, double click on the Ventura icon, and within a minute, Ventura is running on your computer screen.

Dialog Boxes

You must learn how to work with the dialog boxes that appear when running Ventura. Because the dialog boxes that appear in Ventura conform to Windows protocol, once you learn how to work in a dialog box, you can do so in any Windows-based program.

Ventura displays dialog boxes many times when you select an item from the menu. These dialog boxes may request information from you, or they may provide information to you. For example, if you want to place a Ruling Box Around a Frame, Ventura needs to know the thickness and position of the rule. So Ventura displays a dialog box presenting the information, and you must complete it to set the Ruling Box Around information.

Ventura also uses dialog boxes to display additional information and warnings or to explain why a request could not be completed.

Most dialog boxes contain options, which request different kinds of information. After all requested information is supplied, you choose a command button to complete the command.

To move within a dialog box:

Click the mouse pointer on the option you want to move.

or

Press Tab to move forward, or press Shift+Tab to move in the opposite direction.

Text Boxes

A text box is a rectangle where you type information.

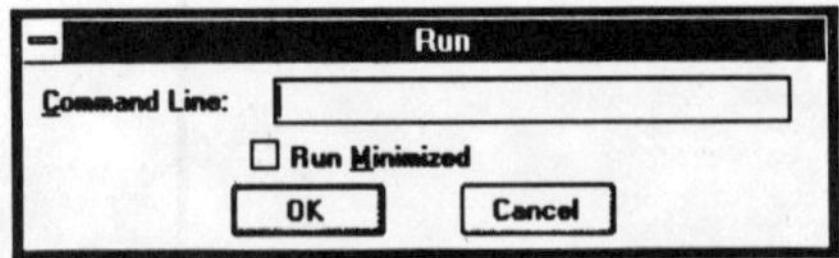

When you move to an empty text box, an insertion point appears within the box, on the left side. The text you type starts at this point, where a flashing vertical bar is located. If the text box already contains text when you move to it, all the text in the box is automatically selected and any text you type replaces it. You can also use Backspace or Delete to edit and make any corrections.

To move into a text box:

Move the mouse pointer to the desired text box and click.

Command Buttons

Command buttons launch an immediate action. For example, you can select Cancel, which instantly dismisses the dialog box. Command buttons marked with an ellipsis (...) open another dialog box so more information can be supplied.

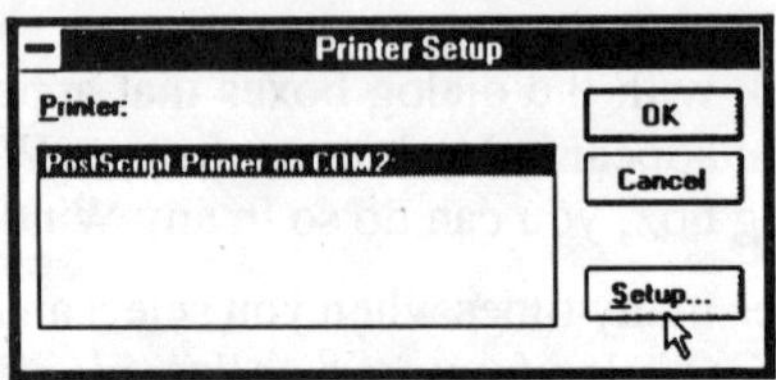

To select a command button:

Click the command button.

or

Press Tab to move to the command button, and press Spacebar or Enter.

Drop-Down List Boxes

A drop-down list box appears as a rectangular box with the current option highlighted with the box. An arrow in the square box at the right opens into a list of all available choices when selected. If there are more choices than can fit in the drop-down list box, scroll bars are available to scroll through the entire list.

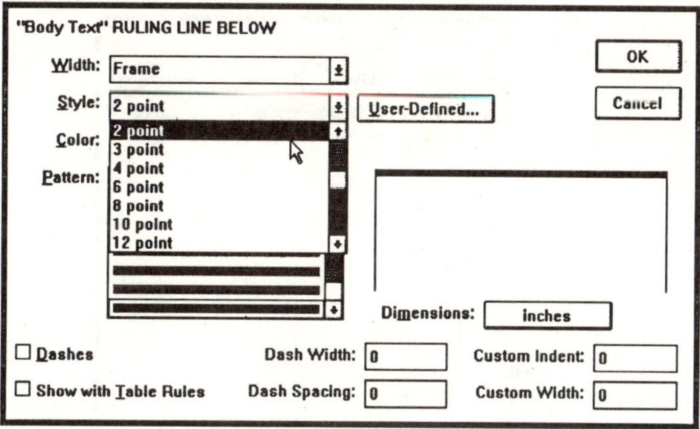

To open a drop-down list box and select an item:

1. Click on the arrow at the right side of the drop-down box to open the drop-down list box.
2. Click the up or down scroll arrow to scroll through the list to locate the desired item.
3. Click on the desired item within the list.

Option Buttons

Option buttons are available in some dialog boxes. You can select one option from a list at a time. The selected option has a black dot within the button. By pointing and clicking on another option, you can select it. When selected, the black dot appears in the new option button.

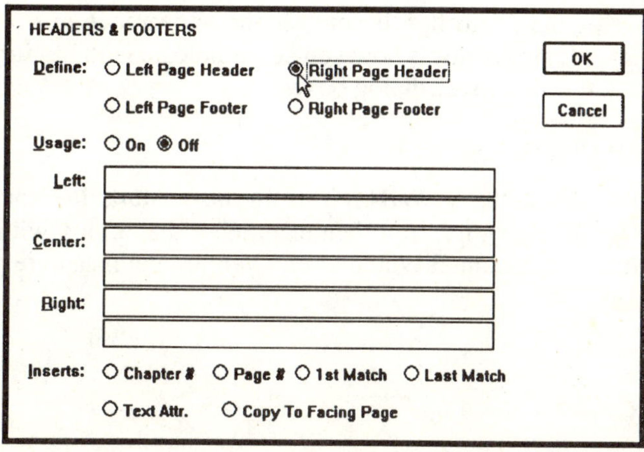

Check Boxes

Check boxes offer a list of options you can switch on and off. You can select as many or as few check box options as are desired. To select a check box, click on the box. An x appears within the box. To remove an x and unselect the check box, simply click on the box again.

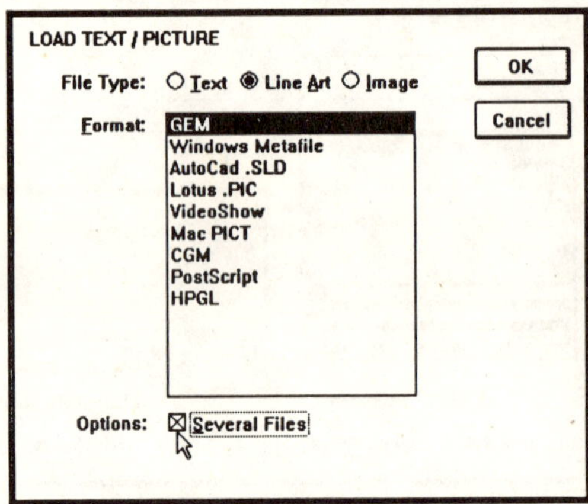

There are many additional things to learn about Microsoft Windows, and you should familiarize yourself with Windows to maximize your efficiency with Ventura. Refer to the *Microsoft Windows User's Guide* or Wordware Publishing's *Illustrated Microsoft Windows 3.0* for complete information about working with Windows whenever you have questions.

APPLICATIONS

Windows is how Ventura Publisher presents graphic based screens to you on your computer. As you work within these screens, you build your documents. Finally, after you have created the document and have its appearance as desired, it is time to print the document. The printing operation is totally controlled by Windows.

Look at Windows as the controller. It controls the appearance of your screens, and it controls your printer. It also controls how you communicate with Ventura by using dialog boxes, and you work within those dialog boxes.

TYPICAL OPERATION

In this activity, you delete the VPWIN.INF from the Ventura directory. Then you start Windows from the DOS prompt. You then examine a dialog box within Windows and finally start Ventura. It is assumed Windows and Ventura Publisher are properly installed on your computer.

1. Type **DEL C:\VENTURA\VPWIN.INF** at the DOS prompt, and press **Enter**.
2. Type **WIN** at the DOS Prompt, and press **Enter**. Within a few moments, you see the Windows screen.

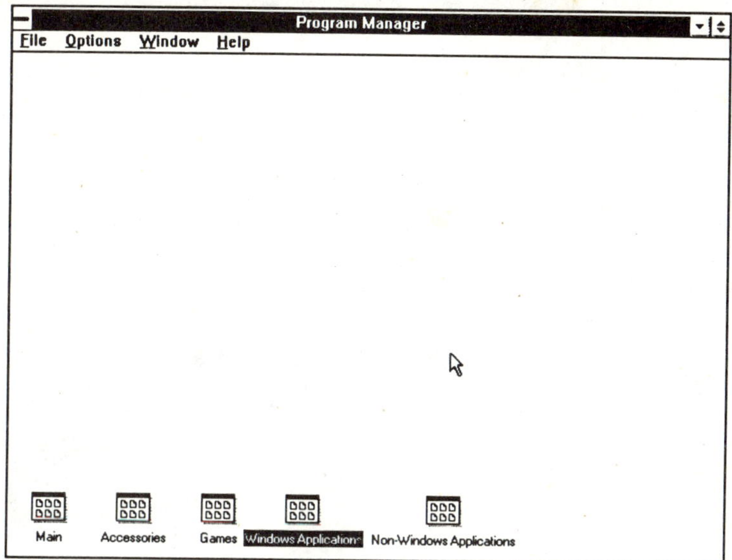

3. Point to **Help** in the Program Manager and click and hold the mouse button.
4. Move to the **About Program Manager** selection within the Help menu and release the mouse button. Your screen should resemble this illustration:

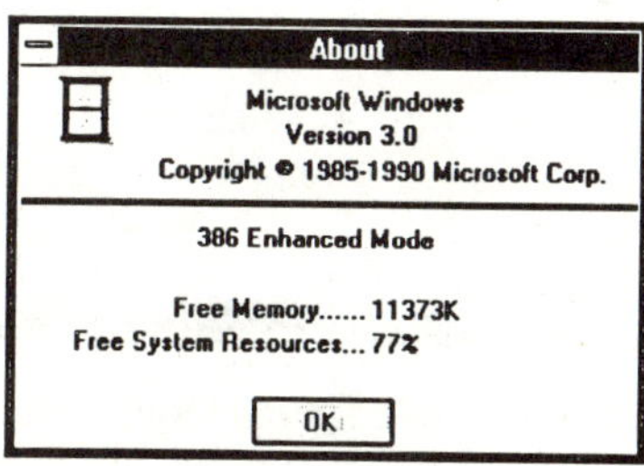

5. Click **OK** to dismiss the About dialog box.

6. Double click on the **Windows Applications** icon. Your screen should resemble this illustration:

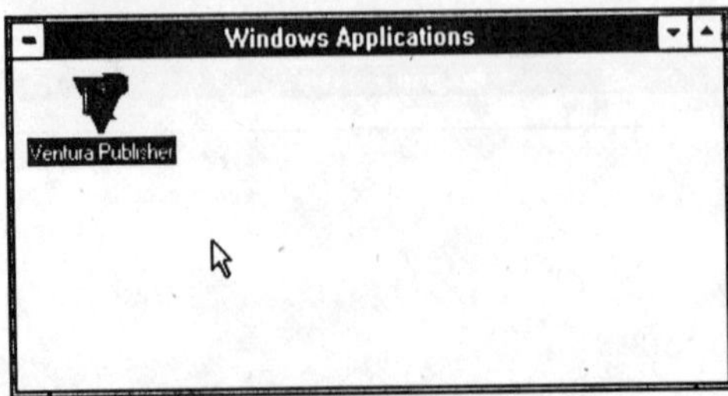

7. Double click on the **Ventura Publisher** icon. Within a few moments, the Ventura Publisher main screen appears:

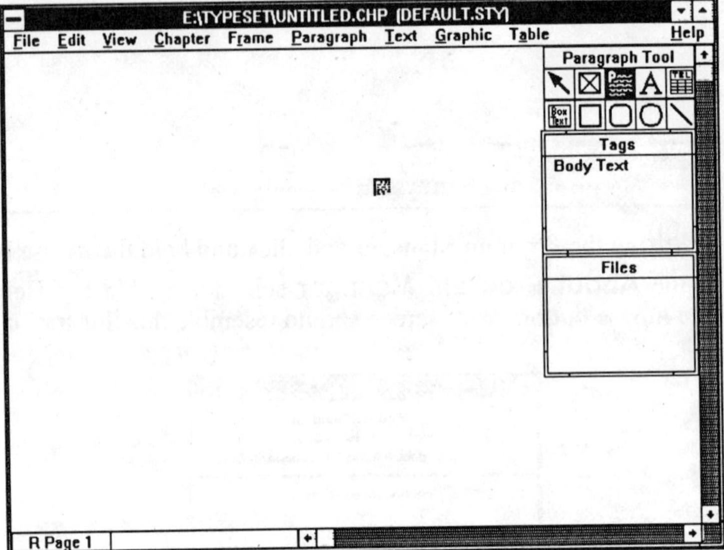

8. Turn to Module 81 to continue the learning sequence.

Appendix A
TERMS AND DEFINITIONS

Term	*Definition*
80286	The microprocessor chip (CPU) used in AT type computers.
8088	The microprocessor chip (CPU) used in PC/XT type computers.
Asynchronous	A term used to describe the way information is sent using a modem.
Ascender	The upward stroke of lowercase letters, such as h, k, l, and t.
ASCII	Acronym for American Standard Code for Information Interchange; 7-bit code that refers to the 256 characters that are used to represent the letters, numbers, control characters, and graphics symbols; the first 128 ASCII are standardized, the upper 128 differ between packages and computer models.
Baseline	The imaginary line that type sits on.
Baud rate	The speed of communications handled by the printer or modem, usually measured in bits per second.
Bits/Bytes	BIT: constructed from the words BInary digiT, the term refers to a single digit of a binary number (0/1), BYTE: (8 bits) the number of bits required to encode one character of information in any given computer system.
Bit map	The pattern of dots that makes up a digitized image.
Bug	An unintentional error in a program.
Button	One of the choices within a dialog box such as OK or Cancel.
CAD	Computer Aided Design/Computer Aided Drafting.
Camera-ready	Graphic layouts that are ready for mass reproduction.
Case	A choice between normal uppercase and lowercase, all capitals, and small capitals.
CGA	Color Graphics Adapter; the graphics card that controls a color monitor with a resolution of 320 x 200 pixels.
Click	To quickly press and release the mouse button.
Click and hold	To press and hold the mouse button.
Clipboard	A temporary holding area where items can be cut or copied. Ventura has three clipboards: one each for graphics, text, and frames.

Term	*Definition*
Compatible	Having the same characteristics and capabilities of an IBM PC; able to use software written to run on an IBM PC.
Computer system	This refers to the entire hardware package and would most properly include all software as well.
Computerese	A kind of confused gobbledegook double talk language only computer experts or hackers can understand.
Configuration	A complete hardware setup, usually consisting of a system unit, disk drives, a monitor, a keyboard, and a printer.
CPU	Central Processing Unit; the part or parts of computer hardware that carry out data manipulation (processing or moving data) and control the sequence of operations performed by the computer; the "brain" of the computer.
Crop	To eliminate unwanted portions of a picture.
Crop marks	Marks that indicate the outside edges of a page.
Cursor	A visible marker used to represent the current position on the display screen.
Daisywheel	An impact printer mechanism, which is usually a 4" diameter metal or plastic wheel with molded characters on the outer perimeter producing good quality printing.
Database	A collection of related information, which is usually filed in a memory area where the data can be easily retrieved.
Desktop publishing (DTP)	The use of a personal computer to generate near typeset quality documents.
Dialog box	Some commands, when accessed, require different options to be selected in order to complete the command. In order to make those various selections available within a command, the program displays a dialog box. When a command is listed in a menu followed by an ellipsis (...), a dialog box will appear when the command is selected.
Double click	To press and release the mouse button two times very rapidly.
Double-sided publication	A publication that, when printed, will be printed on both sides of the paper.
DPI	Dots Per Inch.
Drag	To press and hold the mouse button, and then move the mouse, dragging an object on the computer screen from one location to another.
Drop capital	A large capital letter used at the beginning of some paragraphs.
EGA	Enhanced Graphics Adapter; the graphics card that controls an Enhanced Color Monitor with a resolution of 640 x 350 pixels.

Term	*Definition*
Em	A space the width of the M character in the font.
En	A space the width of the N character in the font. An En is exactly one-half the width of an Em.
Fixed disk	A hard disk; a sealed disk drive with greater capacity and speed than a floppy disk drive.
Floppy disk	An oxide-coated, flexible plastic magnetic recording medium; access time is slow and capacity is small; it is used to record information in the form of binary digits.
Flush left	Aligning the text along the left margin, with the right margin of the text jagged.
Flush right	Aligning the text along the right margin, with the left margin of the text jagged.
Font	A specific typeface including a size and style. For example, Swiss 12 point Italic or Dutch 10 point Bold.
Format	The command used to prepare a disk to accept data; the style of letters such as bold, italic, or underline.
Function key	One of the special keys located on the side or top of a computer keyboard; these keys perform special functions or actions when used in different applications.
Greek	A computer function that converts lines of text into a series of unreadable lines. By doing so, the computer runs faster, rather than building each small line of text.
Gutter	The white space between columns of text.
Hard disk	A mechanical mechanism on which a magnetic secondary-storage medium is mounted to make its data accessible to the computer; a drive contains all electrical and mechanical components necessary to read or write data on its medium; (same as fixed disk or winchester disk).
Hardware	The physical devices included in a computer system.
Hyphenation	The breaking of a word at the end of a line of text at the word's syllables.
Icon	A picture or graphical representation of an action or object.
Image	A picture which is composed of individual dots created with a "paint" program or with a scanner.
Indent	The white space at the beginning of the paragraph, on the first line.
Interface	A device that allows the computer to work with the outside world; a shared boundary between two systems or two devices.
Italic	Slanted type often used to emphasize specific text.
Justified	Text where both the left and right margins are aligned.

Term	Definition
Kerning	The reduction of space between letters of a word.
Keyboard	The part of a computer which looks like a typewriter and allows communication between operator and computer.
Kilobyte (K)	Generally used to describe the storage capacity of a computer's RAM memory or disk storage. 1024 bytes (210); for most purposes "1000" bytes.
LAN	Local Area Network; a communications system that interconnects computer equipment within a limited geographical area.
Landscape	Horizontal or wide page orientation.
Laser printer	A printer that uses technologies similar to photocopiers for printing; fast, quiet, high quality, high price.
Layout	The overall design of a page.
Leading	The amount of space between the lines of text.
Letterspacing	The amount of space between the letters of a word.
Lowercase	The use of small letters, such as g, s, m, and h.
Mainframe	Refers to the central control and processor of any large computer complex; the largest type of computer.
Menu Bar	The area of the top of the computer screen where the various menus can be accessed.
MDA	Monochrome Display Adapter; the card that controls a monochrome monitor (one color); usually cannot display graphs.
Megabyte	1024 Kilobytes; a million bytes; usually refers to the storage capacity of a hard disk drive.
Microcomputer	Refers to a complete computer system built around a microprocessor CPU; a desktop computer; a personal computer.
Modem	MOdulator/DEModulator; a device for changing serial binary numbers into a signal that can be transmitted over standard telephone lines, or the reverse; device that allows different computers to "talk" to each other.
Monitor	The TV like set which contains the CRT (screen) for you to look at as you work at the keyboard.
Mouse	An input device that is used to move the cursor around the screen in order to carry out various operations.
MS-DOS	MicroSoft Disk Operating System.
Network	An intercommunicating group of computer systems and/or terminals.
Operating system	The system software that makes the computer system run; an organized collection of techniques and procedures to supervise and control the running of all other programs.

Term	*Definition*
Orphan	A line of text left alone on the bottom of a page or a column.
PC AT	A personal computer with an 80286 CPU.
PC XT	A personal computer with an 8088 CPU and usually a hard disk.
PC-DOS	IBM's personal computer disk operating system.
PC	A personal computer with an 8088 CPU.
Paragraph	A character, a word, a group of words, a sentence, or a group of sentences that end with a required carrier return. The required carrier return is placed in the text each time the Enter key is selected.
Pica	A pica is approximately 1/6 of an inch. There are 12 points in a pica. The pica is a measurement used by printers.
Plotter	An output device similar to a printer but used mainly for printing graphic images by moving a pen around on the paper.
Point	A point is approximately 1/72 of an inch. The point is a measurement used by printers.
Port	The connection point in the computer for peripherals, such as the mouse, monitor, and printer.
Portrait	Vertical or tall page orientation.
PostScript	A language used to describe how to print a page which consists of both text and pictures.
Pop-up menu	A menu that pops up when selected. These menus are found within a dialog box.
Printer	The hardware which prints the data on paper.
Programming	A predefined method for using and combining language and a set of instructions or symbols in the writing of a program.
Program	A set of commands or steps that control the actions of the computer.
Proportional spacing	A font where the width of each letter is different. For example, the M is much wider than the i.
PS/2	IBM's Personal System/2 computers, which have replaced the PC line of personal computers.
Pull-down menu	A menu that drops down so commands can be accessed. The menu drops down when pointed to by the mouse.
RAM	Random Access Memory; a kind of internal memory whose locations can be accessed and the contents retrieved with the same access time for all locations; the computer memory where calculations and processing take place; data stored in RAM memory is lost when the power is turned off
Register marks	Alignment marks which are used by a printer when printing more than one color on a sheet of paper.

Term	*Definition*
ROM	Read Only Memory; memory from which it is possible to read information but onto which data cannot be written; data stored in ROM memory remains when the power is turned off
Rule	A line used as a divider between text or pictures.
Rulers	A measuring device located on the left and top of the computer screen work area.
Sans serif	A typeface without serifs, such as Helvetica or Swiss.
Scanner	A device which converts a paper drawing or picture into a computer image.
Scroll bars	The bars positioned along the right and bottom borders of the screen. Scroll bars are used to move the portion of the page that is visible. By using the mouse, the page can be moved.
Serif	The short lines at the end of the main strokes of letters. Some typefaces are called serif, such as Times or Dutch.
Software	The programs that cause the computer to perform specific functions.
Spreadsheet	A type of application software used mainly for analysis.
SQL	Structured Query Language; an IBM relational database product and query/reporting language.
Style sheet	A file that contains specific information used to control the format and appearance of a document. Information regarding the format of paragraphs, the page layout, and columns is some of the data stored within a style sheet.
Tag	The format that establishes the appearance of a paragraph.
Terminal	Any device for providing input and/or output to and/or from a computer.
Thin space	A space half the size of an En.
Title bar	The bar that appears at the top of the screen and displays the current chapter file and current style sheet being used.
Type style	One or more of the following: normal, italics, boldface, underlined, strikethru.
Typeface	A family of fonts where all letters, numbers, and symbols have a uniform appearance. Century Schoolbook is one example of a family of type.
Underlying page	A special frame common to all pages within a Xerox Ventura Publisher document and permanent part of the style sheet. The underlying page controls the overall appearance of the entire document.
Uppercase	Capital letters such as G, J, B, and M.

Term	*Definition*
User friendly	An abused term which refers to software that is supposed to be easy to operate.
User	Someone who uses a computer.
VGA	Video Graphics Array, the latest graphic technology being used in the PS/2 computer.
Widow	A line left alone at the top of a page or a column.
Width table	A table that contains information about the fonts.
Winchester disk	A hard or fixed disk drive.
Word processing	A type of software application which is used for the creation, changing, and storing of text.
Word spacing	Adding spacing between words to fill a text line, making it look justified.
WYSIWYG	An acronym meaning What You See Is What You Get. WYSIWYG means the final copy generated from your printer will look like what appears on your computer screen.

Appendix B
TEXT ATTRIBUTE CODES

Ventura translates, displays and prints text attributes, such as boldface and underline, from each word processor it supports. For example, any text assigned Bold in WordPerfect 5.0 is automatically assigned Bold when imported into Ventura. And any text attributes added using Ventura's Text Editing mode are stored in the text file, and the codes are stored in the word processor's native file format.

Ventura can create a much wider range of text attributes than any word processor. Those attributes are also stored in the word processor text file, using the codes shown below.

For example, the beginning of medium italic text is set by inserting <MI> directly before the text to be italicized.

You can insert the text attribute code in your word processor. To do so, simply insert the code between the left and right angle brackets. For example, type this text in your word processor:

This is an example of <U>underlined<D> text that would create text in Ventura that looked like this:

> This is an example of underlined text.

The text attribute can be set for any of the basic attributes, typeface, point size, kerning, offset, and color.

Basic Attributes

The basic text attribute codes are:

Code	*Attribute*	*Code*	*Attribute*
<B>	Bold weight type	<S>	Small type
<D>	Normal weight type	<U>	Underline
<I>	Italic type	<X>	Strikethrough
<L>	Light weight type	<=>	Double underline
<M>	Medium weight type	<^>	Superscript
<O>	Overscore	<v>	Subscript

The attributes can be used alone or in combination. For example, <B> can be entered to begin bold, or <BIU> can be entered to begin bold italic underline text.

All attributes are terminated at the end of a paragraph, even if the Resume Normal code <D> is not found.

Also, all previous attributes are terminated anytime new attributes are set. For example, consider this sentence:

The man jogged down the street.

To assign bold only to the word "man" type:

The <B>man<D> jogged down the street.

To assign bold only to the word "man" and underline to "jogged," type:

The <B>man <U>jogged<D> down the street.

To assign bold to both "man" and "jogged," and underline to the word "jogged," type:

The <B>man <BU>jogged<D> down the street.

Of course, if you are using a supported word processor, simply enter the command in your word processor as desired, and Ventura will translate the word processor code automatically for you.

Typeface

To set the typeface, type <Fnnn> where nnn is the number of the typeface desired. The numbers and typefaces are:

Number	*Typeface*	*Number*	*Typeface*
1	Courier	39	Cheltenham
2	Swiss (like Helvetica)	50	Helvetica Narrow
14	Dutch (like Times)	51	Avant Garde
20	New Century Schlbk	52	Optima
21	Palantino	53	Korinna
22	Garamond	54	Helvetica Light
23	Bookman	55	Helvetica Black
24	Lubalin	56	Franklin Gothic
25	Souvenir	57	Franklin Gothic Heavy
26	Benguiat	58	Helvetica Cond. Light
27	Glypha	59	Helvetica Cond.
28	Friz Quadrata	60	Helvetica Cond. Black
29	Zapf Chancery	100	American Typewriter
30	Trump Mediaeval	101	Machine
31	Melior	103	Prestige Elite
32	Galliard	104	Orator
33	New Baskerville	105	Letter Gothic
34	Goudy	128	Symbol
35	Park Avenue	129	Zapf Dingbats
36	Bodoni	130	Sonata
37	Bodoni Poster	255	Reset to typeface for tag
38	Century Old Style		

To set the point size, type <Pnnn> where nnn is the number of points. The maximum point size available is 254. <P255> resets the point size to that specified in the paragraph tag.

Kerning

To begin the kerning value, type <Knnn> where nnn is any value between -127 and +127. Replace n with the amount of left horizontal shift, measured in 1/300th of an inch. The measurement is used to reset the kerning to zero.

Use <B%n> to Kern/Track the text, and replace n with the number of Ems to add (positive values of n) or subtract (negative number of n) between each character in the selected text. Place <D%0> to mark the end of the text which should be kerned or tracked.

Baseline Jump

To make the baseline jump up or down, type <Jnnn> where nnn is the number of points to shift the baseline. The n may range from 1 to 256. Use <J0> to reset the Baseline Jump to zero.

Color

To set the color of text, type <Cnnn> where nnn is the number of the color to use. The numbers and colors are:

Number	*Color*	*Number*	*Color*
0	White	4	Blue
1	Black	5	Cyan
2	Red	6	Yellow
3	Green	7	Magenta

Use <C255> to reset the color to the color assigned in the tag.

Other Inserted Text

There are some other text codes that can be inserted. They are:

Code	*Text Attribute*
<$B0>	Box (Hollow)
<$B1>	Box (Filled)
<->	Discretionary Hyphen
<_>	Em Space
<~>	En Space
<+>	Figure Space
<R>	Line Break
<N>	Nonbreaking Space
<$R[P#]>	Page Number
<|>	Thin Space

Appendix C
TAGGING TEXT WITH A WORD PROCESSOR

Ventura Publisher's Text Editing function was not designed for extensive word processing. It should be used for "fine-tuning" text, making final editions, deletions, and other minor changes.

When you must enter large amounts of text, it is always better to use a regular word processor. You can then import the text that was prepared in the word processor into Ventura for formatting.

In the same manner, it is normally better to use a word processor to tag the text, rather than using Ventura's Paragraph Tagging function. This is because tagging paragraphs with a word processor is faster than tagging with Ventura.

When a paragraph is tagged with a word processor, the same information is typed that Ventura automatically adds to a text file when text is tagged with Ventura.

For example, you have two headline tags in your style sheet called H1 and H2 for tagging level one and two headlines. You are working with the following text:

> Desktop Publishing Training
> This document contains the four-part plan designed to train our employees in desktop publishing techniques.
> Classroom Training
> This section contains our plan to establish formal classroom training.
> Training Consultant
> This section contains our recommendation to use the services of a training consultant to train our employees in the use of Xerox Ventura Publisher.

If you use Ventura's paragraph tagging function to format the first headline as a level one headline, Ventura adds the paragraph tag's name to the word processing file:

> @H1 =

so the text file appears:

> @H1 = Desktop Publishing Training

Ventura adds this text to the word processing file if you are using Paragraph Tagging to format the next two headlines as level two headlines.

> @H1 = Desktop Publishing Training
> This document contains the four-part plan designed to train our employees in desktop publishing techniques.

@H2 = Classroom Training
This section contains our plan to establish formal classroom training.
@H2 = Training Consultant
This section contains our recommendation to use the services of a training consultant to train our employees in the use of Ventura.

You can tag the paragraphs if you simply type the paragraph tag text with your word processor. The tag text must begin in the very left margin.

A paragraph tag always begins with @ and ends with a space, the = sign, and a space. For example, @Bullet = is a proper tag name for Ventura.

NOTE

The @ *must* always be the first character in the line at the beginning of a tagged paragraph.

Typically, it is best if you keep tag names short. This reduces the amount of paragraph tag text that clutters the computer screen as you edit your text file with a word processor. For example, suppose that in the previous example you use the words HEADLINE 1 and HEADLINE 2 for the level one and two headline tags. Your file would now look like this:

@HEADLINE 1 = Desktop Publishing Training
This document contains the four-part plan designed to train our employees in desktop publishing techniques.
@HEADLINE 2 = Classroom Training
This section contains our plan to establish formal classroom training.
@HEADLINE 2 = Training Consultant
This section contains our recommendation to use the services of a training consultant to train our employees in the use of Ventura.

The clutter becomes even more obvious and unworkable if your document is heavily tagged with long-named tags. For example, suppose each of the paragraphs under the headline is tagged with SUMMARY 1 for the section summary. The text file now looks like this:

@HEADLINE 1 = Desktop Publishing Training
@SUMMARY 1 = This document contains the four part plan designed to train our employees in desktop publishing techniques.
@HEADLINE 2 = Classroom Training
@SUMMARY 1 = This section contains our plan to establish formal classroom training.
@HEADLINE 2 = Training Consultant
@SUMMARY 1 = This section contains our recommendation to use the services of a training consultant to train our employees in the use of Ventura.

To keep your paragraph tags short, here are some suggested tag names and functions:

Name	*Function*	*Type in Text File*
BY	Byline	@BY =
BL	Bullet List Item	@BL =
DC	Drop Capital	@DC =
C#	Chapter Number	@C# =
HO	Chapter Headline	@HO =
H1	Level One Headline	@H1 =
H2	Level Two Headline	@H2 =
H3	Level Three Headline	@H3 =
H4	Level Four Headline	@H4 =
IH	Hanging Indent	@IH =
IN	Normal Indent	@IN =
QL	Long Quote	@QL =
QS	Short Quote	@QS =
SH	Subheadline	@SH =
SS	Section Summary	@SS =
T1	Table Column One*	@T1 =
T2	Table Column Two*	@T2 =
T3	Table Column Three*	@T3 =

*A table where tag items for each column with a different paragraph tag uses the principles of vertical tabs.

Any paragraph not tagged will be assigned the attributes of Body Text within the current style sheet. Accordingly, you do not need to enter the paragraph tag @BODY TEXT =. Ventura will automatically assign untagged paragraphs to the body text tag.

If you have two paragraphs in a row with the same tag name and the text is not body text, you *must* place the tag name on each paragraph. Paragraph tag names do not carry over to the next paragraph. Ventura recognizes the end of a paragraph by the carriage return.

You must spell the tag name exactly as it appears in the style sheet. For example, Bullet 1 and Bullet1 are two *different* paragraph tags to Ventura. If Ventura cannot match a paragraph tag in your text with one in the current style sheet, it will apply the Body Text tag attributes to the paragraph with the unrecognized paragraph tag and add the new name to the Assignment List.

One tip to accurately placing paragraph tags is to use the Macro feature of your word processor. For example, you could create a macro that automatically types @Headline 1 = each time you need it. Not only will the macro save you the time of typing in the paragraph tag, but it will eliminate a typo or spelling error.

THE BLANK LINES PROBLEM

As you work with a word processor, you naturally press Enter twice at the end of a paragraph: once, to mark the end of the paragraph, and the second time to create a blank line. The blank line between paragraphs makes the finished document more readable. However, Ventura interprets these blank lines—placed between the paragraphs—as paragraphs to be formatted. This creates a real problem when you begin formatting your document.

Consider this example:

You create a headline tag that forces Ventura to always position the headline and first paragraph following the headline on the same page. This prevents a headline from appearing by itself at the bottom of a page.

If the headline appears near the bottom of the page when the document is formatted, the first paragraph of the text actually appears at the top of the next page. This is because Ventura interprets the blank line between the paragraphs, and not the subsequent text, as the next paragraph. Ventura is actually keeping the next paragraph (the blank line) with the headline as requested. But the result is not expected or desired.

In addition, if paragraph spacing is added using Ventura's Spacing command, there may be too much space between paragraphs because of the blank lines.

One approach to this problem is to use Ventura's blank line filter. To use the filter, type this as the very first line of your text file:

@PARAFILTER ON =

This filter causes Ventura to ignore blank lines when a text file is loaded. However, the filter also removes blank lines if you ever save the text file from within Ventura.

The removal of the blank lines, although needed for proper formatting within Ventura, makes your editing task more difficult.

As recommended in the beginning of this book, you should be an experienced word processor user. You should be able to use the Search and Replace commands of your word processor without difficulty. You can use Search and Replace to search for <Carriage Return><Carriage Return> and replace it with <Carriage Return>. Also, to make editing easier, you can reverse the process by searching for <Carriage Return> and replacing it with <Carriage Return><Carriage Return>.

ENTERING OTHER CONTROLS

You can also enter the codes Ventura uses for anchors, footnotes, hidden text (comments), and index entries with your word processor.

Anchors

To enter anchor information, type:

<$&anchorname> to place the frame on the same page as the anchor.

<$&anchorname[v]> to place the frame below the anchor position.

<$&anchorname[^]> to place the frame above the anchor position.

Footnotes

To enter footnote information, type <$FContent of the footnote>.

Hidden Text

To enter hidden text, type <$!Content of hidden text>.

Hidden text is used for comment lines. You never see the hidden text on the screen or in the final Ventura printout. You see it only when you open the text file with your word processor.

Index Entries

To enter index entries, type:

<$IPrimary Entry[Sort Key];Secondary Entry[Sort Key]>

for a regular index entry.

<$SPrimary Entry[Sort Key];See Reference[Sort Key]>

for a "See Also" entry.

Appendix D
COMMAND KEYS

Many of the commands available within Ventura can be accessed by using keyboard shortcuts. Most of these commands are accessed by pressing and holding the Ctrl key and then pressing another key. These are designated in this book as Ctrl-? where ? is the name of the key to press in combination with the Ctrl key.

For some Ventura keyboard commands, you must press two keys in combination with the Ctrl key. For example, to create the copyright symbol ©, you must press and hold the Ctrl key, the Shift key, and then the letter C.

Finally, sometimes, you need only press a single key on the keyboard to execute a command. For example, press End to go to the last page in your Ventura document.

The keyboard commands and their keys in alphabetical order by command name are:

Command	*Key*
Add frame, tag, or set font	Ctrl-2
Assign function keys	Ctrl-K
Bring to Front	Ctrl-A
Cancel (from dialog box)	Ctrl-X
Copy	Shift-Del
Copyright	Ctrl-Shift-C
Cut	Del
Delete <- of the cursor	Backspace
Delete -> of the cursor	Del
Delete Selection line text	Esc
Discretionary Hyphen	Ctrl- -
Double Quote, closed	Ctrl-Shift-]
Double Quote, open	Ctrl-Shift-[
Edit Special Item	Ctrl-D
Em dash	Ctrl-]
Em space	Ctrl-Shift-M
En dash	Ctrl-[
En space	Ctrl-Shift-N
Enlarged View	Ctrl-E
Edit Special Item	Ctrl-D
Figure Space	Ctrl-Shift-F
Fill Attributes	Ctrl-F
Frame Mode	Ctrl-U
Go to Page	Ctrl-G

Command	*Key*
Go to First Page	Home
Go to Last Page	End
Go to Next Page	PgDn
Go to Previous Page	PgUp
Graphic Mode	Ctrl-P
Insert Special Item	Ctrl-C
Line Attributes	Ctrl-L
Nonbreaking Space	Ctrl-Spacebar
Normal View	Ctrl-N
Paragraph Mode	Ctrl-I
Paste	Ins
Recall Last Dialog Box (or Cancel)	Ctrl-X
Redraw Screen	Esc
Reduced View	Ctrl-R
Registered Trademark	Ctrl-Shift-R
Renumber Chapter	Ctrl-B
Save	Ctrl-S
Select All (graphics)	Ctrl-Q
Send to Back	Ctrl-Z
Show/Hide Files List	Ctrl-V
Show/Hide Tabs & Returns	Ctrl-T
Show/Hide Tags List	Ctrl-Y
Show/Hide Toolbox	Ctrl-W
Text Mode	Ctrl-O
Thin space	Ctrl-Shift-T
Trademark	Ctrl-Shift-2
Update Tag List	Ctrl-K

The keyboard commands listed alphabetically are:

Key	*Command*
Backspace	Delete <- of the cursor
Ctrl- -	Discretionary Hyphen
Ctrl-2	Add frame, tag, or set font
Ctrl-A	Bring to Front
Ctrl-B	Renumber Chapter
Ctrl-C	Insert Special Item
Ctrl-D	Edit Special Item
Ctrl-E	Enlarged View
Ctrl-F	Fill Attributes
Ctrl-G	Go to Page
Ctrl-I	Paragraph Mode
Ctrl-K	Update Tag List

Key	*Command*
Ctrl-K	Assign function keys
Ctrl-L	Line Attributes
Ctrl-N	Normal View
Ctrl-O	Text Mode
Ctrl-P	Graphic Mode
Ctrl-Q	Select All (graphics)
Ctrl-R	Reduced View
Ctrl-S	Save
Ctrl-Shift-2	Trademark
Ctrl-Shift-C	Copyright
Ctrl-Shift-F	Figure Space
Ctrl-Shift-M	Em Space
Ctrl-Shift-N	En Space
Ctrl-Shift-R	Registered Trademark
Ctrl-Shift-T	Thin Space
Ctrl-Shift-[	Double Quote, open
Ctrl-Shift-]	Double Quote, closed
Ctrl-Spacebar	Nonbreaking space
Ctrl-T	Show/Hide Tabs & Returns
Ctrl-U	Frame Mode
Ctrl-V	Show/Hide Tags List
Ctrl-W	Show/Hide Toolbox
Ctrl-X	Cancel (from dialog box)
Ctrl-X	Recall Last Dialog Box (or Cancel)
Ctrl-Y	Show/Hide Files List
Ctrl-Z	Send to Back
Ctrl-[	En dash
Ctrl-]	Em dash
Del	Cut (in Frame mode)
Del	Delete -> of the cursor (in Text Editing mode)
End	Go to Last Page
Esc	Redraw screen
Esc	Delete Selection line text
Home	Go to First Page
Ins	Paste
PgDn	Go to Next Page
PgUp	Go to Previous Page
Shift-Del	Copy

Appendix E
CHARACTER SETS

This appendix contains the characters and their decimal and ANSI equivalents that can be displayed and printed with Ventura. There are two character sets—one for regular letters, and one for mathematical and greek characters (SYMBOL). The regular letters are called International and contain many special characters needed for most Romance languages, including English, Spanish, French, Italian, and German.

To use one of these special characters while in Ventura for Windows:

1. Locate the desired character and determine the ANSI equivalent from the chart.
2. Press and hold Alt and enter the ANSI equivalent using the keys on the numeric keypad. Do not use the numbers above the letters.
3. After the number has been entered, release Alt. The character appears on the screen in the International font.
4. To display a Symbol character, select the text, press Ctrl-2 to select the Set Font Attributes dialog box, then choose the Symbol font.

The type of printer, as well as available fonts, determines the final result.

You can also insert a special character decimal code into your text file with your word processor. To do so, type the decimal equivalent of the special character between the left and right angle brackets. For example, suppose you wanted to display the copyright symbol. Simply type <189>. Decimal <189> is converted to ANSI 0169 when the file is displayed in Ventura. When Ventura formats the text, the copyright symbol will be placed in the document.

CAUTION

Do not use the Alt key to enter a decimal equivalent in the text file, as the interpretation of keyboard entries is performed by Windows and not by Ventura.

Decimal	ANSI	International	Symbol
32	032		
33	033	!	!
34	034	"	∀
35	035	#	#
36	036	$	∃
37	037	%	%
38	038	&	&
39	039	'	∋
40	040	(	(
41	041	)	)
42	042	*	∗
43	043	+	+
44	044	,	,
45	045	-	−
46	046	.	.
47	047	/	/
48	048	0	0
49	049	1	1
50	050	2	2
51	051	3	3
52	052	4	4
53	053	5	5
54	054	6	6
55	055	7	7
56	056	8	8
57	057	9	9
58	058	:	:
59	059	;	;
60	060	<	<
61	061	=	=
62	062	>	>
63	063	?	?
64	064	@	≅
65	065	A	A
66	066	B	B
67	067	C	X
68	068	D	Δ
69	069	E	E
70	070	F	Φ
71	071	G	Γ
72	072	H	H
73	073	I	I
74	074	J	ϑ
75	075	K	K
76	076	L	Λ
77	077	M	M
78	078	N	N
79	079	O	O
80	080	P	Π
81	081	Q	Θ
82	082	R	P
83	083	S	Σ
84	084	T	T
85	085	U	Y
86	086	V	ς
87	087	W	Ω
88	088	X	Ξ
89	089	Y	Ψ
90	090	Z	Z
91	091	[	[
92	092	\	∴
93	093	]	]
94	094	^	⊥
95	095	_	_
96	096	‘	
97	097	a	α
98	098	b	β
99	099	c	χ

Decimal	ANSI	International	Symbol	Decimal	ANSI	International	Symbol
100	0100	d	δ	132	0228	ä	⁄
101	0101	e	ε	133	0224	à	∞
102	0102	f	φ	134	0229	å	ƒ
103	0103	g	γ	135	0231	ç	♣
104	0104	h	η	136	0234	ê	♦
105	0105	i	ι	137	0235	ë	♥
106	0106	j	ϕ	138	0232	è	♠
107	0107	k	κ	139	0239	ï	↔
108	0108	l	λ	140	0238	î	←
109	0109	m	μ	141	0236	ì	↑
110	0110	n	ν	142	0196	Ä	→
111	0111	o	ο	143	0197	Å	↓
112	0112	p	π	144	0201	É	°
113	0113	q	θ	145	0230	æ	±
114	0114	r	ρ	146	0198	Æ	″
115	0115	s	σ	147	0244	ô	≥
116	0116	t	τ	148	0246	ö	×
117	0117	u	υ	149	0242	ò	∝
118	0118	v	ϖ	150	0251	û	∂
119	0119	w	ω	151	0249	ù	•
120	0120	x	ξ	152	0255	ÿ	÷
121	0121	y	ψ	153	0214	Ö	≠
122	0122	z	ζ	154	0220	Ü	≡
123	0123	{	{	155	0162	¢	≈
124	0124	|	|	156	0156	£	…
125	0125	}	}	157	0165	¥	|
126	0126	~	~	158	0164	¤	—
127	0127			159	0136	ƒ	↵
128	0199	Ç		160	0225	á	ℵ
129	0252	ü	ϒ	161	0237	í	ℑ
130	0233	é	′	162	0243	ó	ℜ
131	0226	â	≤	163	0250	ú	℘

Decimal	ANSI	Inter-national	Symbol	Decimal	ANSI	Inter-national	Symbol
164	0241	ñ	⊗	194			®
165	0209	Ñ	⊕	195		°	©
166	0170	ª	∅	196	0150	–	™
167	0186	º	∩	197	0151	—	∑
168	0191	¿	∪	198	0176	°	⎛
169	0147	“	⊃	199	0193	Á	⎜
170	0148	”	⊇	200	0194	Â	⎝
171			⊄	201	0200	È	⎡
172			⊂	202	0202	Ê	⎢
173	0161	¡	⊆	203	0203	Ë	⎣
174	0171	«	∈	204	0204	Ì	⎧
175	0187	»	∉	205	0205	Í	⎨
176	0227	ã	∠	206	0206	Î	⎩
177	0245	õ	∇	207	0207	Ï	⎪
178	0216	Ø	®	208	0210	Ò	
179	0248	ø	©	209	0211	Ó	〉
180			™	210	0212	Ô	∫
181			∏	211			⌠
182	0192	À	√	212			⎮
183	0195	Ã	·	213	0217	Ù	⌡
184	0213	Õ	¬	214	0218	Ú	⎞
185	0167	§	∧	215	0219	Û	⎟
186			∨	216		Ÿ	⎠
187			⇔	217	0223	ß	⎤
188	0182	¶	⇐	218		Ž	⎥
189	0169	©	⇑	219		ž	⎦
190	0174	®	⇒	220		/	⎫
191	0153	™	⇓	221			⎬
192	0132	„	◊	222			⎭
193	0133	…	〈				

Appendix F
EQUATION COMMANDS

Xerox Ventura Publisher offers an extensive set of commands when working in the equation editor. These commands permit the creation of many different scientific and mathematical equations.

Command	*Example*	*Result*
braces	text~roman{text}	$\mathit{text}\ \mathrm{text}$
/	x~=~a/b	$x = {}^a/_b$
above	(see *pile*)	
back	y back 120 x	$x\,y$
ccol	(see *maatrix)*	
cpile	(see *pile*)	
down	y down 100 x	y $\ \ x$
from	(see *sum*)	
fwd	y fwd 100 x	$y \quad x$
int	int sub 0 sup inf {^1 over x^dx}	$\int_0^\infty \frac{1}{x}\,dx$
inter	C~=~A inter B	$C = A \cap B$
lcol	(see *matrix*)	
left	left {text right}	$\left\{ text \right\}$
	left {a sub b sup c right}	$\left\{ a_b^c \right\}$
lineup	(see *mark*)	
lpile	(see *pile*)	
mark	y sub n+1~mark=~y sub n^+^1	$y_{n+1} = y_n + 1$
	y sub 0~lineup=~0	$y_0 = 0$
	y sub {last}~lineup=~inf	$y_{last} = \infty$

Command	*Example*	*Result*
matrix	matrix {ccol{a above b} ~ccol {c above d}}	$\begin{matrix} a & c \\ b & d \end{matrix}$
over	a over {b^+^c}	$\dfrac{a}{b+c}$
pile	rpile { 0 above 2x above 0 } ~~lpile { x < 0 above 0 <=x <=1 above 1<x }	$\begin{matrix} 0 & x<0 \\ 2x & 0<=x<=1 \\ 0 & 1<x \end{matrix}$
prod	prod from {i~=~1} to inf X sub i	$\prod_{i=1}^{\infty} X_i$
rcol	(see *matrix*)	
right	left { rpile { {x~+~y} above x above x sup 2} right }	$\left\{ \begin{matrix} x+y \\ x \\ x^2 \end{matrix} \right\}$
rpile	(see *pile*)	
sqrt	sqrt {x sup 2^+^y sup 2}	$\sqrt{x^2+y^2}$
sub	a sub b	a_b
	a sub b sub c	a_{b_c}
sum	sum from {i~=~1} to inf X sub i	$\sum_{i=1}^{\infty} X_i$
sup	a sup b	a^b
	a sup b sup c	a^{b^c}
	a sub b sup c	a_b^c
	a sup b sub c	a^{b_c}
to	(see *sum*)	
union	C~=~A union B	$C = A \cup B$
up	y up 100 x	$\begin{matrix} & x \\ y & \end{matrix}$

Appendix G
VENTURA EXERCISES

1. About This Book
   a. What is a module?
   b. What hardware is required to use Ventura?
   c. Describe the contents of the modules.
   d. Is a mouse required to use Ventura?
   e. What other programs should you be proficient with before you begin learning Ventura?
2. Ventura Publisher Overview
   a. What is desktop publishing?
   b. What is a "camera-ready" document?
   c. How is Ventura equal to a graphic designer's layout table?
   d. What type of documents can be produced with Ventura?
   e. Describe how the author views learning Ventura.
   f. What is WYSIWYG?
   g. Is there such a thing as true WYSIWYG?
   h. Describe at least one laser printer limitation.
   i. How do you install Ventura?
   j. How do you start Ventura?
   k. List ten of the thirteen parts of the Ventura screen.
   l. What is the title bar?
   m. Describe the scroll bars, how they can be used, and where they are located.
   n. What is a Side-bar?
   o. Name the five typical mouse operations.
   p. How many different mouse cursor shapes are there in Ventura?
   q. What is a frame?
   r. What is a paragraph tag?
   s. What are Ventura pull-down menus?
   t. What is a dialog box?
   u. Describe a pica and a point.
   v. What is a style sheet?
   w. What are Ventura's modes of operation?
3. Sample Session
   a. What is the purpose of the Sample Session?
   b. Why should Ventura not be used as a word processor?
   c. Why must a specific extension be used as a filename extension on a text file?
   d. What is the VP.INF file?

e. Why was VP.INF removed?
f. Describe the procedure to load a text file.
g. Describe the procedure to select Text Attributes.
h. Describe the procedure to alter the style sheet.
i. Describe the procedure to use another style sheet.
j. Describe the two methods of changing views.
k. Describe how to insert a new page in a Ventura document.
l. How is a Ventura chapter saved?
m. Describe how to quit Ventura.

4. Add New Tag
   a. Describe the paragraph tagging function of Ventura.
   b. How are tag attributes changed?
   c. How many types of tags are there in Ventura Publisher?
   d. Describe the procedure to add a new tag in Ventura Publisher.
   e. What does Ctrl-2 do?

5. Alignment
   a. Name the four types of alignment available in Ventura.
   b. What is a relative indent?
   c. What is an outdent?
   d. What is an indent?
   e. Where is the Alignment command located in Ventura Publisher?
   f. What effect can rivers of white space have on your documents?

6. Anchors & Captions
   a. What is the difference between an anchor and a caption?
   b. Can an anchor and caption be assigned to the underlying page frame?
   c. What is the Table Counter and the Figure Counter?
   d. How is the Anchors & Captions command accessed?
   e. Describe the procedure for setting an anchor.
   f. Describe the procedure for creating a caption.

7. Attribute Overrides
   a. What is the purpose of having an Attribute Overrides command?
   b. List five attributes that can be added with the Attribute Overrides command.
   c. Describe the procedure for changing text attributes by using the Attribute Overrides command.

8. Auto-Numbering
   a. What is auto-numbering?
   b. Can auto-numbering be assigned to text located in frames?
   c. List five different numbering schemes Ventura can create.
   d. What paragraph tag is created for auto-numbered text?

e. Describe the procedure for changing the text attributes of auto-numbered text.
f. Describe the procedure for setting auto-numbering in a Ventura chapter.
g. How is the Renumber command related to the auto-numbering command?
h. Where is the Auto-Numbering command located?

9. Box Character

a. What is a box character?
b. Why is the Box Character available in Ventura?
c. Where is the box character command located?
d. What is the keyboard shortcut to access the command to create a box character?

10. Breaks

a. What is a break?
b. What is the difference between a line break and a paragraph break?
c. Where is the Breaks command located?
d. When would column breaks be used?
e. What is Allow Within, as it pertains to Breaks?
f. Describe why and how breaks are used to force a paragraph to the top of a new page.

11. Bring to Front, Send To Back

a. What can be sent to the back or brought to the front in Ventura?
b. What is the keyboard shortcut to Send to Back?
c. What is the keyboard shortcut to Bring to Front?

12. Browse Chapter

a. What is the Browse command?
b. Where is the Browse command available?
c. How can you tell when a chapter has been opened using the Browse command?

13. Chapter Menu

a. List 8 of the 12 commands available in the Chapter menu.
b. What was the Chapter menu called in earlier versions of Ventura?
c. Where are the Page Layout, Auto-Numbering, Chapter Typography, and Footnote settings stored?

14. Chapter Typography

a. What is chapter typography?
b. What is a widow?
c. What is an orphan?
d. What is the difference between Chapter Typography and Frame Typography?
e. What is a baseline?
f. What is column balance?

15. Column Snap
    a. Define Column Snap.
    b. Define Line Snap.
    c. Where are the Column and Line Snap commands located?
    d. How does the grid affect Column and Line Snap?

16. Cross References
    a. What is a cross reference?
    b. Where is the Cross Reference option located?
    c. Describe the procedure to insert a cross reference.

17. Cut/Copy/Paste
    a. What are the Cut/Copy/Paste commands used for in Ventura?
    b. What is the function of Cut?
    c. What is the function of Paste?
    d. What is a clipboard?
    e. How many clipboards are used by Ventura?
    f. How is the Shift key used with Cut/Copy/Paste?
    g. What are the keyboard shortcuts used to access Cut/Copy/Paste?
    h. Describe how Copy/Paste can save you time when working with Ventura.

18. Define Colors
    a. Name the three elements that color can be assigned to in Ventura.
    b. What determines the color of your final printed page?
    c. What mode must Ventura be in before Define Colors can be accessed?

19. Edit Menu
    a. Describe the Edit menu and how it changes options when Ventura is in different modes.
    b. What options are available in Edit menu when Ventura is in Paragraph mode?

20. Equations
    a. What is the purpose of equations?
    b. Describe the steps to insert an equation.
    c. What is the editing screen?
    d. When is Ctrl-D used?

21. Exit
    a. Describe the purpose of the Exit command.
    b. Where is Exit located?
    c. What effect does Exit have on the VP.INF file?

22. File Menu
    a. List eight commands available in the File menu.
    b. Categorize the main functions of the commands available in the File menu.

23. File Type/Rename
    a. What is the File Type/Rename command?
    b. Describe the procedure for using this command.

24. Fill Attributes
    a. What is fill?
    b. What is a Fill Attribute?
    c. What is the keyboard shortcut used to access the Fill Attributes dialog box?
    d. Where is the Fill Attributes command located?
    e. What is a transparent graphic?

25. Font
    a. Define font.
    b. Where is the Font command located?
    c. What can be selected in the Font dialog box?
    d. What is a strike-thru?

26. Footnote
    a. What is a footnote?
    b. What is a number template?
    c. Name the tags Ventura creates for use with footnotes.
    d. Where is the footnote information stored?
    e. Where is the Footnote command located?

27. Footnote Settings
    a. What is the purpose of the Footnote Settings command?
    b. Does Ventura automatically adjust the space required to place the footnotes at the bottom of the page?
    c. Describe three options available in the Footnote Settings dialog box.
    d. Where is the footnote information stored?
    e. Where is the Footnote Setting command located?

28. Fractions
    a. Why is the Fraction command used to create fractions?
    b. What is a true typographical fraction?
    c. Describe the procedure to create a fraction.

29. Frame Background
    a. Define frame background.
    b. What two attributes can be selected in the Frame Background dialog box?
    c. Explain what a screen is.

30. Frame Menu
    a. List eight commands available in the Frame menu.
    b. What mode must Ventura be in before the commands in the Frame menu are available for selection?

31. Frame Typography
    a. What is frame typography?
    b. Define Move Down to 1st Baseline By.
    c. When is the Frame Typography command used?
32. Go To Page
    a. What is the Go To Page command?
    b. Name the two ways available to access the Go To Page command.
    c. List the four keyboard shortcuts available to help move between pages.
    d. How do you stop the execution of a Go To Page command?
33. Graphic Menu
    a. List five of the seven commands available in the Graphic menu.
    b. What mode must Ventura be in before the various commands in the Graphic menu can be accessed?
34. Grid Settings
    a. What is a grid?
    b. Where is the Grid Settings command located?
    c. What is grid snap?
    d. What is vertical spacing in a grid?
35. Headers & Footers
    a. What is a header?
    b. Name the three parts of each header and footer in a Ventura document.
    c. Describe the procedure for inserting a page number in a footer on both left and right pages.
    d. Can header information be copied to a footer?
    e. Explain how text attributes can be added to a footer.
36. Image Settings
    a. What is an image setting?
    b. Define halftone.
    c. What is a screen angle?
    d. Explain the term lines per inch.
    e. What is TIFF?
    f. Define gray scale image.
37. Insert/Edit Anchor
    a. What is a frame anchor?
    b. Describe the procedure to insert a frame anchor.
    c. What is the advantage of using frame anchors?
    d. How is the Insert/Edit Anchor option used?

38. Insert/Edit Index
    a. What is an index?
    b. Describe the use of the Insert/Edit Index command.
    c. What is a two-level index?
    d. Why should the index information be placed at the end of a paragraph?
    e. What is an index entry?
    f. How does Ventura use the Index option of the Manage Publication command to create an index from the various index entries?
    g. How many levels are there to the index?

39. Insert/Edit Special Item
    a. What is a special item?
    b. What tool must be selected to use the Insert/Edit Special Item command?
    c. What is the keyboard shortcut to access the Insert/Edit Special Item command?
    d. List seven of the nine special items.
    e. Describe the procedure to insert a special item.
    f. How is a special item deleted?

40. Insert/Remove Page
    a. Describe the procedure to remove a page.
    b. Where is the Insert/Remove Page command located?

41. Insert Row/Column
    a. Describe the procedure to add a new column.
    b. Where are new rows placed within the table?
    c. Where are new columns placed within the table?

42. Insert Table
    a. Where can a table be placed within a chapter?
    b. If a table has been created, how do you change the numbers of rows or columns?
    c. How is an existing table edited or changed?
    d. Name the three generated tags created by Ventura Publisher and used in tables.
    e. How is alignment used in a table?

43. Join/Split Cells
    a. What does the Join Cell command do?
    b. Describe the procedure to split a cell.
    c. What can happen to some text in a cell when the cell is split or joined?
    d. Why must columns be adjusted before the chapter is saved?

44. Line Attributes
    a. Define the term line attributes.
    b. What is the keyboard shortcut to access the Line Attributes command?
    c. Explain Defaults in the Line Attributes dialog box.
    d. Describe the procedure to assign color to a previously created line.

45. Line Snap
    a. What is line snap?
    b. Where is the Line Snap command located?
    c. Why should line snap be used?

46. Load Different Style
    a. Explain when the Load Different Style command is used.
    b. Where is the Load Different Style command located?

47. Load Text/Picture
    a. Describe the purpose and use of the Load Text/Picture command.
    b. Name the three general types of files that are loaded with this command.
    c. What should you do with a text file before you use the Load Text/Picture command?

48. Manage Publication
    a. What is the Manage Publication command?
    b. What is a PUB file?
    c. Where is the Manage Publication command located?
    d. Describe the procedure to make an index in Manage Publication.
    e. Describe how to copy a chapter with the Manage Publication command.

49. Manage Width Table
    a. Why is the Manage Width Table command used?
    b. What is a face?
    c. When two width tables are merged together, must they both be for the same printer?
    d. Describe how this command can be used to automatically download fonts to your printer.

50. Margins & Columns
    a. What is the Margins & Columns command?
    b. What is the maximum number of columns permitted in a frame or column?
    c. Where is the Margins & Columns command located?
    d. What is the difference between Calculated Width and Actual Frame Width?

51. New
    a. Where is the New command located?
    b. Describe when New is used.

52. Open Chapter
    a. What is a chapter?
    b. Describe the procedure to open a chapter in Ventura.
    c. What is the filename extension that Ventura recognizes as a chapter?
    d. Where is the Open Chapter command located?

53. Page Size & Layout
    a. Describe the purpose of this command.
    b. What is the difference between landscape and portrait page orientation?
    c. Where is the Page Size & Layout command located?
54. Paragraph Menu
    a. List 9 of the 13 commands available in the Paragraph menu.
    b. What mode must Ventura be in before the commands in the Paragraph menu can be accessed?
55. Paragraph Tagging
    a. What is the purpose of tagging paragraphs?
    b. What is a tag?
    c. Where are paragraph tags saved?
    d. Can the Body Text tag be deleted?
    e. Describe the procedure to assigning text attributes to a paragraph tag.
56. Paragraph Typography
    a. What is paragraph typography?
    b. How does paragraph typography differ from frame typography and chapter typography?
    c. List five options available in the Paragraph Typography dialog box.
    d. What is automatic kerning?
    e. Define letter spacing and how and why it is used.
    f. What is tracking?
    g. What is an Em?
    h. Define Grow Inter-Line to Fit.
57. Print
    a. List five options available in the To Print dialog box.
    b. Define collated copies.
    c. What are crop marks?
    d. Describe spot color overlays.
    e. Define shrink & overlap.
    f. Describe the procedure for printing only page 7 of a 20-page chapter.
58. Re-Anchor Frames
    a. What does the Re-Anchor Frames command do when executed?
    b. How is an anchor created?
    c. Why should each page be checked after executing the Re-Anchor Frames command?
59. Remove Text/File
    a. Explain the use of the Remove Text/File command.
    b. Where is the Remove Text/File command located?
    c. When a file is removed, is it deleted from the disk?
    d. Explain why an unused file should be removed from the Files Window.

60. Renumber Chapter
    a. Define the purpose of the Renumber Chapter command.
    b. Where is the Renumber Chapter command located?

61. Repeating Frame
    a. What is a repeating frame?
    b. Explain why a repeating frame is used.
    c. Describe the procedure for assigning captions to a repeating frame.
    d. Where is the repeating frame command located?
    e. Describe the procedure for creating a repeating frame.

62. Revert to Saved
    a. What is the Revert to Saved command?
    b. Where is the Revert to Saved command located?
    c. When would you use the Revert to Saved command?

63. Ruling Line Above, Line Below, Box Around
    a. What do the Ruling Line Above, Ruling Line Below, and Box Around commands do?
    b. What is the maximum amount of ruling lines available in these commands?
    c. What is the purpose of the display area in the Ruling Line dialog box?
    d. Describe the procedure to change the ruling lines to dashes.

64. Save
    a. What is the Save command?
    b. What is the keyboard shortcut to access the Save command?
    c. Where is the Save command located?
    d. What does Ventura do when the Save command is executed?

65. Save As
    a. What is the Save As command?
    b. What does Ventura do when the Save As command is executed?
    c. Where is the Save As command located?

66. Save Style As
    a. Describe the purpose of the Save Style As command.
    b. Why should a changed or modified style sheet be saved under a new name?
    c. What is the filename extension Ventura uses to identify a style sheet?
    d. Where is the Save Style As command located?

67. Select All
    a. What is the Select All command and how is it used?
    b. What is the keyboard shortcut to Select All?
    c. What mode must Ventura be in before Select All can be accessed?

68. Set Column Width
    a. Describe the two ways the width of any column within a table can be adjusted.
    b. What is the Variable Width command?
    c. Describe how Alt is used to set the column width.

69. Set Preferences
    a. What is Set Preferences command?
    b. What is greeking?
    c. How can Ventura make backup copies of your files?
    d. Describe the procedure to adjust the double-click speed.
    e. What is on-screen kerning?
    f. What is a generated tag?

70. Set Ruler
    a. What is the Set Ruler command?
    b. Which menu contains the Set Ruler command?
    c. What is a pica?
    d. What is a point?
    e. How many points are in an inch?
    f. How many picas are in an inch?
    g. How many points are in a pica?
    h. What is the zero point?
    i. How is the zero point moved?

71. Set Tint
    a. What does the Set Tint command do?
    b. What colors are available within Set Tint?
    c. Describe the procedure to set tint.

72. Show/Hide Pictures, Show Rulers, Column Guides, Tabs & Returns, Loose Lines, Header & Footer
    a. What is the Show Rulers command?
    b. What is the Show Column Guides command?
    c. What is the Show Loose Lines command?
    d. What is the Show All Pictures command?
    e. Does Ventura run faster or slower when the pictures are shown?

73. Show On All Pages
    a. What does the Show On All Pages command do?
    b. Do graphics repeat in the same position on each page?
    c. Contrast the difference between Show On All Pages and Repeating Frame.

74. Sizing & Scaling
    a. What does the Sizing & Scaling command do?
    b. Which mode must Ventura be in to access the Sizing & Scaling mode?
    c. What is vertical padding?

d. How can the mouse be used to scale a picture?
e. What are the settings to make sure a picture prints exactly as scanned?
f. How can the Sizing & Scaling command be used to exactly position a frame on a page?

75. Spacing
    a. What is leading?
    b. What is a temporary margin?
    c. What mode must Ventura be in to access the Spacing command?
    d. What is interline spacing?
    e. Define how and when the In From Right and In From Left options should be used.
    f. What happens when a paragraph has been over-leaded?
    g. What happens when a paragraph has been under-leaded?

76. Special Effects
    a. What two special effects are available in Ventura?
    b. What mode must Ventura be in before the Special Effects command can be accessed?

77. Tab Settings
    a. What is the maximum number of tabs that can be set in one paragraph tag Ventura?
    b. What must be at the end of a line of tabs?
    c. What is a leader tab?
    d. Name the four types of tabs available in Ventura.
    e. Why is justification not used for text lines with tab settings?
    f. Define leader spacing.

78. Table Menu
    a. What is a table?
    b. What is a cell?
    c. What is a column?
    d. What is a row?
    e. What is a spreadsheet?
    f. Does Ventura allow cells to be formatted in a different style?
    g. Name seven of the ten options available in the Table menu.
    h. Describe the procedure to create a table.

79. Text Editing
    a. What operations can be completed when in Text Editing mode?
    b. What is subscript?
    c. Describe the procedure for creating a block of text.
    d. What is the keyboard shortcut to access Text Editing mode?
    e. What does Normal do when selected in the Side-bar?

80. Text Menu
    a. Name seven options available within the Text menu.
    b. Name five options available from the Insert Special Item command.
    c. What tool must be selected before the options within the Text menu can be accessed?

81. Toolbox
    a. Why is the Frame Tool used?
    b. How many files can be placed within a frame?
    c. Which tool is used for selecting, moving, resizing, copying, and deleting frames?
    d. What is the underlying page frame?
    e. What is the difference between the underlying page frame and a frame?
    f. Which tool allows you to design, create, change, and assign attributes to the paragraphs within your document?
    g. What is a paragraph tag?
    h. What is a style sheet?
    i. What is a generated tag?
    j. How many graphic tools are there?
    k. What is the Table Tool?
    l. Describe why you may want to use the Text Tool.

82. Toolbox Window
    a. What is the Toolbox?
    b. How many tools are available within the Toolbox?
    c. Name the tools available within the Toolbox Window.
    d. What does Ctrl-W do?

83. Update Counter
    a. What is the primary purpose of this command?
    b. List six different number formats available.
    c. Explain update method.

84. Update Tag List
    a. List four of the five tools available in the Update Tag List dialog box.
    b. Why are function keys assigned to tags?
    c. Describe the procedure to remove a tag.

85. Vertical Rules
    a. What is a vertical rule?
    b. Describe the procedure for setting a vertical rule in Ventura.
    c. Describe the procedure for precisely positioning the vertical rule within a frame.
    d. Where is the Vertical Rules command located?

86. View Menu
    a. How many different views are available within Ventura?
    b. List the keyboard shortcuts for the various views available within Ventura.
    c. What is a facing page?
    d. Can frames be dragged from one page to another when in facing page?

87. Views
    a. What is a View command?
    b. What does Ctrl-E do?
    c. What does Ctrl-F do?
    d. What is Facing Pages View?
    e. Can frames be dragged across pages when in Facing Pages View?

88. Windows
    a. Can you start or operate Xerox Ventura Publisher Windows Edition without first starting and running Microsoft Windows?
    b. What is a graphic user interface?
    c. How do you start Windows from DOS?
    d. What is an icon?
    e. What is a scroll bar?
    f. What is a dialog box?

Index